THE EMOTIONAL POLITICS OF THE ALTERNATIVE LEFT

In the 1970s, a multifaceted alternative scene developed in West Germany. At the core of this leftist scene was a struggle for feelings in a capitalist world that seemed to be devoid of any emotions. Joachim C. Häberlen offers here a vivid account of these emotional politics. The book discusses critiques of rationality and celebrations of insanity as an alternative. It explores why capitalism made people feel afraid and modern cities made people feel lonely. Readers are taken to consciousness raising groups, nude swimming at alternative vacation camps, and into the squatted houses of the early 1980s. Häberlen draws on a kaleidoscope of different voices to explore how West Germans became more concerned with their selves, their feelings, and their bodies. By investigating how leftists tried to transform themselves through emotional practices, Häberlen gives us a fresh perspective on a fascinating aspect of West German history.

JOACHIM C. HÄBERLEN is Assistant Professor of Modern Continental European History at the University of Warwick, whose research focuses on protest movements and the history of emotions. He is the author of *Vertrauen und Politik im Alltag: Die Arbeiterbewegung in Leipzig und Lyon im Moment der Krise, 1929–1933/38* (2013), numerous academic articles, and an essay on the politics of friendship between Germans and refugees (*Wie aus Fremden Freunde werden*; 2018). He edited *Politics of Authentic Subjectivity: Countercultures and Radical Movements across the Iron Curtain, 1968–1989* (2018).

NEW STUDIES IN EUROPEAN HISTORY

EDITED BY

PETER BALDWIN, *University of California, Los Angeles*
CHRISTOPHER CLARK, *University of Cambridge*
JAMES B. COLLINS, *Georgetown University*
MIA RODRÍGUEZ-SALGADO, *London School of Economics
and Political Science*
LYNDAL ROPER, *University of Oxford*
TIMOTHY SNYDER, *Yale University*

The aim of this series in early modern and modern European history is to publish outstanding works of research, addressed to important themes across a wide geographical range, from southern and central Europe, to Scandinavia and Russia, from the time of the Renaissance to the present. As it develops the series will comprise focused works of wide contextual range and intellectual ambition.

A full list of titles published in the series can be found at:
www.cambridge.org/newstudiesineuropeanhistory

THE EMOTIONAL POLITICS
OF THE ALTERNATIVE LEFT

West Germany, 1968–1984

JOACHIM C. HÄBERLEN

University of Warwick

CAMBRIDGE
UNIVERSITY PRESS

CAMBRIDGE
UNIVERSITY PRESS

University Printing House, Cambridge CB2 8BS, United Kingdom

One Liberty Plaza, 20th Floor, New York, NY 10006, USA

477 Williamstown Road, Port Melbourne, VIC 3207, Australia

314–321, 3rd Floor, Plot 3, Splendor Forum, Jasola District Centre, New Delhi – 110025, India

79 Anson Road, #06–04/06, Singapore 079906

Cambridge University Press is part of the University of Cambridge.

It furthers the University's mission by disseminating knowledge in the pursuit of education, learning, and research at the highest international levels of excellence.

www.cambridge.org
Information on this title: www.cambridge.org/9781108471749
DOI: 10.1017/9781108559201

© Joachim C. Häberlen 2018

First published 2018

Printed and bound in Great Britain by Clays Ltd, Elcograf S.p.A.

A catalogue record for this publication is available from the British Library.

ISBN 978-1-108-47174-9 Hardback

Every effort has been made to contact the relevant copyright-holders for the images reproduced in this book. In the event of any error, the publisher will be pleased to make corrections in any reprints or future editions.

Contents

v

Figures

Acknowledgements

I am grateful to the numerous friends, colleagues and institutions that have supported me during researching and writing this book. The project took off at the Centre for the History of Emotions at the Max Planck Institute for Human Development, Berlin, where I was lucky not only to benefit from the generous financial support it offered, but also from the intellectually inspiring environment. In particular, I wish to express my gratitude to its director, Ute Frevert, to Margrit Pernau, Monique Scheer, Benno Gammerl, Uffa Jensen, Daniel Brückenhaus, Philipp Nielsen, and to the extremely helpful staff at the Institute. I finished the project at the University of Warwick, which since then has become my academic home due to friendly and welcoming colleagues. Discussions I had with Claudia Stein (though she remains sceptical about all the fuss regarding emotions), Rebecca Earle, David Lambert, Ben Smith, Mark Knights, Mark Philp, and Charles Walton have challenged me to think about theoretical approaches to history. The transition to Warwick was also supported by a Marie Curie Career Integration Grant by the European Union that supported further archival research. I equally benefited from the opportunity to present my work at different conferences and colloquia, notably at the University of Tübingen, the University of Sheffield, the Free University Berlin, and the University of Basel. The discussions with the participants of these colloquia were highly stimulating. I also made students of my module on politics of protest in Europe read the manuscript. The discussions we had about the project were indeed amongst the most sophisticated, and some comments and suggestions made it into the text. It speaks to the high quality of students at Warwick.

Mark Philp, Neil Gregor, Mathew Thomson, and Christiane Reinecke read the entire book manuscript and provided me with helpful comments. So did Moritz Föllmer and Jake Smith, with whom I had countless discussion about the West German left and its sometimes weird but fascinating political practices. The two anonymous peer reviewers provided me with helpful comments to revise the manuscript.

Archivists at various places helped me by pointing me to sometimes obscure publications, especially Punx at the Papiertiger Archiv in Berlin. The hours spent in the small archive were always highlights of the week. I'm also grateful to the former activists who talked to me about their experiences. When I attended a meeting to commemorate the thirtieth anniversary of the squatting movement of 1980/1981, I was struck by the profound sense of happiness I felt amongst those present. I don't know if those activists would agree with me, but it seemed to me that they had done something right in their lives.

Introduction

In January 1980, the West Berlin radical left-wing magazine *radikal* published an article, entitled 'subjective mishmash', about the relation between subjectivity and politics.[1] Exploring the entanglement and disentanglement of political and personal issues within the radical left, the text provides an intriguing perspective on the history of the West German left since 1968. According to the anonymous author, protestors in 1968 'regarded their personal difficulties as a result of capitalist society'. Students went to the streets to demonstrate against the Vietnam War not only because of a 'rational and conscious, but also [because of] an emotional solidarity with the fighting Vietnamese people'. Having learned from Wilhelm Reich, a Freudian Marxist popular amongst student activists in the 1968 revolt, that sexuality remained fundamentally repressed in a capitalist society, activists were as much concerned with their orgasm as with imperialist warfare. But by the early 1970s, things changed, the author wrote. Dieter Duhm's popular book on 'Fear in Capitalism', which had already reached its 11th edition in 1975, replaced Wilhelm Reich's work as common reading within the left.[2] 'Everyday, interpersonal fears' rather than 'sexual difficulties' now dominated the conversations amongst leftists, the *radikal* author noted. The change also affected how leftists dealt with their personal difficulties. Whereas Reich and those student activists following him had hoped that professional psychiatrists might provide emotional support, activists now sought to 'collectively liberate themselves'

[1] Anon., 'statt eines Forums: subjektiver Mischmasch', *radikal* 74 (11 January–1 February 1980), 16.
[2] See Dieter Duhm, *Angst im Kapitalismus: 2. Versuch der gesellschaftlichen Begründung zwischenmenschlicher Angst in der kapitalistischen Warengesellschaft* (Lampertheim: Küber, 1973); Wilhelm Reich, *Der sexuelle Kampf der Jugend* (Berlin: Verlag für Sexualpolitik, 1932); Wilhelm Reich, *Was ist Klassenbewusstsein? Ein Beitrag zur Diskussion über die Neuformierung der Arbeiterbewegung* (Kopenhagen: Verlag für Sexualpolitik, 1934); Reich, *Die Funktion des Orgasmus: Zur Psychopathologie und zur Soziologie des Geschlechtslebens* (Amsterdam: Thomas de Munter, 1965); Wilhelm Reich, *Die sexuelle Revolution* (Frankfurt a.M.: Fischer, 1966).

I

by working and living together. Thus consciousness-raising and therapy groups became popular, and left-wing psychotherapist Horst-Eberhardt Richter's advice book 'Learning Goal: Solidarity' became a bestseller.[3] Political and personal issues, the author's narrative implies, had become deeply entangled in the radical left.

The author's own biography reflected this entanglement, as well as the practical problems it entailed. As did many other leftists, the author joined various groups, a bookshop group, a communal living group (*Wohngemeinschaft*), and group dynamics sessions. All those groups had ended frustratingly. The meetings of the bookshop groups seem to have dealt rather little with the business of the bookshop. Instead, members used the meetings to discuss their psychic state of mind, tellingly referring to the meetings as 'psychos'. Some participants looked for more trust in the group, while others wanted to act out their aggressions, and still others wanted to 'practice primal screaming [*Urschrei*]'. Soon enough, people left the group and tried 'massage-, acupuncture- or bioenergy groups'. The communal living group, too, disbanded after 'nightlong psycho-rummaging'. Such experiences were, the author claimed, rather typical in the left, resulting in a 'reprivatization of subjectivity' either in 'dyadic relations [*Zweierbeziehungen*] or in groups concerned with soul and belly'. An avalanche of books 'promised [leftists] individual liberation: group dynamics to *Gestalt* therapy, meditation and massaging were part of what was offered'. While these groups dealt with personal problems, others engaged in politics, but demanded that 'feelings had to be discarded' for political work. According to the author's account, politics and subjectivity were separated by the late 1970s, a development he found deeply worrying. If people dealt with their frustrating experiences on their own, he alleged, those experiences might easily be regarded as personal weaknesses and failures. But if they were published in a magazine like *radikal,* it would become clear that not only personal frustrations were at stake, but 'violence, power, and impotence'. The anonymous author thus called for the magazine's readers to submit reports about their personal experiences that might initiate a communication about those experiences. This would ultimately reveal their political rather than merely individual nature.

As a case in point, *radikal* republished an article that had originally been published in 1977 by the Frankfurt-based *Andere Zeitung*, in which an

---

[3] Horst-Eberhardt Richter, *Lernziel Solidarität* (Reinbek bei Hamburg: Rowolt, 1974).

anonymous author described why she had thrown a Molotov cocktail into a department store.[4] This was not an act of political protest in the conventional sense, for example protesting against some sort of scandal, the author argued. Rather, she had thrown the Molotov cocktail out of a 'heavy party frustration'. Apparently, she had attended a rather boring party where people had not been able to talk to each other because, the author alleged, they were afraid of admitting how 'damaged' they were. To deal with this party frustration, she decided to throw a Molotov cocktail, called rather cloyingly *Molli*, into a department store. It turned out to be a transformative act, as she did not only through the *Molli*, but also all her 'liquefied fear and damagedness' out of herself. After a fearful escape, she cheerfully danced with her friends and comrades at home. Throwing the Molotov cocktails, the author finally admitted, had not brought them closer to socialism, but it had personally helped her, because she had 'experienced' that the slogan 'destroy what's destroying you', a song by the left-wing band Ton Steine Scherben, was true.[5] Her inflammatory way of dealing with the 'heavy party frustration' thus became political because she regarded the inability to communicate openly about their fears as a political problem.

The pieces published by *radikal* and the *Andere Zeitung* provide fascinating insights into the political project of the alternative left in West Germany after 1968, the central theme of this book. Alternative leftists, I argue, developed an understanding of the political for which subjectivity and feelings were central. In contrast to traditional Marxist thinking that had criticized capitalism as a form of exploitation,[6] new leftists charged capitalism with instituting a 'domination of rationality' that left no space for dreams, desires, or (positive) feelings and their expression, that only created fear, boredom, and frustration, and thus 'damaged' both individual personalities and personal relations. Developing this peculiar critique of capitalist modernity, leftists redrew the map of the political and reimagined

---

[4] Anon., '. . . und dann habe ich einen Molli in ein Kaufhaus geworfen . . .', *Andere Zeitung* 12 (February 1977), 16, reprinted in *radikal* 74 (11 January–1 February 1980), 17. See also the discussion in Joachim C. Häberlen and Jake Smith, 'Struggling for Feelings: The Politics of Emotions in the Radical New Left in West Germany, c. 1968–84', *Contemporary European History* 23 (2014).

[5] On Ton Steine Scherben, see Timothy Brown, 'Music as a Weapon? "Ton Steine Scherben" and the Politics of Rock in Cold War Berlin', *German Studies Review* 32 (2009).

[6] For an extensive discussion of traditional Marxism, see Moishe Postone, *Time, Labor, and Social Domination: A Reinterpretation of Marx's Critical Theory* (Cambridge: Cambridge University Press, 1993), 3–83. On the history of the left in general, see also Geoff Eley, *Forging Democracy: The History of the Left in Europe, 1850–2000* (Oxford: Oxford University Press, 2002), 13–118.

political alliances and hostilities on this map. Of course, old enmities persisted. New leftists were anti-capitalist, anti-fascist, and against oppression and exploitation, at home and in the world. But the underlying logic that divided the political world in friends and foes changed. In this political universe, a capitalist, technocratic and deeply male rationality constituted the enemy, while the realm of dreams, wishes and feelings constituted the friend. For leftists, feelings as the 'radical other' of rationality had a subversive and untameable potential that would disturb the clean and ordered world of rational capitalism.[7] A first goal of this book is to make sense of radical leftist politics as a struggle of feelings against the powers of rationality. Emphasizing the role of emotions for the radical left is thus not to provide a depoliticized perspective, but to argue that leftist politics was crucially about emotions.

But leftists did not stop at criticizing capitalism for the emotional suffering it caused. Struggling for feelings also meant that leftists tried to fix their 'damaged' personalities and to recuperate the feelings that were, as they claimed, buried under capitalist rationality – for example by throwing a Molotov cocktail that would liberate the arsonist from her fears. In numerous consciousness-raising groups, called *Selbsterfahrungsgruppen*, or 'self-experience groups' in German, and collective living projects, leftists attempted to learn new emotional styles that were based on the open expression and performance of feelings.[8] Exploring this therapeutic-political project of self-remodelling is a second key goal of the book. To accomplish their goal of escaping from the emotional dearth of capitalism, leftists developed a variety of communicative and bodily practices that would yield, or so they hoped, the feelings of intimacy and intensity they missed so desperately under capitalism. These practices are best interpreted, I argue, as emotional experiments, that is, as attempts to produce specific feelings; and as it happens with experiments, those could succeed or fail. Drawing on an understanding of emotions as practices, the book provides insights into the production of feelings as a process of trial and error.[9]

---

[7] Current affect studies make strikingly similar arguments about the political potential of affects (rather than emotions). It would be worthwhile to investigate the intellectual roots of affect studies in this regard.

[8] On the idea of emotional styles, see Benno Gammerl, 'Emotional Styles: Concepts and Challenges', *Rethinking History* 16 (2012).

[9] On 'trying emotions', see Pascal Eitler and Monique Scheer, 'Emotionengeschichte als Körpergeschichte: Eine heuristische Perspektive auf religiöse Konversionen im 19. und 20. Jahrhundert', *Geschichte und Gesellschaft* 35 (2009).

The book thus seeks to offer an interpretation of what I consider the central political project of the alternative left: its struggle for feelings. Focusing on this simultaneously political and self-transformative project of the radical left, the book also provides further insights into the history of the Federal Republic 'after the boom'.[10] Indeed, as the *radikal* author noted, new leftists were not alone in trying to transform themselves in a therapeutic way. Contemporary observers noted a veritable 'psychoboom', as all kinds of therapy groups mushroomed in the 1970s.[11] In spheres of life ranging from child raising to sports, West Germans became more concerned with their selves, their feelings, and their bodies.[12] Scholars have interpreted these developments in terms of emerging cultures or 'regimes' of subjectivity that shape how people can and should relate to themselves, how they form their selves. Scholars interested in the formation of the contemporary self have often turned to the 1970s, when a new a culture of subjectivity emerged that emphasized autonomy and authenticity as much as effervescence and playfulness.[13] Not least in the alternative left, and the

---

[10] Anselm Doering-Manteuffel and Lutz Raphael, *Nach dem Boom: Perspektiven auf die Zeitgeschichte seit 1970*, 2nd edn (Göttingen: Vandenhoeck & Ruprecht, 2008). See, for arguments along somewhat similar lines, Thomas Raithel, Andreas Rödder, and Andreas Wirsching, eds., *Auf dem Weg in eine neue Moderne? Die Bundesrepublik Deutschland in den siebziger und achtziger Jahren* (Munich: R. Oldenbourg Verlag, 2009); Andreas Rödder, *Wertewandel und Postmoderne: Gesellschaft und Kultur der Bundesrepublik Deutschland 1965–1990* (Stuttgart: Stiftung Bundespräsident-Theodor-Heuss-Haus, 2004); Anselm Doering-Manteuffel, Lutz Raphael, and Thomas Schlemmer, eds., *Vorgeschichte der Gegenwart: Dimensionen des Strukturbruchs nach dem Boom* (Göttingen: Vandenhoeck & Ruprecht, 2016); Konrad H. Jarausch, ed., *Das Ende der Zuversicht? Die siebziger Jahre als Geschichte* (Göttingen: Vandenhoeck & Ruprecht, 2008); Morten Reitmayer and Thomas Schlemmer, eds., *Die Anfänge der Gegenwart: Umbrüche in Westeuropa nach dem Boom* (Munich: Oldenbourg, 2014). See also the discussion in Vierteljahrshefte für Zeitgeschichte, Eckart Conze, 'Sicherheit als Kultur: Überlegungen zu einer "modernen Politikgeschichte" der Bundesrepublik Deutschland', *Vierteljahrshefte für Zeitgeschichte* 53 (2005); Rüdiger Graf and Kim Christian Priemel, 'Zeitgeschichte in der Welt der Sozialwissenschaften: Legitimität und Originalität einer Disziplin', *Vierteljahrshefte für Zeitgeschichte* 59 (2011); Hans Maier, 'Fortschrittsoptimismus oder Kulturpessimismus? Die Bundesrepublik in den 1970er und 1980er Jahren', *Vierteljahrshefte für Zeitgeschichte* 56 (2008); Paul Nolte, 'Jenseits des Westens? Überlegungen zu einer Zeitgeschichte der Demokratie', *Vierteljahrshefte für Zeitgeschichte* 61 (2013); Andreas Rödder, 'Das "Modell Deutschland" zwischen Erfolgsgeschichte und Verfallsdiagnose', *Vierteljahrshefte für Zeitgeschichte* 54 (2006).

[11] On the 'psychoboom', see Maik Tändler, *Das therapeutische Jahrzehnt: Der Psychoboom in den siebziger Jahren* (Göttingen: Wallstein, 2016).

[12] See for example the contributions in Pascal Eitler and Jens Elberfeld, eds., *Zeitgeschichte des Selbst: Therapeutisierung – Politisierung – Emotionalisierung* (Bielefeld: transcript, 2015); Sabine Maasen et al., eds., *Das beratene Selbst: Zur Genealogie der Therapeutisierung in den 'langen' Siebzigern* (Bielefeld: transcript, 2011).

[13] See Andreas Reckwitz, *Das hybride Subjekt: eine Theorie der Subjektkulturen von der bürgerlichen Moderne zur Postmoderne* (Weilerswist: Velbrück, 2006), 441–499. Reckwitz particularly emphasizes the effervescent and playful elements of the contemporary 'creative' subject that emerged in the counterculture during the 1960s and 1970s. See also Detlef Siegfried, 'Die

numerous encounter and therapy groups associated with it, a regime of subjectivity developed that required people to work on their selves, to be creative and autonomous. While leftists imagined the autonomous self in opposition to capitalism, scholars noted, as Ulrich Bröckling put it, that the 'counterculture after 1968, despite its anti-capitalist intentions, turned out to be a laboratory of entrepreneurial dispositions [*Verhaltensorientierungen*]. The reconciliation of living and working that the alternative movement proclaimed becomes a reality for the new entrepreneurs [*Selbstständige*] by work extending to all aspects of life [*als Ausgreifen der Arbeit auf alle Aspekte des Lebens*].' The 'entrepreneurial' or 'neoliberal self', this indicates, is not a particularly gruesome form of (self-)exploitation imposed upon from above. Rather, the 'entrepreneurial self could become a hegemonic figure only because it built on a collective desire for autonomy, self-realization and non-alienated labour'.[14] Put bluntly, what was intended as an anti-capitalist project only contributed to the transformation of capitalism, Bröckling's argument suggests.[15]

By investigating how leftists tried to transform themselves through emotional practices, this book, too, contributes to an understanding of changing regimes of subjectivity. Yet it also seeks to go beyond this interpretative framework in two distinct ways. First, the book highlights how leftists not only formulated implicit or explicit requirements what had to be done to be 'authentic' or 'autonomous', thus participating in the creation of a new form of (self-)governing, but also developed the foundations for a critique of this form of governmentality. At least some leftists were deeply critical about the normative requirements the demands for 'spontaneity' and 'authentic emotionality' created, and worried that the concern with improving the self would only internalize and thereby strengthen the grip of capitalism.[16] Second, by exploring the microdynamics of experimenting with feelings, the book emphasizes the often contingent and ambivalent outcomes of leftist emotional practices. A focus on what

---

Entpolitisierung des Privaten: Subjektkonstruktionen im alternativen Milieu', in *Privatisierung: Idee und Praxis seit den 1970er Jahren*, ed. Norbert Frei and Dietmar Süß (Göttingen: Wallstein, 2012).

[14] Ulrich Bröckling, *Das unternehmerische Selbst: Soziologie einer Subjektivierungsform* (Frankfurt a.M.: Suhrkamp, 2007), 58. See also the discussion of the 'new spirit of capitalism' and its relation to the protests of 1968 by Luc Boltanski and Eve Chiapello, *The New Spirit of Capitalism* (London: Verso, 2005), 167–213. On the reception of their work, see Paul du Gay and Glenn Morgan, eds., *New Spirits of Capitalism? Crises, Justifications, and Dynamics* (Oxford: Oxford University Press, 2013).

[15] See, for a similar argument, Tändler, *Therapeutische Jahrzehnt*, 251.

[16] See the polemic by Joachim Bruhn, 'Unter den Zwischenmenschen', in *Diktatur der Freundlichkeit: Über Bhagwan, die kommende Psychokratie und Lieferanteneingänge zum wohltätigen Wahnsinn*, ed. Initiative Sozialistisches Forum (Freiburg: Ça-Ira-Verlag, 1984).

being and being seen as 'authentic and autonomous' required can hardly grasp this emotional productivity.[17] The book thus provides an interpretation of the radical left in West Germany during the 1970s that emphasizes its highly experimental and productive character.

In the remainder of this introduction, I first provide a brief outline of the contours of the radical, or rather alternative left, during the 1970s: who belonged to this leftist milieu, and what sort of networks shaped the alternative left. In a second step, I discuss how scholars have interpreted the post-1968 New Left drawing on various theoretical approaches, and how my approach relates to this scholarship. To conclude, I explain how the book proceeds and on which sources it draws.

The Contours of the Alternative Left

In many ways, the alternative left of the 1970s was a product of the revolts around 1968, revolts that have been studied elsewhere in great detail.[18] There is no need to retell a familiar story in any detail here. Suffice it to highlight a few characteristics of those revolts that are essential for an understanding of the alternative left during the 1970s. Importantly, it would be misleading to speak about *the* student movements of 1968. It was, in fact, a highly diversified movement. While boundaries between different factions within the student movement were fluid and never entirely clear, it is nevertheless possible to identify two distinct tendencies. On the one hand, radical students tried to develop a critical-scientific understanding of 'late capitalism'.[19] They read and discussed the work of

---

[17] In this regard, the argument put forward in this book differs from Sven Reichardt, *Authentizität und Gemeinschaft: Linksalternatives Leben in den siebziger und frühen achtziger Jahren* (Berlin: Suhrkamp, 2014).

[18] See only Timothy S. Brown, *West Germany and the Global Sixties: The Antiauthoritarian Revolt, 1962–1978* (Cambridge: Cambridge University Press, 2013); Timothy Brown and Lorena Anton, eds., *Between the Avant-Garde and the Everyday: Subversive Politics in Europe from 1957 to the Present* (New York: Berghahn, 2011); Belinda Davis et al., eds., *Changing the World, Changing Oneself: Political Protest and Collective Identities in West Germany and the U.S. in the 1960s and 1970s* (New York: Berghahn, 2010); Martin Klimke, Jacco Pekelder, and Joachim Scharloth, eds., *Between Prague Spring and French May: Opposition and Revolt in Europe, 1960–1980* (New York: Berghahn, 2011); Axel Schildt and Detlef Siegfried, eds., *Between Marx and Coca-Cola: Youth Cultures in Changing European Societies, 1960–1980* (New York: Berghahn, 2006); Belinda Davis, 'What's Left? Popular and Democratic Political Participation in Postwar Europe', *American Historical Review* 113 (2008); Martin Klimke and Joachim Scharloth, eds., *1968 in Europe: A History of Protest and Activism, 1956–1977* (New York: Palgrave Macmillan, 2008); Ingrid Gilcher-Holtey, ed., *1968 – Vom Ereignis zum Gegenstand der Geschichtswissenschaft*, Geschichte und Gesellschaft, Sonderheft (Göttingen: Vandenhoeck & Ruprecht, 1998).

[19] Brown, *West Germany*, 19–20.

thinkers like Karl Marx and rediscovered Marxist theorists like Karl
Korsch as well as contemporary sociology, eagerly and endlessly debating
theoretical questions of Marxism-Leninism, the role of the university or
imperialism. On the other hand, activists developed a critique of the
'poverty' of everyday life, not least by drawing on thinkers such as Herbert
Marcuse, but also the acerbic critique of the Situationist International.[20]
They criticized the alienated and deeply boring world of consumer capitalism that offered nothing but false happiness, and regarded their personal
and sexual problems, as the anonymous *radikal* author had remarked, as
just as important, and hence political, as the Vietnam War. Unlike those
activists concerned with seemingly serious issues like imperialism and
war, these 'antiauthoritarian' activists celebrated hedonism and individual
liberation; they sought to provoke the establishment rather than engaging
in serious discussions with its representatives.[21]

When the wave of protests of 1968 came to an end in West Germany
and the student movement broke apart, two distinct factions emerged that
can be vaguely mapped onto these two tendencies and that would characterize the West German radical left during the 1970s. Believing that the
movement of 1968 had failed because it had not been able to mobilize
workers, numerous students joined so-called *K-Gruppen*, most famous
among them the *Kommunistischer Bund Westdeutschland*. These were
communist groups of various allegiances – Marxist-Leninist, Stalinist,
Trotskyite, Maoist – that criticized capitalist class society and agitated for
a communist revolution.[22] These groups typically pursued sober and
serious politics, denying that personal issues like sexuality or feelings
should play a major role in political activism as these would only drive
workers away. On the other hand, a plethora of 'nondogmatic' groups
developed out of the antiauthoritarian wings of the student movement.[23]
Unlike the 'dogmatic' groups that seemed to have a clear idea of how the
path to change and revolution might look like, those nondogmatic groups

[20] Herbert Marcuse, *Eros and Civilization: A Philosophical Inquiry into Freud* (London: Routledge,
    1987 [1956]); Guy Debord, *The Society of the Spectacle* (New York: Zone Books, 1995); Raoul
    Vaneigm, *The Revolution of Everyday Life* (London: Rebel Press, 2003); Ken Knabb, ed., *Situationist
    International Anthology* (Berkeley: Bureau of Public Secrets, 1981).
[21] See Joachim Scharloth, *1968: Eine Kommunikationsgeschichte* (Paderborn: Wilhelm Fink, 2011),
    348–351.
[22] Gunnar Hink, *Wir waren wie Maschinen: Die bundesdeutsche Linke der 70er-Jahre* (Berlin: Rotbuch
    Verlag, 2012); Autorenkollektiv, *Wir warn die stärkste der Partein: Erfahrungsberichte aus der Welt
    der K-Gruppen* (Berlin: Rotbuch-Verlag, 1977).
[23] See in addition to the literature mentioned in footnote 18, Michael März, *Linker Protest nach dem
    Deutschen Herbst: Eine Geschichte des linken Spektrums im Schatten des 'starken Staates', 1977–1979*
    (Bielefeld: transcript, 2012).

Figure 1   'The small but fine difference between the capitalist (1), the orthodox-communist (2) and the alternative (3) way to the sun, to freedom . . .'
(*radikal* 50/51, December 1978/January 1979, 8.)

made an explicit point of not having such a plan; instead, they believed in developing alternative forms of living and thus the foundations of a better society already in the present, for example by founding urban and rural communes, small self-managed businesses, bookshops, cafés, or anti-authoritarian kindergartens. Change would not happen, they believed, in a large-scale revolution, but in small steps that required people to change themselves.[24] This nondogmatic, or 'alternative' left, is the subject of this book.

Outlining the contours of the alternative left is a challenging endeavour. There was no organization with enrolled and dues-paying members, designated leaders or a political program, but an amorphous milieu with fluid and unclear boundaries that encompassed a variety of groups that included local initiatives, parts of the women's and gay movements,[25] consciousness-raising and therapy groups, activists in urban anarchist circles as well as rural communes, and a subcultural scene with political bands, theatre groups, and other artists.[26] Members of the alternative milieu shared a common lifestyle. They lived in communal apartments, celebrated informal personal styles, rejected consumer culture and, in general, authority. Some people in the milieu were involved in numerous activities for several years, while others only joined a local initiative or

---

[24] Walter Hollstein, 'Autonome Lebensformen: Über die transbürgerliche Perspektive der Jugendbewegung', in *Aussteigen oder rebellieren: Jugendliche gegen Staat und Gesellschaft*, ed. Michael Haller (Reinbek bei Hamburg: Rowohlt, 1981), 203. Quoted in Reichardt, *Authentizität*, 876.

[25] On the women's movement, see Kristina Schulz, *Der lange Atem der Provokation: Die Frauenbewegung in der Bundesrepublik und in Frankreich* (Frankfurt a.M.: Campus, 2002); Kristina Schulz, '1968: Lesarten der "sexuellen Revolution"', in *Demokratisierung und gesellschaftlicher Aufbruch: Die sechziger Jahre als Wendezeit der Bundesrepublik*, ed. Matthias Frese, Julia Paulus, and Karl Teppe (Paderborn: Ferdinand Schöningh, 2003); Kristina Schulz, 'Echoes of Provocation: 1968 and the Women's Movements in France and Germany', in *Transnational Moments of Change: Europe 1945, 1968, 1989*, ed. Gerd-Rainer Horn and Padraic Kenney (Lanham, MD: Rowman & Littlefield, 2004); Andrea Bührmann, *Das authentische Geschlecht: Die Sexualitätsdebatte der neuen Frauenbewegung und die Foucaultsche Machtanalyse* (Münster: Westfälisches Dampfboot, 1995); Imke Schmincke, 'Sexualität als "Angelpunkt" der Frauenbewegung? Zum Verhältnis von sexueller Revolution und Frauenbewegung', in *Sexuelle Revolution? Zur Geschichte der Sexualität im deutschsprachigen Raum seit den 1960er Jahren*, ed. Peter-Paul Bänziger et al. (Bielefeld: transcript, 2015); Eva-Maria Silies, 'Ein, zwei, viele Bewegungen? Die Diversität der neuen Frauenbewegung in den 1970er Jahren der Bundesbewegung', in *Linksalternative Milieus und neue soziale Bewegungen in den 1970er Jahren*, ed. Cordia Baumann, Stefan Gehrig, and Nicolas Büchse (Heidelberg: Winter, 2011). On the gay movement, see Sebastian Haunss, *Identität in Bewegung: Prozesse kollektiver Identität bei den Autonomen und in der Schwulenbewegung* (Wiesbaden: Verlag für Sozialwissenschaften, 2004); Andreas Pretzl and Volker Weiß, eds., *Rosa Radikale: Die Schwulenbewegung der 1970er Jahre* (Hamburg: Männerschwarm Verlag, 2012).

[26] For a good overview of the left-wing artist scene, see Brown, *West Germany*, 155–233.

group for a brief period; some had previously been active in the dogmatic *K-Gruppen*, while others turned their back on the alternative milieu to join these groups, to focus exclusively on esoteric practices, or to join the *Aktionsanalytische Aktion* under Otto Mühl.[27] Given the nature of sources, tracking individual life stories is usually impossible, unless individual authors wrote about their political biography. This book, however, is not interested in life stories, but in the political visions and practices that were developed within the alternative left. Seeking to understand the political project of the alternative milieu as a whole, the book draws on diverse examples to highlight shared ideas and practices rather than differences between different groups.

The terminology employed to describe this milieu was not always clear. Some political groups, especially in Northern Germany, described themselves as nondogmatic, in distinction to the dogmatic *K-Gruppen*. Others referred to themselves as 'Spontis', for example in Frankfurt am Main and in Heidelberg. Finally, the term 'alternatives [*die Alternativen*]' emerged at the end of the 1970s. Scholars, too, have employed different concepts to describe these groups. Some have addressed them as parts of New Social Movements, thus emphasizing the variety of political issues and campaigns these groups were involved in, ranging from sexual liberation to environmentalism.[28] Pursuing a more holistic approach that is less interested in political campaigns, but in a common search for authenticity and warmth in this milieu, Sven Reichardt has described those leftist groups as an 'alternative milieu'.[29] For the most part, this study follows Reichardt's terminology, though it also refers to these groups as radical or

---

[27] On Mühl, see Reichardt, *Authentizität*, 686–699. It should be noted, however, that many leftists criticized Mühl's AAO as fascist.

[28] See Cordia Baumann, Stefan Gehrig, and Nicolas Büchse, eds., *Linksalternative Milieus und Neue Soziale Bewegungen in den 1970er Jahren* (Heidelberg: Universitätsverlag Winter, 2011); Joachim Raschke, *Soziale Bewegungen: Ein historisch-systematischer Grundriss* (Frankfurt a.M.: Campus, 1985); Roland Roth and Dieter Rucht, eds., *Die sozialen Bewegungen in Deutschland seit 1945: Ein Handbuch* (Frankfurt a.M.: Campus, 2008); Dieter Rucht, *Modernisierung und neue soziale Bewegungen: Deutschland, Frankreich und USA im Vergleich* (Frankfurt a.M.: Campus, 1995); Michael M. Zwick, *Neue soziale Bewegungen als politische Subkultur: Zielsetzungen, Anhängerschaft, Mobilisierung – eine empirische Analyse* (Frankfurt a.M.: Campus, 1990); Roland Roth and Dieter Rucht, *Neue soziale Bewegungen in der Bundesrepublik Deutschland* (Bonn: Bundeszentrale für Politische Bildung, 1987); Karl-Werner Brand, Detlef Büsser, and Dieter Rucht, *Aufbruch in eine andere Gesellschaft: Neue soziale Bewegungen in der Bundesrepublik* (Frankfurt a.M.: Campus, 1983).

[29] Reichardt, *Authentizität*. See also the essays in Sven Reichardt and Detlef Siegfried, eds., *Das Alternative Milieu: Antibürgerlicher Lebensstil und linke Politik in der Bundesrepublik Deutschland und Europa 1968–1983* (Göttingen: Wallstein, 2010).

nondogmatic leftists, reflecting that the terminology in the sources is anything but coherent.

If anything shaped the contours and boundaries of this alternative milieu, it was the vast number of magazines and newspapers that formed a (counter-) public sphere of the milieu.[30] In 1981, observers counted 390 magazines or newspapers associated with the alternative scene, with a total print run of 1.6 million. Many of these magazines referred to each other, republished texts first published in another magazine, or published advertisements for each other. These cross-references suggest, differences and conflicts notwithstanding, the existence of a sphere of communication that was essential for the constitution of the alternative milieu. Tracing the links between magazines enables us to get a sense of who was part of this milieu and who was not, though boundaries were never entirely clear. At the core of this network of publications were local magazines, known as *Stadtblätter* – magazines that reported about local events such as parties, concerts or movie screenings as well as about the activities of local initiatives working on a range of topics, from the urban development to solidarity with so-called Third World movements; they also published small adds by people offering free rooms in communal apartments or looking for intimate relations. Typically, these magazines opened their pages for contributions from readers and the local scenes and thus enabled diverse local groups, whether they were gay groups or environmental initiatives, to communicate with each other. Such magazines existed in major university cities with a strong alternative scene, for example the *Blatt* in Munich, *Pflasterstrand* in Frankfurt, or *'s Blättle* in Stuttgart, to name only a few; various *Infos* of 'undogmatic groups' in different cities, such as *Info BUG* in West Berlin or *Carlo Sponti* in Heidelberg, fulfilled a similar function, though they focused more explicitly on political topics. The alternative public sphere also included more theoretical magazines like *Autonomie: Materialien gegen die Fabrikgesellschaft* or *Schwarze Protokolle*, as well as magazines by the women's movement like *Courage* or the *Frauenjahrbücher*, and the gay movement, like *HAW Info* and *Emanzipation*, and occasionally even local high school newspapers by left-leaning students. In their totality, these publications provide insights into the diversity of issues with which the alternative left was concerned, ranging from struggles against imperialism to healthy food, new-ageism and new forms of intimate and sexual relations.

---

[30] On the alternative press, see with further references Reichardt, *Authentizität*, 223–315.

These publications also provide a glimpse into the size of the milieu. The publication numbers themselves are telling, and, given that the count dates from 1981, a number of magazines that had ceased publication by that time would have to be added. Otherwise, we have to rely on the estimates of contemporary observers. According to one estimate from 1980, some eighty thousand people were active in alternative projects of some kind. A much larger number professed to be following an at least partially alternative lifestyle. A survey in 1979 for example estimated that between 10 and 15 per cent of West German teenagers belonged to the alternative milieu; another survey from 1980 found that 2.7 million people between fourteen and fifty-four were 'alternatives', and another 3.4 million people were open to alternative ideas. Not surprisingly, most 'alternatives' were university students, mostly studying humanities or social sciences, as anecdotal evidence suggests. In addition to large cities with a strong leftist scene like West Berlin, Frankfurt or Munich, university cities like Heidelberg, Freiburg or Göttingen were centres of the alternative milieu. People in these local scenes often knew each other, disregarding their distinct political affiliations. They went to the same parties, the same concerts, and read the same local publications. The predominance of students in the alternative milieu also indicates that most activists were members of the educated middle classes. Activists with working-class backgrounds were a rarity within the milieu, and often had a hard time fitting in. It was also a predominantly white milieu, despite the fascination with the Third World and 'native', supposedly more authentic peoples that can be found amongst alternative leftists. Foreign students and immigrant workers were largely absent in the alternative left. The alternative milieu was a minority phenomenon, these numbers indicate. Yet it was anything but a small and marginal minority that joined this milieu, as its popularity amongst students and educated young adults suggests.[31]

The alternative milieu that developed in the years after 1968 reached its apogee in the mid to late 1970s, though elements of alternative lifestyles continued to exist into the 1980s. The main chapters of this book thus discuss the alternative milieu without inquiring about chronological dynamics. This basic continuity notwithstanding, an important change can be noted in the wake of the German Autumn of 1977, the abduction

---

[31] For numbers, see ibid., 41–48; Siegfried, 'Entpolitisierung', 124–125; Sven Reichardt and Detlef Siegfried, 'Das Alternative Milieu: Konturen einer Lebensform', in *Das Alternative Milieu: Antibürgerlicher Lebensstil und linke Politik in der Bundesrepublik Deutschland und Europa 1968–1983*, ed. Sven Reichardt and Detlef Siegfried (Göttingen: Wallstein, 2010).

and murder of Hanns-Martin Schleyer and the subsequent death of imprisoned RAF members, when a sense of despair took hold in the alternative milieu.[32] The fact that many nondogmatic new leftists were considered RAF 'sympathizers' by the state only increased this impression. Publishers of leading magazines, for example *Info BUG* from West Berlin, faced prosecution for allegedly supporting terrorism. The nondogmatic left had hit, activists felt, an impasse. In this situation, a group of Berlin activists decided to organize a large gathering, called TUNIX (literally, 'Do Nothing') Congress.[33] To everyone's surprise, some twenty thousand people showed up. Timothy Brown and Karrin Hanshew have suggested that the TUNIX Congress marked the end of a period of radical left-wing struggles.[34] This is, at best, half the story. The congress marked a turning point for the alternative milieu that signalled not only an end of an era of left-wing politics, but also a new phase of activism. Some activists turned to politics in the more traditional sense and pushed for the formation of the Green Party.[35] Others turned away from political issues and came to focus entirely on transforming their selves, for example by in the context of New Age groups.[36] Yet there was also a sense of new potentials for radical activism emerging out of TUNIX, which moved beyond the politics of the alternative left. This renewed sense of activism culminated in the wave of militant protests and squatting in West German cities like Freiburg and West Berlin, but also in Zurich in Switzerland. These events are the subject of the final chapter.

---

[32] On terrorism, see for example Sarah Colvin, *Ulrike Meinhof and West German Terrorism: Language, Violence, and Identity* (Rochester, NY: Camden, 2009); Sebastian Gehrig, 'Sympathizing Subcultures? The Milieus of West German Terrorism', in *Between Prague Spring and French May: Opposition and Revolt in Europe, 1960–1980*, ed. Martin Klimke, Jacco Pekelder, and Joachim Scharloth (New York: Berghahn, 2011),; Leith Passmore, *Ulrike Meinhof and the Red Army Faction: Performing Terrorism* (New York: Palgrave Macmillan, 2011); Karrin Hanshew, *Terror and Democracy in West Germany* (Cambridge: Cambridge University Press, 2012); Petra Terhoeven, *Deutscher Herbst in Europa: Der Linksterrorismus der siebziger Jahre als transnationales Phänomen* (Berlin: De Gruyter Oldenbourg, 2016).

[33] See März, *Linker Protest*.

[34] Brown, *West Germany*, 354–362, Hanshew, *Terror and Democracy in West Germany*, 241–252. For a perspective from a radical geographer, see Alex Vasudevan, *Metropolitan Preoccupations: The Spatial Politics of Squatting in Berlin* (Chichester, UK: John Wiley and Sons, 2016), 86–97.

[35] See Silke Mende, *'Nicht rechts, nicht links, sondern vorn': Eine Geschichte der Gründungsgrünen* (Munich: Oldenbourg, 2011).

[36] See for example Pascal Eitler, '"Alternative" Religion: Subjektivierungspraktiken und Politisierungsstrategien im "New Age" (Westdeutschland 1970–1990)', in *Das Alternative Milieu: Antibürgerlicher Lebensstil und linke Politik in der Bundesrepublik Deutschland und Europa, 1968–1983*, ed. Sven Reichardt and Detlef Siegfried (Göttingen: Wallstein, 2010).

Understanding the Alternative Left: Historiography and Theory

The broadly defined New Left in West Germany has been the subject of an extensive scholarship, both in English and German. Much of this work is characterized by a focus on the student revolts around 1968. Scholars have investigated both the complicated histories that led to the protests, and the impact of those revolts on West German society in the years to come. Yet the years from 1967 to 1969, when the student revolt in West Germany reached its apogee, remain at the centre of the narrative, even though historians have extended their chronological horizon and have come to question how radical a rupture those revolts really were.[37] Recent studies have provided us with an increasingly complex understanding of the dynamics of protest and revolt around 1968. Scholars have explored the role of rituals for questioning symbolic and social power, the reaction of the establishment and the state to the revolts, the transnational connections activists fostered with their comrades in the United States as well as with students from Third World countries studying in Germany, the importance of protests around issues of consumption, or the specificities of local dynamics.[38] As interesting and important as many of these studies are, their narrative focus on 1968 is also limiting. On an empirical level, we read all too often about the familiar leading figures of 1968 – Rudi Dutschke, Daniel Cohn-Bendit, K. D. Wolff, Dieter Kunzelmann or Bahmann Nirumand –, the same journals, such as *Kursbuch* or *konkret*, and the same organizations, like the *Sozialistischer Studentenbund*

---

[37] See Axel Schildt, Detlef Siegfried, and Karl Christian Lammers, eds., *Dynamische Zeiten: Die 60er Jahre in den beiden deutschen Gesellschaften* (Hamburg: Christians, 2000); Klaus Weinhauer, 'Zwischen Aufbruch und Revolte: Die 68er Bewegung und die Gesellschaft der Bundesrepublik Deutschland der sechziger Jahre', *Neue Politische Literatur* 3 (2001); Norbert Frei, *1968: Jugendrevolte und globaler Protest* (Munich: Deutscher Taschenbuchverlag, 2008).

[38] See for example and with useful discussions of the historiography, Martin Klimke, *The Other Alliance: Student Protest in West Germany and the United States in the Global Sixties* (Princeton: Princeton University Press, 2010); Quinn Slobodian, *Foreign Front: Third World Politics in Sixties West Germany* (Durham, NC: Duke University Press, 2012); Katja Nagel, *Die Provinz in Bewegung: Studentenunruhen in Heidelberg 1967–1973* (Heidelberg: Verlag für Regionalkultur, 2009); Wolfgang Kraushaar, *1968 als Mythos, Chiffre und Zäsur* (Hamburg: Hamburger Edition, 2000); Aribert Reimann, *Dieter Kunzelmann: Avantgardist, Protestler, Radikaler* (Göttingen: Vandenhoeck & Ruprecht, 2009); Susanne Rinner, *The German Student Movement and the Literary Imagination: Transnational Memories of Protest and Dissent* (New York: Berghahn, 2013); Alexander Sedlmaier, *Consumption and Violence: Radical Protest in Cold-War West Germany* (Ann Arbor, MI: University of Michigan Press, 2014); Scharloth, *1968*; Andrea Wienhaus, *Bildungswege zu '1968': Eine Kollektivbiografie des Sozialistischen Deutschen Studentenbundes* (Bielefeld: transcript, 2014); Stefanie Pilzweger, *Männlichkeit zwischen Gefühl und Revolution: Eine Emotionsgeschichte der bundesdeutschen 68er-Bewegung* (Bielefeld: transcript, 2015); Vasudevan, *Metropolitan Preoccupations*.

Deutschlands (SDS) or *Kommune 2*. Until recently, scholars who move beyond the focus on 1968 have tended to focus on terrorism and the Red Army Faction. Geoff Eley, in a telling statement, for example remarked that the decade between 2 June 1967, when Benno Ohnesorg was killed by a police officer during a demonstration against the Shah, and the 'German Autumn' of 1977 forms a coherent period.[39] Indeed, as Joachim Scharloth has quipped, it has become difficult to say something new about 1968.[40]

The dual focus on the student revolts of 1968 and terrorism that culminated in 1977 is also limiting conceptually. Both the student revolts and terrorism are typically interpreted within the democratization (or, in its more cultural version, liberalization) framework, an interpretative framework that also dominates much of the historiography of West Germany more broadly.[41] On the one hand, scholars have claimed that the student revolts had a democratic impulse and, even more importantly, ultimately democratizing effects. According to this interpretation, students succeeded in overcoming the authoritarian and antidemocratic structures that had still existed in the early Federal Republic. Even if the radically democratic impulses were not all realized, the revolting students helped implement a democratic culture. Some scholars have even argued that the revolt presented a 're-foundation of the Second Republic' that ultimately strengthened democratic legitimacy of the West German state.[42] Most recently, Timothy Brown has presented such a history of West Germany's 'antiauthoritarian revolt', stressing the radical 'antiauthoritarian and self-organizational imperatives' activists followed and that called for a radical, participatory democracy.[43] On the other hand, scholars have denounced the students as fundamentally antidemocratic. West Germany became a stable democracy not because, but despite of the revolting students.[44] It

---

[39] 'Forum: 1977, The German Autumn', *German History* 25 (2007). The chronological argument goes back to Gerd Koenen, *Das rote Jahrzehnt: Unsere kleine deutsche Kulturrevolution 1967–1977* (Cologne: Kiepenheuer & Witsch, 2001).

[40] Scharloth, *1968*.

[41] See the discussion of the historiography in ibid., 14–20, Slobodian, *Foreign Front*, Vasudevan, *Metropolitan Preoccupations*, 7–12. For a general interpretation of West German history as a successful democratization, see most importantly Edgar Wolfrum, *Die geglückte Demokratie: Geschichte der Bundesrepubik Deutschland von ihren Anfängen bis zur Gegenwart* (Stuttgart: Klett-Cotta, 2006).

[42] Claus Leggewie, '1968 ist Geschichte', *Aus Politik und Zeitgeschichte* B 22–23 (2001). For a discussion, see Scharloth, *1968*, 16.

[43] Brown, *West Germany*, 17–19.

[44] See for example Eckart Conze, *Die Suche nach Sicherheit: Eine Geschichte der Bundesrepublik Deutschland von 1949 bis in die Gegenwart* (Munich: Siedler, 2009), 357. See also Kurt Sontheimer, 'Gegen den Mythos der 68er', *Die ZEIT* 6 (8 February 2001), 34, and Kurt

proved able to resist a more or less dangerous, antidemocratic threat. Even the wave of terrorism in the late 1970s has been placed into this context. As Karrin Hanshew has forcefully argued, the state's successful but moderate response to terrorism allowed both conservatives and leftists to make peace with the Federal Republic that had demonstrated that it was able to deal with terrorism without having recourse to brutal oppression.[45]

A less political and more cultural version of this argument puts the revolts of 1968 in the context of an alleged 'liberalization' of society and a fundamental change in social norms.[46] 'Postmaterialist' values replaced older desires for material well-being and safety, scholars have claimed, while social norms and manners, for example regarding sexuality, became less rigid, at least in part as a result of the student movement. Acceptance of extramarital sexual relations, homosexuality, and informal dress or communicative codes increased, and society as a whole allegedly became more liberal.[47] Critics of this argument have, however, pointed out that many of these processes were well underway by the mid-1960s. 'The rebels of 1968 stormed barricades that had been abandoned by their former defenders', as Philipp Gassert put it.[48] Whether the revolting students

Sontheimer, *So war Deutschland nie: Anmerkungen zur politischen Kultur der Bundesrepublik* (Munich: C.H. Beck, 1999). For a discussion, see Scharloth, *1968*, 17.

[45] See Hanshew, *Terror and Democracy in West Germany*; Hanshew, '"Sympathy for the Devil?" The West German Left and the Challenge of Terrorism', *Contemporary European History* 21 (2012).

[46] See the essays in Ulrich Herbert, ed., *Wandlungsprozesse in Westdeutschland: Belastung, Integration, Liberalisierung 1945–1980* (Göttingen: Wallstein, 2002); Matthias Frese, Julia Paulus, and Karl Teppe, eds., *Demokratisierung und gesellschaftlicher Aufbruch: Die sechziger Jahre als Wendezeit der Bundesrepublik* (Paderborn: Ferdinand Schöningh, 2003). For an account of West German youth culture along somewhat similar lines, see Detlef Siegfried, *Time Is on My Side: Konsum und Politik in der westdeutschen Jugendkultur der 60er Jahre* (Göttingen: Wallstein, 2006). The foundational text for the debate regarding 'changing values' is Ronald Inglehart, *The Silent Revolution: Changing Values and Political Styles among Western Publics* (Princeton: Princeton University Press, 1977). For a good discussion of the debate, see David Templin, *Freizeit ohne Kontrollen: Die Jugendzentrumsbewegung in der Bundesrepublik der 1970er Jahre* (Göttingen: Wallstein, 2015), 10–11. See also Bernhard Dietz, Andreas Rödder, and Christopher Neumaier, eds., *Gab es den Wertewandel? Neue Forschungen zum gesellschaftlich-kulturellen Wandel seit den 1960er Jahren* (Munich: Oldenbourg, 2014); Andreas Rödder and Wolfgang Elz, eds., *Alte Werte – neue Werte: Schlaglichter des Wertewandels* (Göttingen: Vandenhoeck & Ruprecht, 2008); Tobias Sander, 'Der Wertewandel der 1960er und 1970er Jahre und soziale Ungleichheit: Neue Befunde zu widersprüchlichen Interpretamenten', *Comparativ: Zeitschrift für Globalgeschichte und vergleichende Gesellschaftsforschung* 7 (2007).

[47] See for example Karl-Heinz Bohrer, '1968: Die Phantasie an die Macht? Studentenbewegung – Walter Benjamin – Surrealismus', in *1968 – Vom Ereignis zum Gegenstand der Geschichtswissenschaft*, ed. Ingrid Gilcher-Holtey (Göttingen: Vandenhoeck & Ruprecht, 1995), 300. For a discussion, see Scharloth, *1968*, 15–16.

[48] Philipp Gassert, 'Narratives of Democratization: 1968 in Postwar Europe', in *1968 in Europe: A History of Protest and Activism, 1956–1977*, ed. Martin Klimke and Joachim Scharloth (New York: Palgrave Macmillan, 2008), 315.

are given democratic credit or not, whether their actions are viewed as having a liberalizing impact or not, the revolts of 1968 are thus integrated into master narratives of West-Germany history that depict the Federal Republic as a state and society on the ultimately successful path into the family of liberal, western democracies.

This interpretation of West German history in general and the revolts around 1968 has been questioned in recent years. Scholars have noted the teleological and highly normative character of those success stories of democratization and liberalization.[49] Nina Verheyen has, for example, criticized the normative 'democratization' narrative. Instead, she has called for historicizing the linkage between democracy and discussing by showing how American occupation forces tried to teach Germans in the aftermath of World War II how to discuss in order to turn them into good democratic citizens. Interpreting West Germany's discursification as part of a successful democratization would simply replicate a historically peculiar understanding of how democracy requires such forms of communication; it would also overlook that discussions were not free of domination, *pace* Jürgen Habermas, but privileged those who had the necessary skills to succeed in such discussions. Verheyen's study thus historicizes the democratization narrative itself.[50] With regards to the revolts of 1968, linguist Joachim Scharloth makes a related argument. He focuses on communicative styles, noting that informal styles of communication, both verbally and physically, became more common in the wake of the student revolts. Addressing each other with the informal *Du*, people performed a personal intimacy – 'doing buddy', as Scharloth calls it. The informal communicative style he analyzes seemed to be less formal and less rigid, but nevertheless followed its own strict rules. Interpreting it as another aspect of a 'fundamental liberalization', that is the reduction or abolishment of rules regulating social interaction, would be utterly misleading.[51] Just like Verheyen, Scharloth moves beyond the democratization narrative and thus offers one way out of the highly politicized and ultimately unproductive debates whether '1968' had democratizing effects or not.

---

[49] See for example the work by Dominik Rigoll, *Staatsschutz in Westdeutschland: Von der Entnazifizierung zur Extremistenabwehr* (Göttingen: Wallstein Verlag, 2013). See also the work by Konrad Jarausch, who argues that contemporary history needs to provide an explanation for the problems of the present: Konrad H. Jarausch, 'Verkannter Strukturwandel: Die siebziger Jahre als Vorgeschichte der Probleme der Gegenwart', in *Das Ende der Zuversicht? Die siebziger Jahre als Geschichte*, ed. Konrad H. Jarausch (Göttingen: Vandenhoeck & Ruprecht, 2008).

[50] Nina Verheyen, *Diskussionslust: Eine Kulturgeschichte des 'besseren Arguments' in Westdeutschland* (Göttingen: Vandenhoeck & Ruprecht, 2010).

[51] Scharloth, *1968*.

Sven Reichardt has recently provided us with an innovative interpretation of a leftist movement that points beyond questions of democratization and liberalization.[52] Given the importance of Reichardt's monumental study, which addresses the same subject as this book, it is worth discussing his arguments in some detail. Drawing on the work of Michel Foucault, Reichardt proposes to analyze the 'alternative milieu' as a 'regime of subjectification, in which self-shaping [*Selbstmodellierung*] was turned into life-politics [*Lebenspolitik*]'.[53] At the core of this self-shaping was the desire for 'authenticity', which included a desire for authentic feelings. Reichardt's study is an attempt to identify the 'genealogies, forms, practices, constellations and discursive negotiations of the grasp on the self'. In other words, he seeks to understand how alternative subjects 'performatively created themselves' as 'authentic', and how this concept was used 'strategically' as a tool of power.[54] On a theoretical level, Reichardt invokes Foucault's argument that freedom and coercion are not mutually exclusive, but related to each other; the alternative regime of subjectivity, that is, both enabled and required individuals to care for themselves. This perspective offers a 'mediating alternative', Reichardt claims, between the two interpretations of the alternative culture as either liberating or restrictive and, at worst, totalitarian. Reichardt thus sets out to analyze the 'complexes of knowledge and practices', '"with which individuals are typified as individuals and that admonish them to comply to their obligation of individualization."'[55] However, as scholars drawing on Foucault sometimes tend to do, Reichardt effectively stresses the coercive elements that are often concealed behind a rhetoric of liberation. As Reichardt puts it:

> Within the left-alternative milieu, people not only had the right to live self-realized [*selbstverwirklicht*], but also the duty to render account of themselves, and to convey these insights into the self to others ... The self-therapeutization was intended as a project for the liberation of the alienated individual, but unfolded in the practice of the democratic panopticism a norming effect and became a management of the self.[56]

---

[52] Reichardt, *Authentizität*.   [53] Ibid., 68.   [54] Ibid., 67.
[55] Ibid., 67. Reichardt quotes Bröckling, *Unternehmerische Selbst*, 24.
[56] Reichardt, *Authentizität*, 67–71. For further critiques of the liberalization paradigm along such Foucauldian lines, see Jens Elberfeld, 'Subjekt/Beziehung: Patriarchat – Partnerschaft – Projekt. Psychowissen und Normalisierungspraktiken im Diskurs der Paartherapie (BRD 1960–1990)', in *Das Selbst zwischen Anpassung und Befreiung: Psychowissen und Politik im 20. Jahrhundert*, ed. Uffa Jensen and Maik Tändler (Göttingen: Wallstein, 2012), 113–114; Jens Elberfeld, 'Befreiung des Subjekts, Management des Selbst: Therapeutisierungsprozesse im deutschsprachigen Raum seit den

Reichardt's work has many merits. By focusing on practices of subjectification, he avoids both praising the alternative left as part of the fundamental liberalization of West German society and denouncing it as a 'totalitarian project'. Instead, he highlights how power and freedom, and the relation between these two, changed. In the alternative milieu, 'external coercion was replaced by an internalized coercion that pretended to be liberty'. [*An die Stelle des Fremdzwangs trat ein Selbstzwang, der sich als Freiheit ausgab*].[57] It turns our attention to a broad variety of communicative, bodily and emotional practices, to phenomena such as consciousness raising and therapy groups and New Ageism in the alternative left, that so far have received little attention.[58] Both conceptually and empirically, Reichardt's work is a landmark study that advances our understanding of the left during the 1970s and postwar West German history more generally.

Reichardt's book can be situated within a larger trend in German scholarship that, building on the work of Michel Foucault as well as cultural sociologists like Andreas Reckwitz, Ulrich Bröckling, or Sabine Maasen, investigates the history, or rather, as Pascal Eitler and Jens Elberfeld emphasize, the genealogy of the contemporary self.[59] This scholarship seeks to understand the demands a society or group of people imposes upon human beings to be recognized as 'authentic', 'as a self that is recognized and accepted by others as well'.[60] Crucially, studies pursuing this approach do not limit their perspective to ways in which human beings are governed by others (*Fremdführung*), but turn to forms of 'self-governing' (*Selbstführung*). People are not only subjected to specific requirements of self-formation or 'subject-cultures', but people subject themselves to those requirements. Only by adopting these requirements and thereby reproducing but also transforming them, the argument goes, does a society emerge in a performative way. To study those practices of

1960er Jahren', in *Zeitgeschichte des Selbst: Therapeutisierung – Politisierung – Emotionalisierung*, ed. Pascal Eitler and Jens Elberfeld (Bielefeld: Transcript, 2015), 81–82; Marcel Streng, 'Führungsverhältnisse im Hungerstreik: Ein Kapitel zur Geschichte des westdeutschen Strafvollzugs (1973–1985)', in *Zeitgeschichte des Selbst: Therapeutisierung – Politisierung – Emotionalisierung*, ed. Pascal Eitler and Jens Elberfeld (Bielefeld: Transcript, 2015), 145.

[57] Reichardt, *Authentizität*, 887.

[58] See also the contributions in Reichardt and Siegfried, eds., *Alternative Milieu*.

[59] See Reckwitz, *Hybride Subjekt*; Bröckling, *Unternehmerische Selbst*; Sabine Maasen, *Genealogie der Unmoral: Zur Therapeutisierung sexueller Selbste* (Frankfurt a.M.: Suhrkamp, 1998); Eitler and Elberfeld, eds., *Zeitgeschichte*.

[60] Pascal Eitler and Jens Elberfeld, 'Von der Gesellschaftsgeschichte zur Zeitgeschichte des Selbst – und zurück', in *Zeitgeschichte des Selbst: Therapeutisierung – Politisierung – Emotionalisierung*, ed. Pascal Eitler and Jens Elberfeld (Bielefeld: transcript, 2015).

subjectification, scholars have looked at how people shaped, or tried to shape their selves, how they shaped their feelings and psyche in therapeutic contexts, and their bodies through sports or medicine. In particular, scholars have explored how a knowledge about the body, the mind and feelings was created that people could and should use to form their individual bodies, minds and feelings. A variety of studies have addressed the therapy boom of the 1970s, questions of sexuality and sexual self-formation, drug consumption and as ascetic practices, self-formation at the workplace or in religious contexts.[61] What has emerged in the present is, it seems, a regime of subjectification that requires people to constantly work on themselves and to take care of themselves – physically, mentally and emotionally. In the 'democratic panopticum' of contemporary governmentality, everyone has to become an 'entrepreneur of the self', constantly engaged in self-observation and self-improvement.[62]

This is a highly stimulating and theoretically sophisticated body of literature.[63] Yet I also see problems, both with regards to the theoretical framework and to how at least some empirical studies proceed. Sociologists like Reckwitz and Bröckling, who, drawing on Michel Foucault themselves, provide much theoretical inspiration for historical studies, are primarily interested in forms of knowledge that regulate the formation of subjectivities, in the scripts of subjectivity that people can enact; they are not interested in what actual human beings do. Using the metaphor of a classroom, Bröckling for example explains that the genealogical perspective he is advocating is not interested in what a student does in the class room, but in how various institutions and people, including the student herself, try to make her do certain things and not do other things.[64] Conceptually, this perspective strikes me as ultimately incoherent, as neither what the

---

[61] See the contributions in Maasen et al., eds., *Beratene Selbst*; Eitler and Elberfeld, eds., *Zeitgeschichte*; Uffa Jensen and Maik Tändler, eds., *Das Selbst zwischen Anpassung und Befreiung: Psychowissen und Politik im 20. Jahrhundert* (Göttingen: Wallstein, 2012); Thomas Lemke, Susanne Krasmann, and Ulrich Bröckling, eds., *Gouvernementalität der Gegenwart: Studien zur Ökonomisierung des Sozialen* (Frankfurt a.M.: Suhrkamp, 2000); Jens Elberfeld and Marcus Otto, eds., *Das schöne Selbst: Zur Genealogie des modernen Subjekts zwischen Ethik und Ästhetik* (Bielefeld: transcript, 2009).

[62] Bröckling, *Unternehmerische Selbst*; Ulrich Bröckling, 'Das demokratisierte Panopticon: Subjektivierung und Kontrolle im 360° Feedback', in *Michel Foucault: Zwischenbilanz einer Rezeption. Frankfurter Foucault-Konferenz 2001*, ed. Axel Honneth and Martin Saar (Frankfurt a. M.: Suhrkamp, 2003).

[63] See my discussion in Joachim C. Häberlen, 'The Contemporary Self in German History (Review Article)', *Contemporary European History*, forthcoming.

[64] Ulrich Bröckling, 'Regime des Selbst – Ein Forschungsprogramm', in *Kulturen der Moderne: Soziologische Perspektiven auf die Gegenwart*, ed. Thomas Bonacker and Andreas Reckwitz (Frankfurt a.M.: Campus, 2007), 134.

student does, nor the institutions that try to regulate what she does, can be understood in isolation. What we need is, I suggest, a study that considers both the forms of knowledge that shape a subjectivity, and what people do with this knowledge, not least because what people do with this knowledge ultimately shapes that knowledge itself.[65]

Empirically, Reckwitz and Bröckling turn to sources that advise people on what they are supposed to do and what not – to guidance literature, for example, but also to theoretical texts such as the work of Herbert Marcuse, Guy Debord, or Gilles Deleuze, which Reckwitz uses to describe the 'hedonistic' subject he sees emerging in the 1960s.[66] In the end, this approach results in a 'relatively static sociological grand-scale model', as Maik Tändler rightly remarks.[67] Historical studies that use guidance and advice literature but ignore what exactly people do with this literature arguably face a similar problem.[68] Reichardt's work is different in this regard insofar as he does analyze what people did and moves beyond looking at merely theoretical texts. Nevertheless, the picture he ultimately draws is remarkably static, too. Indeed, his prose is telling. It is full of the impersonal German *man*: one wanted, one should, one had to. Thus emerges the impression of rather strict norms and constraints of what people had to do to be authentic, but no sense of anyone 'doing' the 'doings'.

This book shares a certain scepticism vis-à-vis narratives of democratization and liberalization that ignore less formal but by no means less powerful forms of constraint. Indeed, studies of contemporary selfhood have provided a useful alternative to such success stories. Nevertheless, the book is equally sceptical about replacing a narrative of democratization with a narrative of the formation of a neoliberal or, for that matter, hedonistic subjectivity that comes with its own norms and requirements. Ultimately, such interpretations fail to grasp ambivalences and contingencies. Instead, the book argues for looking at the 1970s as a period of experimentation. Rather than interpreting the 1970s as a 'prehistory' of the present, or, more precisely, the prehistory of a present regime of subjectivity, the book seeks to regain a sense of the openness of the 1970s.

---

[65] In a programmatic text, Andreas Reckwitz acknowledges that individuals practise their subjectivity in idiosyncratic ways. Yet he suggests that studies might pay attention to such idiosyncracies in passing, but should nevertheless focus on socially dominant forms. See Andreas Reckwitz, 'Auf dem Weg zu einer praxeologischen Analyse des Selbst', in *Zeitgeschichte des Selbst: Therapeutisierung – Politisierung – Emotionalisierung*, ed. Pascal Eitler and Jens Elberfeld (Bielefeld: Transcript, 2015), 44–45.

[66] Reckwitz, *Hybride Subjekt*, 441–499.   [67] Tändler, *Therapeutische Jahrzehnt*, 39.

[68] See for example the contributions in Jensen and Tändler, eds., *Selbst*; Eitler and Elberfeld, eds., *Zeitgeschichte*.

Discussing the emotional politics of the alternative left, the book explores how leftists 'tried out' feelings, sometimes succeeding and sometimes failing, based on an understanding of politics for which feelings played a central role.

To make sense of leftist emotional practices, the book first examines how leftists imagined their political world. Leftists divided their political world into two camps: on the one side, they saw the forces of rationality that structured and categorized all aspects of life; not least, capitalism was, leftists argued, based on the principles of rationality. The critique of capitalism leftists developed, in other words, was a critique of rational capitalism. In the other proverbial camp, leftists located the forces of anything that remained outside the reach of rationality: dreams, desires, fantasies and above all feelings that challenged and questioned the domination of rationality. Understanding the logic of this political discourse highlights the centrality of feelings for leftist politics, both in terms of their critique of capitalism and, even more importantly, in terms of leftist political practices. Recuperating the feelings that were, according to leftist thinking, buried under the rationality of capitalism became a central goal for leftist practices.[69] This conceptualization of the political can hardly be understood in terms of democratization. Alternative leftists in the 1970s did not struggle for a more democratic world, in whatever sense, but for liberating feelings. Alternative left thus placed questions of subjectivity at the centre of their politics. Indeed, it would be interesting to trace the current scholarly concern with subjectivity and the political potential of feelings to its origins in the alternative milieu of the 1970s. It is, after all, not by chance that thinkers like Michel Foucault, but also Gilles Deleuze and Félix Guattari were widely read in the scene.[70]

Producing feelings of intimacy and intensity was thus crucial for alternative activism, not only because these feelings were missing in the capitalist world leftists inhabited, as they saw it, but because such feelings had a subversive potential. As Reichardt notes, expressing one's feelings was an essential requirement of practising an authentic subjectivity in the alternative milieu. Yet, whereas Reichardt emphasizes the informal requirements that governed how people could and had to practice an emotionally authentic subjectivity, this study is interested in the production of

[69] See also Häberlen and Smith, 'Struggling'.
[70] See in this context the study about the important leftwing publisher Merve by Philipp Felsch, *Der lange Sommer der Theorie: Geschichte einer Revolte* (Munich: Beck, 2015). See also Philipp Felsch, 'Merves Lachen', *Zeitschrift für Ideengeschichte* 2 (2008); Philipp Felsch, 'Der Leser als Partisan', *Zeitschrift für Ideengeschichte* 6 (2012); Uwe Sonnenberg, *Von Marx zum Maulwurf: Linker Buchhandel in Westdeutschland in den 1970er Jahren* (Göttingen: Wallstein, 2016), 319–320.

emotions in the alternative left. In other words, I ask what leftists did '*in order to* have [those] emotions' they missed in the capitalist word they considered emotionally void.[71] Conceiving of emotions as practices, as Monique Scheer has suggested, the book shares an interest in practices with the studies of subjectivities discussed earlier. But my perspective is more microscopic, as it were. To use Bröckling's metaphor, I am not only interested in how various institutions try to regulate what the student does, but also in how the students reacts to and interacts with these demands. By looking as closely as possible at what people did to feel, or, put more radically, how people *tried* to 'do' the feelings they desired, we can gain a sense of the openness and contingencies of emotional production. Studying the alternative left from a history of emotions perspective that seeks to reconstruct practical attempts to feel differently yields a more nuanced and more fluid picture of the 1970s. The book is thus less interested in the formation of a particular regime of subjectivity, but rather in how leftists during the 1970s tied to produce feelings in a fluid and contingent process.

Seen from this perspective, the alternative left appears as a space for experimenting with feelings in multiple ways.[72] Indeed, trying to 'recuperate' feelings became an imperative in the alternative left; but how to do so was open to discussion. And what worked for producing feelings and what did not was never clear. Talking freely about feelings was one way of producing these feelings, albeit a problematic and often considered insufficient one. Leftists regarded feelings as something deeply bodily and sensual, and hence developed a variety of bodily and sensual practices that would allow activists both to feel their bodies and to feel *with* their bodies. The book is thus as much a contribution to the history of emotions in postwar Germany as a contribution to the history of the body.[73]

To make sense of how leftists tried to produce feelings, we also need to understand precisely how they held capitalism responsible for limiting them.

---

[71] Monique Scheer, 'Are Emotions a Kind of Practice (and Is That What Makes Them Have a History)? A Bourdieuan Approach to Understanding Emotion', *History and Theory* 51 (2012): 194. The history of emotions is a thriving field. For a discussion of the literature, see Nicole Eustace et al., '*AHR* Conversation: The Historical Study of Emotions', *American Historical Review* 117 (2012); Jan Plamper, *The History of Emotions: An Introduction*, trans. Keith Tribe (Oxford: Oxford University Press, 2015). See also, with special attention to emotions in protest movements, Joachim C. Häberlen and Russell A. Spinney, 'Introduction', *Contemporary European History* 23 (2014).

[72] See Joachim C. Häberlen and Maik Tändler, 'Spaces for Feeling Differently: Emotional Experiments in the Alternative Left in West Germany during the 1970s', *Emotion, Space and Society* 25 (2017).

[73] See Eitler and Scheer, 'Emotionengeschichte'. See also the contributions to Netzwerk Körper, ed., *What Can a Body Do? Praktiken und Figurationen des Körpers in den Kulturwissenschaften* (Frankfurt a.M.: Campus Verlag, 2012).

To this end, the book makes use of the concept of 'emotional regimes' that historian of emotions William Reddy has suggested, though my usage deviates from Reddy's theorization.[74] Reddy argues that unspecific 'thought material' has to be transformed into specific emotions, notably through speech acts. For example, I might have somewhat unspecified feelings for a friend. Only by saying 'I love you' does this unspecified thought material turn into an actual emotion, that is, love. Reddy calls this speech act an 'emotive', an act that does not merely describe an emotion, but creates it by giving it shape. Precisely how this thought material can be turned into specific emotions, by whom and in which social contexts, is subject to an emotional regime. The implication of this argument is that an emotional regime not only shapes how, when, and where we can express our emotions, but the very emotions we can experience.

Without subscribing to Reddy's conception of emotions themselves, I find his notion of emotional regimes highly suggestive. Alternative leftists would arguably have claimed that capitalism constituted such an emotional regime, as capitalism prevented people from expressing their feelings and produced nothing but fear, boredom and loneliness, even though these feelings could not be expressed. This, however, is not to say that capitalism really produced such emotional structures. Rather, in analyzing capitalism in such terms, leftists effectively created an emotional regime of their own scene that regulated how they should feel and talk about feelings. We can thus observe the practical creation of an emotional regime in the left; this in itself was a way to produce and practice the negative emotions of capitalism. Alternative leftists, that is, really did feel bored, lonely and afraid, precisely because they thought that this is how they would normally feel in a capitalist society; but understanding how capitalism produced such feelings also allowed them to develop a variety of practices that would help them to overcome feelings of boredom and fear and thus to feel differently.

Chapter Outline and Sources

The book is divided into five chapters, with the first and last chapter providing a chronological frame for the three central chapters that discuss the emotional politics and practices of the alternative milieu in a

---

[74] William M. Reddy, *The Navigation of Feeling: A Framework for the History of Emotions* (Cambridge: Cambridge University Press, 2001), 94–111, 122–130. For the political implications of his work, see William M. Reddy, 'Emotional Liberty: History and Politics in the Anthropology of Emotions', *Cultural Anthropology* 14 (1999).

synchronic fashion. The first chapter traces the traditions, in Germany and elsewhere, on which the alternative left built. A look into an imagined alternative bookshelf is instructive in this regard, where we might find, next to the thick blue volumes of the *Marx Engels Werke*, novels by Hermann Hesse, the works of Herbert Marcuse who linked psychoanalysis with Marxism,[75] of American Beat poets like Allen Ginsburg or French Situationists such as Guy Debord. These writings point to a tradition of criticizing modern society that goes, at least, back to the German life reform and youth movement around 1900, if not to German romanticism.[76] Simultaneously, life reformers, the youth movement as well as nonconformist teenagers in postwar West Germany, developed various ways of practising an emotionally and bodily more 'authentic' subjectivity. Tracing both the critiques of a supposedly inauthentic society and the practices of 'authentic' subjectification these movements developed, Chapter 1 enables us to understand the alternative left in a long-term context that reaches beyond the borders of Germany.

The following three chapters dealing with the alternative left during the 1970s constitute the core of the book. They proceed in a synchronic manner, examining the alternative left's political project and its search for intimacy and intensity from different angles. Chapter 2 begins with a reconstruction of the political map of the alternative left. It shows how leftists construed their politics as a struggle against the domination of rationality, which required, so to speak, the mobilization of feelings, dreams, and fantasies. Rationality divided and categorized the world in an ultimately reductive manner, leftists argued; feelings, dreams, and fantasies, by contrast, disrupted this well-ordered world.[77] Being mindful of critical voices within the alternative left, the chapter provides an account of how alternative leftists thought about the political. The third chapter then examines more specifically how living in a capitalist world felt, according to leftists. If we were to believe leftist publications, life under capitalist conditions was full of permanent fear; capitalism damaged both personalities and personal relations; and finally, modern cities produced not only fear, but also isolated people from each other, while the grey

---

[75] See Anthony D. Kauders, 'Drives in Dispute: The West German Student Movement, Psychoanalysis, and the Search for a New Emotional Order, 1967–1971', *Central European History* 44 (2011).

[76] See Thomas Tripold, *Die Kontinuität romantischer Ideen* (Bielefeld: transcript, 2012).

[77] See in this context the highly inspiring work by Kristin Ross, *May '68 and Its Afterlives* (Chicago: University of Chicago Press, 2002). She highlights how important the overcoming of social categories and boundaries was for French activists in 1968.

monotony of concrete resulted in a sensual deprivation. Discussing feelings under capitalism in such terms, leftists effectively created emotional norms of how one would normally feel under capitalism. The chapter argues that leftists practiced this emotional regime within their own milieu, that is to say that leftists not only expected themselves and their comrades to feel afraid and isolated in capitalism, but indeed did feel so.

Chapter 4 investigates precisely how leftists tried to produce the feelings of intimacy and intensity they missed in capitalism. It is here that we encounter the emotional experiments that characterized the alternative left, for example in the numerous consciousness-raising groups or in communes and youth centres. As leftists sought to feel their bodies in a different and unfragmented way, the chapter pays particular attention to bodily practices. Engaging in these practices of intimacy, activists arguably worked on transforming their emotional and bodily selves, in a way to 'fix' their 'damaged' personalities. Yet leftists also experimented with feelings in a different, less transformative manner when they tried to find ways of producing extraordinary feelings of intensity that would, for a brief moment, fill the emotional void of capitalism. This happened, for example, during excessive parties, but also during demonstrations and riots, when protestors sought to overcome fear in moments of confrontations with the forces of order. These practices, too, can be analyzed as emotional experiments. Finally, the chapter turns towards critics of therapeutic politics within the radical left who wondered whether such practices did anything to actually change the world. These critics worried about a depoliticization of the left that turned into a mere self-experience group. Paying attention to processes of depolitization is thus as important to understanding how issues of subjectivity were politicized.[78]

In contrast to Chapters 2 to 4, the final fifth chapter that serves as a culmination has a chronological perspective. Taking the German Autumn of 1977 and the TUNIX Congress in West Berlin in February 1978 as its starting points, the chapter argues that by the late 1970s not only a sense of despair took hold amongst leftists, but also a hope for new radical activism beyond the therapeutic politics of the alternative left. This desire for new activism culminated in the urban revolts of 1980–1981, which the chapter discusses at length, specifically in Zurich, Freiburg and most importantly West Berlin, where hundreds of houses were squatted by early 1981. These

---

[78] See, with some emphasis on processes of depoliticization, which are more difficult to track, most recently Eitler and Elberfeld, 'Gesellschaftsgeschichte', 25–26. See also Andrew Bergerson et al., 'The Contours of the Political', *German History* 33 (2015).

revolts were moments of intense emotional exuberance, which the chapter explores. Drawing on William H. Sewell, Jr.'s and Victor Turner's work, the chapter proposes interpreting these revolts as liminal events for which transgressing boundaries, though not for the sake of arriving on the other side, was central. By looking at the aesthetics of the movement, at practices of collective living in squatted houses, and at confrontations with the forces of order, the chapter seeks to understand the production of feelings of intensity. Not least, this focus on brief moments of exuberance implied a radically different temporality of the politics of the revolt, as protestors were not primarily concerned with changing either society or the self, but with what happened at the moment of transgression. The chapter is thus not interested in historical change, but in understanding the intensity of a peculiar moment.[79]

To make these arguments, the book draws on different sources, most importantly about seventy left-wing periodicals from the early 1970s to the early 1980s, but also books published by left-wing authors, ranging from children's books, novels, reports to theoretical texts. These sources provide insights into how alternative leftists construed their political universe, how they created an emotional knowledge about the feelings capitalism allegedly produced, and, crucial for the praxeological approach of this study, into how leftists engaged in various bodily and emotional experiments trying to generate the feelings of intimacy and intensity they missed in capitalism. Leftist magazines frequently provided very detailed accounts of activities such as group meetings, life in communes, or demonstrations that allow a precise reconstruction of emotional practices. Additionally, I have made use of a limited number of oral history interviews in Chapter 5, as well as visual representations. For a historical study of emotions, the predominant reliance on written sources might be surprising choice. It might seem that more extensive oral history interviews and audio-visual sources might have provided more immediate access to feelings. Without denying that such sources can be used very effectively, it strikes me as problematic to privilege such sources over written sources; neither images, nor photos, nor oral history interviews provide a more immediate access to feelings of the past. For the praxeological approach this study follows, the detailed accounts of leftist activities provide an ideal source. Indeed,

---

[79] See also Joachim C. Häberlen, 'Sekunden der Freiheit: Zum Verhältnis von Gefühlen, Macht und Zeit in Ausnahmesituationen am Beispiel der Revolte 1980/81 in Berlin', in *Ausnahmezustände: Entgrenzungen und Regulierungen in Europa während des Kalten Krieges*, ed. Dirk Schumann and Cornelia Rauh (Göttingen: Wallstein, 2015).

reconstructing practices based on audiovisual material or oral history interviews would arguably have been more difficult.

Drawing primarily on these sometimes-obscure left-wing magazines rather than on the more popular publications of the New Left, such as *Kursbuch* or *konkret* (though I draw on those as well), has the advantage of providing insights into what more or less ordinary members of the leftist scene thought and did. Sometimes the arguments individual authors made might be idiosyncratic and hardly representative. Yet, based on a kaleidoscope of different voices, it is possible to reconstruct a more complex and nuanced image than by only referring to the opinion leaders in the scene. Not least, the variety of sources allows us to see contradictions and contestations within the leftist milieu that might get lost in the pages of the mainstream left-wing journals.

A Note on Translations

Alternative leftists often wrote in a highly informal and colourful way that is not always easy to translate into English. To give a taste of the sources, I have tried to stay as close to the German original as possible. In particularly important instances, I provide the German original in brackets.

CHAPTER I

Wholeness and Exuberance

In May 1978, the Berlin-based *BUG Info* (*Berliner Undogmatischer Gruppen*), the city's most widely read alternative magazine, invited its readers to travel to Monte Verità at Lago Maggiore in Switzerland. 'We will gather celebrating, dancing, thanking and commemorating', the invitation pronounced. A number of anniversaries were to be celebrated, most notably the 77th anniversary of the foundation of the rural commune (*Landkommune*) at Monte Verità in 1900, but also, as the invitation explained, the 100th birthdays of its founder, Gusto Arthur Gräser (who was, in fact, only one of several founders); 'its poet', Hermann Hesse; 'its psychologist', Otto Gross; 'its revolutionary', Erich Mühsam; and the 'pioneer of female emancipation', Franziska von Reventlow; as well as the 'dancer and fighter pioneer of female emancipation', Isadora Duncan.

> Come to the ball of dreams in Baladrume, on the traces of Hermann Hesse and Gusto Gräser, through the valley of peace to the heathen's cave to the rock of the holy ape ... [Come to] the dance of green power, to the mountain and valley, to the folk and joy festival [*Volks- und Freudenfest*] of alternative dreamers ... [Come to] market and fair, dance and theatre, music and magic, saying and singing, hiking and going, gaming and fighting, to desire, love and exuberance, to the great going-with-one-another [*Miteinandergang*], to the holy wrapping-each-other [*Ineinanderschlag*] ... come to Monte Verità, come to Ascona, come![1]

The organizers promised nothing, but hoped that, if enough people would show up, numerous 'working groups [*Arbeitsgruppen*]' would be formed on various themes of concern for the alternative movement, such as ecology, the Third World, soft (*sanfte*) technologies, but also 'women and mothers', 'dance, music, theatre', 'self presentation, self experience', 'psychotherapies', or 'religion today: east and west'.

---

[1] Anon., 'Fiesta, Ascona, Monte Verità', in *BUG Info* 1021, 22 May 1978, 3. The magazine was slightly renamed to *BUG Info* after internal conflicts at *Info BUG* in December 1977.

The festival took place again in the following years. But not everything went well, as Margret from Munich explained in the aftermath of the August 1980 festival in the local *Blatt*.[2] On the positive side, people engaged in a variety of interesting activities. For many, music, 'a medium independent of language', played a major role. Others did 'something like gymnastics, mixed with breathing exercises, Tai Chi, Eurhythmia'. However, problems emerged soon enough. A local farmer, while allegedly an anarchist himself, complained that he did not want to see women walking around with bare breasts, and that attendees had contaminated his font by brushing their teeth in it. The increasingly dire food situation at the festival gave reason for conflict amongst the attendees. The festival ended prematurely after only two days.

The festival provides an interesting glimpse into the complexity of the alternative left and the themes activists were interested in, ranging from the liberation struggles in the Third World, to overcoming the limitations of (rational) language by playing music. At least some activists saw themselves and their 'desire, love, and exuberance' as part of a longer tradition, though by no means always uncritically. The organizers of the festival, a group from the Swabian village of Schelklingen, considered the aforementioned left-wing life reformers (*Lebensreformer*), whether they were dancers, psychologists, or founders of the Monte Verità community, an inspiration for the present. Others, however, pointed out that the community at Monte Verità had turned into a profit-oriented business rather quickly, and worried that the same might happen to the alternative left.[3] Critics saw a dangerous parallel between desires to return to nature that were popular in the early twentieth century, and a contemporary fascination with oriental mysticism. This step, they argued, was not a mingling of leftist politics and mysticism, but a replacement of the former by the latter. Even Erich Mühsam, celebrated by the group from Schelklingen, had in fact written a highly critical and sarcastic account the community at Ascona.[4]

The festival at Ascona points us, critical voices aside, to the traditions alternative leftists could and did build upon for developing their critique of an inauthentic world that lacked spaces for feelings and desires. Taking a look at an imaginary leftist bookshelf as its starting point, this chapter

---

[2] Margret, 'Monte Verità, eine Reise zum Berg der Reformen, oder: zum Bermudadreieck des Geistes', in *Das Blatt* 178, 15–28 August 1980, 18–20.

[3] For a critique, see Anon., 'Monte Verità: Wohl eher beängstigende Gedanken zu einer Ausstellung', in *Traumstadt* 5, n.d., probably spring 1979, 20–22.

[4] Erich Mühsam, *Ascona: Eine Broschüre* (Locarno: Carlson, 1905 [reprint, Berlin: Verlag Klaus Guhl, 1982]).

explores some of these traditions. Coming mostly from educated middle-class backgrounds, leftists were often eager readers. On their bookshelves, we might find the heavy blue volumes of the *Marx-Engels-Werke* next to Michael Ende's *Momo*, a children's book,[5] and the writings of Carlos Castaneda about his encounters with Mexican Native American shamanism in northern Mexico. For the purposes of this chapter, I focus on those texts that allow us to reconstruct the intellectual traditions on which alternative leftists built.[6] These included, not surprisingly, thinkers such as Wilhelm Reich and Herbert Marcuse, who combined Marxism with Freud, but also less widely known leftist Freudians like Otto Gross and Siegfried Bernfeld, who were rediscovered in the 1970s. Turning from theory to fiction, we might find the works by American Beat Poets like Allan Ginsberg and Jack Kerouac who formulated an artistic critique of the lack of authenticity in modern American society. Perhaps less often read, but nevertheless influential for the formation of alternative politics was the Situationist International who had criticized modern everyday life for its deadly boredom.

Most surprisingly, however, we might find books associated with German life reform movement that had emerged around 1900. Indeed, books like Hans Paasche's *Die Forschungsreise des Afrikaners Lukanga Mukara ins innerste Deutschlands*, originally published in 1921, or Erich Scheurmann's *Der Papalagi: Die Reden des Südsee-Häuptlings Tuiavii aus Tiavea*, originally published in 1920, had politicized more people in the alternative scene than Marx and Engels, activist Klaus-Bernd Vollmar argued in *Ulcus Molle*. Using fictional 'savages' from Africa and the South Sea, both authors provided a critique of contemporary German society describing it as deeply unhappy due to Germans' alienation from nature. While Germans were engaged in purposeless businesses, they lost the connection to their own bodies, the authors suggested. Lungs and air were filled with smoke, bodies were covered with tight clothes, and people lived in stone cages. Europeans did not use money to purchase things that might make them happy, the authors charged, but bought useless things. Constantly under the pressure to work, they had no time to actually enjoy

---

[5] See my discussion in Joachim C. Häberlen, 'Ingrid's Boredom', in *Learning How to Feel: Children's Literature and Emotional Socialization, 1870–1970*, ed. Ute Frevert et al. (Oxford: Oxford University Press, 2014).

[6] On left-wing book publishers in the 1970s, see Uwe Sonnenberg, *Von Marx zum Maulwurf: Linker Buchhandel in Westdeutschland in den 1970er Jahren* (Göttingen: Wallstein, 2016). A good source to get a sense of what leftists were reading is the magazine *Ulcus Molle*, an 'information service' for the alternative scene that discussed relevant (old and new) publications.

life. And instead of simply regarding everyone as a human being, people had to be categorized according to their profession, which made them single-minded, both fictional characters criticized.[7]

While the influence of writers like Herbert Marcuse and Situationist Guy Debord on the New Left is widely recognized, the life reform movement of the early twentieth century is rarely considered in histories of the post-1968 left. Only Christoph Conti, an author with clear sympathies for the alternative left, argued in 1984 that the life reform movement, the youth movement that emerged slightly later, and the alternative movement of the 1970s, were all 'alternative movements' who said 'farewell to the bourgeoisie'.[8] This chapter thus presents a prehistory of the alternative left that differs from most accounts of New Left in West Germany. While scholars have frequently turned to subcultures like the *Halbstarke* and *Gammler*, student protests in the early 1960s, and the of role foreign students for mobilizing West German students, the chapter suggests considering the alternative left of the 1970s as part of a longer tradition that reaches back to the alternative life reform movement at the turn of the century.[9]

Discussing life reformers and the youth movement, Freudian Marxists, Beat Poets, and the Situationist International, the chapter inquires why alternative leftists in the 1970s found such movements inspiring for their own political project. The chapter thus works on two consciously dissonant temporal registers. It is at one and the same time historical as it is giving a historical narrative that leads to the alternative left of the 1970s, and genealogical as it is looking back from the 1970s to trace where elements of alternative politics and subjectivities come from.[10] In different ways, all the groups and movements under discussion here developed

---

[7] KBV (=Klaus Bernd Vollmar), 'Politische Überlegungen zur Alternativliteratur', in *Ulcus Molle* Sonderinfo 3, December 1976, 10–16. He was referring to Hans Paasche, *Die Forschungsreise des Afrikaners Lukanga Mukara ins innerste Deutschlands* (Hamburg: Verlag Junge Menschen, 1921); Erich Scheurmann, *Der Papalagi: Die Reden des Südsee-Häuptlings Tuiavii aus Tiavea* (Buchenbach: Felsen-Verlag, 1920). Both books were republished in the 1970s.

[8] Christoph Conti, *Abschied vom Bürgertum: Alternative Bewegungen in Deutschland von 1890 bis heute* (Reinbek bei Hamburg: Rowohlt, 1984). See also briefly Sven Reichardt, *Authentizität und Gemeinschaft: Linksalternatives Leben in den siebziger und frühen achtziger Jahren* (Berlin: Suhrkamp, 2014), 58.

[9] For conventional views, see Timothy S. Brown, *West Germany and the Global Sixties: The Antiauthoritarian Revolt, 1962–1978* (Cambridge: Cambridge University Press, 2013); Quinn Slobodian, *Foreign Front: Third World Politics in Sixties West Germany* (Durham, NC: Duke University Press, 2012).

[10] See Maren Möhring's suggestive comment that a history of the present has to start at the turn of the century: Maren Möhring, 'Ethnic Food, Fast Food, Health Food: Veränderungen der Ernährung und Esskultur im letzten Drittel des 20. Jahrhunderts', in *Vorgeschichte der Gegenwart: Dimensionen*

critiques of (capitalist) modernity that evolved around the notion that the conditions of modern society inhibited an 'authentic' life, that is, a life 'according to (human) nature'. These authors and activists criticized what they perceived as the domination of abstract rationality, exemplified by urban living conditions that damaged and deformed individual subjects, their bodies, and their feelings. This was not, as traditional Marxism would have it, a critique of class society and exploitation, but a critique of the social conditions that shape human subjectivity. For alternative leftists more concerned with their 'living practices [*Lebenspraxis*]' than with big theories, as Vollmar had noted, such critiques were highly appealing.[11] And these movements offered more than just critiques on which leftists in the 1970s could build; they also offered models for living a more authentic life, for example by openly showing feelings or searching for permanent transgressions. All this made those movements deeply fascinating for alternative leftists longing for a life that would break with what they perceived as the domination of abstract rationality.

Placing the alternative left in these traditions, however, does not mean that leftists in the 1970s simply reproduced what others had done before them. Both the critiques of the inauthentic world and what people did in order to live an authentic life changed dramatically. Life reformers, for example, sought to create healthy and wholesome bodies, whereas the Beat Poets celebrated fragmentation and ecstasy. Investigating a variety of precursors of the alternative left thus also highlights how leftists in the 1970s were innovative and produced something genuinely new. Above all, alternative leftists of the 1970s conceived of their search for an authentic life as something deeply political and anti-capitalist. Life reformers and Beat Poets had, by contrast, rarely regarded their critiques of the inauthentic world or their efforts to live a more authentic life as political. Freudian Marxists like Reich and Marcuse and the Situationist International, however, began to formulate a different understanding of the political for which questions of subjectivity became central; working on the self thus came to be regarded as an inherently political act. Analysing these issues, the chapter contributes to an understanding of how the 'personal' *became* political, an understanding of the political that not only implied that 'changing the self' would be necessary for 'changing the world', but also that regimes of subjectivity could and should become the object of political

des *Strukturbruchs nach dem Boom*, ed. Anselm Doering-Manteuffel, Lutz Raphael, and Thomas Schlemmer (Göttingen: Vandenhoeck & Ruprech, 2016), 331.
[11] Vollmar, 'Politische Überlegungen'.

critique. The chapter, in other words, also provides an outline of a genealogy of a peculiar understanding of the political and the politics of subjectivity.[12]

While the first three sections of the chapter discuss these more distant and literary influences – the life reform and youth movements; Freudian-Marxist thinkers; and Beat Poets and the Situationist International – the final section turns to teenage subcultures in West Germany that more immediately preceded the revolts of 1968 and the subsequent emergence of the alternative left: the *Halbstarke* and *Gammler*. These subcultures did not leave traces on leftist bookshelves, but the counterhegemonic practices of subjectivity developed in these groups informed the later alternative left. They are thus part of the genealogy this chapter outlines.

'A Rediscovery of the Body': Life Reformers and the Youth Movement

In 1900, a small group of men and women decided to turn their backs on bourgeois life. Hoping to escape from 'the old social order, or rather disorder, with the goal of a more personal life and a more personal way of living' and pursuing a 'desire for freedom', as Ida Hofmann-Oedenkoven wrote, they searched for a place to build a rural commune.[13] They finally found it at Lago Maggiore in Switzerland, where they found the commune of Monte Verità that the leftists from Schelklingen celebrated some eight decades later. To fulfil their 'desire for freedom', the members of the commune abolished private property, ploughed the land together, and followed a vegetarian diet. Working half or completely naked, they hoped to experience freedom from restrictive clothing in a bodily sense. Soon enough, the commune became famous and attracted numerous visitors, among them literary authors like Hermann Hesse – who later wrote about his experiences at Ascona in *Demian* – and Gerhard Hauptmann, dancers like Rudolf von Laban and Isadora Duncan, and Max Weber.[14]

[12] See also the contributions in Uffa Jensen and Maik Tändler, eds., *Das Selbst zwischen Anpassung und Befreiung: Psychowissen und Politik im 20. Jahrhundert* (Göttingen: Wallstein, 2012)

[13] Ida Hofmann-Oedenkoven, *Monte Verità: Wahrheit ohne Dichtung* (Lorsch: Karl Röhm, 1906), 7. Quoted in Ulrike Voswinckel, *Freie Liebe und Anarchie: Schwabing – Monte Verità. Entwürfe gegen das etablierte Leben* (Munich: Allitera-Verlag, 2009), 13.

[14] On Monte Verità, see Yme Kuiper, 'On Monte Verità: Myth and Modernity in the Lebensreform Movement', in *Myths, Martyrs, and Modernity: Studies in the History of Religions in Honour of Jan N. Bremmer*, ed. Jitse Dijkstra, Justin Kroesen, and Yme Kuiper (Leiden, ND: Brill, 2010); Voswinckel, *Freie Liebe*; Harald Szeemann, ed., *Monte Verità: Lokale Anthropologie als Beiträge*

The commune at Monte Verità was part of a broader life reform movement, in the context of which also Paasche and Scheurmann had published their books. The life reform movement was a complex and diverse phenomenon. It included a variety of associations and leagues (*Bünde*) that all promoted reforming individual life in one way or another to make it more 'healthy', ranging from a vegetarian diet to natural healing, (nude) swimming, and sun bathing.[15] In the absence of any central organization, it is impossible to provide accurate numbers of how many people joined these various associations and leagues. All in all, the mostly middle-class membership of these organizations reached several hundred thousands, though it is unclear how active individual members were.[16] Mostly, these associations promoted a way of living that would be 'according to nature [*naturgemäß*]' by organizing lectures or by providing members with an opportunity to engage in their preferred activities, be it vegetarian cooking or naked sunbathing. Around the same time, the youth movement, most famously the *Wandervogel* emerged, first in Berlin, then in other German cities.[17] Even though the youth movement frequently distanced itself from the life reformers, it shared similar ideals of a life 'according to nature' in modern society. Mostly, those teenagers – initially mostly boys, though later girls joined – wanted to escape from parental and school authorities.[18] To this

zur Wiederentdeckung einer neuzeitlichen sakralen Topographie (Milan: Electa Editrice, 1979); Gernot Böhme, 'Monte Verità', in *Die Lebensreform: Entwürfe zur Neugestaltung von Leben und Kunst um 1900*, ed. Kai Buchholz et al. (Darmstadt: haeusser-media, 2001).

[15] About the life reform movement and its attempts to create healthy bodies, see in general Wolfgang R. Krabbe, *Gesellschaftsveränderung durch Lebensreform: Strukturmerkmale einer sozialreformersichen Bewegung im Deutschland der Industrialisierungsperiode* (Göttingen: Vandenhoeck & Ruprecht, 1974); Diethart Kerbs and Jürgen Reulecke, eds., *Handbuch der deutschen Reformbewegungen, 1880–1933* (Wuppertal: Hammer, 1998); Kai Buchholz et al., eds., *Die Lebensreform: Entwürfe zur Neugestaltung von Leben und Kunst um 1900*, 2 vols. (Darmstadt: haeusser-media, 2001); Eva Barlösius, *Naturgemäße Lebensführung: Zur Geschichte der Lebensreform um die Jahrhundertwende* (Frankfurt a.M.: Campus Verlag, 1997); Marc Cluet and Catherine Repussard, eds., *'Lebensreform': Die soziale Dynamik der politischen Ohnmacht* (Tübingen: Francke Verlag, 2013); Avi Sharma, *We Lived for the Body: Natural Medicine and Public Health in Imperial Germany* (DeKalb, IL: Northern Illinois University Press, 2014).

[16] On organizational matters and the social profile of the life reform movement, see Krabbe, *Gesellschaftsveränderung*, 131–166; Barlösius, *Lebensführung*; Matthew Jefferies, 'Lebensreform: A Middle-Class Antidote to Wilhelminism?', in *Wilhelminism and Its Legacies: German Modernities, Imperialism, and the Meanings of Reform, 1890–1930*, ed. Geoff Eley and James Retallack (New York: Berghahn Books, 2003).

[17] On the youth movements, see most recently Rüdiger Ahrens, *Bündische Jugend: Eine neue Geschichte, 1918–1933* (Göttingen: Wallstein, 2015). See also Thomas Rohkrämer, *Eine andere Moderne? Zivilisationskritik, Natur und Technik in Deutschland, 1880–1933* (Paderborn: Schöningh, 1999), 141–156; Peter Stachura, *The German Youth Movement: An Interpretative and Documentary History* (London: Macmillan, 1981).

[18] Rohkrämer, *Andere Moderne?*, 143–145. See in general also Marion E. P. de Ras, *Körper, Eros und weibliche Kultur: Mädchen im Wandervogel und in der Bündischen Jugend* (Pfaffenweiler: Centaurus,

end, they hiked through Germany, 'rediscovering' both nature and rural life, and, even more importantly, their own bodies.[19]

A lithography published by Eduard Bilz, a renowned naturopath, in his 1905 book *Der Zukunftsstaat* (translated as *The State of the Future*), neatly illustrates the social critique of the life reform movement, and the future society life reformers envisioned that would ensure 'everybody's happiness and carefree living', as the subtitle of Bilz's book stated.[20] The left side of the picture depicts 'today's society': a chained young girl; workers in a factory labouring for ten hours a day, as the inscription says; a bedroom with closed windows, sickness, smokers, and the family of an alcoholic; overcrowded mental institutions and prisons; and violence. The right half, by contrast, depicts the 'people in the state of the future'. It shows a young girl with a torch, men celebrating 'liberty, equality, fraternity', women in wide and shoulder-free dresses performing a round dance in open nature, bare-breasted men working for three hours in a garden, and a 'happy family'. At the centre of the illustration stand lightly dressed men and women and naked children enjoying nature – picking fruits, praising the sun, swimming in the river and dancing together.

The lithography captures a social critique common amongst life reformers. At the core of this critique was the notion that urban, industrial society, but also more fundamentally the domination of rationality and 'bloodless science' prohibited people from living according to their nature.[21] In the modern world, 'words, concepts, and abstraction' ruled, but not senses and aesthetics, Robert Breuer, a left leaning life reformer,

---

1988). For an interesting source, see Leopold Fulda, *Im Lichtkleid! Stimmen für und gegen das gemeinsame Nacktbaden von Jungend und Mädchen im Familien- und Freundeskreise* (Rudolstadt: Verlag Gesundes Leben, 1924).

[19] On hiking on the life refom movement, see Judith Baumgartner, 'Licht, Luft, Sonne, Bergwelt, Wandern und Baden als Sehnsuchtsziele der Lebensreformbewegung', in *Die Lebensreform: Entwürfe zur Neugestaltung von Leben und Kunst um 1900*, ed. Kai Buchholz et al. (Darmstadt: haeusser-media, 2001).

[20] F. Eduard Bilz, *Der Zukunftsstaat: Staatseinrichtung im Jahre 2000. Neue Weltanschauung. Jedermann wird ein glückliches und sorgenfreies Dasein gesichert* (Leipzig: F. E. Bilz Verlag, 1904). The image is reproduced and discussed in Klaus Wolbert, 'Die Lebensreform – Anträge zur Debatte', in *Die Lebensreform: Entwürfe zur Neugestaltung von Leben und Kunst um 1900*, ed. Kai Buchholz et al. (Darmstadt: haeusser-media, 2001); Diethart Kerbs, 'Die Welt im Jahre 2000: Der Prophet von Oberlößnitz und die Gesellschafts-Utopien der Lebensreform', in *Die Lebensreform: Entwürfe zur Neugestaltung von Leben und Kunst um 1900*, ed. Kai Buchholz et al. (Darmstadt: haeusser-media, 2001).

[21] Quote from Charly Strässer, quoted without reference in Michael Andritzky, 'Einleitung', in *'Wir sind nackt und nennen uns Du'. Von Lichtfreunden und Sonnenkämpfern. Eine Geschichte der Freikörperkultur*, ed. Michael Andritzky and Thomas Rautenberg (Giessen: Anabas, 1989), 5.

Figure 2   'The people in the state of the future'.
(Friedrich Eduard Bilz, *Der Zukunftsstaat*.)

wrote in an essay called 'Beauty as *Weltanschauung*'.[22] The ideals depicted
in the lithography would have resonated with alternative leftists in the
1970s. Unlike them, however, life reformers argued that modern, rational
life was unnatural. Bilz for example claimed that men were guided 'by their
modern reason, which is however an artificial product that originates
from specific social relations that are not in accordance with nature [*den
jeweiligen naturwidrigen Verhältnissen entspringt*]'. Animals, by contrast,
would live according to their instincts, which, Bilz claimed, never erred.[23]
Along similar lines, reform pedagogue Gustav Wyneken praised the
youth movement that would break with the 'autarchy [*Alleinherrschaft*]
of reason' by promoting the acting out of a 'passionate affirmation of drives
[*leidenschaftlicher Triebbejahung*]'. Disregarding cultural conventions, the

---

[22] Robert Breuer, 'Schönheit als Weltanschauung', *Deutsche Kunst und Dekoration* 23 (1908/09): 154.
Quoted in Kai Buchholz, 'Lebensreform und Lebensgestaltung: Die Revision der Alltagspraxis', in
Die Lebensreform: Entwürfe zur Neugestaltung von Leben und Kunst um 1900, ed. Kai Buchholz et al.
(Darmstadt: haeusser-media, 2001), 363.
[23] Bilz, *Zukunftsstaat*, 361.

youth movement called for the 'emancipation of life', Wyneken rejoiced.[24] The rationalization of the world, these authors implied, and following them a number of modern scholars studying those movements, had left no space for instincts and emotionality – an argument many leftists would have subscribed to.[25] Living a life according to nature was thus rendered impossible, unless people made conscious efforts to reform their lives. Yet the celebration of a natural life did not imply a general rejection of modernity and a desire to recreate to premodern living conditions.[26] Rather, both life reformers and the youth movement wanted to create conditions for such a life *within* modern society. Tellingly, they frequently relied on scientific arguments when proposing more healthy life styles.

Most importantly, life reformers were concerned about the natural health of the human body that was, in their understanding, damaged in modern society. Reforming life would thus require working on the body.[27] One way to achieve this was to change dietary habits.[28] In particular, life reformers called for stopping eating meat. For example, in the foreword of a vegetarian cookbook, Joseph Springer argued that apes, evolutionarily closest to humans, lived by a diet consisting mostly of fruits. Eating meat was therefore, he argued, not part of human nature, as the fact that 'exotic' peoples in Australia or Africa had not eaten meat until Europeans had arrived would prove.[29] For Springer and other life reformers, eating meat poisoned the body, especially kidneys and liver, and caused illnesses such as gout and rheumatism.[30] Meat consumption also influenced people's mood. Killing animals, Springer argued, resulted in a 'dulling of empathy

---

[24] Gustav Wyneken, 'Der weltgeschichtliche Sinn der Jugendbewegung', in *Der Kampf für die Jugend*, ed. Gustav Wyneken (Jena: Diederichs, 1919). Quoted in Rohkrämer, *Andere Moderne?*, 155.

[25] See for example Rohkrämer, *Andere Moderne?*; Michael Andritzky and Thomas Rautenberg, eds., *'Wir sind nackt und nennen uns Du': Von Lichtfreunden und Sonnenkämpfern. Eine Geschichte der Freikörperkultur* (Giessen: Anabas, 1989).

[26] Rohkrämer, *Andere Moderne?*, 151–152.

[27] See above all the pioneering study by Maren Möhring, *Marmorleiber: Körperbildung in der deutschen Nacktkultur (1890–1930)* (Cologne: Böhlau, 2004). See also Ulrich Linse, 'Das "natürliche" Leben: Die Lebensreform', in *Erfindung des Menschen: Schöpfungsträume und Körperbilder, 1500–2000*, ed. Richard van Dülmen (Vienna: Böhlau, 1998); Sharma, *We Lived for the Body*.

[28] See for example Sabine Merta, *Schlank! Ein Körperkult der Moderne* (Stuttgart: Franz Steiner Verlag, 2008), 50–54; Karl E. Rothschuh, *Naturheilbewegung, Reformbewegung, Alternativbewegung* (Darmstadt: Wissenschaftliche Buchgesellschaft, 1983), 109–117; Krabbe, *Gesellschaftsveränderung*, 50–77; Judith Baumgartner, 'Ernährungsreform', in *Handbuch der deutschen Reformbewegungen, 1880–1933*, ed. Diethart Kerbs and Jürgen Reulecke (Wuppertal: Hammer, 1998); Judith Baumgartner, both 'Vegetarismus' and 'Antialkoholbewegung', in *Handbuch der deutschen Reformbewegungen, 1880–1933*, ed. Diethart Kerbs and Jürgen Reulecke (Wuppertal: Hammer, 1998).

[29] Anna Springer, *Vegetarisches Kochebuch. Mit einer Einleitung: 'Wie sollen wir leben?' von Joseph Springer* (Berlin: Verlag Lebensreform, 1907), II.

[30] Ibid., VI–VIII, XI.

and brutalization'. Mikhail Bakunin, a Russian anarchist whom Springer characterized as a 'state theorist', had even claimed that it would be 'a small step from killing animals to killing human beings'.[31] Eating meat, life reformers believed, had direct consequences for people's emotional state. Along similar lines, reformers criticized drinking alcohol and smoking tobacco as modern vices that destroyed the body, a critique we can also find in the *Wandervogel* movement that used it to distance itself from the alcohol-consuming student fraternities.[32]

Bourgeois fashion was another feature of modern society that life reformers believed to be deeply harmful for the body.[33] Eduard Bilz for example criticized that women had to carry trains and wear corsets, that children were not allowed to walk barefoot if the weather was appropriate, and that men were wearing hats. Such clothes, and especially the corset, literally deformed the body; they shielded the skin from the sun and prevented it from breathing.[34] Heinrich Pudor, one of the key figures in the nudity movement and later on a vigorous anti-Semite, claimed that 'a collar divides human beings into a living and a dead part. It prevents damps and mists that are raising from the entire body and that want to discharge themselves there [at the collar] from being dispensed, it prevents the communication between head and body, it prevents that the flows of life [*Lebensströme*] move from head to body, and from body to head, it constitutes the genuine mark of Cain of the modern rational man [*Kopfmenschen*], who has forgotten to carry his body into life [*der seinen Leib in das Leben vergessen hat mitzunehmen*].'[35] Tight bourgeois fashion that did not expose the body to nature was equally harmful to male genitalia, life reformers worried. Writing in 1927, H. Sietzer described how the average penis of a 'European man' would look like: 'grey-greenish colour of decay, because only very few are willing to expose this part of the body that

---

[31] Ibid., IX–X.
[32] See for example Krabbe, *Gesellschaftsveränderung*, 37–47; Baumgartner, 'Antialkoholbewegung'; Rohkrämer, *Andere Moderne?*, 147.
[33] Rothschuh, *Naturheilbewegung*, 119–132; Ras, *Körper*, 17–18, 47–48; Astrid Ackermann, 'Kleidung, Sexualität und politische Partizipation in der Lebensreformbewegung', in *'Lebensreform': Die soziale Dynamik der politischen Ohnmacht*, ed. Marc Cluet and Catherine Repussard (Tübingen: Francke Verlag, 2013); Karen Ellwanger and Elisabeth Meyer-Renschhause, 'Kleidungsreform', in *Handbuch der deutschen Reformbewegungen, 1880–1933*, ed. Diethart Kerbs and Jürgen Reulecke (Wuppertal: Hammer, 1998).
[34] Bilz, *Zukunftsstaat*, 4–5, 16.
[35] Heinrich Pudor, 'Die Nacktheit in Kunst und Leben', *Der Eigene* (1906), 16, quoted in Lothar Fischer, 'Getanzte Körperbefreiung', in *'Wir sind nackt und nennen uns Du': Von Lichtfreunden und Sonnenkämpfern. Eine Geschichte der Freikörperkultur*, ed. Michael Andritzky and Thomas Rautenberg (Giessen: Anabas, 1989), 106.

constitutes the worst source of sweat to air and sun; the acid remnants of sweat lixiviate [*auslaugen*] the flesh and give it this disgusting colour as well as often a sickening odour'.[36] Finally, life reformers criticized what living conditions did to the human body. In line with their critique of bourgeois fashion, they bemoaned that sleeping in dark rooms with no windows kept bodies away from fresh air, which would make them sick.[37] To sum up their critique, life reformers believed that, under the conditions of rational modernity, people would be incapable of listening to their bodies and instincts, and thus living a healthy and authentic life true to human nature.

These critiques of modern society called for a response that would 'liberate' the body from the impositions of modern society. Indeed, sympathetic observers of the youth movement like Gustav Wyneken interpreted the movement as 'the body's struggle for liberation'.[38] Along similar lines, Charly Strässer claimed that the movement wanted 'to liberate life in order to liberate all energies against the mechanization that kills everything that has a soul, to liberate all powers for truly creative acting, for deeds that tremble from the faith and fortune that is enclosed in the body. [*Sie will die Befreiung des Leibes, um alle Energien gegen die alles Beseelte ertötende Mechanisierung, alle Kräfte zu wahrhaft schöpferischem Tun freizubekommen, zu Taten, die durchbebt sind von dem Glauben und dem Glück, die im Leib verschlossen liegen.*][39] Scholars have at times rather uncritically replicated this rhetoric. Michael Andritzky for example claims that the youth movement had constituted a 'revolt of the body'.[40]

Employing a Foucauldian approach, Maren Möhring has criticized such liberation narratives and instead argued that bodies were produced as 'natural' and hence 'normal'.[41] In her landmark book, *Marmorleiber*, Möhring carefully reconstructs bodily practices, such as doing nude gymnastics, as

[36] H. Sieker, 'Fünf Sätze zu einer Hygiene der Ehe', *Junge Menschen* 7 (July 1927), 172, quoted in Ras, *Körper*, 47.

[37] Kai Buchholz and Renate Ulmer, 'Reform des Wohnens', in *Die Lebensreform: Entwürfe zur Neugestaltung von Leben und Kunst um 1900*, ed. Kai Buchholz et al. (Darmstadt: haeusser-media, 2001).

[38] Wyneken, 'Sinn', reproduced in Werner Kindt, ed., *Grundschriften der deutschen Jugendbewegung* (Düsseldorf, Cologne: Eugen Diederichs Verlag, 1963), 148–162, quote 152. Quoted in Conti, *Abschied*, 111.

[39] Charly Strässer, quoted without reference in Andritzky, 'Einleitung', 5.

[40] Ibid.; Klaus Wolbert, 'Körper: Zwischen animalischer Leiblichkeit und ästhetisierender Verklärung der Physis', in *Die Lebensreform: Entwürfe zur Neugestaltung von Leben und Kunst um 1900*, ed. Kai Buchholz et al. (Darmstadt: haeusser-media, 2001), 339.

[41] Möhring, *Marmorleiber*, 23–24, 120–121, and throughout. See along similar lines Cornelia Klose-Lewerentz, 'Der "ideale Körper" und seine "Herstellung": Körperdiskurse der Lebensreformbewegung zwischen Utopie und Normativität', in *'Lebensreform': Die soziale Dynamik der politischen Ohnmacht*, ed. Marc Cluet and Catherine Repussard (Tübingen: Francke Verlag, 2013).

technologies of power that were anything but liberating. I concur with Möhring's critical analysis that such practices could and should be considered technologies of power; yet this is only half the story. We should be careful not to dismiss claims of 'liberation' too easily. Instead, I would propose that we can reconstruct not only how 'natural' or 'authentic' bodies, but also how 'liberated' bodies were historically produced. Crucial in this regard would be to avoid any notion of genuinely authentic bodies (or feelings, for that matter) that could be 'liberated'. This, however, does not mean that the (historically constructed) 'liberation' of bodies was any less real. From this perspective, we could analyse the creation of both 'liberated' and 'normal' bodies as a simultaneous process that enforced a historically specific 'discipline of liberation' onto the body; we could then write multiple histories of liberation, instead of placing the history of life reform or youth movement into a grand liberation narrative. At the same time, the praxeological focus on the *production* of authenticity and liberation provides a way to eschew rather unproductive debates about the 'reactionary' nature of the life reform and youth movements.[42] By contrast, this perspective enables us to reconstruct what authentic feelings and an authentic body looked like, or, to put it more sharply, how authenticity and liberation were practised in specific historical contexts. It allows us to place the practices that alternative leftists developed in the 1970s into a longer history, but also to see how their practices of subjective liberation diverged from those of their antecedents. In what follows, I analyse how life reformers and youth movement activists practically created their 'liberated' bodies.

Life reformers' detailed and specific critique of the ills of the modern world usually implied very specific steps to 're-form' the body in a more 'natural' way. If eating meat would harm the body and result in a bloodthirsty character, then avoiding meat and living by a vegetarian or even vegan diet was the obvious solution. Similarly, the critique of tight bourgeois fashion that did not expose the body to nature called for clothes that did. Wearing loose and pragmatic clothes or going naked altogether was then only a logical conclusion. Promoting nudity – naked swimming,

---

[42] See for example Wolbert, 'Lebensreform'; Arno Klönne, 'Eine deutsche Bewegung, politisch zweideutig', in *Die Lebensreform: Entwürfe zur Neugestaltung von Leben und Kunst um 1900*, ed. Kai Buchholz et al. (Darmstadt: haeusser-media, 2001). A classical study along these lines is George Mosse, *The Crisis of German Ideology: Intellectual Origins of the Third Reich* (New York: Grosset & Dunlap, 1964). On politics in the youth movements, see Ahrens, *Bündische Jugend*, 77–98. See also the contributions in Gideon Botsch and Josef Haverkamp, eds., *Jugendbewegung, Antisemitismus und rechtsradikale Politik: Vom Freideutschen Jugendtag bis zur Gegenwart* (Berlin: De Gruyter Oldenbourg, 2014).

naked gymnastics, or doing gardening work nakedly – was one of the key activities of the life reform movement, as numerous photos of naked men and women engaging in those activities show.[43] One former member of the youth movement for example recalled:

> We were forced to wear strange, stiff white linen rings, long, black pipes we put on our legs, and something made of sleaze was put on our head . . . Suddenly our body lost its patience. It put shoes and socks, trousers and collar to a tree and jumped naked into the forest. Thus hatred against these strange shells [Hüllen] flared up. But now the naked body stood in the sun, and the wind touched it as if it did not believe it . . . Oh, what a vigour that flows through the body when it drinks, utterly naked, the wind.[44]

Going naked, the author argued, would liberate the body. Freeing the body from clothes did not only expose it to the sun and fresh air, but it restored agency to the body itself. In this sense, members of the life and youth movements conceived of their activities as a revolt of the body itself.[45]

Other practices that would liberate the body included hiking, popular among the youth movement, or dancing.[46] The community at Monte Verità was famous not least for attracting avant-garde dancers like Isadora Duncan, Rudolf von Laban, and Mary Wigman, who used dancing to 'liberate' their body and soul.[47] Rudolf von Laban for example wanted to revive the 'sense of dancing that existed in every human being, but that was trapped under the "ballast" of civilization'.[48] More focused on herself, Mary Wigman hoped that through dancing, her true inner self, 'the witch – the being rooted deeply in the earth, in its uninhibited instinctiveness [Triebhaftigkeit], in its insatiable lust for life, animal and woman at the same time' could come to the fore.[49] Dancing was thus a way to practise an authentic and liberated subjectivity. In the youth movement, dancing

---

[43] See the photos in Buchholz et al., eds., Lebensreform. On the nudity movement, see, Möhring, Marmorleiber; Rolf Koerber, 'Freikörperkultur', in Handbuch der deutschen Reformbewegungen, 1880–1933, ed. Diethart Kerbs and Jürgen Reulecke (Wuppertal: Hammer, 1998); Wolbert, '"Unbekleidet"'.

[44] Quoted, without reference, in Andritzky, 'Einleitung', 5.

[45] See ibid. See critically Möhring, Marmorleiber, 23–24.

[46] On the role of dancing in the life reform movement, see Gabriele Brandstetter, 'Ausdruckstanz', in Handbuch der deutschen Reformbewegungen, 1880–1933, ed. Diethart Kerbs and Jürgen Reulecke (Wuppertal: Hammer, 1998).

[47] See the excellent article by Hedwig Müller, 'Tanz der Natur: Lebensreform und Tanz', in Die Lebensreform: Entwürfe zur Neugestaltung von Leben und Kunst um 1900, ed. Kai Buchholz et al. (Darmstadt: haeusser-media, 2001). See also Natalia Stüdemann, Dionysos in Sparta: Isadora Duncan in Russland. Eine Geschichte von Tanz und Körper (Bielefeld: transcript, 2008).

[48] Müller, 'Tanz', 332.

[49] Mary Wigman, Die Sprache des Tanzes (Stuttgart: Battenberg, 1963), 40–41. Quoted in Müller, 'Tanz', 333–334.

played a similarly important role. At the Hohe Meißner gathering in 1913, where between two and three thousand members of the movement met, participants often preferred to dance rather than to listen to the speeches. Initially disgusted, reform pedagogue Gustav Wyneken later praised this: 'He who sits all day between the walls of a school or who walks around the stony streets of the cities, has no real body, he runs like a cart on stony tracks. As a revolt against this, as a celebration of the rediscovery of the body and a renewed covenant with it – this is how I interpreted the dancing at the Meißner. [*Wer den ganzen Tag zwischen den Wänden der Schule sitzt oder in den steinernen Straßen der Städte umherläuft, der hat eigentlich gar keinen Körper, er läuft wie ein Wagen in steinernen Gleisen. Als eine Auflehnung hiergegen, als eine Feier des Wiederfindens des eigenen Körpers und des neuen Bundes mit ihm deute ich mir die Tanzerei vom Meißner.*]'[50]

Liberating the natural body was not merely an individual task, but also an interpersonal endeavour. Life reformers and *Wandervogel* activists wanted to relate not only to their own bodies in a more natural way, but also to those of their friends and comrades. Discussions about gender relations are particularly revealing in this regard. After initial hesitations, at least some groups in the *Wandervogel* admitted girls, who would eventually join boy groups on their hiking trips, and swim and dance naked with the boys without feeling shame.[51] Going naked would, as one *Wandervogel* put it, allow them to be 'entirely free, entirely in the nature, without all the stuff that irrationality, immorality and artificiality have burdened us with. [*Wir wollen doch einmal ganz frei sein, ganz in der Natur, ohne alles, was uns Unverstand, Unsittlichkeit und Unnatur angehängt hatte.*]'[52] According to the youth movement, the shame attached to nudity was deeply unnatural. Importantly, as many scholars have stressed, the celebration of shame-free nudity in both the life reform and youth movements was an attempt to desexualize nudity.[53] In *Wandervogel* groups, relations between girls and boys would remain 'comradely' and asexual. Only after World War I and at the fringes of the youth movement did some Viennese groups, influenced by socialist Eduard Bernfeld, to whom I return in the next section, call for open sexuality.

For *Wandervogel* members, being naked was not only a way to create an authentic and liberated body, but also to produce intimate and hence

---

[50] Wyneken, 'Sinn', quoted in Rohkrämer, *Andere Moderne?*, 154–155. See also Ras, *Körper*, 19; Conti, *Abschied*, 113.

[51] On girls in the *Wandervogel*, see Ras, *Körper*, esp. 47–48.

[52] Fulda, *Lichtkleid*, 10, quoted in Koerber, 'Freikörperkultur', 103.

[53] Krabbe, *Gesellschaftsveränderung*, 99.

natural feelings. Former *Wandervogel* member Otto Piper, for example, recalled how he and his comrades had 'walked hand in hand, flung [their] arms around a friend's neck, scuffled to feel the other's bodily vitality, hugged each other and cried together or kissed each other, full of emotion [*vor Rührung*]. That had always been part of human life; only the recent time with its marked intellectualism had abandoned this', Piper remarked. Bodily closeness was a way of showing, sharing, and practising emotions; it was a way to 'feel' the other and his vitality.[54] Physical intimacy had to be complemented by communicative intimacy. A publication of the nudity movement (literally, the free-body-culture [*Freikörperkultur*] movement) was, for example, entitled 'We Are Naked and Call Us *Du* ', that is, the informal German 'you'.[55] Living a life according to nature called, as this brief discussion has shown, for a variety of bodily, emotional, and communicative practices that liberated the body and produced an intimate relation with one's own body as well as with friends and their bodies.

In the 1970s, alternative leftists could turn to the dropouts who gathered at Monte Verità and authors such as Hans Paasche and Erich Scheurmann to both formulate their critique of a society they deemed overly rational and hostile to feelings, and find inspiration for developing practices that would yield the feelings of bodily intimacy that they missed in capitalism. Indeed, life reformers' critique of a rational and scientific world that left no space for instincts and feelings and that harmed bodies sounds remarkably similar to the critique of rationality that alternative leftists formulated in the 1970s. Given these parallels, interpreting the alternative left as part of a longer search for authenticity in a world perceived as deeply inauthentic makes more sense than integrating it into a narrative of postwar liberalization. But while alternative leftists, too, sought to develop less rational, more emotional, and more 'holistic' ways of living, both their critique of modern society and the practices they engaged in to create more wholesome and healthy bodies radically differed from what life reformers had propagated. Shaping strong, natural, and healthy bodies by exposing them to the sun and fresh air, or by eating a vegetarian diet and avoiding alcohol and tobacco, was nothing leftists strove for. While they complained about industrial food and preferred

---

[54] Otto Piper, 'Rückblick auf den Wandervogel', in *Wandervogel und Freideutsche Jugend* , by Gerhard Ziemer and Hans Wolf (Bad Godesberg: Voggenreiter Verlag, 1961 [Niederschrift, 1959]), reproduced in Kindt, ed., *Grundschriften*, vol. 2, 215–230, here 224. See also Rohkrämer, *Andere Moderne?*, 144.

[55] Adolf Koch, *Wir sind nackt und nennen uns Du! Bunte Bilder aus der Freikörperkulturbewegung* (Leipzig: Ernst Oldenburg Verlag, 1932).

wide, comfortable clothes to the dress codes of bourgeois society, they also enjoyed cigarettes, beer, and wine. Attitudes towards sexuality differed as well, of course. Leftist magazines frequently published photos of naked men, women, and children – but to naturalize sexuality rather than to desexualize healthy, nude bodies.

Most importantly, life reformers and alternative leftists had radically different political attitudes and indeed understandings of politics. While there were left-wing life reformers and youth movement groups, many others shared *völkisch*-nationalist and anti-Semitic ideas that had, of course, no place in the alternative left, even though some leftists in the 1970s embraced notions of *Heimat*.[56] While scholars have for a long time focused on the more or less right-wing ideologies of the life reform and youth movements, recent scholarship has inquired the body politics of the life reform movement, arguing that by trying to produce 'natural' and hence 'normal' bodies in a historically specific way, movements like the nudist movement effectively disciplined the body, which made these movements inherently political. What was considered healthy and natural had deeply political implications, for example with regard to the health of the 'national body'.[57] The step from cleansing individual bodies from 'unhealthy' food to cleansing the national bodies from 'unhealthy' people was indeed a short one, as Michael Andritzky has noted.[58] Leftists in the 1970s did not care about the national body. But they, too, tried to shape authentic and healthy bodies and feelings. It is indeed not by accident that both Maren Möhring in her work on the life reform movement and Sven Reichardt have turned to Michel Foucault to analyse how movements that claimed to liberate bodies and feelings had a highly disciplinary and coercive character. However, while life reformers typically regarded their activities as apolitical, liberating bodies and feelings from their oppression in capitalist and rationalist society was a crucial element of leftists' political program in the 1970s. The personal, that is, had become political. Considering the alternative left as part of a longer search for an authentic life in an inauthentic world thus does not mean that alternative leftists simply replicated the life reform movement. While life reformers around 1900 and leftists in the 1970s shared a critique of a world dominated by science and rationality and longed for liberated bodies and intimate

---

[56] See the discussion in Rohkrämer, *Andere Moderne?*, 126–127, 148–149; Botsch and Haverkamp, eds., *Jugendbewegung*. For a more positive evaluation of the life reform movement, see Wolbert, 'Lebensreform'.

[57] See Möhring, *Marmorleiber*.   [58] Andritzky, 'Einleitung', 7.

feelings, they differed with regards to liberating bodies and producing feelings of intimacy.

Instincts and Politics: Freudian Marxists

In 1912, one of the founding members of the *Wandervogel*, Hans Blüher, published a book that caused a massive outrage within the youth movement: *The German Wandervogel Movement as an Erotic Phenomenon: A Contribution to an Understanding of Sexual Inversion.*[59] In a distinctly Freudian manner, Blüher argued for a broad understanding of sexuality. The times had passed, he posited, when sexuality was understood as being located in genital organs and directed toward reproduction. With this understanding of sexuality in mind, he sought to explain the *Wandervogel* movement. Most teenage boys in this movement, he observed, had at least temporarily no interest in girls, but a desire for other boys, which he interpreted in sexual terms. The erotic ideal he found in the *Wandervogel* was a 'young, brown human being [*Mensch*] with a somewhat savaged travelling suit, a feather in the hat, a rucksack on the back, and a guitar full of ribbons' – an image somewhat reminiscent of hippies in the 1970s. Admiring this quaint fashion, *Wandervogel* leaders could 'bona fide believe in the "asexuality" of their desires'.[60] At the end of the book, he called the legalization of 'sexual inversion', a term he preferred vis-à-vis homosexuality.[61] It is certainly not surprising that most *Wandervogel* groups vigorously rejected the book.[62]

Blüher was only one of several thinkers at the fringes of the life reform and youth movements who turned to Freud's teachings and questioned the desexualization of the body.[63] While Blüher was particularly attracted by Freud's broad understanding of sexuality that was not limited to genital, reproductive sexuality, others sought to explore what they considered the political implications of psychoanalytic theory. According to Freud, sexual

---

[59] Hans Blüher, *Die deutsche Wandervogelbewegung als erotisches Phänomen: Ein Beitrag zur Erkenntnis der sexuellen Inversion. Mit einem Vorwort von Dr. med. Magnus Hirschfeld* (Berlin: Verlag Bernhard Weise, 1912). For an extended discussion of Blüher's work and the reactions he faced in the youth movement, see Claudia Bruns, *Politik des Eros: Der Männerbund in Wissenschaft, Politik und Jugendkultur* (Cologne: Böhlau, 2008).

[60] Blüher, *Wandervogelbewegung*, 39–40.   [61] Ibid., 108–121.

[62] See Otto Piper, 'Rückblick auf den Wandervogel', in *Dokumentation der Jugendbewegung, vol 2: Die Wandervogelzeit*, ed. Werner Kindt (Düsseldorf and Cologne: Diederichs, 1968), 224; Bruns, *Politik*, 338–358.

[63] See Uffa Jensen, 'The Lure of Authenticity: Emotions and Generation in the German Youth Movement of the Early 20th Century', in *History by Generations: Generational Dynamics in Modern History*, ed. Harmut Berghoff et al. (Göttingen: Wallstein, 2013).

drives have to be suppressed and sublimated in order to enable the process of civilization; civilization thus inherently causes psychic discomfort, because natural drives have to be suppressed. Freud, of course, believed that this suppression was a necessity. No political or social revolution would be able to change this situation and thus solve the problems that came with suppressing desires. Some of his students, however, saw this differently, most famously Wilhelm Reich, but already before him Otto Gross and Siegfried Bernfeld.[64] Especially Reich and Bernfeld attempted to link Marxist with Freudian thinking, a line of thinking that was later, after World War II, further developed by Herbert Marcuse and Reimut Reiche.[65] These thinkers explored what they considered the politically revolutionary potential of psychoanalysis; even more importantly, they also claimed that seemingly 'personal' problems, notably with regard to sexuality, were in fact deeply social, and hence of political importance. The solution of these seemingly individual problems therefore required political action. Freudo-Marxists fundamentally re-shaped the contours of the political. Questions of sexuality, instincts, and feelings moved to the centre of politics and a potential political liberation.

Wilhelm Reich and Herbert Marcuse have long been recognized as influential thinkers for the German student movement around 1968. While they were less popular during the 1970s, their ideas about the political, and especially the political significance of sexuality and sexual desires, informed the politics of the alternative left. During the 1970s, leftists also rediscovered the work of Gross and Bernfeld, though this does of course not mean that they were widely read in the alternative left.[66] By looking at the writings of Gross, Bernfeld, Reich and Marcuse, we can thus understand the intellectual genealogy of the politics of the alternative left.

The critiques of modern society Gross, Bernfeld, Reich and later Marcuse formulated of course differed in many ways from the arguments made by life reformers and *Wandervogel* activists. Neither of these thinkers was concerned with fashion, dietary habits, or nudity. But both life reformers and Freudian

---

[64] See the discussion in Uffa Jensen, 'Die Utopie der Authentizität und ihre Grenzen: Die Politisierung der Psychoanalyse im frühen 20. Jahrhundert', in *Das Selbst zwischen Anpassung und Befreiung: Psychowissen und Politik im 20. Jahrhundert*, ed. Uffa Jensen and Maik Tändler (Göttingen: Wallstein, 2012).

[65] On Reich and Reiche and their influence in the New Left, see Dagmar Herzog, *Sex after Fascism: Memory and Morality in Twentieth-Century Germany* (Princeton: Princeton University Press, 2005), 152–162; Kauders, 'Drives in Dispute'.

[66] Otto Gross, *Von geschlechtlicher Not zur sozialen Katastrophe* (Hamburg: Edition Nautilus, 2000); Siegfried Bernfeld, *Antiautoritäre Erziehung und Psychoanalyse: Ausgewählte Schriften*, 3 vols. (Frankfurt a.M.: März Verlag, 1969–1971).

Marxists argued that an essential part of human nature was repressed in modern society, and both sought for ways to enable a life that was more 'according to human nature', and thus more 'authentic', even if Freudo-Marxists hardly used this term. Yet they differed with regard to their understanding of what constituted human nature, and hence the solutions they proposed. In contrast to most life reformers, Freudo-Marxists considered sexuality to be an essential but repressed aspect of human nature, and unlike life reformers, they did not believe in individually 're-forming' life (and bodies), but in the necessity of radical changes of social and political structures. Creating the conditions for a life 'according to human nature', which implied for Freudo-Marxist thinkers a liberation of sexual desires, would be the central objective of a socio-political revolution. While this would ultimately be a political task, particularly Wilhelm Reich also argued that psychoanalytical therapy might help overcoming the repression of sexual desires. This combination of psychoanalytic thinking with (Marxist) politics was highly appealing to new leftists in Germany and elsewhere, because it gave political meaning to projects of personal and sexual transformation. Working on the self, to use a different terminology, became immanently political.[67] While looking at life reformers has helped us reconstruct the genealogy of alternative subjectivities, looking at Freudian-Marxist thinkers helps us outline the genealogy of alternative politics of subjectivity.

One of the first to draw political conclusions from Freud's teachings was Otto Gross, a left-wing psychoanalyst with anarchist leanings who had spent some time at the community of Monte Verità in the early 1900s.[68] In Gross's reading, Freud's insights into the human psyche had enabled a new ethics that called for the 'real knowledge of one self and the other'.[69] This knowledge would allow people to truly understand each other and thus escape the 'infinite final loneliness' that individuals experienced.[70] The ethics he developed called for a genuine revolution that would, unlike all the previous revolutions, do away with the ultimate source of authority,

---

[67] See the insightful study of Herbert Marcuse by Roland Roth, *Rebellische Subjektivität. Herbert Marcuse und die neuen Protestbewegungen* (Frankfurt a.M.: Campus, 1985), 84–85. Roth emphasizes that Marcuse was not alone in rehabilitating the political power of 'fantasy, utopia, and subjectivity', as writers like Raoul Vaneigm and Henri Lefebvre in France played an equally important role.

[68] See Voswinckel, *Freie Liebe*, 47–50. On Gross, see also Raimund Dehmlow, 'Gefährten: Otto Gross und Franz Jung', in *Von geschlechtlicher Not zur sozialen Katastrophe*, by Otto Gross (Hamburg: Edition Nautilus, 2000); Emanuel Hurwitz, *Otto Gross: Paradies-Sucher zwischen Freud und Jung* (Frankfurt a.M.: Suhrkam, 1979); Jensen, 'Utopie', 47–52.

[69] Otto Gross, 'Zur Überwindung der kulturellen Krise', in *Von geschlechtlicher Not zur sozialen Katastrophe*, by Otto Gross (Hamburg: Edition Nautilus, 2000 [1913]), 59.

[70] Otto Gross, 'Ludwig Rabiners "Psychoanalyse"', in *Von geschlechtlicher Not zur sozialen Katastrophe*, by Otto Gross (Hamburg: Edition Nautilus, 2000 [1913]), 62.

that is, in his view, the 'paternal law'. 'Today's revolutionary, who envisions, with the support of the psychology of the unconscious, the relations among the sexes in a free and happy future, struggles against rape in its most original form, against the father and his law. The coming revolution will be a revolution for the maternal law', he wrote in 1913.[71] Only this revolution would enable humans to live to their full, natural potential. Gross therefore considered 'all of humanity' to be the 'clinic' for psychoanalysts. Individual psychoanalysis would provide would only be the 'clinical preparation' that liberated potential revolutionaries.[72] Gross, however, never sought to combine Marxist thinking with psychoanalysis – Nietzsche and Schopenhauer were his theoretical references, in addition to Freud – even though he showed sympathies for the Russian revolution after World War I and joined the German Communist Party (KPD) in Berlin.[73]

Siegfried Bernfeld, a second important thinker to consider, was more involved with the Marxist working-class movement.[74] A member of the Viennese youth movement, Bernfeld had been strongly influenced by the ideas of Gustav Wynecken; he also expressed sympathies for Hans Blüher and his Freudian interpretation of the youth movement. In Bernfeld's mind, it was the youth movement's achievement to 'sense that the sexual question was as a public, social ill'.[75] Above all, Bernfeld was active as reform pedagogue in Vienna. In the 1970s, his writings were re-published by the left-wing publisher März Verlag as a contribution to the theory of anti-authoritarian child rearing.[76] Bernfeld was also the first to consider an integration of Marxism and psychoanalysis. Both theories argued, he noted, historically, materialistically, and dialectically. Psychoanalysis explained individual behaviour by examining the individual's biography, that is, its history, up to the earliest childhood; it rejected any absolute 'higher' or 'moral' values, but explained them as a result of 'lower' phenomena, such as sexual desires, which makes it materialistic; and it worked with polar concepts, such as Eros and the death drive, which

---

[71] Gross, 'Überwindung', 62.   [72] Gross, 'Psychoanalyse', 64.

[73] See Otto Gross, 'Zur neuerlichen Vorarbeit: vom Unterricht', in Von geschlechtlicher Not zur sozialen Katastrophe, by Otto Gross (Hamburg: Edition Nautilus, 2000 [1913]); Otto Gross, 'Die kommunistische Grundidee in der Paradiessymbolik', in Von geschlechtlicher Not zur sozialen Katastrophe, by Otto Gross (Hamburg: Edition Nautilus, 2000 [1913]); Dehmlow, 'Gefährten', 187.

[74] On Bernfeld and left-wing psychoanalysis in Vienna, see Jensen, 'Utopie', 52–58.

[75] Siegfried Bernfeld, 'Die Psychoanalyse in der Jugendbewegung', Imago 5 (1919). Reprinted in Bernfeld, Antiautoritäre Erziehung, vol. 3, 108–115, here 112.

[76] Bernfeld, Antiautoritäre Erziehung.

makes psychoanalysis in Bernfeld's view dialectic.[77] Despite his Marxism, however, Bernfeld never developed a political program that placed the liberation of sexual desires at its core.

This crucial step was made by Wilhelm Reich, arguably the most influential Freudo-Marxist thinker for the student revolts around 1968. Reich had developed his ideas in the 1920s, when he actively supported the German Communist Party, even though his calls for a sexual revolution remained marginal. Being mostly forgotten by the time of his death in 1957, he was rediscovered by radical students a decade later. The unauthorized reprints of *Die Funktion des Orgasmus, Massenpsychologie des Faschismus, Die sexuelle Revolution,* and others printed by students, were quickly sold and widely discussed amongst students.[78] Similar to members of the life reform movement, Reich believed that modern, in his terms capitalist society made it impossible for people to live according to their nature. Building on Freud's theory, however, he regarded sexual desires as an essential part of human nature. The 'organic drive apparatus, especially the sexual chemistry' produced, Reich argued, 'bodily excitements' that longed for 'relaxation'.[79] Reich, that is, developed an ultimately biological understanding of sexuality, with a particular focus on both male and female genitalia.[80] Being able to achieve genital orgasms during heterosexual intercourse, an ability Reich defined as 'orgiastic potency', would characterize sexually 'healthy' men and women.[81] The problem was, however, that social reality prohibited the satisfaction of these desires. Unlike Freud, Reich held the specific social conditions of capitalism responsible for the suppression of sexual desires. The repression of desires required, Reich argued, 'a great amount of psychic energy', which would inhibit the development of intellectual and critical abilities. In this sense, sexual repression stabilized the capitalist system.[82] But the political consequences of sexual repression went further. The 'psychic organism', Reich claimed, had to protect itself with an 'armour' against the demands of both

---

[77] Siegfried Bernfeld, 'Sozialismus und Psychoanalyse', *Der Kampf: Sozialdemokratische Monatsschrift* 19 (1926). Reprinted in Bernfeld, *Antiautoritäre Erziehung,* vol. 2, 490–497.

[78] See Herzog, *Sex,* 152–162.

[79] Wilhelm Reich, *Dialektischer Materialismus und Psychoanalyse* (Copenhagen: Verlag für Sexualpolitik, 1934), 15.

[80] For a radical critique of Reich's biological reading of Freud, see Wilhelm Burian, *Sexualität, Natur, Gesellschaft* (Freiburg: Ca-Ira-Verlag, 1985), 45–46, 55–59.

[81] See Wilhelm Reich, *Die Funktion des Orgasmus: Zur Psychopathologie und zur Soziologie des Geschlechtslebens* (Amsterdam: Thomas de Munter, 1965). See in general the intellectual biography by Burian, *Sexualität.*

[82] Wilhelm Reich, *Der sexuelle Kampf der Jugend* (Berlin: Verlag für Sexualpolitik, 1932), 99.

its internal drives and the external morality; it had to make itself 'cold'. This armour, he argued, was 'the most important reason for people's loneliness [*Vereinsamung*] in the midst of a collective life'.[83] This 'moral regulation of natural, biological desires' created 'secondary, sick, and asocial drives', such as sadism and the lust for violence.[84] Ultimately, these sadist tendencies resulted in the rise of Fascism in Germany, Reich proposed, thus linking the repression of genital sexuality with Nazism.[85]

Liberating sexual desires, which would enable people, and especially teenagers, to live a life that would be in accordance with their nature, was the central goal of Reich's politics. Sexual education and the 'realization of an ability for sexual pleasure' would be 'a cardinal question of social life', he wrote in 1945.[86] After the revolution, a communist society would allow the satisfaction of people's sexual desires, he hoped; then, women would no longer be sexually exploited by their husbands.[87] Before these goals could be achieved, Reich wanted to 'politicize the sexual question', especially for the youth.[88] Teenagers, both male and female, were in Reich's understanding particularly damaged by both the repressive sexual morality, and by the sheer lack of opportunities to engage in 'healthy' sexual activities, notably the lack of apartments where they could have sex without being interrupted by their parents. In the early 1930s, Reich became an active member of the German Communist Party, where he believed to find support for his program of sexual 'liberation'.[89] Addressing the everyday concerns of teenagers, which were mostly sexual and not solely material, would motivate them in a struggle against capitalism, he claimed. Reich thus encouraged young communists to openly talk about their 'sexual problems' and to create the conditions for a more fulfilled sexual life within the communist organization.

Scholars have mostly looked at Reich's influence on students' sexual politics. However, Reich's work also raised the question of what politics is about, as he himself was clearly aware of. Most people think of 'politics' as 'diplomatic negotiations between small and large powers', or as parliamentary proceedings, but remain disinterested in these issues that are far away

---

[83] Wilhelm Reich, *Die sexuelle Revolution* (Frankfurt a.M.: Fischer, 1966), 28–29.   [84] Ibid., 44.

[85] See Wilhelm Reich, *Massenpsychologie des Faschismus: Zur Sexualökonomie der politischen Reaktion und zur proletarischen Sexualpolitik* (Copenhagen: Verlag für Sexualpolitik, 1933).

[86] Reich, *Sexuelle Revolution*, 264.   [87] Reich, *Sexuelle Kampf*, 148–149.   [88] Ibid., 123.

[89] On the Reich and his often overestimated role in the 'sexpol movement', see Marc Rackelmann, 'Wilhelm Reich und der Einheitsverband für proletarische Sexualreform und Mutterschutz: Was war die Sexpol?', *Emotion: Beiträge zum Werk von Wilhelm Reich* 11 (1993); Atina Grossmann, *Reforming Sex: The German Movement for Birth Control and Abortion Reform, 1920–1950* (Oxford: Oxford University Press, 1995), 124–132.

from their everyday life, Reich argued. Communist propaganda, he remarked critically, often replicated this 'bourgeois form of politics', for example by giving boring lectures on the 'economic background of the coming war', or by mechanically relating questions of everyday life to high politics. By contrast, the 'sexpol movement', that is, the sexual political movement within the German Communist Party that Reich claimed to have inspired, 'developed the necessity of a social revolution based on subjective needs (*Bedürfnisse*), based all political questions on the "if" and "how" of the satisfaction of the needs of the masses', which included sexual needs. Reich, in other words, sought to challenge the 'absolute antagonism between the personal and the political' that was common for communist politics. 'Not only do most personal questions exist which are, at the same time, most typical questions of the social order, such as the question of sexual relations or the questions of residence for the youth, but politics as such is nothing else but the praxis of different interests of needs [*Bedürfnisinteressen*] of the different social strata and the different age groups of society.'⁹⁰ Based on his explicitly biological understanding of human nature, Reich developed a concept of politics that put sexual desires and other feelings such as loneliness at its core, both in terms of his political utopias and his practical politics in the sexpol movement. Politics therefore had to address, Reich believed, workers' everyday life. In the 1920s and early 1930s, this remained a minority position; it resonated, however, with radical students in the 1960s and 1970s who wanted to revolutionize everyday life.

Wilhelm Reich was not the only intellectual who, during the 1920s and 1930s, drew on Freud to develop a critical theory of society. Thinkers associated with the so-called Frankfurt School similarly interpreted society with Freudian concepts.⁹¹ Most important in the context of this chapter is Herbert Marcuse, another author who was widely read amongst radical students in the 1960s.⁹² Facing persecution by the Nazis, Marcuse fled

---

⁹⁰ Wilhelm Reich, *Was ist Klassenbewusstsein? Ein Beitrag zur Diskussion über die Neuformierung der Arbeiterbewegung* (Kopenhagen: Verlag für Sexualpolitik, 1934), 36–37.

⁹¹ For a history of the Frankfurt School, see Martin Jay, *The Dialectical Imagination: A History of the Frankfurt School and the Institute of Social Research, 1923–1950* (Berkley, Los Angeles: University of California Press, 1996).

⁹² On Marcuse's influence on the student movement, see Roth, *Subjektivität*, 165–291; Alexander Sedlmaier, *Consumption and Violence: Radical Protest in Cold-War West Germany* (Ann Arbor, MI: University of Michigan Press, 2014), 61–94; John Abromeit, 'The Limits of Praxis: The Social-Psychological Foundations of Theodor Adorno's and Herbert Marcuse's Interpretations of the 1960s Protest Movements', in *Changing the World, Changing Oneself: Political Protest and Collective Identities in West Germany and the U.S. in the 1960s and 1970s*, ed. Belinda Davis et al. (New York: Berghahn, 2010); Hanning Voigts, *Entkorkte Flaschenpost: Herbert Marcuse, Theodor W. Adorno und*

first to Switzerland and then, in 1934, to the United States, where he wrote the majority of his books that would become influential in the New Left on both sides of the Atlantic, most notably *Eros and Civilization: A Philosophical Inquiry into Freud* (1955) and *The One-Dimensional Man* (1964).[93] In the remainder of this section, I turn to Marcuse's *Eros and Civilization* to explore his peculiar understanding of the political for which questions of authentic subjectivity were central and that in many ways anticipated the politics of the alternative left.

At the core of Marcuse's philosophical inquiry into Sigmund Freud's theory of desires was the attempt to uncover the potential for imagining an emancipated society in which repressing desires was no longer necessary. To this end, Marcuse distinguished between a repression of desires that was biologically 'basic', that is necessary, and a 'surplus' repression of desires that was dictated by historically specific social conditions.[94] Repressing desires was, as Freud had argued, necessary to succeed in the struggle for survival and therefore for social and cultural progress. Only the repression of desires would enable people to redirect their energies towards productive work that did not immediately satisfy desires. How much work, and thus how much repression of desires, was necessary, however, depended on social and technological factors. In this sense, Marcuse claimed to have uncovered a 'historical-social component' of what Freud had called the 'reality principle'.[95] This historical understanding of repression implied that, if society changed, repressing desires would no longer be necessary to such an extent. In Marcuse's view, the development of the forces of production and the process of automation had indeed made most physical labour unnecessary. Repressing desires, which once had been necessary to make people work hard, had become unnecessary.[96] Under these conditions, work could become play, desires could be fulfilled and sublimated, and the body could become a source of pleasure; people would not have to fear death, but might choose it at the right moment. Marcuse thus presented a utopian vision of a society in which individuals no longer suffered from the tensions between a struggle for being and the fulfilment of desires. Human beings

---

der Streit um die Neue Linke (Münster: LIT Verlag, 2010). On the intellectual context, see Tim B. Müller, *Krieger und Gelehrte: Herbert Marcuse und die Denksystem im Kalten Krieg* (Hamburg: Hamburger Ediition, 2010), 586–600, 627–649.

[93] Herbert Marcuse, *Eros and Civilization: A Philosophical Inquiry into Freud* (London: Routledge, 1987 [1956]); Herbert Marcuse, *One-Dimensional Man: Studies in the Ideology of Advanced Industrial Society* (Boston: Beacon Press, 1964).

[94] Marcuse, *Eros*, 35.   [95] Ibid.   [96] Ibid., 102–103.

would be 'whole', rationality and fantasies would be reconciled.[97] Marcuse thus envisioned a 'complete' subjectivity that would no longer be shattered by internal contradictions and struggles.

This re-reading of Freud had also consequences for an understanding of the political.[98] As Marcuse stressed in the book's preface, psychological problems had become inherently political problems, an understanding of the political that, of course, resembled Wilhelm Reich's, even though Marcuse never quoted Reich.[99] Marcuse's focus on the (historically unnecessary) repression of desires meant that fantasies and dreams, in which those usually repressed desires survived, turned into a potentially subversive and revolutionary force against the dominating, and ultimately irrational, reality principle of capitalist society: the performance principle.[100] Overcoming this principle would constitute a genuine revolution. Once this had been achieved, the 'pleasure principle' would reign, and people would be able to live according to their inner nature, in particular with regard to their sexuality. Indeed, sexuality would be radically transformed in a society 'beyond the reality principle'. The necessity to work under the performance principle had resulted, Marcuse argued, in the limitation of sexuality to genitalia and the desexualization of the rest of the body that was needed for work, but could no longer be a source of (sexual) pleasures. So-called 'perversions', illegitimate sexual desires that did not focus on genitalia, were reminders of a polymorph sexuality that had characterized childhood, but that had to be suppressed in adult life. Once the unnecessary suppression of desires had ended, the entire body would become a source of (sexual) pleasure again. Under these circumstances, even productive work would transform into a form of play that people could enjoy with their entire bodies.[101]

When Marcuse was writing *Eros and Civilization* in 1955, he believed that the 'new' subjectivity would be possible only after radical social changes. To indicate that there was such a potential, he had to draw on mythologies. Witnessing the student movements around 1968, however, Marcuse came to regard them as empirical prove of 'the possibility of new ways of experiencing, which constitute the sensual core of a revolutionary subjectivity', as Roland Roth argued in his 1985 analysis of Marcuse's thinking. The 'new movements' had, according to Roth's rather

---

[97] Ibid., 193, 235–237. See in general Part II, 'Beyond the Reality Principle', and especially Chapter 11, 'Eros and Thanatos', for Marcuse's vision of a reconciliation of desires and rationality.
[98] Roland Roth sees this very clearly. See Roth, *Subjektivität*, esp. 210, 216, 249.
[99] Marcuse, *Eros*, xi.   [100] Ibid., 142–144.   [101] Ibid., 199–205.

sympathetic analysis, realized Marcuse's vision of a different ground of politics by revolting 'against the crippling of human senses under capitalism' and by making 'nature', that is above all human nature, part of politics again.[102] Marcuse, Roth suggested, had anticipated an understanding of the political that alternative leftists in the 1970s.

Artistic Critiques of Inauthentic Life

Around the same time that Marcuse was gaining popularity among students in Western Europe and the United States, avant-garde artist groups like the Beat Poets and the Situationist International emerged that pursued a similar agenda of 'politically rehabilitating fantasy, utopia and subjectivity'.[103] These artists, too, believed in the politically subversive force of imaginations, dreams, and desires in a world dominated by a mind-dulling rationality, a world that lacked, according to Beat Poets, 'vitality' as well as spiritual and emotional fulfilment.[104] Popular amongst alternative leftists, the Beat Poets provided a vision of a transgressive and fluid subjectivity that differed from the ideals of a 'healed' and wholesome subjectivity Reich and Marcuse had to offer.[105] Leftists were also inspired by both Beat Poets' and Situationists' celebration of exuberance and ecstasy. Whereas Reich and Marcuse had been influential for the more theoretically inclined parts of the student movement, radical artists played a more prominent role in the emerging countercultural scene. Beat poets were read by West German *Gammler*, to be discussed in the next section, while the Situationist International and its critique of the 'society of the spectacle'

---

[102] Roth, *Subjektivität*, 249–250.

[103] Ibid., 85. For the general countercultural context, see Gerd-Rainer Horn, *The Spirit of '68: Rebellion in Western Europe and North America, 1956–1976* (Oxford: Oxford University Press, 2007), 5–53.

[104] Sharin N. Elkholy, 'Introduction', in *The Philosophy of the Beats*, ed. Sharin N. Elkholy (Lexington, KY: University Press of Kentucky, 2012), 5.

[105] See for example Peter Schult, 'Musik ist eine Waffe', in *Das Blatt* special issue, n.d., probably March 1976; Herbert Röttgen, 'Die Entdeckung des Körpers und der neuen Sexualität', in *Das Blatt* 94, 10 May–2 June 1977; Rädli, '[Title illegible]', in *Das Blatt* 111, 23 December 1977–12 January 1978, 24; cover page of *Ulcus Molle* 7/8, 1979; Review of 'Keroauc, Die Schrift der goldenen Ewigkeit', in *Ulcus Molle* 1/2, 1981, 79. See also Christiane Thurn and Herbert Röttgen, eds., *Die Rückkehr des Imaginären: Märchen, Magie, Mystik, Mythos, Anfänge einer anderen Politik* (Munich: Trikon-Dianus Buchverlag, 1981), 12. Beat poets were attractive for non conformists throughout Europe, see for example Vaneigm, *The Revolution of Everyday Life*, 86, 138, 253; Klaus Hegemann, *Allen Ginsberg: Zeitkritik und politische Aktivitäten* (Baden-Baden: Nomos-Verlagsgesellschaft, 2000), 125; Primo Moreni and Nanni Balestrini, *Die goldene Horde: Arbeiterautonomie, Jugendrevolte und bewaffneter Kampf in Italien* (Berlin: Assoziation A, 2002), 56–74.

(Guy Debord) influenced not only the May 1968 events in France, but also key figures of the West German antiauthoritarian revolt like Dieter Kunzelmann.[106] Beat Poets and the Situationist International were thus part of the intellectual heritage on which the alternative left could build, though in particular the writings of the Beat Poets are rarely considered in studies of the West German left.

Beat poets are conventionally portrayed as one of the crucial intellectual sources of American counterculture after World War II, even though their radicalness has recently been questioned.[107] Radical or not, Beat Poets placed questions of subjectivity at the core of their critique of modern life, which makes them an important part of the story this chapter is telling about the emergence of alternative politics of subjectivity. To explore their critique of modern life, Allen Ginsberg's 1956 poem *Howl*, a central text for the Beat Poets and popular around the globe, can serve as an example.[108] The poem, divided in three parts, opens with mourning: 'I saw the best minds of my generation destroyed by madness', followed by multiple descriptions of how these 'best minds' had vanished. At the opening of the second part, which is most interesting with regard to his social critique, Ginsberg asked: 'What sphinx of cement and aluminium bashed open their skulls and ate up their brains and imagination?', and answered: 'Moloch'. In what follows, Ginsberg constructs an opposition between an impenetrable urban and industrial world, and the 'brains' and 'imagination' of individual minds – an opposition we find within the radical left of the 1970s as well. The description of the urban 'Moloch' provides further insights into his critique of modern society. 'Moloch, whose mind is pure machinery', he exclaimed. In the 'Moloch' of a rationalist society, imagination and intuition had no place. The very materiality of urban life symbolized the domination of the 'Mind': the 'skyscrapers' that stand 'in the long streets like endless Jehovas' and the 'thousand blind windows' that function as 'eyes' for this mind. The

[106] On Kunzelmann, see Aribert Reimann, *Dieter Kunzelmann: Avantgardist, Protestler, Radikaler* (Göttingen: Vandenhoeck & Ruprecht, 2009), 43–123.
[107] For a critical perspective, see Manuel Luis Martinez, *Countering the Counterculture: Rereading Postwar American Dissent from Jack Kerouac to Tomás Rivera* (Madison: The University of Wisconsin Press, 2003).
[108] On the poem and its popularity, see Jonah Raskin, *American Scream: Allen Ginsberg's* Howl *and the Making of the Beat Generation* (Berkeley: University of California Press, 2004); Jason Shinder, ed., *The Poem That Changed America: 'Howl' Fifty Years Later* (New York: Farrar, Straus and Giroux, 2006). The poem itself can be found, for example, in Allen Ginsberg, *Howl, and Other Poems* (San Francisco: City Lights Pocket Bookshop, 1956).

'Moloch' shapes the poet's feelings, as sitting inside 'Moloch' makes him 'lonely'. It also deprives him of his body – 'Moloch in whom I am consciousness without a body'; it 'frightened me out of my natural ecstasy'. Ginsberg, and with him other Beat poets, bemoaned, the poem suggests, the domination of rationality under which individuals suffered spiritually, emotionally, and bodily. The poem, and its critique of modern, urban society as a 'Moloch', provided alternative leftists in 1970s West Germany with a rhetoric they eagerly took up, frequently describing the cities they were living in as 'Molochs', as Chapter 3 discusses.

Beat Poets searched for opportunities to live a more 'authentic' life in this world seemingly lacking authenticity. They looked for a 'new consciousness' in situations of instability and fluidity, which they found in practises such as travelling, taking drugs, experimenting with sex, or meditating, which made them attractive for alternative leftists who were frequently hitchhiking around Europe and showed a similar fascination with drugs, sexual experiments, and 'eastern' bodily techniques like meditating.[109] Jack Kerouac, a second key figure of the Beat Generation, famously travelled to the American West and Mexico, hoping and believing to find 'authenticity' among social outcasts and non-whites, as the fictionalized account of travels in his *On the Road* suggests.[110] In multiple instances, as Steve Wilson observes, Kerouac equated the 'outsider status with authenticity: his description of the farmers, waitresses, and hobos he meets on his first trip west'. The authenticity he found in African-American culture, particularly in jazz, was characterized by valuating 'the intense moment over tradition, intuition over reason shaped by education', and a celebration of the body, which simply appeared as 'evil' in 'Anglo' culture, as Wilson put it. Creating an authentic self required not merely 'studying' these outcasts, but becoming one of them.[111] Along these lines, Ed D'Angelo suggests that the Beat poets' contacts with the criminal underworld, namely with drug dealers and addicts, as well as their own drug consumption, including experiments with LSD, constituted a descent into the underworld of the 'of the unconsciousness. The beats, in this

---

[109] See for example the journalistic account on West Germany by Margret Kosel, *Gammler, Beatniks, Provos: Die schleichende Revolution* (Frankfurt a.M.: Verlag Bärmeier & Nickel, 1967).

[110] Jack Kerouac, *On the Road* (London: Penguin, 1991). The book was first published in 1957 by Viking Press, New York. On the book, see Hilary Holladay and Robert Holton, eds., *What's Your Road, Man? Critical Essays on Jack Kerouac's* On the Road (Carbondale, IL: Southern Illinois University Press, 2009).

[111] Steve Wilson, 'The Author as Spiritual Pilgrim: The Search for Authenticity in Jack Kerouac's *On the Road* and the *Subterraneans*', in *The Beat Generation: Critical Essays*, ed. Kostas Myrsiades (New York: Peter Lang, 2001), 81.

respect, resemble shamans or mystics who transgress the bounds of social rules and conventions in their lonely journey beyond the walls of the city, into the forest, up the mountain, and into the belly of the beast.'[112]

Acts of transgression were central for the Beats' vision of authenticity. In their contacts with outcasts, they transgressed social boundaries; consuming drugs, they transgressed bodily boundaries; travelling, they transgressed both spatial and temporal boundaries. Erik Mortensen for example has pointed out how the actions of Dean Moriarty, one of the main characters of *On the Road*, are 'rationally fragmented' by a precise schedule, but not in order to produce, as in a capitalist regime of production, but in an attempt to fulfil his 'desires'. Moriarty's fragmented time is thus 'figured in an economy of ecstasy, not of oppression ... Dean's conception of time is shifted away from past and future and towards an ever-changing present.' Mortensen considers this, with Heidegger, an 'authentic' experience of time. Mobility in space was another form of transgression in which Beats found authenticity. Constant mobility implied, as Klaus Hegemann suggests, escaping social control and inclusion. It was on the road, he claims, where Kerouac found 'it' – that is, spiritual fulfilment and authenticity.[113] Finally, writing itself had a defiant quality for Beat poets. Not only did they report about transgressive experiences in their poetry and novels, but the very process of writing could be (bodily and temporally) transgressive. Jack Kerouac for example wrote his *On the Road* famously under the influence of stimulants within a mere three weeks. From the Beats' perspective, such acts of transgression could be subversive, as they lay bare what constituted human authenticity and what had been buried in the world of the 'Moloch': ecstasy, dreams, and imagination. This celebration of exuberance and transgressions made the Beat Poets popular not only within the American counterculture, but also amongst West German radical leftists.

Around the same time the Beat Poets developed their critique of modern American culture, radical artists and writers in Europe formed the Situationist International (SI).[114] They formulated both a sharp critique of the boredom of everyday life in Western consumer societies that

---

[112] Ed D'Angelo, 'Anarchism and the Beats', in *The Philosophy of the Beats*, ed. Sharin N. Elkholy (Lexington, KY: University Press of Kentucky, 2012), 231.

[113] Hegemann, *Ginsberg*, 98.

[114] On the Situationist International, see Horn, *Spirit*, 5–13; Thomas Hecken and Agata Grzenia, 'Situationism', in *1968 in Europe: A History of Protest and Activism, 1956–1977*, ed. Martin Klimke and Joachim Scharloth (New York: Palgrave Macmillan, 2008); Sadie Plant, *The Most Radical Gesture: The Situationist International in a Postmodern Age* (London: Routledge, 1992); McKenzie Wark, *The Beach Beneath the Street: The Everyday Life and Glorious Times of the Situationist International* (London: Verso Books, 2011). On the intellectual context in France, see Ingrid

informed the protests around 1968, especially in France, and an ideal of a revolution that would enrich life. Situationists, too, condemned modern society as inauthentic and argued that only a fundamental revolution of everyday life might restore an authentic life. The writings of the SI thus provided the European left with a critical analysis for which feelings – above all, boredom – played a fundamental role. While direct references by alternative leftists to Situationist texts are rare, many of the critical arguments West German leftists made in the 1970s resonate with what Situationist authors had written.

Officially formed in 1957, the SI included a number of artists, such as Asgar Jorn, Constant Nieuwenhuys, Ralph Rumney and his London Psychogeographical Association, and, most prominently, French writer Guy Debord. In the following years, the SI built a network that spanned most of Western Europe. In Germany, for example, the Munich-based Gruppe SPUR, to which later Kommune 1 member Dieter Kunzelmann belonged, became part of the Situationist International.[115] Soon enough, however, the SI under Guy Debord's leadership began to split and exclude members and factions that wanted, as the charge went, to make use of the organization to further their artistic careers. Until 1966, it remained a rather obscure group. This changed when students in Strasbourg published the Situationist manifesto *The Misery of Student Life* and made use of the student union's funds to freely distribute ten thousand copies of the pamphlet.[116] Subsequently, the SI and its ideas not only influenced the May 1968 uprisings in France, but also the alternative and nondogmatic left elsewhere in Europe, such as the Provos of Amsterdam.[117]

Gilcher-Holtey, 'Die Phantasie an die Macht': Der Mai 68 in Frankreich (Frankfurt a.M.: Suhrkamp, 1995), 46–81.

[115] On the Gruppe SPUR, see Mia Lee, 'Gruppe Spur: Art as a Revolutionary Medium during the Cold War', in *Between the Avant-Garde and the Everyday: Subversive Politics in Europe from 1957 to the Present*, ed. Timothy Brown and Lorena Anton (New York: Berghahn, 2011). See also Frank Böckelmann and Herbert Nagel, eds., *Subversive Aktion: Der Sinn der Organisation ist ihr Scheitern* (Frankfurt a.M.: Verlag Neue Kritik, 1976).

[116] Horn, *Spirit*, 12–14. On the influence of situationists in the French student movement of 1968, see also Gilcher-Holtey, 'Phantasie an die Macht', 143–153.

[117] On the Amsterdam Provos, see Richard Kempton, *Provo: Amsterdam's Anarchist Revolt* (Brooklyn: Autonomedia, 2007); Niek Pas, 'Subcultural Movements: The Provos', in *1968 in Europe: A History of Protest and Activism, 1956–1977*, ed. Martin Klimke and Joachim Scharloth (New York: Palgrave Macmillan, 2008); Niek Pas, 'Mediatisation of Provo: From a Local Movement to a European Phenomenon', in *Between Prague Spring and French May: Opposition and Revolt in Europe, 1960–1980*, ed. Martin Klimke, Jacco Pekelder, and Joachim Scharloth (New York: Berghahn, 2011). On Provos in Frankfurt, who developed out of a local *Gammler* scene, see Detlef Siegfried, *Time Is on My Side: Konsum und Politik in der westdeutschen Jugendkultur der 60er Jahre* (Göttingen: Wallstein, 2006), 413–428.

In numerous texts, Situationists described the modern, industrial world as deeply alienating and inauthentic. 'Private life' had been 'deprived' of 'life itself', Guy Debord claimed. 'People are as deprived as possible of communication and of self-fulfilment; deprived of the opportunity to make their own history', he wrote in May 1961.[118] Even though material conditions had improved, the 'possibilities of everyday life' had not.[119] Life had been, as Raoul Vaneigm put it, replaced by 'emotionally dead survival'. Survival, in the mere biological sense, was easy given the provision of the welfare state. And yet, ordinary people might already be 'dying of boredom' and pushed to suicide.[120] This fundamental critique of modern 'survival' provided the perspective from which Situationists analysed various aspects everyday life. Most prominently, they formulated a sharp critique consumer society. The material 'wealth of consumer goods impoverishes authentic life', wrote Vaneigm, first, because it replaced 'authentic life with *things* ', and second because people could no longer 'be attached to these things, precisely because they have to be *consumed*, i.e., destroyed'. Relations to things were equally deprived of meaning in the sphere of production, in which it was 'useless to expect even a caricature of creativity from the conveyor belt'.[121] Personal relations, too, lacked authentic meaning. Living in isolation, people had 'nothing in common except the illusion of being together',[122] their relationships lacked 'authentic direct communication', wrote Guy Debord.[123] People simply performed a multiplicity of fragmented roles, but without any genuine passion, compensating 'for the lack of life'.[124] Finally, the critique of inauthenticity extended to modern cities that had turned in 'cemeteries of reinforced concrete' in which the 'masses of the population are condemned to die of boredom'.[125] Everyday life was, to sum up the Situationist argument, in all its aspects inauthentic and horribly boring. A revolutionary change of society would therefore have to fundamentally affect people's everyday life. It had to 'enrich' their 'deprived' lives.

---

[118] Guy Debord, 'Perspectives for Conscious Changes in Everyday Life', in *Situationist International Anthology*, ed. Ken Knabb (Berkeley: Bureau of Public Secrets, 1981 [1961]), 95.

[119] Anon., 'The Sound and the Fury', in *Situationist International Anthology*, ed. Ken Knabb (Berkeley: Bureau of Public Secrets, 1981 [1958]), 47.

[120] Vaneigm, *The Revolution of Everyday Life*, 83.   [121] Ibid., 54; emphasis in the original.

[122] Ibid., 39.

[123] Guy Debord, 'Theses on Cultural Revolution', in *Situationist International Anthology*, ed. Ken Knabb (Berkeley: Bureau of Public Secrets, 1981 [1958]), 54.

[124] Vaneigm, *The Revolution of Everyday Life*, 139.

[125] Constant, 'Another City for Another Life', in *Situationist International Anthology*, ed. Ken Knabb (Berkeley: Bureau of Public Secrets, 1981 [1959]), 71.

Individual life was not only deprived of meaning in this inauthentic society, but also, and perhaps more importantly, deeply fragmented, Situationists posited. As Guy Debord declared: 'This society tends to atomize people into isolated consumers and to prohibit communication. Everyday life is thus private life, the realm of separation and spectacle.'[126] Not least, Situationists held the gaze of (social) sciences that viewed society 'through specialized fragments' responsible for this fragmentation of life.[127] Labelling every fragment in biological or social categories, language failed to 'communicate anything but facts emptied of their authentically lived content'.[128] In this sense, scientific, nonpoetic language remained inauthentic as it was incapable of grasping the authentic essence of its objects. Similarly important was the fragmentation of space and time. Situationists particularly criticized the separation of work and leisure in cities and the relegation of play and leisure to a sphere that was limited 'in space, in time and in qualitative depth'.[129] Time, too, was fragmented into 'a series of tiny points', Situationists argued, and then integrated into a 'specific order of succession', though without constituting a unitary whole. In the society of the capitalist spectacle, every activity had its designated time. 'This is the temporality of work, progress, productivity, production deadlines, consumption and planning. The spectacle's time: time for a kiss, snapshot time', wrote Vaneigm.[130]

Given the alienation and fragmentation that characterized capitalist society, Situationists came to regard genuine subjectivity as 'most crucial revolutionary demand'. Situationists like Raoul Vaneigm were remarkably optimistic in this regard. In the midst of the inauthentic world, 'beneath the fragmentation of the self', an authentic subjectivity survived, hidden 'in the heart of each human being', he wrote. For Situationists, the desires, dreams, passions, and spontaneous creativity that constituted the core of an authentic subjectivity had the potential to challenge and question the inauthentic world. Hence, the subversive 'reversal of the perspective' that Vaneigm called for meant to 'base everything on subjectivity and to follow one's subjective will to everything'. Situationists, these examples show, divided their political universe into an inauthentic, capitalist world and an authentic subjectivity hidden beneath the surface of this world; their

---

[126] Debord, 'Perspectives', 93.   [127] Ibid.

[128] Raoul Vaneigm, 'Basic Banalities (Part 2)', in *Situationist International Anthology*, ed. Ken Knabb (Berkeley: Bureau of Public Secrets, 1981 [1963]), 168.

[129] Anon., 'Instructions for an Insurrection', in *Situationist International Anthology*, ed. Ken Knabb (Berkeley: Bureau of Public Secrets, 1981 [1961]), 85.

[130] Vaneigm, *The Revolution of Everyday Life*, 226.

political project can be described as an attempt to retrieve authenticity in an inauthentic world and to create the conditions for genuine subjectivity. And Vaneigm saw reason for hope, since alienation was never complete. The 'subjective refusal' was able to shatter alienations 'every day for an instant, for an hour, for the space of a dream'. Subjective, 'authentic' experience and the expression of creativity were, from this perspective, inherently revolutionary. The inauthentic world, for example, caused 'an insatiable desire for human contact' that was fulfilled in love. 'Sometimes I think', Vaneigm wrote, 'that nothing else is real, nothing else is human, as the feel of a woman's body, the softness of her skin, the warmth of her cunt'. In his mind, the adventure of love could be 'a search for the Northwest Passage out of inauthenticity'. Similarly, creativity, and thus art, would be 'revolutionary in its essence', because the artist would follow his 'desire to increase his share of dreams in the objective world of others', at least as long as they had not totally succumbed to 'aesthetic assimilation'.

To develop an authentic subjectivity, Situationists argued, it was necessary to overcome the separations that characterized the inauthentic world – between different roles, between work and pleasure and the spaces devoted to them,[131] or the fragmentation of linear time. Situationists celebrated moments and practices that facilitated an 'immediate experience' of the world as instances of authentic life. Central for this project was the idea of *détournement*, literally a diversion, but often translated as 'subversion'. By reversing relations between time and space, a different, more authentic and imaginative experience would become possible.[132] In his *The Revolution of Everyday Life*, Vaneigm provides an example of what this might entail in practice. One night, he recalls, he and his friends wandered through the Palais de Justice in Brussels. As they drifted through the building, 'the labyrinth of corridors, staircases and suite after suite of rooms' – a 'monstrosity', symbolizing fragmentation and power –, they imagined how the building might be transformed into a 'fantastic funfair, into a sunny pleasure dome'. With the 'power of our imagination', they 'occupied', at least for a time, the 'enemy's territory'. 'Daydreaming subverts the world', Vaneigm concluded, in this case in a spatial sense.[133] Exploring and imagining space in such a way created a situation for a subjective experience; it allowed desires and dreams to surface.

---

[131] Guy Debord, 'Situationist Theses on Traffic', in *Situationist International Anthology*, ed. Ken Knabb (Berkeley: Bureau of Public Secrets, 1981 [1959]), 69.
[132] Vaneigm, *The Revolution of Everyday Life*, 185–189.   [133] Ibid., 264–267.

Experiencing the world in a more 'immediate' way also required overcoming the separation between bodies, their senses, and the world. Not
least, a different language would be necessary to convey 'authentically lived
content'. To achieve this, Vaneigm called for a 'poetic language' that
would not merely convey information, but would function as a 'mirror
of the senses' and a 'sensual language'.[134] Situationists also hoped to relate
to the world with their bodies. Vaneigm's discussion of Jazz, which he
thought to resemble the 'improvisation in everyday life', provides an
instructive example in this regard. In contrast to Western music, that is
perceived 'aurally', Jazz is experienced through 'bodily movement',
Vaneigm claimed.[135] Listening to jazz, he argued, thus provides access to
the world in a different and more immediate way. Moreover, it facilitates a
different experience of time. According to Vaneigm, jazz music is characterized by a 'discontinuity' that results from 'ecstatic centres of gravity out
of time with musical rhythm and meter proper'. This ruptures the linear
and 'empty' time that structures the inauthentic world. Finding such
disruptive moments 'of creativity, of pleasure, of orgasm', moments that
slip away from the structured, linear time, was a central goal for Situationists, as those moments enabled authentic experiences.[136] Children
provided a sort of role model for a different experience of time. Their time
is, Vaneigm wrote, 'swollen by subjectivity, by passion, by dreams
inhabited by reality'. For Vaneigm, childhood was a promise for a better
world: 'The semi-barbarity of our bodies, our needs, and our spontaneity –
that is, our childhood, as refined by consciousness' provides access to a
world 'never so much as dreamed of by the bourgeoisie'.[137]

Both Beat Poets and Situationists provided leftists with critiques of the
modern world that depicted it as deeply inauthentic, fragmented, boring,
and devoid of exuberant feelings. Simultaneously, they developed visions
of a fluid and transgressive subjectivity that were extremely attractive for
alternative leftists, even though Situationists criticized practices such as
drug consumption or the 'cult of speed' that were propagated by Beat
Poets as only partial and hence false solutions. West German leftists were
inspired by the celebration of intensely experienced moments that contained a subversive potential in the sterile and boring world of the present,
because moments of exuberance could disturb the order of society in
which everything functioned according to well-defined roles and rules.
Not least, this celebration of intense moments altered the temporality of
politics, something we will re-encounter within the alternative left. While

---

[134] Ibid., 103.   [135] Ibid., 195.   [136] Ibid., 227.   [137] Ibid., 221–222.

still longing for a world in which an 'authentic' subjectivity would become possible, Beat Poets and Situationists were more concerned with the present, and the intensity of moments, than with an abstract future. In that sense, they anticipated the politics of the moment popular amongst leftists in the 1970s and early 1980s.

Rebellious Teenagers: *Halbstarke* and *Gammler*

While Beat Poets and Situationists criticized postwar capitalist society on a theoretical and artistic level, nonconformist teenagers in the Western world began to rebel in more practical ways. In West Germany, the so-called *Halbstarke* made news during the mid-to-late 1950s.[138] These mostly male teenagers challenged social norms in postwar Germany that called for orderly behaviour, for emotional restraint and quietness, by listening to rock 'n' roll music, dressing up like American movie star James Dean or musician Elvis Presley, riding mopeds in large groups, and occasionally, most famously after concerts and movie screenings, rioting. This was neither an exclusively German phenomenon, nor was it entirely new. In the Netherlands, the *nozems* were similarly rebellious; in France they were known as *blousons noir*, and in the United States as *Greasers*.[139] Being mostly of working-class background, they drew upon traditions of nonconformist working-class groups that reached back to the Weimar Republic and continued during the Third Reich in groups such as the *Edelweißpiraten* in Cologne or the *Wilde Meuten* in Leipzig, who refused to be integrated into the Hitler Youth and preferred to listen to American jazz music. In West Germany, the *Halbstarken* phenomenon reached its apogee in 1956–57, but then declined rapidly. Yet teenagers and young adults continued to rebel against social norms. In Schwabing, a Munich neighbourhood with a long history of bohemian subculture, riots broke out in June 1962 after the police had tried to disperse a group of teenagers playing music in the streets. In the following days, hundreds of protestors, young workers, and apprentices, as well as students, engaged in street

---

[138] See in general Thomas Grotum, *Die Halbstarken: Zur Geschichte einer Jugendkultur der 50er Jahre* (Frankfurt a.M.: Campus Verlag, 1994); Sebastian Kurme, *Halbstarke: Jugendprotest in den 1950er Jahren in Deutschland und den USA* (Frankfurt a.M.: Campus Verlag, 2006); Jürgen Zinnecker, '"Halbstarke" – Die andere Seite der 68er-Generation', in *Protestierende Jugend: Jugendopposition und politischer Protest in der deutschen Nachkriegsgeschichte*, ed. Ulrich Herrmann (Weinheim: Juventa, 2002).

[139] See, with further references, Horn, *Spirit*, 23–32.

battles with the police.[140] In the mid-1960s, yet another youth phenomenon developed, the so-called *Gammler*, who 'bummed around' in streets
of Berlin, Frankfurt or Munich (again, in Schwabing), and refused to
adhere to norms of productivity.[141]

These groups did not produce artistic or theoretical texts alternative
leftists could draw on to develop their critique. Instead, they contributed
to the formation of alternative subjectivities in a more practical fashion.
Detlef Siegfried, who has written one of the most comprehensive studies of
the relation between politics and consumption in postwar West German
youth cultures, places these subcultures and especially their musical styles
into a narrative of democratization. Dancing styles like the Skiffle, for
example, were 'democratic and egalitarian', Siegfried claims, as everyone
could learn them without much formal training.[142] Siegfried as well as
other scholars have therefore drawn a line from those subcultures to the
protests of 1968, especially with regard to the *Gammlers* in West Berlin,
who provided the proverbial hummus for the emerging anti-authoritarian
scene.[143] While arguments that these youth cultures provided the ground
for the protests in the late 1960s and 1970s are convincing, I propose a
different interpretative framework. Instead of integrating these nonconformist teenagers into a master narrative of political democratization
and cultural liberalization, I discuss them as an important part of the
genealogy of alternative subjectivities. More so than before, the practices
of alternative subjectification, such as excessive dancing or particular
hairstyles, in the postwar years caused conflicts with parental and official
authorities. Arguably, such conflicts contributed to the politicization
of alternative subjectivities, and hence the formation of a new form of
political struggles against what Michel Foucault called a 'government of
individualization'.[144]

In contrast to the life reformers, Freudian Marxists or avant-garde
artists, neither *Halbstarke* nor *Gammler* made many theoretical statements
that criticized the postwar world as 'inauthentic'. Sympathetic observers,
however, interpreted the phenomenon in those terms. They regarded the

[140] See Gerhard Fürmetz, ed., '*Schwabinger Krawalle*': *Protest, Polizei und Öffentlichkeit zu Beginn der
60er Jahre* (Essen: Klartext, 2006).
[141] See Siegfried, *Time*, 399–413.   [142] Ibid., 109–110.
[143] See Brown, *West Germany*, 62–68. For an international perspective, see Horn, *Spirit*, 23–32;
Roland Roth, '"Die Macht liegt auf der Straße": Zur Bedeutung des Straßenprotests für die neuen
sozialen Bewegungen', in *Straße und Straßenkultur: Interdisziplinäre Beobachtungen eines
öffentlichen Sozialraumes in der fortgeschrittenen Moderne*, ed. Hans-Jürgen Hohm (Konstanz:
Universitätsverlag Konstanz, 1997), 203.
[144] Michel Foucault, 'The Subject and Power', *Critical Inquiry* 8 (1982).

rebellious teenagers as a reaction to a repressive world that lacked spaces to express 'authenticity'. Using a language that strikingly resembles the arguments made by reform pedagogues during the interwar period, psychologist Curt Bondy for example argued in 1957 that teenagers in the 'urban, industrial society' were subject to numerous restrictions at school and at work, where they found no community that could fulfil their 'needs for contacts'. All in all, he wrote, 'our society calls for a rational, restricted behaviour that leaves little space for spontaneously expressing feelings and desires'.[145] Given the lack of written statements by teenagers themselves, we need to turn to the bodily and emotional practices that *Halbstarke* and *Gammler* developed to understand how they disrupted the 'restricted behaviour' and 'spontaneously' expressed feelings.

Just like life reformers and youth movement activists, *Halbstarke* and *Gammler* tried to live a more authentic life, attempting to liberate bodies as well as feelings. In contrast to life reformers, however, livening in accordance with nature or more healthily played no role for them. Rather, *Halbstarke* and *Gammlers'* way of living authentically resembled the authenticity that Beat Poets, whose work was popular amongst *Gammler*, and Situationists envisioned and that was characterized by both excessiveness and fragility. As in many (sub)cultures, including the youth movement, fashion played a central role for liberating the body from (social) restrictions. But for *Halbstarke* and *Gammler*, this did not mean wearing loose clothes that allowed the body to move freely or that would expose it to the sun. Instead, *Halbstarke* teenagers stereotypically wore blue jeans, t-shirts, checked shirts and jackets, short cut satin blousons, cowboy boots, and, their most distinct sign, black leather jackets.[146] Especially blue jeans that had been designed as working trousers and t-shirts, originally designed by the American army as underwear, expressed, as Sebastian Kurme has noted, a 'desire for wilder and more excited life than that of their parents'.[147] While the *Halbstarke* style was elaborate and potentially rather expensive, *Gammler* dressed in worn-out and shabby clothes suitable for a life in parks and streets, in rejection to bourgeois norms.[148] Though *Halbstarke* and *Gammler* looked radically different, their fashion expressed a similar desire for a life free from social restrictions.

Perhaps even more importantly than dressing up, practices of movement provided *Halbstarke* and *Gammler* with an opportunity to pursue their goal of living a liberated and excessive life. *Halbstarke* teenagers

---

[145] Grotum, *Halbstarken*, 149.   [146] Kurme, *Halbstarke*, 189.   [147] Ibid., 284–285.
[148] Kosel, *Gammler*, 10–11, Siegfried, *Time*, 399–404.

notoriously rode their mopeds in large groups through the cities, at times accosting passersby. When a group of fifty *Halbstarke* noisily started their mopeds, yelling and chanting, a former *Halbstarke* recalled, it was an emotionally intense moment, full of exuberance, such that they were even 'worse than being intoxicated [*schlimmer als ein Rausch*]'.[149] *Gammler* on the other hand were famous for travelling, either within cities without any specific goal, or on a global scale from one country to another, travelling as far as Afghanistan.[150] Reminiscent of the Beat Poets, both groups defied expectations of purposeful movement in space. Dancing, a practice that we already encountered in the discussion of the life reform and youth movements, was equally important for liberating the *Halbstarke* body. The fast, artistic, and openly sexualized moves that characterized popular rock 'n' roll dances broke with norms of both male and female decency and restraint. Dancing up to the point of physical exhaustion and beyond was a way of disrupting, as Thomas Grotum remarked, the 'normal rules of space and time', both bodily and socially, because teenagers stayed up late.[151] Jazz, though a different musical genre, left-wing pedagogue Helmut Kentler wrote echoing Raoul Vaneigm, liberated 'the desire for rhythm that had long been suppressed by the beat of machines'.[152] Finally, dancing was also a way to break with expectations of emotional restraint, especially during concerts and movie screenings, where any form of 'emotional excitement' was considered inappropriate, and could result in an intervention of security forces.[153] All these (bodily) practices – dressing up, riding mopeds in large groups, roaming through the city, fast dances that did not adhere to the rules of classical dance – can be considered ways of performing an excessive and liberating subjectivity that supposedly disrupted the bodily and emotional restraints of postwar society.

In contrast to life reformers who sought to create healthy and strong bodies and selves by freeing them from the restrictions of bourgeois morality, the liberated self of *Halbstarke* and *Gammler* was deeply instable and fragile. Not least, this defied dominant understandings of strong masculinity.[154] Photographs of both *Halbstarke* and their American role

---

[149] Kurme, *Halbstarke*, 288.
[150] Kosel, *Gammler*, 14, Siegfried, *Time*, 405–411, Brown, *West Germany*, 62–63.
[151] Grotum, *Halbstarken*, 201.   [152] Quoted in Siegfried, *Time*, 111.
[153] Kurme, *Halbstarke*, 328. See also Wilfried Breyvogel, 'Provokation und Aufbruch der westdeutschen Jugend in den 50er und 60er Jahren: Konflikthafte Wege der Modernisierung der westdeutschen Gesellschaft in der frühen Bundesrepublik', in *Protestierende Jugend: Jugendopposition und politischer Protest in der deutschen Nachkriegsgeschichte*, ed. Ulrich Herrmann (Weinheim: Juventa, 2002), 449–453.
[154] On changing masculinities, see Siegfried, *Time*, 255–264.

models typically showed them in insecure and (emotionally) vulnerable positions, as Sebastian Kurme stressed.[155] *Halbstarke*, as many contemporary observers remarked, avoided any 'jerking [*ruckhaft*] and stiff movements', but moved their 'entire body' in 'elastic' ways.[156] *Gammler* similarly avoided stiff bodily postures and talking in a direct or even commanding way; instead, they kept their bodies relaxed and spoke in an informal way.[157] Hairstyles were another way of questioning ideals of a strong masculinity. The *Gammlers'* long hair is of course famous in this regard. But also the great efforts *Halbstarke* placed on styling their hair, and especially on the sideburns they adopted from Elvis Presley, were considered emasculating: a 'real' man would not spend that much time on styling his hair.[158] Among nonconformist teenagers, we can thus observe the emergence of an alternative subjectivity that resembled the life reform and youth movement in its focus on the liberation of bodies and feelings. This liberated subjectivity, however, looked markedly different in its emphasis on fluidity, excess, and exuberance, as well as instability and insecurity.

None of the alternative subjectivities discussed in this chapter emerged without conflicts. Yet the level of conflict surrounding *Halbstarke* and *Gammler* was exceptional. Reactions to dancing may highlight the difference. Nude avant-garde dancers before and after World War I at times faced criticism, and the more popular dancing culture of the youth movement might have been derided, but these dances never gave, it seems, reason for public concern. Instead, reform minded pedagogues like Gustav Wyneken praised it as a reawakening of the body. Rock 'n' roll music and dancing in postwar West Germany, by contrast, worried parents, observers, and authorities. The artistic and sexualized dancing constituted, in the words of a teacher, 'erotic excesses [*Ausschreitungen*]'.[159] Concerts and film screenings famously resulted in riots. Watching rock 'n' roll movies, teenagers often left their seats to dance themselves. When security forces intervened to uphold order, riots started.[160] Following a movie screening in Bremen for example, some hundred teenagers had formed a circle, in the midst of which teenagers performed artistic rock 'n' roll dances to

---

[155] Kurme, *Halbstarke*, 286.

[156] Curt Bondy and Jan Braden, *Jugendliche stören die Ordnung: Bericht und Stellungnahme zu den Halbstarkenkrawallen* (Munich: Juventa-Verlag, 1957), 25. Quoted in Kurme, *Halbstarke*, 193.

[157] See the documentary by Peter Fleischmann, 'Herbst der Gammler', (Germany: 1967).

[158] Kaspar Maase, *BRAVO Amerika: Erkunden zur Jugendkultur der Bundesrepublik in den fünfziger Jahren* (Hamburg: Junius, 1992), 120–121; Siegfried, *Time*, 108.

[159] Friedl Schröder, 'Gefahr und Not der Halbstarken', in *Allgemeine Deutsche Lehrerzeitung* 8 (1956), 326–328, quoted in Grotum, *Halbstarken*, 201.

[160] Kurme, *Halbstarke*, 338.

improvised music. When a man saw his daughter dancing, he intervened and dragged her away, causing other teenagers to accost him, so that he had to escape into a tram.[161] Sexualized dancing was not the only reason for conflict. The famous Elvis quiff became a regular source of conflict between parents and their sons, while youth magazine *Bravo* mocked male teenagers as unmanly who had not shaved their sideburns.[162] Later on, the *Gammlers'* rejection to regularly work as well as their general attire – long hair, shabby clothes, living in the streets – made ordinary citizens infamously call for new gas chambers, comments which rebelling students in 1968 would have to face as well.[163]

Clashes between *Halbstarke* teenagers and the forces of order are certainly the most obvious indication of the level of conflict this subculture caused. Sebastian Kurme has counted at least 350 riots involving *Halbstarke* in both East and West Germany between 1955 and 1958, with a particular peak in September 1956, which saw twenty-four riots with fifty or more participants. Exceptionally large riots took place later in November in Gelsenkirchen, with more than 1,500 teenagers participating, and in December in Dortmund, where some 1,100 battled the police. Concerts or movie screenings often provided the context for first clashes, which were frequently followed by at least another night of rioting. Kurme thus concludes that teenagers expected and hoped for the 'spectacle' to continue.[164] A few years later, in June 1962, the situation exploded in Munich-Schwabing. Even though the Schwabing riots had little to do with the *Halbstarke* riots a few years earlier, it is nevertheless worth looking at them in conjunction. The Schwabing riot resembled at least some *Halbstarke* riots, in that music played a central role in its beginning. Yet it was not a concert that marked the starting point, but the police's attempt to arrest five street musicians playing after 10pm, which had resulted in complaints by neighbours. During the following days, between ten thousand and twenty thousand people, mostly young workers, apprentices, and teenagers, clashed with the police, while many more acted as spectators. It was, it seems, a rather joyous atmosphere, as people danced and celebrated in the streets. Tellingly, one young couple was convicted for having danced in the streets instead of clearing them when ordered by the police.[165]

---

[161] Grotum, *Halbstarken*, 141–142.
[162] Maase, *BRAVO Amerika*, 120–121; Siegfried, *Time*, 108.   [163] See Siegfried, *Time*, 411–413.
[164] Kurme, *Halbstarke*, 206–209.
[165] Stefan Hemler, 'Aufbegehren einer Jugendszene: Protestbeteiligte, Verlauf und Aktionsmuster bei den "Schwabinger Krawallen"', in *'Schwabinger Krawalle': Protest, Polizei und Öffentlichkeit zu Beginn der 6oer Jahre*, ed. Gerhard Fürmetz (Essen: Klartext, 2006), 47–48.

Historians have debated the reasons of these riots and their place within histories of protest in West Germany.[166] Recent scholarship on both the *Halbstarke* and the Schwabing riots has put them into a context of Americanization and the rise of a consumer society. Teenagers rejected the desires for stability and the concomitant demands for emotional restraint that were predominant in postwar West Germany. Instead, they wanted to enjoy the riches and possibilities consumer society had to offer, scholars have argued. In this sense, Kurme sees tension between social norms that were not in line with the consumer possibilities a socially and economically modernizing society had to offer.[167] Along similar lines, Stefan Hemler has argued against the notion that the Schwabing riots were a first protest against consumer society. To the contrary, he considers them the result of a clash between a westernized, consumption-oriented youth that had been restricted in its desires (to celebrate at night outside) and the restrictive forces of the state.[168] Ultimately, both Kurme and Hemler place the protests and riots within the context of a society that changed socioeconomically, but not in terms of dominant cultural norms. In their reading, rebellious teenagers were, so to speak, in line with socio-economic changes to which social and cultural authorities had not yet adapted. While the emerging consumer society arguably provided a material background, and made 'hedonistic' lifestyle choices in general more popular, these interpretations run the risk of reducing the riots to a reaction to economic changes. Considering the riots through the lens of a struggle for alternative subjectivities provides a different perspective.

One way to read the various conflicts would be to consider the hostile reactions by both parental and state authorities as attempts to suppress a new, counterhegemonic subjectivity. Along these lines, Wolfgang Kraushaar for example argued in 1986 that the 'Beat Generation' with 'its expressive musical style and sexualized body language that had thoroughly disturbed the older generation' was beaten up in Schwabing.[169] Without framing the issue in terms of subjectivities, Kaspar Maase somewhat similarly argues that the *Halbstarke* movement resulted the 'democratization of a bodily ideal' emphasizing 'laxity' that had previously existed

---

[166] See the contributions in Fürmetz, ed., *'Schwabinger Krawalle'*.

[167] Kurme, *Halbstarke*, 328–329.   [168] Hemler, 'Aufbegehren', 56–57.

[169] Wolfgang Kraushaar, 'Time Is on My Side: Die Beat-Ära', in *Schock und Schöpfung. Jugendästhetik im 20. Jahrhundert*, ed. Willi Bucher and Klaus Pohl (Darmstadt: Luchterhand, 1986). Quoted in Gerhard Fürmetz, 'Die "Schwabinger Krawalle" von 1962: Vom Ereignis zum Forschungsgegenstand', in *'Schwabinger Krawalle': Protest, Polizei und Öffentlichkeit zu Beginn der 6oer Jahre*, ed. Gerhard Fürmetz (Essen: Klartext, 2006), 11.

amongst (sub)proletarian youths, but that now saw a 'generalization and legitimization' previously unknown.[170] With regard to conflicts concerning hairstyles or dancing, as in Bremen, this interpretation seems indeed plausible. Yet it can hardly explain why teenagers joyfully participated in those riots. Scholars who have worked on these riots have noted the 'desire for experience [*Erlebnissuche*]' or the sense for adventure common amongst rebellious teens. All too often, such desires are understood as being simply part of any youth rebellion, as Stefan Hemler has claimed.[171] In contrast to such ultimately dehistoricizing views, the 'desire for experience' needs to be interpreted as part of a historically specific search for authentic experiences in a world conceived as 'inauthentic'. As we have seen, avant-garde artists as well as rebellious teenagers claimed that the world they were living in was 'Moloch', ruled by pure rationality, devoid of any genuine 'experience' or feelings. Acts of bodily and spatial transgressions could yield excessive and authentic feelings nonconformist teenagers otherwise missed. Riots were one, perhaps particularly radical form of practising this 'excessive' subjectivity. The 'desire of experience', the playful and exuberant elements of the rioting should not be dismissed as being an inherent aspect of any youth rebellion, but should be considered as a central aspect of a historically peculiar form of subjectivity. Dancing in public spaces during a riot for example can be read as a bodily practice disrupting the spatial order, reminiscent of the Beat Poets' and the Situationist International's attempts to make space fluid and to defy capitalist orders of space. At the same time, expressing both joyful and sad feelings openly constituted a challenge of the emotional regime that prohibited such expressions. The riot provided, to put it pointedly, an opportunity for an 'authentic' experience that otherwise seemed not to exist.

This raises the question how political the various forms of protest – including hairstyles, dancing, and rioting – were. Most commentators agree that, at least in a traditional sense, the *Halbstarke* or Schwabing riots were apolitical. Only occasionally did *Halbstarke* voice a protest against the remilitarization of West Germany; other *Halbstarke*, however, readily volunteered for the new army. Despite somewhat paranoid suspicions by the security forces, the riots were not instigated by the recently outlawed Communist Party, as Thomas Grotum stresses.[172] The Schwabing riots, too, were not about politics, even though some students later protested against police brutality that did not fit with their image of a

---

[170] Maase, *BRAVO Amerika*, 119.   [171] Hemler, 'Aufbegehren', 50–51.
[172] Grotum, *Halbstarken*, 129–130.

democratic state.[173] In the traditional sense, the riots had thus little to do with politics, commentators agree. From a Foucauldian perspective, however, that considers the body a central object of inherently political relations of power, these revolts were fundamentally about politics, as Sebastian Kurme has argued. Teenagers who danced seemingly without any constraint to rock 'n' roll music evaded, he claims, 'the microphysics of power that wanted to control and subdue their bodies'; thus, they 'positioned themselves symbolically' – and, one could add, bodily – 'against the social forces that wanted to see them subdued to discipline'. 'To listen to that music', Kurme quotes Philip Ennis, 'to dance to that music, and to make that music was a political act without being political'.[174] The initially harsh response by the state might indeed suggest that the state itself considered the *Halbstarke* a political danger. Yet, by defining teenagers' rebellious behaviour as 'normal' part of adolescence, the rioting was turned in a mere psychological problem that needed to be dealt with, but that did not constitute a political problem, as Kurme notes.[175]

Kurme's discussion points to an important issue: the contested emergence of a new understanding of what was political and what was not. What people did with their bodies, not least how they used their bodies to express feelings, became an issue of public and hence political concern. A brief comparison with the life reform and youth movements is instructive in this regard. Both life reformers and youth movement activists around 1900, and rebellious teenagers in the 1950s and 1960s, sought to rediscover and liberate their bodies through practices such as excessive dancing, clothing, or particular hairstyles. Yet only in the postwar period did such practices cause public outcries and conflicts. Though neither *Halbstarke* nor *Gammler* framed their actions in political terms, we can look at them as one step in the development of a peculiar form of struggle 'against forms of subjection'. No doubt, life reformers and the youth movement struggled against forms of subjection as well, but only in the postwar years did these issues gain political meaning. Kurme's argument that dancing teenagers sought to evade the 'microphysics of power' is based on exactly this new understanding of the political, which itself needs to be

---

[173] See Stefan Hemler, 'Anstoß für die Studentenbewegung? Warum die "Schwabinger Krawalle" wenig mit "1968" zu tun haben', in *'Schwabinger Krawalle': Protest, Polizei und Öffentlichkeit zu Beginn der 6oer Jahre*, ed. Gerhard Fürmetz (Essen: Klartext, 2006); Esther Arens, 'Lektion in Demokratie: Die "Schwabinger Krawalle" und die Münchner "Interessengemeinschaft zur Wahrung der Bürgerrechte"', in *'Schwabinger Krawalle': Protest, Polizei und Öffentlichkeit zu Beginn der 6oer Jahre*, ed. Gerhard Fürmetz (Essen: Klartext, 2006).

[174] Kurme, *Halbstarke*, 333–334.   [175] Ibid., 336–338.

historicized. The *Halbstarke* and *Gammler* are thus not only of interest because of the rise of a new form of an 'alternative' subjectivity on which leftists of the 1970s could draw, but also because these movements indicate that a new form of *political* struggles began to develop that would also be constitutive for the alternative left. Placing *Halbstarke* and *Gammler* into the context of an emerging consumer society, as valuable as this interpretation is, cannot grasp this development.

Conclusion

When leftists in the 1970s tried to develop warm, emotional alternatives to the cold and rational world of capitalism, they could build on a variety of intellectual and practical traditions, ranging from the life reform movement to subcultures of the 1960s like the *Gammler*, from Freudian Marxists like Wilhelm Reich to the Beat Poets. Indeed, the alternative left was part of a tradition of movements that longed for authentic feelings in a world that seemed to be hostile to feelings and anything that could not be rationally grasped. Examining these traditions is important in order to understand the intellectual and practical sources on which leftists could draw for their politics, but also to see more clearly in what ways leftists in the 1970s broke with those traditions and developed something new.[176]

The movements and authors discussed in this chapter influenced leftist thinking in different ways. Authors of the life reform movement like Hans Paasche or the community who gathered at Monte Verità provided a general critique of urban civilization that had alienated humans from their bodies and feelings, and had thus made impossible a healthy life according to human nature. However, this critique was never phrased in explicitly political terms. Freudian Marxists, some of whom were themselves influenced by life reformist ideas, made this step. They argued that sexual desires were suppressed in a capitalist society; liberating those desires and thus enabling humans to live a life according to their (sexual) nature was thus the key goal of the political revolution they called for. The political program that Reich and Marcuse formulated implied a fundamental rethinking of the political. Rather than grounding their politics in a critique of class-based exploitation, Freudian Marxists made the individual and its oppressed desires central for their politics. Beat Poets and the

---

[176] For a discussion of the long-term continuity of ideals of authenticity from romanticism to the alternative movement, see Thomas Tripold, *Die Kontinuität romantischer Ideen* (Bielefeld: transcript, 2012).

authors of the Situationist International introduced yet another element of critique into leftist thinking. Broadening the perspective beyond the focus on sexuality typical for Freudian Marxists, these thinkers criticized the modern world for being deeply boring, devoid of intense feelings of exuberance. Rather than searching for ways to 'heal' the 'damaged' individual, both Beat Poets and Situationists celebrated, albeit in different ways, moments of bodily and emotional intensity and exuberance that would disrupt the boring normalcy of the modern world. Rejecting stiff bourgeois norms and pursuing an instable and transient lifestyle, *Halbstarke* and *Gammler* finally put the ideals of a fragmented subjectivity that above all Beat Poets had propagated into practice.

In the 1970s, alternative leftists incorporated elements of these traditions into their political project. They, too, criticized modern society for preventing genuine feelings and human relations. But unlike life reformers, they did not long for creating healthy and strong bodies, and, again in contrast to life reformers, leftists framed their critique of modern society as a critique of capitalism that, they argued, damaged individual personalities. Leftists thus built upon the understanding of the political both Reich and Marcuse and the Situationist International had developed for which the individual subject had been central. Indeed, as we will see, fixing 'damaged' personalities became of one of the central goals of alternative politics. But leftists also drew on the Beats' and Situationists' celebration of intense moments and forms of transgressions. In these situations, they believed, the rational order of capitalism might be suspended, if only for brief moments. In different ways, life reformers and the youth movements, Freudian Marxists, Beat Poets and Situationists, as well as *Halbstarke* and *Gammler*, thus set the stage for the alternative left of the 1970s.

CHAPTER 2

Feelings against Reason

In July 1980, *Ulcus Molle*, an 'information service' for the alternative left that informed about new publications of interest to the 'scene' and reviewed selected titles, included a book by Lutz Seiler entitled *Grenzüberschreitungen: Zur Sprache des Wahnsinns* (*Transgressions: On the Language of Insanity*) into its catalogue.[1] Seiler's book is, at least ostensibly, not concerned with politics. Rather, it discusses in a somewhat incoherent manner various 'literary products of schizophrenics',[2] ranging from authors as diverse as August Strindberg and Antonin Artaud, Maria Erlenberger and Robert Musil. To make his arguments, Seiler also drew on non-Western thinkers and traditions, such as Zen Buddhism and Native American 'mysticism', as well as on French philosophers like Michel Foucault, Gilles Deleuze and Felix Guattari, who were becoming increasingly popular within the alternative left. The book appeared only after the alternative left had reached its apogee, and it does not seem to have been broadly discussed within the scene; it was certainly not an intellectually brilliant work. Nevertheless, the book's discussion of insanity as the 'radical other' of a rationalized world reflects in many ways alternative political thinking of the late 1970s. It may thus serve as a first example to illuminate how alternative leftists imagined the conflicts that shaped their political world.

At the outset of his book, Seiler construed an opposition between 'rationality' and what he considered 'excluded from it, that is, emotions, the dream, excesses, insanity' – an exclusion rationality in fact needs to 'constitute itself', Seiler argued.[3] In his account, rationality is deeply alienating. Language has limited people's capacity to grasp the world. Quoting Erich Fromm's book *Psychoanalysis and Zen Buddhism*,[4] Seiler

---

[1] 'Katalog', in *Ulcus Molle* 7/8, 1980, 51.
[2] Wolfgang Seiler, *Grenzüberschreitungen: Zur Sprache des Wahnsinns* (Giessen: Focus, 1980), 7.
[3] Ibid.   [4] Erich Fromm, *Zen Buddhism & Psychoanalysis* (New York: Harper, 1960).

claimed that people 'believe to feel', but in reality only 'think these feelings'. When people believe that they 'grasp reality, it is only their brain-ego that grasps it, while the entire human being, its eyes, its hands, its belly does not grasp anything'.[5] On a more abstract level, Seiler criticized the 'the dualistic thinking of the West' that functions in strict binaries – 'inside and outside, good and evil, pain and lust, movement and rest, nothingness and cosmos' – but is incapable of imagining unity, since it lacks the experience of such a unity.[6] Only schizophrenics are capable of experiencing this world in a fundamentally different, more immediate, and less alienated way, Seiler argued. In Seiler's thinking, schizophrenics and their relation to the world serve as the radical other. Pivotal for creating a different relation to the world is the 'experience of dying' that Seiler's authors described, no matter whether they were schizophrenics in the clinical sense, drug users, or mystics. Talking about dying, however, Seiler did not have biological death in mind, but the dissolution of the stable subject.[7] For Seiler, this form of 'dying' can become an ecstatic experience, during which the subject that rationally perceives the world destabilizes and can thus experience the world in a different manner. It is a moment when the schizophrenic's 'Id' surfaces; then, the schizophrenic is nothing but 'pure immediacy; there is no yesterday or tomorrow for him'.[8] Echoing Raoul Vaneigm's discussion of language, Seiler also claimed that schizophrenics develop a 'tonal' language that is full of invented words, which gives them access to the world in a way the abstract 'normal' language is incapable of. As the stable subject dissolves, the difference between inner and outer world disappears, and thus an experience of unity becomes possible. In this situation, schizophrenics, drug users, or mystics can 'make rhizomes', a term that Seiler clearly took from Gilles Deleuze and Felix Guattari.[9] In Western culture with its monopoly on rational thinking, Seiler concluded, only the 'schizophrenic collapse' can provide a way to 'enlightenment' (a term he put in quotation marks). Other cultures, by contrast, for example in Mexico, that had not banned 'irrationality that is *not* irrational', served him as positive alternative role model, since they still aspire to an 'enlightenment' in this more 'cosmic' sense.[10]

---

[5] Seiler, *Grenzüberschreitungen*, 28. See also the depiction of physical labor in the youth novel by Gerd-Gustl Müller, *Der Job: Roman* (Munich: Weismann Verlag, 1977). For a discussion, see Joachim C. Häberlen, 'Ingrid's Boredom', in *Learning How to Feel: Children's Literature and Emotional Socialization, 1870–1970*, ed. Ute Frevert et al. (Oxford: Oxford University Press, 2014).
[6] Seiler, *Grenzüberschreitungen*, 79–80.   [7] Ibid., 78–9.   [8] Ibid., 59.
[9] Ibid., 84, also 65 and throughout on Deleuze and Guattari.   [10] Ibid., 90–91.

Though Seiler's book was never a canonical text for the radical left, it encapsulates what I call the political imagination of the alternative left. Exploring this political imagination is at the heart of this chapter. To grasp this political imagination, it may be helpful to think about 'the political' as a terrain that can be mapped. On this terrain, we might identify hostile forces: forces that are for or against democracy; for or against authority; for or against capitalist exploitation; for or against equality, to name only a few examples.[11] Seiler's book, however, indicates that alternative leftists mapped their political world in a rather different way. Their imagined political map was characterized, this chapter argues, by a conflict between the dominating forces of rationality, and everything that remained beyond rationality, such as dreams, desires, or feelings. Radical leftists, in other words, conceived of themselves as struggling for the liberation of feelings in a society deemed deeply anti-emotional. This political imagination was based on a particular understanding of rationality and its (deeply problematic) power. According to leftists, the power of rationality rested on its ability to categorize, to separate, and thus to limit individuals; feelings and desires, by contrast, had the power to disrupt such categorizations.[12] Whereas the 'cold' technocratic and bureaucratic world of rationality dissected people and disrupted personal connections, the 'warmth' of feelings could overcome those separations and hence foster relations of solidarity and intimacy.[13]

Struggling against the categorizing power of rationality had important implications for what 'doing politics' meant. If political activism was a struggle against the power of rationality, then anything that might

[11] This 'friend-foe' distinction is obviously central to Carl Schmitt's thinking about the political. See Carl Schmitt, *Der Begriff des Politischen. Text von 1932 mit einem Vorwort und drei Corollarien* (Berlin: Dunker und Humblot, 1987). See, for a discussion of different approaches of how to think about the political and its history, Seyla Benhabib, ed., *Democracy and Difference: Contesting the Boundaries of the Political* (Princeton: Princeton University Press, 1996); Judith Butler and Joan W. Scott, eds., *Feminists Theorize the Political* (New York; London: Routledge, 1992); Ute Frevert and Heinz-Gerhard Haupt, eds., *Neue Politikgeschichte: Perspektiven einer historischen Politikforschung* (Frankfurt a.M.: Campus Verlag, 2005); Thomas Mergel, 'Überlegungen zu einer Kulturgeschichte der Politik', *Geschichte und Gesellschaft* 28 (2002); Tobias Weidner, *Die Geschichte des Politischen in der Diskussion: Das Politische als Kommunikation* (Göttingen: Wallstein, 2012); Ulrich Bröckling and Robert Feustel, eds., *Das Politische denken: Zeitgenössische Positionen* (Bielefeld: transcript, 2010).

[12] See, from the perspective of changing cultures of subjectivity, the discussion in Andreas Reckwitz, *Das hybride Subjekt: eine Theorie der Subjektkulturen von der bürgerlichen Moderne zur Postmoderne* (Weilerswist: Velbrück, 2006), 455–468.

[13] For a discussion of alternative semantics of 'cold' and 'warmth', see Sven Reichardt, *Authentizität und Gemeinschaft: Linksalternatives Leben in den siebziger und frühen achtziger Jahren* (Berlin: Suhrkamp, 2014), 186–203.

undermine the categorizations that rationality imposed was potentially subversive. This may help us understand why leftists were politically interested in insanity, drug taking, and non-Western religions, as these were all possibilities of disrupting 'Western' rationality. Yet alternative leftists were not simply 'anti-rational', but more specifically critical about the separations and limitations that a *categorizing* rationality created. The interesting and perhaps paradoxical implication of this critique was that it could also be applied to the very differentiation between rationality and emotionality. The critique of categorization contained, in other words, an inherent potential for self-critique, which we will encounter both in the theoretical discussions of the alternative left that are the subject of this chapter and in the more practical attempts to challenge the domination of rationality to be discussed in subsequent chapters.

The chapter analyses the political project of the alternative left as a struggle against a categorizing rationality that imposed limitations upon people's imaginations, dreams and desires. This analysis shows, the chapter argues, the inadequacy of interpretations of radical leftist politics as an 'antiauthoritarian' struggle for more 'participatory' democracy. Such interpretations fail to grasp how radically the alternative left challenged conventional understandings of politics.[14] In his recent study of the 'antiauthoritarian' revolts from the early 1960s to the late 1970s in West Germany, Timothy Brown for example notes, correctly, that protestors sought to question and challenge authority in all spheres of life. Thus, not only the authority of the state was called into question, but also the authority of parents and men. In Brown's reading, this critique was based on a 'scholarly-scientific [*wissenschaftlich*] imperative', that is, it was based on the confidence in rational arguments.[15] His account might be adequate for the student revolts around 1968; it fails, however, to grasp the fundamental rethinking of the political within the alternative left since the early 1970s that provided a new theoretical basis for challenging the authority of parents and men: For alternative leftists, parents and, even more so, men were representatives of the powers of rationalization par excellence. Far

---

[14] For such narratives, see only Philipp Gassert, 'Narratives of Democratization: 1968 in Postwar Europe', in *1968 in Europe: A History of Protest and Activism, 1956–1977*, ed. Martin Klimke and Joachim Scharloth (New York: Palgrave Macmillan, 2008). See the introduction for a more extensive discussion of this literature.

[15] Timothy S. Brown, *West Germany and the Global Sixties: The Antiauthoritarian Revolt, 1962–1978* (Cambridge: Cambridge University Press, 2013), 19–20. On the importance of rationally arguing in the student movement, see also Nina Verheyen, *Diskussionslust: Eine Kulturgeschichte des 'besseren Arguments' in Westdeutschland* (Göttingen: Vandenhoeck & Ruprecht, 2010), 244–298.

from struggling for a more 'participatory' democracy, alternative leftists of the 1970s questioned the very foundation of democracy: rational arguments. The chapter thus argues that the radical left should not be studied as part and parcel of a struggle for a viable or participatory democracy. Rather, it proposes that examining the political project of the alternative left – the 'liberation of feelings' against the forces of a categorizing rationality – may help us understand the emergence of a new form of politics in which issues of subjectivity became central.[16]

The chapter thus provides an intellectual history of what alternative leftists called a 'new politics'. Drawing on philosophical texts that influenced alternative discussions, notably the work of Deleuze and Guattari, as well as theoretical debates in leftist publications, the first section discusses leftists' critique of the categorizing powers of rationality and what leftists envisioned as a subversive alternative. In a second step, the chapter looks at imagined 'friends' and 'foes' of the alternative left. It tries to make sense of the strange lists of potential allies in the struggle against rationality leftists magazines published, which could include groups as diverse as women, the insane, animals, Bedouins, or erotomanes. Having discussed this imagined political landscape, the chapter investigates what distinguished the 'new politics' leftists imagined from the 'old politics' of traditional leftist parties. It analyses what the 'politics of the first person' entailed beyond a mere extension of the political into the private sphere. Finally, the chapter turns to critics of this 'new politics' and the celebration of feelings and irrationality. Privileging feeling over thinking, these sceptics worried, merely introduced new and equally problematic separations and categorizations that needed to be overcome.

The Critique of Rationality

Seiler's book was not the only text published by radical leftists during the late 1970s that criticized the rationality of capitalist society, nor was it the only text to look for ways of transgressing and subverting the categories of rationality. Reminiscent of the Beat Generation literature, leftists of the 1970s frequently invoked images of 'morasses' that, knowing no strict boundaries, could undermine the strict hierarchies of capitalist society.

---

[16] On the politicization of the subject, see for example Jens Elberfeld, 'Befreiung des Subjekts, Management des Selbst: Therapeutisierungsprozesse im deutschsprachigen Raum seit den 1960er Jahren', in *Zeitgeschichte des Selbst: Therapeutisierung – Politisierung – Emotionalisierung*, ed. Pascal Eitler and Jens Elberfeld (Bielefeld: transcript, 2015).

They turned to 'savage' traditions that had not (yet) excluded the unconscious and magical elements of thinking and living that had no place in a rational society. For example, Hans-Peter Duerr's *Traumzeit* (*Times of Dreams*), an investigation into traditions of magical and mythic thinking, called for a rediscovery of the 'borderlands' between civilization and wildness, while an anthology about the 'return of the imaginary', edited by Christiane Thurn and Herbert Röttgen in 1981, looked at 'fairy tales, magic, mystic, myth' as the 'beginning of a different politics'.[17] Here we can see how New Ageism that seemed to question the rational foundations of modern society became politically attractive for alternative leftists.[18] Gilles Deleuze and Félix Guattari's *Rhizome*, a German translation of which was published in 1977 by the small left-wing publisher Merve in West Berlin, provided the philosophical foundation for this fascination with moments of transgression.[19] *Rhizome* is a complex and rich text, and the discussion here cannot do justice to its philosophical critique of the traditions of 'Western' thought. Instead, I read their work as a redrawing of the political map, arguing that it could become so immensely popular

---

[17] Hans Peter Duerr, *Traumzeit: Über die Grenze zwischen Wildnis und Zivilisation* (Frankfurt a.M.: Syndikat, 1978); Christiane Thurn and Herbert Röttgen, eds., *Die Rückkehr des Imaginären: Märchen, Magie, Mystik, Mythos, Anfänge einer anderen Politik* (Munich: Trikon-Dianus Buchverlag, 1981). The volume included contributions, amongst others, from Hans Peter Dürr, Sergius Golowin, Peter Mosler, Dirk van Gunsteren, and Hadayatullah Hübsch. See also the extremely popular work by Carlos Castaneda and, less so, by Sergius Golowin, for example Carlos Castaneda, *Eine andere Wirklichkeit: neue Gespräche mit Don Juan* (Frankfurt a.M.: S. Fischer, 1973); Carlos Castaneda, *Die Lehren des Don Juan: ein Yaqui-Weg des Wissens* (Frankfurt a.M.: S. Fischer, 1973); Carlos Castaneda, *Reise nach Ixtlan: die Lehre des Don Juan* (Frankfurt a.M.: S. Fischer, 1975); Sergius Golowin, *Hexen, Hippies, Rosenkreuzer: 500 Jahre magische Morgenlandfahrt* (Hamburg: Merlin-Verlag, 1977).

[18] On New Ageism in the alternative left and beyond, see, with further references, Pascal Eitler, '"Alternative" Religion: Subjektivierungspraktiken und Politisierungsstrategien im "New Age" (Westdeutschland 1970–1990)', in *Das alternative Milieu: Antibürgerlicher Lebensstil und linke Politik in der Bundesrepublik Deutschland und Europa, 1968–1983*, ed. Sven Reichardt and Detlef Siegfried (Göttingen: Wallstein, 2010); Pascal Eitler, '"Selbstheilung": Zur Somatisierung und Sakralisierung von Selbstverhältnissen im New Age (Westdeutschland 1970–1990)', in *Das beratene Selbst: Zur Genealogie der Therapeutisierung in den 'langen' Siebzigern*, ed. Sabine Maasen et al. (Bielefeld: transcript, 2011); Pascal Eitler, 'Privatisierung und Subjektivierung: Religiöse Selbstverhältnisse im "New Age"', in *Privatisierung: Idee und Praxis seit den 1970er Jahren*, ed. Norbert Frei and Dietmar Süß (Göttingen: Wallstein, 2012); Reichardt, *Authentizität*, 807–831; Michael Mildenberger, *Die religiöse Revolte: Jugend zwischen Flucht und Aufbruch* (Frankfurt a.M.: Fischer Verlag, 1979).

[19] Gilles Deleuze and Félix Guattari, *Rhizome* (Berlin: Merve, 1977). Rhizome is the introduction of their larger work *A Thousand Plateaus*, from which I will quote: Gilles Deleuze and Félix Guattari, *A Thousand Plateaus*, trans. Brian Massumi (Minneapolis: University of Minnesota Press, 1987). On the reception of Deleuze and Guattari in West Berlin, see also Felsch, *Lange Sommer*, 115, 121–127. On the French context, see Julian Bourg, *From Revolution to Ethics: May 1968 and Contemporary French Thought* (Montreal: McGill-Queen's University Press, 2007).

within the leftist scene because it expressed how alternative leftists imagined the political.

Deleuze and Guattari's small book provides a radical critique of Western thinking that the authors describe as the 'tree model'. In this mode of thinking (and writing books), either a single, strong 'root', or a multiplicity of small 'roots', structures everything that follows. The ramifications of this foundational thought – the metaphorical 'leaves of the tree' – are nothing but copies of the original roots, Deleuze and Guattari argue. Hierarchies of knowledge, stable centres of power, and significance form the centre of such trees, in Deleuze and Guattari's vision. The *rhizome* then constitutes the alternative: a system of the multiple that is not created by adding an ever-increasing number of dimensions ('n + 1'), but by subtracting the singularity ('n – 1'). 'A rhizome as subterranean stem is absolutely different from roots and radicals. Bulbs and tubers are rhizomes', Deleuze and Guattari write.[20] They find rhizomes in the worlds of botany and animals: rats' burrows 'in all their functions of shelter, supply, movement, evasion and breakout' serve as an ideal example for a rhizome. Unlike trees, rhizomes have no centres, no 'relation to the One as subject or object', no 'points or positions', but only 'lines' and 'assemblages'.[21] The lines of the rhizome may be interrupted or end up in a cul-de-sac, but this does not matter: elsewhere, new lines will sprawl. Wishes and desires, the sources of rhizomes according to Deleuze and Guattari, will continue producing the rhizome in new and unforeseen ways. A rhizome is thus not a copy of anything, but rather an ever-evolving map with multiple entry points; unlike the stable and coherent 'tree', a rhizome knows no fixed boundaries at its fringes.

Deleuze and Guattari's *Rhizome* is not merely a critique of a particular mode of thinking, but of a society for which the 'tree structure' of thinking was constitutive in every way. This ranges from the usage of seed plants, 'even those with two sexes', which the authors considered as emblematic for how the tree model shapes not only agriculture, but sexuality itself as '[seed plants] subjugate sexuality to the reproductive mode', to the state as the political form of modernity par excellence, which in their eyes is nothing less but the 'tree of power. For a long time in history, the state was a model for the book and thinking: logos . . . What a pretension of the state . . . to root man.' Only the rhizome and its nomadic 'war machinery' can subvert this 'state-tree'. In the 'arborescent culture', where everything is founded on roots, only 'underground stems and aerial roots,

---

[20] Deleuze and Guattari, *Plateaus*, 21.   [21] Ibid., 6–7.

adventitious growths and rhizome' have the potential to be 'beautiful or loving or political'. Making rhizomes can thus dissolve the fixed categorizations of the arborescent culture. 'The rhizome, on the other hand, is the liberation of sexuality not only from reproduction but also from genitality', Deleuze and Guattari claimed. In short, they longed for unbound desires that produce rhizomes and can subvert a society dominated by 'logos'.

Deleuze and Guattari's book found a receptive audience in the West German left, at least amongst those who were more theoretically inclined, as Günter Pitz remarked in the Frankfurt journal *diskus*, even though he claimed that the French philosophers 'tumbled only in a reduced shape through Germany'.[22] Perhaps most tellingly, a left-wing bar in Berlin named itself *Rhizom*.[23] In Munich, Herbert Röttgen, a central figure for the local scene (he had cofounded the publishing house *Trikont Verlag*, had coedited the important theoretical journal *Autonomie: Materialien gegen die Fabrikgesellschaft*, and had frequently contributed to Munich's biweekly alternative magazine *Das Blatt*), even identified the alternative left as the rhizome. In the wake of the German Autumn of 1977, he reflected on how the New Left had developed since the late 1960s. The classical understanding of (leftist) politics, that is, challenging the state by mobilizing the masses, had been thrown overboard by 1973, Röttgen claimed. Instead, the time of 'autonomy' began. Individual needs and desires 'to change the totality and thus everyday life', that is, 'subjectivity' took precedent. Politics as a means to achieve a revolution in the future was given up in favour of developing a 'radically different way of life' here and now. Rather than agitating the masses, the left had 'built networks, multiple channels, had developed a milieu, occupied niches and cracks, in order to undermine the state, to make it crumbling and fragile, instead of smashing it'. By not committing and defining themselves, the alternative left remained intangible. Thus, an alternative network, 'entangled in multiple ways', emerged. What many leftists perceived as impotence was in reality 'a revolutionary field that could determine itself based on abundance and positivity: the body, the spirit, radically different ways of life, being a woman'. A 'morass', as the state would call it, of 'alternative approaches' slipped into the 'state's walling' – 'women, children, the elderly, gays, men's groups, dispersed leftists, film makers or regionalists'. Philosophically speaking, Deleuze had identified, Röttgen noted, this 'morass' as the rhizome. For Röttgen, that is, this alternative leftist scene was the revolutionary rhizome.[24]

---

[22] Ibid., quotes 18, 24, 15.   [23] See, e.g., *radikal* 92, 5/1981, 30.
[24] Herbert Röttgen, 'Sumpf', in *Das Blatt* 107, 4–17 November 1977, 14–15.

A year later, Röttgen published, together with Florian Rabe, a less well-known author,[25] the book *Vulkantänze* (*Volcano Dances*). The book, which also included a more critical perspective on Deleuze and Guattari's rhetoric of 'desiring machines',[26] is both a sharp and insightful critique of the radical left in West Germany, addressing the alternative scene as well as the more dogmatic *K-Gruppen*, and an attempt to inspire an alternative, anti-rational critique of society. The book opens with the description of the myth (and two mythological figures, the centaur and the forest nymph). When the myth was still alive, the authors claimed, humankind had not yet completely distanced itself from 'being animal'. At this stage, which marked the 'apogee of humankind itself', humankind had existed in a space between 'the sensual and reason, [between] word and image, [between] emotion and thinking'. But the myth had been killed. 'The murderers, these are reason with its axe that separates everything, the tearing apart of human beings into body and corpse [*Leib und Körper* – the difference in German is not exactly clear either], the destruction of its freedom and its passions. And the state, that's this bleak death that wants everything to settle down, and that subordinates everything to utilitarian thinking.' The myth's murderers' 'ten lances' were the sciences, among them anatomy 'that dissects bodies', astronomy that denied that stars could influence a person's character, jurisprudence that 'incarcerated all great affects of human beings', and philosophy that 'respected only reason and held the sensual in contempt'.[27] Pure reason and the institutions that enforced it, namely the state, 'gassed every corner', indeed, 'life' itself, with its 'lack of emotions'.[28] For Röttgen and Rabe, this suggests, a utilitarian and categorizing rationality constituted the proverbial enemy of emancipatory politics.

In this world ruled by 'the laws of rationality and reason [*der Vernunft und des Verstandes*]', the myth as a 'form of emotional thinking' became the 'only means of revolutionary politics'.[29] Yet not all myths have this emancipatory potential. Röttgen and Rabe were clearly aware of how fascists had appealed to myths and irrational thinking, a tradition that reached in their account back to George Sorel. But the working-class movement also had its myths: Lenin, Stalin, and, the biggest myth of all,

---

[25] According to reviewer G. Rossi, Rabe was only an alias for Röttgen, and Röttgen was the sole author of the book, see G. Rossi, 'Der Tanz um einen erloschenen Vulkan', in *Das Blatt* 123, 23 June–6 July 1978, 25.

[26] Herbert Röttgen and Florian Rabe, *Vulkantänze: Linke und alternative Ausgänge* (Munich: Trikont-Verlag, 1978), 76.

[27] Ibid., 8.   [28] Ibid., 95.   [29] Ibid., 9, 19.

the working class itself. These were not the myths Röttgen and Rabe called for. Refusing to criticize those myths – after all, myths were beyond rational critique – they rather envisioned different myths: 'Myths of desires, anti-state myths, Dionysian myths of ecstasy, colourful image-maps of our feelings, magical myths of love, myths of adventures.' Against the 'monotheism of the socialist movement', they invoked a 'polytheism'; the earth they imagined was populated by 'animal-humans, cunning foxes, steppenwolves [*Steppenwölfe*, arguably a reference to Hermann Hesse's book of the same title],[30] presaging toads, proud eagles, singing female dogs'. 'Our myth reflects the variety of revolutionary movements that revolts against the great unitary myth, the Moloch' – note the reference to Ginsburg! – 'the all-dominating spider.' To challenge the laws of reason and rationality, but also to prevent people from falling for the destructive myths of fascism, a reactivation of the 'laughing myth' was necessary, Röttgen and Rabe argued.[31]

Vulkantänze hardly provides a political theory in any conventional sense; it discusses neither institutional authority or legitimacy, nor the emergence of a political will. Yet, by distinguishing friend and foe, Röttgen and Rabe effectively mapped the political field. Both rationality as a force that categorized, hierarchized and thus separated, and the monolithic myths of fascism and socialism constituted the enemy. Against these enemies, Röttgen and Rabe sided with the 'plurality' of myths that derided authorities – the West Berlin *Kommune 1* that had made fun of the court and the American anarchist *Youth International Party* of the late 1960s, commonly known as the Yippies, who ceremoniously elected a pig as president of the United States, served as role models for this subversive plurality. These myths could become revolutionary, Röttgen and Rabe's rhetoric suggests, because they blurred the categorizations and separations reason had enforced. The opposition between rationality and feelings the book construed constituted, of course, a rather clear categorization itself, something Röttgen and Rabe were remarkably aware of. To the 'critics' and rationalists' surprise', as they wrote somewhat ironically, they thus equally argued against 'dreamers [*Schwärmer*]', 'against all too colourful images, against silver foggy-threads [*silberne Nebelfäden*]', using precisely the weapon they had just 'condemned': '*reason*'. 'Where only passions vibrate, we start longing for *critique*.' After all, they refused to being seduced by the 'sweet melodies' of feelings, which would only lead them away from reality.[32] It is this simultaneity of both radically appealing to myths as a revolutionary

---

[30] Hermann Hesse, *Der Steppenwolf* (Berlin: S. Fischer, 1927).
[31] Röttgen and Rabe, *Vulkantänze*, 16–18.   [32] Ibid., 89.

force *and* criticizing the naïve celebration of passions and feelings within the left that makes *Vulkantänze* an insightful source for the radical left in West Germany.

Conceiving of politics as a struggle of feelings and dreams against the domination of rationality was of course not an invention of the late 1970s, as the preceding chapter has shown. Already French students during the May 1968 protests had demanded: 'Power to the Imagination.'[33] In West Germany, students who argued and discussed rationally and 'scientifically' were arguably more typical.[34] However, within the antiauthoritarian parts of the extra-parliamentary opposition, notably in the *Kommune 1*, a critique of such 'serious' forms of politics emerged as well.[35] In *radikalinski*, a West Berlin student magazine aligned to the anarchist magazine *Linkeck*, secondary school students defended their idea of revolutionary politics that would not be subordinated to serious student politics. 'We won't let anyone plan with us. We have started the revolution with ourselves. We think and feel revolutionary and act accordingly. We do what pleases us. We make experiments. We don't know any boundaries. We don't limit ourselves.'[36] Radical politics was, for these young leftists, not about following a strategic plan to revolution, but making experiments based on subjective desires and wishes. In contrast to Röttgen, who had claimed that a decisive shift had taken place around 1973, the editors of *Carlo Sponti*, from Heidelberg, the university town in southwest Germany, argued in January 1977 that in the early 1970s, numerous activists of the student revolts joined the *K-Gruppen* in an attempt to 'overcome the antiauthoritarian period'. The 'subjective element', the desire for dreams and feelings, was thus sidelined, though it never entirely disappeared.[37]

These slightly diverging chronologies notwithstanding, it is clear that by the late 1970s, critiques of a functionalist and categorizing rationality came to dominate much of the alternative leftist discourse. For example, in 1979, Martin Lüdke observed the disappearance of any 'confidence in

---

[33] See Andrew Feenberg and Jim Freedman, *When Poetry Ruled the Streets: The French May Events of 1968* (Albany, NY: State University of New York Press, 2001); Ingrid Gilcher-Holtey, '*Die Phantasie an die Macht': Der Mai 68 in Frankreich* (Frankfurt a.M.: Suhrkamp, 1995); Kristin Ross, *May '68 and Its Afterlives* (Chicago: University of Chicago Press, 2002).

[34] See above all Verheyen, *Diskussionslust*, 244–298; Brown, *West Germany*, 19–20; Joachim Scharloth, *1968: Eine Kommunikationsgeschichte* (Paderborn: Wilhelm Fink, 2011), 211–253, 269–308.

[35] See the semi-fictitious account by Peter Mosler, *Was wir wollten, was wir wurden: Studentenrevolte, 10 Jahre danach* (Reinbek bei Hamburg: Rowohlt, 1977). See also Rolf Schwendter, *Theorie der Subkultur* (Cologne and Berlin: Kiepenheuer und Witsch 1971); Scharloth, *1968*, 309–353.

[36] Anon., 'Terror', in *Radikalinski* 1, probably September 1968, 7.

[37] Redaktion Carlo Sponti, 'Vorwort', in *Carlo Sponti* 25/26, January 1977, 1–4.

the force of reason'. Marx's 'dialectics of forces and relations of production' found no support any more, not even in the left.[38] Left-wing periodicals such as the *Blatt*, *Pflasterstrand*, or *Ulcus Molle* confirm this impression. In 1979, Rainer Klassen observed in *Ulcus Molle* that the 'scene' was often viewed as 'anti-rational', since the 'brutality of the dominating rationality' only aimed at 'forcing renitent spirits into the streams of insanity'.[39] Making a more theoretical argument, a man named Rädli, frequent contributor to the *Blatt*, wrote that the 'discovery of the laws of nature and society have ... reduced the inner life of human beings. In the age of technology, the soul is suffering from exhaustion [*Auszehrung*].'[40] 'Technological rationality', had created, an anonymous author wrote in *Pflasterstrand*, 'labyrinths in which any self-conscious, autonomous idea of life searches in vain for orientation and survival, just as anything superfluous or non-functional'. At work was an 'efficient, anonymously calculating logic' that was based on the 'will to dominate nature', a will that ultimately also called for the domination of human beings.[41] Grounding emancipatory politics, as Jürgen Habermas did, on reason thus appeared to be utterly misguided, as Gerd Bergfleth argued in *Konkursbuch* in 1978, for 'what defines reason, and in particular reason that makes itself the measure of everything [*die sich zum Maß aller Dinge aufschwingt*], is nothing but *domination*: domination over nature, over human beings, over itself'. Ultimately, Habermas only dreamed of the 'universal domination of rationality', Bergfleth charged.[42] And finally, a self-proclaimed 'alternative man' from Graz, Austria, named Gerhard Fuchs, though not uncritical of the fascination with irrationality in the alternative scene, nevertheless provided criteria from a wrong kind of rationality, such as the 'primacy of the intellect over feelings', the 'tyranny of language and concept', the 'categorization' that disables any openness towards new phenomena and experiences, or the 'rationalization of human relations', which denies basic human needs such as 'unification, a feeling of safety [*Geborgenheit*], security'.[43]

---

[38] W. Martin Lüdke, 'Wildnis und Kultur', in *Unter dem Pflaster liegt der Strand* 6, 1979, 105–132: 107.

[39] Rainer Klassen, 'Aphorismus zur Vernunft', in *Ulcus Molle* 3/4, 1979, 7.

[40] Rädli, 'Verdorrte Seelen', in *Das Blatt* 128, 1–14 September 1978, 24–27.

[41] Anon., 'Grüne Liste – Natur als Politik', in *Pflasterstrand* 18, 3–16 November 1977, 30–32.

[42] Gerd Bergfleth, 'Kritik der Emanzipation', in *Konkursbuch: Zeitschrift für Vernunftkritik* 1, 1978, 13–38, esp. 27.

[43] Gerhard Fuchs, 'Alternativbewegung: Überlgungen zur Diskussion um eine Programmatik der Alternativbewegung', in *Ulcus Molle* 11/12, 1979, 10–15. See also Klaus Bernd Vollmar, 'Politische Überlegungen zur Alternativliteratur', in *Ulcus Molle* Sonderinfo 3, December 1976, 10–16.

This categorizing rationality imposed itself on bodies as well as on the built environment of cities, leftists argued. Writing from a feminist perspective, Christiane Matties noted that putting on a bra and suspenders, the act that 'turns us into women', is also an act of 'containment and separation'. Being a woman means giving up on the ambiguity of being a child. As children, girls want, at least at times and not forever, to become boys or men; they want to be something else, at least for a brief moment, Matties claimed. But when girls turn into women, this ambiguity is sealed off. Adult women are expected to show a certain bodily posture. But when they gave up this posture, when their bodies 'laughed, snorted, giggled, cried' in public, women were no longer women, but merely 'foolish chicks' or 'stupid cows': 'We offered a beastly spectrum'. In a way resonating with Röttgen and Rabe's invocation of 'animal-humans', Matties called for dissolving fixed gender categories and thus criticized the women's movement and its focus on women's sexuality and belly (*Unterleib*).[44] Matties was not alone with her call for the dissolution of fixed boundaries. In *Autonomie*, Matthias Beltz for example blamed the 'factory society' for 'destroying human beings into parts of a machine, into head, belly, and sex'.[45] Reflecting on the funeral of RAF terrorists Gudrun Ensslin, Andreas Baader, and Jan-Carl Raspe, 'three flashingly rouged women' claimed in the *Blatt* that the 'one-eyed' – they might have meant policemen, journalists, or the state and system in general – 'thing-fixers, black-and-white-painters with their super-things' pinch everything that is still alive with their 'cold mechanics'. At the funeral, they witnessed an 'unholy alliance' of police and press that wanted 'to fix us, to imprison us in their either-or'. Just as with Röttgen and Rabe's animal-humans, and Matties's girls who wanted to be boys for a while, these women too longed for a 'liveliness' that could not be fixed: 'we aren't black, we aren't white, sometimes warm, sometimes hot' – but, note, never cold! – 'sometimes young, sometimes old, sometimes sad, sometimes happy, sometimes like this, sometimes like that'.[46] Like many other leftists, these women rejected any fixed categorizations being imposed upon their feelings and bodies, a refusal that was in itself an act of political resistance.

---

[44] Christiane Matties, 'Penthesilea, Annie und die anderen Frauen', in *Konkursbuch: Zeitschrift für Vernunftkritik* 2, 1978, 189–204, quote 189.

[45] Matthias Beltz, 'Abenteuer in der Fabrik. Geschichten aus der Beziehung zwischen Linksradikalen und Arbeiterbewegung', in *Autonomie: Materialien gegen die Fabrikgesellschaft* 9, October 1977, 9–22, esp. 17.

[46] Drei grell geschminkte Frauen, 'Grell geschminkte Lippen – ausdrucksloses Gesicht: das macht geil!', in *Das Blatt* 107, 4–17 November 1977, 13.

Leftists' critique of modern urbanity followed a similar logic.[47] Rationally planned cities, leftists claimed, had turned into deeply boring places. One of the most detailed critiques of modern urbanity was offered in 1980 by the Cologne-based *Office for Anti-Utopian Research* in its 'Time of the Concrete [*Betonzeit*]', a 'pamphlet against the urban environment and its improvements'. Since the times of absolutism, a 'geometry of order, of symmetry, of clarity' had taken hold, the authors argued, a geometry that disciplined 'the bodies, the movements of human beings' and 'turned them into a functioning part of the Great Machinery'.[48] The imposition of this 'geometry' also structured time that had lost its 'fluid character: it freezes into an exactly defined, measurable, homogenous *space*' – an argument reminiscent of the Situationist analysis of urban space under capitalism. At the same time, this 'scientific-rational dissection of time' fragmented 'human beings into exactly separated and calculable functions'.[49] In the 19th century, the authors claimed, factories and neighbourhoods were structured according to the logics of this geometry; in the late twentieth century, this logic also extended to shopping zones that were scientifically structured according to people's ability to process information.[50] The result was a 'landscape of absence', determined by 'the rhythm of time, the rhythm of machines ... the rhythm of alarm clocks, of egg timers, of bus tickets ... of coffee breaks'.[51] In these 'living zones', 'boredom is the public problem no. 1', the *Office* noted. Even though this description of the urban landscape rarely explicitly referred to the categorizing power of rationality, the underlying motif is clear: the powers of a geometrical logic dissected and fragmented life.

In this world governed by the laws of reason and rationality, anything that might undermine the categorizations and fragmentations that rationality imposed upon people had a revolutionary potential. Drawing on the traditions of the Situationist International as well as Herbert Marcuse, leftists celebrated fantasy, dreams, insanity, and desires as the subversive

---

[47] On leftist critiques of modern urbanity in a European context, see Moritz Föllmer, 'Cities of Choice: Elective Affinities and the Transformation of Western European Urbanity from the mid-1950s to the early 1980s', *Contemporary European History* 24 (2015): 587–595. See also Christiane Reinecke, 'Localising the Social: The Rediscovery of Urban Poverty in Western European "Affluent Societies"', *Contemporary European History* 24 (2015).

[48] Büro für anti-utopische Forschungen, *Betonzeit: Ein Pamphlet gegen die Stadtlandschaft und ihre Verbesserungen* (Cologne: Eigenverlag, 1980), 10–11. The pamphlet was clearly inspired by the work of French Marxist Henri Lefebvre and his critiques of modern urbanity, see for example Henri Lefebvre, *The Urban Revolution* (Minniapolis: University of Minnesota Press, 2003). The book was first published in French in 1970; a German translation appeared in 1972.

[49] Büro, *Betonzeit*, 12–13.   [50] Ibid., 18.   [51] Ibid., 4–5.

forces in a rational world. The 'subrealists', a political avant-garde group
from Hamburg, for example defined its 'strategic goals' in the following
way: 'Occupation of all spaces that the old world cannot cover any more:
the dreams, the passions, the anti-productivity of creation, the play, the
delight [*Genuss*], and the nonconsumable wishes.'[52] All the 'new forms of
expressing resistance, disrupting the interactions between men and
women, [the] new forms of demonstrating' the alternative left had
developed 'are eruptions of our fantasy that escape from ruling norms
and turn being crazy and insane into subversive fun', an anonymous
author of the Frankfurt *Pflasterstrand* wrote.[53] Writing from prison to
the *Info Berliner Undogmatischer Gruppen (Info BUG)*, a certain Django
urged his comrades in a somewhat confused text to overcome the fragmentation of 'our hatred / our rage / our sorrow / our longing for
tenderness and love' in a revolt that would involve 'acting out our fears,
lovingly mutual touching, RAGING MOVEMENT'.[54] Reminiscent of
the searches for an 'authentic' life discussed in the previous chapter,
Michael Hiltl noted in *Ulcus Molle* that the common denominator of
the alternative scene was a 'protest against the cultural impoverishment of
human beings in our society, against the suppression and deformation
of human nature (the needs, drives, dreams, sensuality, production,
interpersonal and object relations)'. The 'culturally grounded and hence
internalized domination of the mind of the body and the senses has to be
abolished', Hiltl summarized alternative politics.[55]

Disrupting spatial categorizations was also central for the 'social explosion' the *Office of Anti-Utopian Research* envisioned in 'dream fragments'.
'Small hordes of rebels roam the cities', the *Office* imagined, 'they infiltrate
everything, occupy new spaces and buildings on a daily basis'. The *Office*
dreamed of a complete liberation of 'all prisoners, the children from
kindergartens and foster homes, the animals from the zoo'. Even the
'suppressed musical instruments escape from the stores and run through
the cities. In raving sessions, they unite with the drums of the new savages:
the jerry cans that rest from their work and the barricade-tools of differently sounding cars.' In this revolt, everyone 'changes name, place of living
and identity as often as he wants'. Walls are decorated with images and

[52] 'Selbstdarstellung der Subrealisten', in *Revolte* 14, October 1975, 8–10.
[53] Anon., 'Taylorisierung des Menschen', in *Pflasterstrand* 9, 4–17 May 1977, 30–32.
[54] Django, 'Zwei Briefe aus der Hölle, mit lieben Grüßen vom Teufel', in *Info BUG* 162, 27 June
1977, 17.
[55] Michael Hiltl, 'Steppenwolf: Ein Männerbild aus der "Alternativ"-Szene', in *Ulcus Molle* 7/8, 1979,
20–24.

'poetic exchanges of words', but these are no works of art, but 'screams of an unchained desire'. The spatial organization of factories equally collapses. 'Water battles rage on the shop floors ... An ever-increasing number of workers are found in the wrong shop, participating in secret meetings or giving away stocks. Those who are still eagerly standing at the work bench create products of unseen quality, but for purposes utterly unknown to the company.'[56] Similar to the revolts called for by authors like Röttgen and Rabe or the 'three flashingly rouged women', the revolt the *Office* imagined would disrupt the limitations and categorizations of modern society, in this case its spatial organization.

The alternative left that emerged in the 1970s redefined the political in a peculiar way. For leftists, the capitalist world was dominated by a rationality that categorized everything it touched, from bodies to entire cities. Anything that remained beyond the grasp of rationality, such as feelings, dreams, desires, and fantasies, had a subversive potential, as it could disrupt the order rationality had established. The revolt these anti-rational forces might incite would have little to do with the ideal of a well-planned insurrection. Rather, those would be joyous and exuberant revolts against the logic of capitalism.

Women, Children, the Insane, and Kalmyk: The Rebels against Rationality

It would be an odd alliance that struggled against the laws of reason and rationality. In Röttgen and Rabe's account, the 'mixture of revolt' consisted of: 'women, female foreign workers [*Fremdarbeiterinnen*], erotomans [*Erotomanen*], children, the elderly, prisoners, the insane, animals, Yakis, Turks, Bedouins, [American] Indians, Kalmyk, Montoneros, Australian dock workers, Irish, transvestites ... [sic]'[57] Left-wing magazines appealed to similarly unlikely coalitions. In December 1977, *Pflasterstrand* for example called for a 'gathering of the insane' in Frankfurt next summer. 'An earthquake shall take place, an explosion of the insane, workers, dissidents, women, gays, musicians, militants, Metropolitan Indians, lesbians, communists, socialists, macrobiotics, ecologists, officials [*Beamten*; sic!], freaks, artists, (female) dreamers, fantastics [*Fantasten*], opponents of progress, potheads, fighters and chaotics.'[58] Already a year before that, leftists had declared during a demonstration in Frankfurt that 'we are

---

[56] Büro, *Betonzeit*, 70–77. [57] Röttgen and Rabe, *Vulkantänze*, 75.
[58] Anon., 'Wir rufen die Irren Europas', in *Pflasterstrand* 20, 1–14 December 1977, 24–25.

the insane and utopians!'[59] A list of nouns on the cover page of the Göttingen journal *Politikon* indicates what all these seemingly diverse groups of people might have had in common in leftists' imagination: 'Needs, emancipation, women's movement, immediacy, sexuality, experience, subjectivity.' And on the cover's background, the editors had printed photo of a small, naked and dirty child.[60]

In other texts, leftists concentrated on what opponents of the 'German Sunday peace' might do to disturb this peace.[61] *Pflasterstrand* for example imagined what a 'Green List', long before the Green Party came into being, would do: 'It is nothing but a medium that punches holes into the barriers and walls, into fears and insecurities, it subverts them, pushes them aside, makes them ridiculous, makes them disappear, saws [*ansägt*], redefines them, unveils them as paper tigers, jumps, occupies, hurts, buries, enwraps, tears apart, lets them go to seed [*vergammeln lässt*], plays them their own melody, dances around, makes crazy, yells, paints, turns on [*antörnt*], flies over [*überfliegt*], dissolves them into air, water, animals, human beings . . .'[62] With a slightly different list of verbs, the Hamburg magazine *Große Freiheit* looked forward to the Mayday demonstrations of 1978. 'Out for Mayday', it called its readers to arms, 'yell out, dance out, cuddle out, throw out, drum out [*rausschreien, raustanzen, rausschmusen, rauswerfen, raustrommeln*]', in the rhythm of our heartbeat: rage, hatred, joy, love – together'.[63] The *Blatt* used a variety of activities to differentiate between 'us' and 'them'. 'They defend the power of their class', they have 'walky-talkies, guns, uniforms, data collection, concrete, and loneliness'. The others, the imaginary we, by contrasted, defended their 'lives'; they had 'fantasy' and 'hot clothes', they had 'the joy of being able to hug and trust each other'.[64] The West Berlin *Info BUG* described 'you' and 'us' in similar terms. 'You: the perennial rulers, the fathers, the adults, you, who always know everything better, you managers of death . . . you, with your extreme lack of emotions. You: you are incapable of loving.' It would be a 'new youth' that confronted these 'fathers' and 'adults', a youth that included: 'the women, the sons, the children, the elderly, the insane, the criminals, the terrorists, the anarchos, the gays, the radical leftists – with one word: the excluded, *we*, the friends [*Sympathisanten*] of life, the morass

---

[59] Anon., 'Wer sich nicht wehrt – lebt verkehrt', in *Das Blatt* 72, 18 June–1 July 1976, 4–5.
[60] Cover page, *Politikon* 45, November 1974.   [61] Anon., 'Wir rufen die Irren Europas'.
[62] Anon., 'Das ökologische Manifest', in *Pflasterstrand* 20, 1–14 December 1977, 18–19.
[63] Anon., 'Der Mai ist gekommen – 1. Mai in Hamburg', in *Große Freiheit* 13, June 1978, 8.
[64] Anon., 'Müllimpressionen', in *Das Blatt* 116, 10–23 March 1978, 17.

Figure 3   Cover page of *Politikon* 45, November 1974.

[*Sumpf*] of your dreams, which you try in vain to drain'.[65] The enemy, in other words, might be powerful and armed, but it was lonely and lacked feelings; those challenging the power might not have guns, but they had more attractive clothes and, above all, feelings.

Scholars have often remarked how leftists, most notably the terrorists of the Red Army Faction and their supporters, divided their political word into enemies of humanity, 'the pigs', which included the police as well as capitalists, and 'human beings'.[66] Alternative leftists, too, distinguished between 'us' and 'them', perhaps not surprisingly given how fundamental the distinction between friend and foe is for politics. The way they did so is, however, more surprising and worthy of an exploration. What, after all, might women, the insane, Kalmyk, transvestites, and prisoners have in common, except being marginalized? But it is not merely the composition of these long and at times open-ended lists of potential allies that is remarkable, but the very practice of putting together such lists of potential allies and what they might do. In simply listing these various groups and activities, placing nouns and verbs next to each other without logically connecting them, leftists created, as it were, an alternative to the tree-model of thinking Deleuze and Guattari had criticized. Such lists lacked an explicit unifying principle; they could be expanded, albeit not arbitrarily, by simply adding new groups or activities. Like a rhizome, they were never finished.

This makes the analysis of such lists a paradoxical endeavour. Examining what women, children, the insane, and Bedouins might have in common that made them potential rebels is a search for the unifying principle that alternative leftists wanted to avoid. Here, then, the scholarly logic not only differs from the alternative way of thinking (this, after all, happens all too often), but is *in conflict* with this thinking: it is this scholarly logic that alternative leftists vigorously criticized. There is no way to reconcile this conflict; being aware of it is thus all the more important.

A group that commonly appeared in the lists of potential allies is women; men, by contrast, are never mentioned (though gays and sons are). Women, leftists frequently argued, felt, whereas men only thought. In

---

[65] 'Gewaltige Frauen – Unter der Oberfläche beginnt der Untergrund', in *Info BUG* 172, 5 September 1977, 4–5.

[66] On the RAF's language, see Sarah Colvin, *Ulrike Meinhof and West German Terrorism: Language, Violence, and Identity* (Rochester, NY: Camden House, 2009), 116–148. On the depiction of the police as 'pigs' in the left-wing paper *agit 883*, see also Massimo Perinelli, 'Longing, Lust, Violence, Liberation: Discourses on Sexuality on the Radical Left in West Germany, 1969–1972', in *After the History of Sexuality: German Interventions*, ed. Dagmar Herzog, Helmut Puff, and Spector Scott (New York: Berghahn Books, 2011).

a letter to the West Berlin magazine *radikal* from 1976, a woman named Bettina for example criticized the male authors of numerous articles in a previous edition of the magazine on the women's movement for only explaining what they thought, but not what they felt. 'The patriarchal principle requires the elimination of anything subjective', she claimed. For women, this means 'the denial of their entire identity, which for now is utterly subjective'; for men, by contrast, it means 'the elimination and alienation of subjectivity in their emotional world'. Dealing with autonomous women would only be productive for men if those would 'break with their self-alienated rationalism (which works with concepts like strategy, etc.) and thus self-alienated understanding of politics'.[67] The women's movement, by contrast, had broken with this rationalism, as Elisabeth Matz and Johanna Müller explained in *Politikon* (Göttingen), by demanding that 'empathy [*Mitleid*] is no longer considered a weakness, that feelings are no longer sacrificed to rationality, that peacefulness is no longer regarded as stupidity, and that spontaneity is not looked upon as craziness'.[68]

The Frankfurt-based feminist group *Metropolitan Women*, who were otherwise rather critical of the celebration of 'female irrationality' within the women's movement, nevertheless rejected a 'rigid, male rationality' and instead longed for a revolt to escape from the 'narrowness of order'.[69] When other women from Frankfurt called for the 'invention of happiness', they not only rejected violence, as Karrin Hanshew has pointed out,[70] but also 'machine rationality'. Women, they argued, had always been 'sand in the gears [*Getriebe*] of this machinery'. Women were hence trained to have only 'meekness [*Sanftmut*]'. Genuine happiness, however, was beyond both 'machine rationality' and 'meekness'. To 'invent happiness', chaos would be necessary: 'The age of orderliness is over. Clean apartments, clean self-righteousness, freshly ironed men's shirts, fearful children – that's over.' Chaos and the 'refusal to be logical' were women's weapons of choice in the struggle against rationality.[71] How common the

---

[67] Bettina, 'Antworten einer schönen und sonderbaren Sumpfblüte (Leserbrief)', in *radikal* 6, 21 October 1976, 11. The article was a reaction to three articles by male authors on the women's movement in *radikal* 5, 7 October 1976, 8–9.
[68] Elisabeth Matz and Johanna Müller, 'Wir wollen Brot und Rosen', in *Politikon* 45, probably fall 1974, 12–17: 17.
[69] Metropolitan Women, 'Der Himmel ist auf den Boden gefallen – Die Revolution ist nicht mehr verborgen', in *Autonomie: Materialien gegen die Fabrikgesellschaft* 8, August 1977, 18–23.
[70] Karrin Hanshew, *Terror and Democracy in West Germany* (Cambridge: Cambridge University Press, 2012), 239–240.
[71] Frankfurter Frauen, 'Aufruf an alle Frauen zur Erfindung des Glücks', in *Autonomie: Materialien gegen die Fabrikgesellschaft* 10, January 1978, 10.

association of women with emotionality was within the women's movement is perhaps best exemplified by a sharp critique of this equation that a group called *Militante Panthertanten* formulated. Within the women's movement, emotionality, the *Panthertanten* wrote, was deemed both subversive and harmonizing, as it allegedly helped overcome class differences amongst women. Yet this 'emotionality is domesticated. Its façade is the perennial [*perennierend*] smiling that denies rationality and prohibits thinking.' Women who dared to think and criticize, who made use of their intellectual capabilities, were thus attacked within the women's movement as 'aggressive', the *Panthertanten* complained.[72]

Some leftists like author and filmmaker Alexander Kluge even argued that rationality and emotionality provided the very basis for two distinctly male and female reality principles, as he explained in a discussion after the presentation of his film *Gelegenheitsarbeiten einer Sklavin* in Heidelberg. The film depicts the plight of a woman named Roswitha, married to a leftist but sexist husband. During the course of the film, Roswitha becomes politically active and travels to Portugal, where she wants to document how the construction of a branch factory (*Zweigwerk*) results in the closure of the main factory (*Heimwerk*). After the screening of the film, critics accused Kluge of making fun of Roswitha and depicting her as 'infantile and dumb'. When she travelled to Portugal, Roswitha did not take any photos or bring official documents home to prove her case, but only reported what she saw and trusted that people would believe her. 'No woman is that dumb and naïve', Kluge's critics remarked. Kluge, however, responded that he had tried to show how two different 'reality principles clash in women'. On the one hand, the 'phallus-competing industrial society is based on written proofs, certificates, [logical] deductions [*Herleitungen*], which are all means of domination'. Roswitha's reality principle, by contrast, was based on 'the principles of trust, solidarity, mutual belief, etc.'. Her colleagues would know that she would not betray them. Those who deemed Roswitha's actions infantile were therefore wrong, as they insisted on 'principles that embody domination and suppression, but not solidarity'.[73] For women's reality principle, Kluge's argument implied, empathy and feelings mattered, whereas men merely relied an logics and the evidence that could support such logic – a

---

[72] Die Panthertanten, 'Neue Weiblichkeit in der Frauenbewegung?', in *Schwarze Protokolle* 12, November 1975, 33–36.

[73] C.S. Kulturbrigade, 'Zur Kluge-Veranstaltung vom 17.4.75', in *Carlo Sponti* 11/12, April 1975, 15.

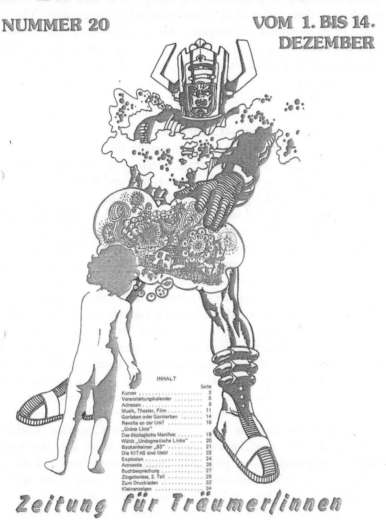

Figure 4   Cover page of *Pflasterstrand* 20, December 1977.

perspective the article in *Carlo Sponti* reporting about the debate seems to have shared.

Another group leftists frequently included into their imagined alliance against rationality were children (that Röttgen and Rabe also included the elderly into their 'mixture of revolt' was rather exceptional). The cover image of *Pflasterstrand* – a 'magazine for dreamers', as it called itself – in December 1977 visualizes the central role children played in the political imaginary of the radical left. A young, naked child (it is shown from the back, which leaves the gender undetermined) confronts a large, presumably male robot. The child apparently dreams of a colourful world, of a nice house in the midst of trees and fantastic flowers; the robot, by contrast, emits greyish smoke. The child's dreams, it seems, function as a 'weapon', which the child launches against the menacing force of the robot. The picture represents leftists' dream of a 'children's revolt' that would be, as Röttgen put it, 'the most radical and most fantastic revolution' to come. In Röttgen's mind, children were predestined to rebel against the adult rational world order, as they still 'perceive the world in an emotional way, they want to conquer the world with feelings, they are still entirely body and soul and not yet consciousness'. This made children the ideal allies in the coming struggle of the 'party of feelings and senses against the party of rationality and alienation'.[74] Leftists also eagerly consumed novels that depicted such rebellions of children against the grey, monotone, and boring world of adults, for example Michael Ende's *Momo*. The book depicts the struggle of a girl of indeterminable age, named Momo, against the 'grey gentlemen' who steal people's time and thus create an efficient but monotone, hectic, and boring world that has no place and time for playing, telling stories, or genuine communication. Only when Momo can defeat the grey gentlemen and return time to the city's inhabitants does life become pleasurable again.[75] Another book praised by leftist journals was French novelist Christiane Rochefort's *Zum Glück geht's dem Sommer entgegen*. The book tells the story of children, in particular two girls, who escape from school and the adult world more generally, sometimes with the help of sympathetic adults, to discover 'love, sexuality', and reclaim their identity against a hostile adult world. The girls learned, as an anonymous reviewer for *Pflasterstrand*

---

[74] Herbert Röttgen, 'Kinderrevolution', in *Das Blatt*, 22 April–5 May 1977, 14–16. The text was republished in *Pflasterstrand*, 13 July–September 1977, 18–20.

[75] Michael Ende, *The Grey Gentlemen*, trans. Frances Lobb (London & Toronto: Burke Books, 1974). See also my discussion in Häberlen, 'Ingrid's Boredom'.

wrote, to 'like themselves, their bodies, the other's body'. However, the 'dividing line' was not simply between adults and children, the reviewer stressed, but between 'the state and with it all those who insist on their authority, their power, and on the other side all those who understand and support the children's longing for freedom'.[76]

Leftists also called for the emancipation of children and demanded a right for children to divorce their parents.[77] The Munich *Blatt* for example reported favourably about the *Indiani Metropolitani* in Rome who had demanded, among other things, that any child 'who is capable of escaping from its parents, even "on all fours"' should be declared legally mature.[78] At times, leftists placed both men and women on the side of rationality. A 'girls' commune' from Berlin for example claimed that it was engaged in a 'nonviolent guerrilla warfare against the emotion-destroying world of women and men, against the adult culture of concrete [*Betonkultur*] with its suicidal shopping streets, its world of plastic, where our desire for free love relationships and cohabitation has no space, particularly for girls'.[79] More commonly, however, leftists imagined both women and children as resisting the anti-emotional world. In his critique of distinctly male violence, Joschka Fischer therefore placed both women and children on 'the other side of the barricade', since both had what male militants lacked as much as the capitalist world: 'fantasy'.[80] For leftists, children thus

---

[76] Christiane Rochefort, *Encore heureux qu'on va vers l'été* (Paris: Grasset, 1975). Published in German as Christiane Rochefort, *Zum Glück gehts dem Sommer entgegen* (Frankfurt a.M.: Suhrkamp, 1977). For reviews, see Anon., 'Bücher: Christiane Rochefort: "Zum Glück gehts dem Sommer entgegen", in *Pflasterstrand* 24, 23 February–8 March 1978, 20–21. See also the reviews in *Traumstadt* 1, March 1978, 7–9, *Lesbenpresse* 7, May 1978, 7, and *BUG Info* 1026, 16.

[77] See, e.g., Micky Remann, 'Nichtwähler aufgepasst', in *Pflasterstrand* 36, 26 August–8 September 1978, 31–32; Peter Laudenbach (14 years), 'Das Jahr des Kindes', in *Pflasterstrand* 46, 27 January–9 February 1979, 27; the brochure *Kinderbefreiungsfront*, summer 1979, published by a group from Pforzheim.

[78] Peter Schult, '. . . der heiße Sommer kam im Februar', in *Das Blatt* 91, 1–21 April 1977, 12–15. The Indiani Metropolitani pamphlet is reprinted, in German, in Alberto Benini, ed., *Indianer und P 38: Italien, ein neues 68 mit anderen Waffen* (Munich: Trikont Verlag, 1978), 85–86. On the *Indiani Metropolitani*, see also Sebastian Haumann, '"Indiani Metropolitani" and "Stadtindianer": Representing Autonomy in Italy and West-Germany', in *Between Prague Spring and French May: Opposition and Revolt in Europe, 1960–1980*, ed. Martin Klimke, Jacco Pekelder, and Joachim Scharloth (New York: Berghahn, 2011); Angelo Ventrone, *'Vogliamo tutto': Perché due generazioni hanno creduto nella rivoluzione 1960–1988* (Rome: Editori Laterza, 2012), 348–351; Pablo Echaurren, *La casa del desiderio: '77: indiani metropolitani e altri strani* (Lecce: Manni Editore, 2005).

[79] 'Mädchenkommune', in *radikal* 81, September 1980, 18.

[80] Joschka Fischer, 'Vorstoß in "primitivere" Zeiten', in *Autonomie: Materialien gegen die Fabrikgesellschaft* 5, February 1977, 52–64, esp. 57.

presented an ideal of a wholesome subject not yet tainted by the forces of rationality and still able to dream and fantasize.

Next to women and children, leftists liked to include non-Western peoples like Bedouins, Kalmyk or Yakis into their lists of potential allies in the struggle against the domination of rationality. If the industrial world of capitalism (and, for that matter, Soviet-style communism) was characterized by a 'machine-rationality', then pre- or nonindustrial 'tribes and clans' might point to an alternative way of living.[81] Like children and women, peoples who were still close to nature would relate to the world not merely with words, but in a sensual and imaginative way. According to an author writing as 'Family Wierpsek' in *Ulcus Molle*, the modern world was 'hooked on progress'. In this world, heart attacks and depressions constantly increased. Yet there were also a growing number of people that tried to find a life that could be 'sensually experienced [*sinnlich erfahrbares Leben*]' and that would be 'manageable in contact with like-minded comrades'. And thus people longed for a life with 'shepherds Greece, with Gypsies in St. Marie de la Mer, with Eskimos or [American] Indians', the author argued. His own experience of living with Gypsies had amounted, he claimed, to a 'wild therapy'; 'the world of my childhood once again enchants me'. Employing a language reminiscent of Röttgen and Rabe's work, he saw artists dressed up as 'half cow, half human being, sluggish fire-breathers, oily chain-blasters', and many others. Amongst the Gypsies and their 'life experience', he found his joy. 'We begin putting together what we used to splittingly analyse [*Wir beginnen zusammenzufügen, was wir sonst spalterisch analysierten*].'[82]

Other leftists found a more emotional and sensual way of life in Latin America. A man named Chris for example had travelled to Lima, Peru, and reported how couples 'snuggled' in the parks. Late in the afternoon, there was an 'erotic haze over the city, a bit of enchantment between work and family home'.[83] Travelling to America was not even necessary for being

---

[81] Familie Wierpsek, 'Bumerang Nr. 3', in *Ulcus Molle* 3/4, 1979, 16–19. For debates about 'alternative' travelling, see also Anja Bertsch, 'Alternative (in) Bewegung: Distinktion und transnationale Vergemeinschaftung im alternativen Tourismus', in *Das Alternative Milieu: Antibürgerlicher Lebensstil und linke Politik in der Bundesrepublik Deutschland und Europa 1968–1983*, ed. Sven Reichardt and Detlef Siegfried (Göttingen: Wallstein, 2010).

[82] Familie Wierpsek, 'Bumerang Nr. 3'.

[83] Chris, 'In Peru: Ein Erfahrungsbericht', in *Pflasterstrand* 28, 20 April–3 May 1978, 30–34. See in also, on leftists' fascination with African-Americans, Moritz Ege, *Schwarz werden: 'Afroamerikanophilie' in den 1960er und 1970er Jahren* (Bielefeld: transcript, 2007); Moritz Ege, 'Becoming-Black: Patterns and Politics of West-German "Afro-Americanophilia" in the Late 1960s', *PORTAL Journal of Multidisciplinary International Studies* 12 (2015).

impressed by the alleged emotionality of Native Americans. After attending an information event in May 1978, a teacher from Frankfurt described how moved he had been by the 'South and North American Indians' who reported about their country and peoples 'by playing, singing and talking – but they talk the way they sing – infinitely gently, patient, softly'. Similar to the way Röttgen had described children, the teacher from Frankfurt suggested that Native Americans relate to the world not through rational discourse, but in a more sensual way. It was enough for him to listen to them, he claimed, to be put into a 'state of strong agitation, of sorrow, rage, joy and expectation'. Rhetorically, he contrasted this emotionally charged experience with the 'brutality of institutions, the omnipresent technic and civilization', against which he and his comrades fought, a collective fight that was, indeed, another source of joy for him.[84] It is then not surprising that leftists listed the 'Indians' fight against Cowboys' alongside the 'human lung's struggle against air pollution [*Abgase und Gestank*], the stomach's and the bile's struggle against plastic-food, poison and pharmacological products, [and] the rebellion of nonsense against the rationality of concrete [*betonierte Vernünftigkeit*]', as an author for *Pflasterstrand* wrote.[85] Tribes and clans, Gypsies, and Native Americans from North and South America all provided examples for a more 'wholesome', natural, emotional, and joyful way of life that had not been torn apart by an analytical and technological rationality.

Perhaps most oddly, but also most tellingly, leftists commonly included the insane (*Irre*, or *Wahnsinnige*) into their lists of allies for the coming revolt; at times, leftists even referred to themselves as 'insane'.[86] For example, the call for a Europe-wide congress in the summer of 1978 in Frankfurt (the congress never took place) referred to 'the insane of Europe

---

[84] Ein Lehrer, 'Über die Schwierigkeit einen Beruf zu haben und manchmal glücklich zu sein. Bericht eines linken Lehrers, Teil 2', in *Pflasterstand* 31, 1–16 June 1978, 33–35.

[85] Micky Remann, 'Nichtwähler aufgepasst', in *Pflasterstrand* 36, 26 August–8 September 1978, 31–32.

[86] Scholars have paid relatively little attention to leftists' fascination with insanity. Exceptions include Franz-Werner Kersting, 'Juvenile Left-wing Radicalism, Fringe Groups, and Anti-psychiatry in West Germany', in *Between Marx and Coca-Cola: Youth Cultures in Changing European Societies, 1960–1980*, ed. Axel Schildt and Detlef Siegfried (New York: Berghahn, 2006); Christian G. De Vito, 'Liminoids, Hegemony and Transfers in the Liminal Experiences in Italian Psychiatry, 1960s–1980s', in *Ausnahmezustände: Entgrenzungen und Regulierungen in Europa während des Kalten Krieges*, ed. Dirk Schumann and Cornelia Rauh (Göttingen: Wallstein, 2015). The *Sozialistische Patienkollektiv* (SPK) that was formed in the early 1970s in Heidelberg is a somewhat different story. Members of the SPK criticzed capitalism as 'ill' and declared that therapy had to be a revolutionary act. Later, members of the SPK joined the Red Army Faction. There is no academic study of the SPK so far.

[*die Irren Europas*]'. Here, the 'insane' functioned as an all-embracive category that included women, children, lesbians, dreamers, and others.[87] West German leftists were inspired by their French and Italian comrades, notably Gilles Deleuze, Félix Guattari, and Gérard Hof, a lesser-known psychiatrist who had worked in Lyon where inmates of a psychiatric hospital had revolted. Celebrating Hof's book, *Hunde wollt ihr ewig sterben*, about the revolt in Lyon,[88] two authors of the *Blatt* named Kristine and Traubi argued that the revolt was not only directed against the hierarchies of the clinic, but against the norms and values of a society in general that had made 'bodily and psychic deprivation' a condition of survival.[89] From this perspective, mental institutions were not simply another form of oppression, but emblematic for a society that relied on psychic oppression. Leftists also believed that insanity had the potential to overcome the separations that rationality had imposed upon the world and hence to create a better and more emotional world. Activists from Heidelberg for example likened the atmosphere at a huge leftist congress in Bologna in February 1977 to a scene from the French-Italian film *Le Roi de Cœur* (*King of Hearts*) by Philipe de Broca.[90] In the film, 'the inmates of a mental institution [*Irrenhaus*] occupied a city for a couple of days and turned it, with a huge flow [*Riesenstrom*] of love, colour and fantasy, into a vastly comfortable home [*urgemütliches Domizil*]'. This was how the congress in Bologna felt: 'everywhere people danced, played, staged theatre plays, made sketches, people from all over Italy met again, greeted each other, total communication "ruled" and nothing else'.[91] Insanity might create, that is, what leftists longed for: the total collapse of all boundaries and separations, the merry chaos of a festival. Indeed, it was only logical that leftists celebrated the insane.

An example from the *Blatt* may finally illustrate how this fascination with insanity, children, and Native Americans was translated into political rhetoric and a utopian vision. The text is, to be sure, exceptional, and the 'desperate part of the [*Blatt's*] editorial team' noted 'with resignation' that they had failed to convince the author to write a text that was 'closer to reality'. But how would they convince an author who argued that 'reality is

---

[87] Anon., 'Wir rufen die Irren Europas'.

[88] Gérard Hof, *Hunde wollt ihr ewig sterben!?* (Munich: Trinkont Verlag, 1976). The French original: Gérard Hof, *Je ne serai plus psychiatre* (Paris: Stock, 1976).

[89] Kristine and Traubi, 'Hundeleben: Internationale der rasenden Narren', in *Das Blatt* 81, 12–25 November 1976, 21.

[90] Philipe de Broca, 'Le Roi de Cœur', (France: 1966).

[91] Panino, 'Der Kongress tanzt', in *Carlo Sponti* 38/39, November 1977, 14.

unreal and utopia is real'? Ostensibly, the text was a report about a cyclists' demonstration in Munich in July 1977. In the author's account, the demonstration began when a boring lecture about statistics was interrupted by a group of masked people who brought a model of a nuclear power plant into the lecture hall – and then the masked demonstrators just disappeared. Suddenly, the author found himself on an open, sunny square, with hundreds of bikers racing around him. 'A shrill Indian cry shook me to the bones. They were colourful, had trailers attached to their bikes: adventurous constructions wobbled in the head wind – a circus!' He felt insane. Finally, the demonstration moved into a subway tube, the author reported, but soon began to climb out of it again. 'When the people reach the open air, they are welcomed by the sun and dancing children – after a long captivity, they return to life as long-time forgotten [*längst Verschollene*].' After this event, the subway tube was closed and the city celebrated a magnificent festival – 'and since this day of the liberation of our era's pest no more clock was seen ... The machine never errs', the report ends.[92] The surreal and somewhat confused text was certainly not appreciated by everyone in Munich's leftist scene. Still, it captures the political visions of the radical left, its utopias, and its enemies. On the utopian (and, for this author, more real) side were dancing children, a circus, and 'Indian cries'; on the 'hostile' side, there was rationality in the form of a statistics lecture, dark subway tubes, and the order of time symbolized by clocks.

The 'mixtures of revolt' radical leftists like Röttgen and Rabe envisioned might look odd; yet, it made sense. In the struggle against an oppressive and fragmenting rationality, all those who were potentially not subdued by this male and adult rationality were welcome allies for the left: women, children, clans and tribes, the insane, perhaps even animals. They would tear down barriers and separations, they would dissolve them, or simply ridicule them. The way leftists composed the 'mixture of revolt' was not as arbitrary and unstructured as the practice of simply listing opponents of rationality might suggest. The opposition between the 'party of feelings and senses' and 'the party of rationality and alienation, as Herbert Röttgen put it,[93] was deeply structured by categories such as gender (female feelings against male rationality), age (childish feelings against an adult rationality), or 'civilization' ('savage' feelings against 'industrial' rationality). The

---

[92] Der Verfasser, 'Die Demonstration der lachenden Gesichter', in *Das Blatt* 99, 15–28 July 1977, 5–8.
[93] Röttgen, 'Kinderrevolution'.

constant rhetoric of dissolving boundaries notwithstanding, leftists created new boundaries and separations. As we will see, numerous leftists were remarkably well aware, and highly critical, of these new separations.

The Politics of Subjectivity

Reimagining politics as a struggle of feelings against the domination of rationality called for different political practices and had implications for the goal of doing politics. It was a new struggle that called for a new politics. 'Old' (and rational) politics sought to create a new order; the new politics of subjectivity, as leftists often called this politics, would dissolve any order. In a way, the distinction between 'old' and 'new' politics can be mapped onto the opposition between feelings and rationality that was so fundamental for leftist thinking. The authors of *Vulkantänze* for example contrasted the 'desire of power in the discourse of order' with the 'power of desire against the order of the discourse', a sentence 'probably written by Foucault', as they remarked. On the one side, which we might describe as the foundation of 'old politics', Röttgen and Rabe saw the 'will to power, the desire for domination, the joy of limiting others'. All 'emotional currents' long for power, they claimed. On the other hand, they saw the 'immense field of human desires: the desire for a multifaceted erotic, for quietness, for play, for sun, for nature – all of them limited and catalogued [*einmaziniert*] by the order of things'. And those encaged wishes long for expansion, not to gain power, but to destroy the order that prevents them from expanding. 'The power of desire against the desire for power.'[94] Creating a different order, the object of 'old politics', was thus anathema for the 'new politics' of the alternative left, which longed instead for a liberation of desires. Nor was the abolishment of want, the central object-ive of the old working-class movement, the goal of a new politics. Rather, Röttgen and Rabe conceived of want as a boundary 'that blocked the realization of our desires'. The 'revolution's sweet melody: *transgression, delimitation*' did not aim at abolishing all want, but at 'shrugging off all the wishes we are carrying inside us. Revolution, we proclaim solemnly, that means for us boiling over, exuding, bursting open as a cloud or thunderstorm, squandering rather than collecting, blowing up armours, melting barbed wire, tearing down fences – in short, excess [*sich verausgaben*].'[95]

[94] Röttgen and Rabe, *Vulkantänze*, 38–39.   [95] Ibid., 49–50. Emphasis in the original.

If perhaps somewhat opaquely, Röttgen and Rabe outlined the contours of the 'new politics', a term alternative leftists frequently used to distinguish their political project and practices from both the 'old left' and the dogmatic *K-Gruppen*. Activists and scholars have described this form of politics as a 'politics of the first person', meaning that 'individual and collective needs' provided the starting point. Issues that immediately affected everyday life in local contexts, for example relating to gender relations or the environment, became the subject of politics, scholars have noted.[96] Yet our understanding of this 'politics of the first person' remains incomplete unless the fundamental role of feelings is taken into account. This is shown at a 1976 congress of the alternative left in Frankfurt, where 'Spontis' and women reminded their audiences about the 'original motif' for the struggle against a 'wrong life', a motif that had been banned by the more dogmatic groups: 'the wish ... the production of desire, which, excluded and declared to be an enemy of work, is supposed to threaten anything it infests. We are no longer driven by hunger for food, but by hunger for freedom, love, fondness, and different ways of interaction [*Verkehrsformen*].'[97] It was not an 'abstract insight into the necessity of socialism', the antiauthoritarian magazine *Hundert Blumen* had argued already in 1973, but 'the experience of psychic misery' and the 'insight into the possibility of overcoming it' that provided the basis for politics. Under capitalist conditions, the desires for 'self-realization in harmony, free of fear and the pressure to perform' could not be fulfilled. Struggling against capitalism would thus be the only way out of this misery.[98] Along similar lines, the Berlin magazine *Traumstadt* explained in 1978 that the rhetoric of 'being immediately concerned [*unmittelbare Betroffenheit*]' had emphasized 'our emotionality as precondition and content of political activism'. Being able to empathize was therefore essential for politics.[99] 'Our own difficulties, problems and needs should be the point of origin for our political activism', rather than the abstract 'problems of society', an author named Caesar declared in the *Frankfurter Gemeine*.[100] The 'politics of the first person' was, then, not simply about issues of direct personal

---

[96] See for example Sebastian Haunss, *Identität in Bewegung: Prozesse kollektiver Identität bei den Autonomen und in der Schwulenbewegung* (Wiesbaden: Verlag für Sozialwissenschaften, 2004), 115. See also Reichardt, *Authentizität*, 55–56.

[97] Anon., 'Bericht über den Pflingstkongress'.

[98] Anon., 'Psychisches Elend und Politische Praxis' in *Hundert Blumen* 9, n.d., probably summer 1973, 6–7.

[99] Anon., 'Gedanken übers Zeitungsmachen', in *Traumstadt* 0, January 1978, 6–8.

[100] Caesar, 'Wer interessiert sich für *deine* Probleme – für *deine* Bedürfnisse?', in *Frankfurter Gemeine* 3/4, July/August 1972, 2.

concern for leftists. Rather, it was based on the assumption that individual desires were suppressed in capitalism, which is why those desires and needs became the ultimate foundation of alternative politics.

Making personal desires the foundation of politics collapsed the boundaries between the private and the political. As Chapter 1 has shown, radical leftists of the 1970s were not the first to question the separation of these spheres. In the 1970s, however, this blurring of the private and the political became a much more central aspect of leftist politics. Most famously, feminists declared that the 'personal is political'. Talking to each other about seemingly personal problems, such as income inequality in couples, in what were rather misleadingly, as American feminist Carol Hanisch stressed, called 'therapy groups', women realized that these were no personal problems, but 'political problems', which meant that they could not be solved individually, but only collectively.[101] Around Europe, women soon embraced this notion of politics and thus extended the 'boundaries of the political' by bringing issues such as sexuality, abortion, or appearance into the political arena.[102] Collapsing the boundaries between the personal and the political, and hence what could be discussed in political groups, did not remain limited to the women's movement. With an 'old understanding of politics', themes like 'love and marriage' had simply not belonged into political groups, the Göttingen *Politikon* remarked in 1974; now, 'relations' were a 'legitimate topic for discussion in political groups'.[103] At times, the demand for new politics caused conflicts. In 1973, a group of West Berlin teenagers rejected the politics of a communist youth organization that had wanted to keep a local youth club free of personal problems, which would only hinder political activism. The teenagers frequenting the youth club, however, refused to distinguish between political and personal problems, and considered the it a place were they could collectively deal with the full range of their issues. Making an argument reminiscent of Wilhelm Reich, they declared that 'all

[101] Carol Hanisch, 'The Personal is Political', in *Notes from the Second Year: Women's Liberation*, ed. Shulamit Firestone and Anne Koedt (New York: Radical Feminism, 1970).

[102] See only Maud Bracke, *Women and the Reinvention of the Political: Feminism in Italy, 1968–1983* (New York: Routledge, 2014); Anna Bull, Hanna Diamond, and Rosalind Marsh, eds., *Feminisms and Women's Movements in Contemporary Europe* (Basingstoke, UK: Macmillan, 2000); Kristina Schulz, *Der lange Atem der Provokation: Die Frauenbewegung in der Bundesrepublik und in Frankreich* (Frankfurt a.M.: Campus, 2002); Andrea Bührmann, *Das authentische Geschlecht: Die Sexualitätsdebatte der neuen Frauenbewegung und die Foucaultsche Machtanalyse* (Münster: Westfälisches Dampfboot, 1995).

[103] Redaktionskollektiv, 'Die Angst, die aus der Ware kam: Persönliche Emanzipation und politische Arbeit', in *Politikon* 45, probably fall 1974, 3–9, esp. 5.

problems', including problems with their living situation, with parents or their sexuality, were a result of the 'exploitation and oppression in this capitalist society'.[104]

Historians have frequently noted that this extension of the political was central for both the women's movement and the New Left more generally.[105] In the context of alternative leftists' struggle for the liberation of desires, however, the collapsing of the boundaries between the private and the political gained a different meaning. In Heidelberg, *Carlo Sponti*, too, criticized the 'distinction between a private and a political existence'. Discussing the 'production of relations' had become an important part of the 'political strategy and praxis', the paper noted. At stake were, as the Frankfurt group *Revolutionärer Kampf* had explained, the revolution of the 'ways of life [*Lebensverhältnisse*]', and the reorganization of 'the entire individual existence'. The way to achieve such a far-reaching program, and particularly the 'false distinction between private and political existence', would be the overcoming of the 'separation of work and sensuality'. The basis for this approach was, according to the Frankfurt Spontis, the 'rediscovery of fantasy as a productive force'.[106] For Spontis, the point of overcoming the 'false distinction' between the private and the political was, this final reference to 'fantasy as productive force' indicates, not simply to recognize that seemingly individual problems required a collective and hence political solution. Rather, they considered personal relations and private life to be inherently political because this was the sphere in which desires and feelings were suppressed, and hence where they might be liberated.

Engaging in emancipatory politics thus required a personal transformation that would allow people to recuperate their feelings and desires. Working on the self became inherently political. British feminist Cathy

---

[104] Anon., 'Der Kampf um das Jugendzentrum', in *Selber Machen: Zeitung des Schöneberger Jungarbeiter- und Schülerzentrums* 2, June 1973, 5–10, esp. 10.

[105] See for example Geoff Eley, 'Wie denken wir über die Politik?' Alltagsgeschichte und die Kategorie des Politischen', in *Alltagskultur, Subjektivität und Geschichte: Zur Theorie und Praxis von Alltagsgeschichte*, ed. Berliner Geschichtswerkstatt (Münster: Westphälisches Dampfboot, 1994); Belinda Davis, 'The Personal is Political: Gender, Politics, and Political Activism in Modern German History', in *Gendering Modern German History: Rewriting Historiography*, ed. Karen Hagemann and Jean H. Quataert (New York: Berghahn Books, 2007); Belinda Davis, 'What's Left? Popular and Democratic Political Participation in Postwar Europe', *American Historical Review* 113 (2008); Gassert, 'Narratives'; Reichardt, *Authentizität*, 140–144; Ursula Krechel, *Selbsterfahrung und Fremdbestimmung: Bericht aus der neuen Frauenbewegung* (Darmstadt, Neuwied: Luchterhand, 1975); Bührmann, *Geschlecht*.

[106] Mad, 'Kunscht, Kultur und die Linken (oder was will Jürgen Herlemann in der Peking-Oper?)', in *Carlo Sponti* 11/12, January/February 1975, 9–12.

Levine for example argued in a text the German anarchist magazine *Schwarze Protokolle* republished, that a simultaneous analysis of the 'inner-psychological chains and the external political structures and the relations between us' would be necessary to successfully challenge the enemy.[107] In his famous critique of violence, published in *Autonomie* in February 1977, later foreign minister Joschka Fischer similarly called upon his comrades to fight the 'inner cop'. The struggle against the 'orgy of violence called late capitalism' required, he argued, an 'immense sensibility for oppression'. Accomplishing this sensibility was itself a revolution against the 'huge monster, the capitalism inside me, my upbringing, my needs, my structures, sexuality, etc.', a monster that had to be defeated before a new sensibility could be realized. What Fischer called for here was an internalization of the political struggle. No longer would his comrades fight an external enemy, but the 'microscopic fascism' that had nested in the 'wishing machines' – a notably Foucauldian and Deleuzian terminology. This internalized struggle required new methods, Fischer argued, that would address the 'unconscious complicity with the established powers', with the 'internalized repression'.[108] Two months later, Uta Schatteburg wrote in the same magazine on 'structures of violence in ourselves'. She diagnosed a fear of change, which was 'experienced as a fear of losing the self'. For 'political-emancipatory activism' to be successful, however, this fear of change had to be overcome. 'Strengthening the subjectivity, strengthening the self and the ego' had thus not a merely 'therapeutic' meaning, but was an 'indispensable part of our political activism', she claimed. Crucially, such a strengthened subjectivity required a 'holistic perception' of both 'rational-verbal and emotional-sensual meanings'.[109] Just like Fischer, Schatteburg considered a personal and emotional transformation to be essential for political struggles.

This personal transformation also had an important bodily component. The 'alternatives' discovery' had included, Rädli wrote in the *Blatt*, 'experiments with the body, the liberation of desires [*Lüste*], pleasures and perceptions, the dismounting of the armour with which life protects itself from orgasms'.[110] Referring to Wilhelm Reich, David Burkhart claimed, also in the *Blatt*, that 'body armours [*Körperpanzer*]' are essential for

---

[107] Cathy Levine, 'Tyrannei der Tyrannei: Zur Strukturlosigkeit in Frauengruppen', in *Schwarze Protokolle* 12, November 1975, 29–32; first published in *Black Rose* 1, fall 1974.
[108] Fischer, 'Vorstoß in "primitivere" Zeiten', 56–57.
[109] Uta Schatteburg, 'Gewaltstrukturen in uns', in *Autonomie: Materialien gegen die Fabrikgesellschaft* 6, April 1977, 10–14.
[110] Rädli, '[Title illegible]', in *Das Blatt* 111, 23 December 1977–12 January 1978, 24.

keeping capitalism alive. Under capitalism, he wrote, people are fundamentally alienated 'from their deepest wishes and longings, from anything living, from the cosmos and their own bodies'. Liberation would hence mean 'getting in contact with the body'. For these reasons, Burkhart argued that an interest in the 'bioenergetic state' of the body, a concept he took from Reich, is never apolitical.[111] To re-establish a different relation with the body, leftists wanted to abolish the 'internalized domination of the mind over the body and senses', as Michael Hiltl observed in a sociology seminar paper about the alternative movement that was republished by *Ulcus Molle* in January 1981. Discovering one's own 'inner world means overcoming the alienation of oneself and, in a social context, [the alienation] of others, it means the rediscovery of a natural sensibility beyond the realm of the sexual'. Dreams, fantasies, and desires would provide guidance on this way.[112]

The 'new politics' radical leftists claimed to develop also differed from 'old politics' with regards to what it could achieve. Typically, alternative leftists refused to formulate any utopian visions for a distant future. Rather, the politics they imagined had a disruptive and transgressive potential in the present. The *Metropolitan Women*, for example, cautioned women not to look for niches as 'places of withdrawal and regression, where the myth of female irrationality might find its place'. Instead, niches should become 'spaces of liberation' whose boundaries had to be 'blown up in the process of transgression. Then they will turn into the house of cheerfulness [*Haus des Heiteren*].'[113] It was not a new social order the *Metropolitan Women* longed for, but constant disruptions. In Hamburg, the *Subrealists*, a situationist inspired group, contrasted labour, the 'core of [mere] survival', with playing, which would facilitate the 'realization of human beings outside commodity structures'. Unlike the 'conditioning techniques' of capitalism that 'destroy the playing attitude of humans' and yield a 'stabilization of stagnancy [*Stillstand*]', the 'revolutionary play of desire' the *Subrealists* called for knew no boundaries; it would be characterized by never-ending 'discovery and adventure'.[114] Along similar lines, author and imprisoned terrorist Peter-Paul Zahl called his fellow leftists to 'respect the old values' again: 'dancing, singing, playing, idleness'.[115]

[111] David Burkhart, 'Wilhelm Reich und die Befreiung', in *Das Blatt* 98, 1–14 July 1977, 15.
[112] Michael Hiltl, 'Soziale Beziehungen in der Alternativbewegung', in *Ulcus Molle*, January 1981, 4–20.
[113] Metropolitan Women, 'Der Himmel ist auf die Erde gefallen'.
[114] 'Definition der Subrealisten', in *Revolte* 15/16, June 1976, 53–55.
[115] Peter-Paul Zahl, 'Nieder mit der Arbeit', in *Info BUG* 130, 1 November 1976, 8–9.

Festivities were occasions par excellence for reinvigorating these values. In *Vulkantänze*, Röttgen and Rabe described them as moments when 'groups, genders and classes that live separately in everyday life establish numerous ties, interweave and interlock, until the state of voluptuousness of communion, of homosexuality, of incest. All and any compulsiveness and efficiency thinking is melted away in a foaming and vibrating mixing pot.' And once the passions turned so intense that they could only be satisfied with violence, a feast might turn into revolution. 'All great rebellions were less strategy, tactics, agitation, organization – they were above all a mass feast, a ball of the devil that made all normalcies dance, a cornucopia of feelings.'[116] No doubt, these are exceptional texts even within the radical left. Nevertheless, the rhetoric of blown-up boundaries, adventures, and vibrating festivities suggests what was at the core of the 'new politics': individually or collectively recuperated feelings and desires that would disrupt the strict categorizations of a rational society.

The search for constant disruptions also points to the peculiar temporality of alternative politics. Rejecting a revolutionary idealism according to which the 'realm of freedom' would come only after a revolution, alternative leftists wanted to start changing life 'here and now'. Historians Sven Reichardt and Detlef Siegfried for example note that alternative leftists wanted to 'practically experiment with socialist ways of living here and now', rather than merely theoretically anticipating them. In countless projects, ranging from urban and rural communes to self-managed shops, alternative leftists attempted to realize visions of a non-alienated and emancipated life in the present.[117] The focus on the 'here and now' was indeed central for leftists. Thomas Schmid for example wrote in Frankfurt-based *diskus* that 'the strength of revolutionary movements is that they do not allow themselves to be put off [*vertrösten lassen*], that they struggle for emancipation today, that they begin to leave the limits of the social forces of domination [*gesellschaftliche Herrschaftsinstrumente*] behind by developing a new form of living'.[118] Along similar lines, an author for the *Info BUG* defined undogmatic leftist politics as 'becoming subjects of history' already 'today, and not only after a revolution'.[119] And in the *Blatt*, Rädli argued that 'we want freedom here and now.

---

[116] Röttgen and Rabe, *Vulkantänze*, 113–114.
[117] Sven Reichardt and Detlef Siegfried, 'Das Alternative Milieu: Konturen einer Lebensform', in *Das Alternative Milieu: Antibürgerlicher Lebensstil und linke Politik in der Bundesrepublik Deutschland und Europa 1968–1983*, ed. Sven Reichardt and Detlef Siegfried (Göttingen: Wallstein, 2010), 23.
[118] Thomas Schmid, 'Phantasie statt Selbstrepression', in *Diskussion* 4, 2 June 1976, 10–15.
[119] 'Was ist undogmatisch? (Leserbrief)', in *Info BUG* 7, 21 April 1974, 12–13.

Politics is only a belief in the future, shit. We want to live, not tomorrow or the day after, but *today*.'[120] This demand to 'revolutionize the everyday *here and now*' also distinguished the alternative left from the dogmatic *K-Gruppen*, who would maintain their 'bourgeois forms of relation [*Verkehrsformen*]' until 'day X' of the revolution, as Michael Hiltl wrote in *Ulcus Molle*.[121]

This radical presentism was intimately tied to the leftist politics of subjectivity. According to Schmid, the crucial 'quality' and 'strength' of a 'new politics' would be the 'consistent [*konsequent*] unfolding of subjectivity' here and now.[122] In a situation in which subjectivity was, according to leftists, suppressed, the very expression of it was both subversive and anticipating a better life. Rädli pushed this presentism even further. Alternative 'discoveries', 'experiments with the body, liberation of desires, pleasures and sensations, slashing of armours with which life protects itself of orgasms', all this helped alternatives to 'live in a different time, in a dimension without history, in the absoluteness of the present'. Alternative leftists, the rhetoric indicates, did not merely try to live an 'emancipated life' already in the present. Rather, the subjective politics of the radical left were, so to speak, a politics against history itself. As Rädli wrote: 'Long live the body of humankind and of earth [*des Menschen und der Erde*], since it eludes the merciless machinery of history. Wishes are timeless, feeling has no history. If society stands at the abyss, only dancing against the grain of time will help.'[123]

Since leftists conceived of politics as a struggle for the 'liberation' of subjective feelings and desires, or, more precisely, a struggle of feelings and desires for their liberation, they regarded any expression of feelings as inherently political. Developing a more emotional language, something already envisioned by Raoul Vaneigm, was a crucial aspect of this. Röttgen and Rabe, for example, called for a more 'sensual' language that would use concepts referring to the body and senses: 'cooking one's ears instead of being attentive'; 'to drool rather than to lust'; 'to swallow rather than to repress' – 'a more than small gesture, but also an element in the great struggle for the recapture of our senses'.[124] Along these lines, though in strikingly abstract terms, an author for *Info BUG* urged his comrades to use a 'genuinely subjective language' that would be able to convey 'lived emotions'.[125] Another author for *'s Blättle* from Stuttgart argued that

---

[120] Rädli, '[Title illegible]'.   [121] Hiltl, 'Steppenwolf'.   [122] Schmid, 'Phantasie'.
[123] Rädli, '[Title illegible]'.   [124] Röttgen and Rabe, *Vulkantänze*, 55–56.
[125] Anon., 'Subjektiver Faktor Sprache', in *Info BUG* 43, 3 February 1975, 12–13.

talking about feelings of strength at a demonstration, rather than providing an intellectual and rational analysis of the political situation, was politically valuable, as it helped breaking through the 'exterior layer of our personality armour'.[126] Similarly, a woman writing for *Lesbenpresse* from West Berlin claimed that talking to other women and learning about 'our preferences and our fears' was genuinely 'doing politics', while 'abstractly theorizing' was not.[127] And talking about feelings was not all that could be subversive in a world supposedly hostile to feelings. Already in 1971, a 'rural commune' from Kucha, close to Nuremberg, under the informal leadership of Raymond Martin, had for example stated: 'If we become happy, that's already revolutionary.' And thus they ran barefoot over the grass to bodily feel this happiness.[128] For the same reason, leftists considered street festivals that helped people overcome their isolation to be politically meaningful.[129] Indeed, any way of acting out 'wishes, demands and fantasies' that could bring activists in conflict with the 'moral boundaries' of society equally attained a political meaning, as Roger Dewald suggested in the *Andere Zeitung*.[130] Chapter 4 examines more closely what leftists did to 'find' feelings they missed so desperately. For now, the important point is that expressing feelings and creating emotionally charged moments was an essential aspect of the 'new politics' leftists propagated.

Scholars have frequently noted an extension of the political sphere into the private during the 1970s, within and beyond the radical left.[131] The feminist slogan that the 'personal is political' perhaps captures this extension best. But the extension was not limited to feminism. Discussing the alternative milieu, Sven Reichardt for example considers the 'subjectivation of the meaning of revolution [*Subjektivierung des Revolutionsverständnisses*] a delimitation [*Entgrenzung*] of the political that encroached on the private sphere and regulated it'.[132] To fully understand this, I propose, we need to place it into the context of leftists' reimagination of the political. Alternative leftists did not simply extend the boundaries of the political into the

---

[126] Dietmar Seeber, 'Die Poesie an die Macht! (Leserbrief)', in *'s Blättle* 23, December 1977/January 1978, 17.

[127] Anon., 'Frauenfest-Lesbenfrust, Lesbenfest-Frauenfrust. Frauenfeste in Heidelberg und Münster', in *Lesbenpresse* 3/1976, 2–3.

[128] Anon., 'Visionen der Freiheit', in *Päng* 4, probably spring 1971, 2.

[129] Anon., 'Bericht über den Pflingstkongress'.

[130] Roger Dewald, 'Leserbrief', in *Die Andere Zeitung* 13, March 1977, 11. The letter was a response to Gaby Weber, 'Der Tanz der Bedürfnisse', in *Die Andere Zeitung* 12, February 1977, 4–5.

[131] See, in addition to the literature already cited, Bernd Faulenbach, 'Die Siebziger Jahre – ein sozialdemokratisches Jahrzehnt?', *Archiv für Sozialgeschichte* 44 (2004): 14–21.

[132] Reichardt, *Authentizität*, 103.

private sphere, but radically re-conceptualized what doing politics was about: it was a struggle for the liberation of feelings in a society dominated by rationality. Only from this perspective of the fundamental reinterpretation of the political does the deep concern with the body, sexuality, personal relations, and feelings within the alternative left make sense. Since the very act of expressing feelings or 'acting out wishes' was inherently political in the sense that it challenged the domination of rationality, the transformation of personal relations had to start *here and now*; otherwise, the governing laws of reason would never be questioned. This understanding of a 'new politics' also distinguished alternative leftists, as they repeatedly stressed, from the dogmatic *K-Gruppen* that had emerged in the early 1970s.[133] Dogmatic groups, alternative leftists criticized, were still clinging to an 'old' understanding of politics in which emotions had no place and which did not address the (emotional) suffering here and now, but merely waited for the day of a final revolution. Tellingly, *Carlo Sponti* bemoaned that Wilhelm Reich had been banned from the German left for a second time when the various small communist parties and groups, such as the Kommunistischer Bund Westdeutschland (KBW), the Deutsche Kommunistische Partei (DKP) or Kommunistische Partei Deutschland (KPD), emerged in the early 1970s.[134]

Depoliticization and Affirmation: Critical Voices

The vision of a 'new politics', a politics that would struggle for the liberation of feelings, for the acting out of dreams, wishes, and desires, for different forms of personal interaction here and now, did not remain uncontested. Within the left, *K-Gruppen* were, not surprisingly, appalled by alternative leftists' politics of feelings and their 'undisciplined' lifestyles. Long hair and short skirts would only, they argued, alienate students from the working class.[135] Yet at times quite sophisticated critiques of the new 'politics of the first person' and the 'mystification' of feelings, desires, or insanity were also formulated within the alternative left. Frequently, those who conceptually grasped the 'new politics' most clearly were also most critical about it. It is debatable whether individual critics like Wolfgang Kraushaar or groups like the feminist *Militante Panthertanten* were themselves part of the alternative left, a claim they might have refuted given how

---

[133] Hild, 'Steppenwolf'.
[134] Redaktion Carlo Sponti, 'Vorwort', in *Carlo Sponti* 26/26, January 1977, 1–4.
[135] See Reichardt, *Authentizität*, 130–133.

harshly they criticized alternative politics. Yet their critiques were often published by alternative papers, and they were debated within the alternative left, which distinguishes them from the critiques of the *K-Gruppen*, which were usually just mocked.

Broadly speaking, two different lines of critique can be identified, even though they often intersected. First, and perhaps most commonly, activists questioned how 'political' the 'new politics' with its focus on 'psychically changing the self [*psychische Selbstveränderung*]' really was.[136] Rather than changing the social structures of capitalism, the search for feelings could be integrated into capitalism, critics worried. While this line of critique questioned the premise of grounding politics on individual desires and their fulfilment, a second line of critique addressed leftists' fascination with transgressions and dissolutions. On the one hand, critics pointed out that the celebration of feelings and the condemnation of rationality only introduced new separations instead of overcoming them. On the other hand, some authors noted the destructive potential of the dissolution of subjectivities. Ultimately, they worried that the focus on feelings would, far from liberating them, only create new internalized norms, indeed a constant concern that we encounter in the following chapters as well.

One of the most sophisticated and certainly most prominent critiques of alternative politics was formulated by Wolfgang Kraushaar, prominent leftist in Frankfurt and editor for the left-wing publisher *Verlag Neue Kritik*. Notably, Kraushaar published his 'Theses on the Relationship between Alternative and Escape Movement' in a volume, edited by himself, on 'Controversies about the Alternative Movement', which also included contributions by prominent members of the alternative left such as Bernd Leineweber or Thomas Schmid, a frequent writer for *Pflasterstrand* and *Autonomie*. Kraushaar's critique should thus not be conflated with *K-Gruppen* polemics, not least because he criticized those groups at least as harshly as he criticized the 'alternative movement'.[137] His theses provide an extremely insightful analysis of the alternative left. Situating the alternative left in the post-1968 history of the West German left, Kraushaar engages with both the (in his view deeply problematic) implications of the alternative 'politics of the first person', and the practical difficulties and informal hierarchies within the scene. He keenly observed a

---

[136] Wolfgang Kraushaar, 'Thesen zum Verhältnis von Alternativ- und Fluchtbewegung: Am Beispiel der frankfurter scene', in *Autonomie oder Ghetto? Kontroversen über die Alternativbewegung*, ed. Wolfgang Kraushaar (Frankfurt a.M.: Verlag Neue Kritik, 1978), 36.

[137] On Kraushaar's critique see also Reichardt, *Authentizität*, 128–130.

number of oppositions that shaped the alternative left: 'consciousness – insanity'; 'struggle – life'; 'rationality – emotionality'; 'intellect – fantasy', to name a few. Yet none of these binaries would adequately describe what happened within the 'New Left': 'No longer social, but rather natural grounds are meant to vouch for an emancipatory process that could not be accomplished in a political struggle. [*Nicht mehr gesellschaftliche, sondern natürliche Gründe sollen einen Befreiungsprozess verbürgen, der im politischen Kampf nicht auszustehen war.*]'[138] Focusing on 'changing the self', alternative leftists imagined, Kraushaar argued, 'a sort of identity in the natural state', which could be recovered. Yet this natural self did not exist; it was always already social.[139] The fundamental problem of the alternative left and its 'politics of the first person' was thus that it ceased to 'negate the existing social relations' of capitalism in favour of merely working on the self, which would not 'subvert existing social relations', but only contribute to a social pacification.[140]

Kraushaar was not alone with his criticism that the alternative left ignored the 'real' social conditions of capitalism and thus failed to engage in serious politics. An author for *Info BUG* mocked the 'demand for immediate happiness, the refusal of any abstinence', which made activists unwilling to undertake any necessary but unpleasant tasks. Worrying about their personal happiness, leftists, the author charged, 'persistently overlooked the conditions for politics in capitalism, understood as an intervention into social relations'.[141] Trying to realize their 'dreams of a human relations free of fear', Lothar Hildebrandt wrote for the *Blatt*, alternatives created islands 'in the midst of roaring capitalism', islands 'where millet blossoms and a fondness not deformed by any repression [reigns]'. The problem with the creation of such islands, however, was, Hildebrandt argued, that activists no longer addressed the social conditions that made the realization of such dreams within society impossible. As long as the struggle for a better, personal life here and now would not include a struggle against those social relations that required people to engage in this 'unwanted struggle', it would remain a mere appeal to the world: 'please let us live that way ...'[142] Similarly, a participant in a discussion in *Pflasterstrand* after the TUNIX Congress of February 1978 bemoaned that people only talked about their 'inner insanity' and the 'abstract, internalized

---

[138] Kraushaar, 'Thesen', 47–48.   [139] Ibid., 36.   [140] Ibid., 30.
[141] 'Wir wollen alles, aber umsonst', in *Info BUG* 37, 16 December 1974, 6.
[142] Lothar Hildebrandt, 'Liebe allein genügt nicht', in *Das Blatt* 75, 30 July–18 August 1976, 18. The text was reprinted in *Info BUG* 117, 10 August 1976, 6.

power' that needed to be grasped, but no longer engaged in a critique of the social relations that produced this insanity.[143] In the women's movement, finally, an author for the Berlin *Lesbenpresse* criticized women's fascination with astrology, not only because it imposed another kind of categories on women, in that sense resembling 'male' psychology, but also because the 'new territory' of astrology was 'innocuous, politically irrelevant, and lacked any realistic relation to the contemporary world'.[144] In all corners of the alternative movement, critics worried that being preoccupied with the self, activists might retreat from the world, but no longer seek to change it. Real politics, they argued, required an intervention into the 'real' social relations of capitalism.

In the worst case, this search for authentic and spontaneous feelings could easily become part of capitalist exploitation, some critics worried. For example, Wolfgang Kraushaar wondered how leftists could still call themselves 'Spontis' after 'spontaneous purchase' had become a 'central category for the work of department store psychologists'.[145] In *Ulcus Molle*, Rainer Klassen noted the 'commercialization' of 'subjective experience'. 'Inwardness, body consciousness, nutrition, mystic, and most recently even: alternatives' all became economically profitable trends.[146] A few months later, Gerhard Fuchs observed, also in *Ulcus Molle*, how 'highly paid trainers' benefited from the number of frustrated activists who hoped to find salvation in one of the many psycho groups.[147] With their search for feelings, leftists contributed to a depoliticization, these critics suggested, that ultimately strengthened capitalism rather than weakening it.[148]

While this line of inner-leftist critique blamed the focus on feelings for losing sight of real politics and the struggle against capitalism, another line of critique argued that by celebrating feelings and condemning reason, leftists only reconfirmed the very categories they sought to challenge. Critical reactions to Deleuze and Guattari's *Rhizome* and its enthusiastic reception in the theoretically inclined sections of the alternative left provide a case in point for this critique. As we have seen, leftists were fascinated by the subversive implications of Deleuze and Guattari's work. Like a rhizome, they hoped to undermine the categories of reigning

---

[143] 'Diskussion über TUNIX, von deutschen und ausländischen Genossen', in *Pflasterstrand* 29, 4–17 May 1978, 23–25.
[144] Anette, 'Ich bin Zwilling – Und wie geht's dir?', in *Lesbenpresse* 7, 1979, 24.
[145] Kraushaar, 'Thesen', 27.   [146] Klassen, 'Aphorismus'.   [147] Fuchs, 'Alternativbewegung'.
[148] On politicizing and depoliticizing tendencies, see Maik Tändler, *Das therapeutische Jahrzehnt: Der Psychoboom in den siebziger Jahren* (Göttingen: Wallstein, 2016), 177–185.

rationality. But not all leftists shared this enthusiasm. In what was ostensibly a critique of Christiane Matties's article in *Konkursbuch*, discussed earlier in the chapter, the *Metropolitan Women* from Frankfurt effectively formulated a critique of 'French theory gurus'. While Matties sought to distance herself from the male 'war machine' of Deleuze and Guattari, she simply replaced this machine with a female 'desiring machine and war machine', the *Metropolitan Women* pointed out. Her rhetoric of destruction was ultimately nothing but a 'totalitarian fantasy of violence that left no space for the diversity of feelings and thoughts'. In the world of (female) 'amoebae' that Matties imagined might break the power of the categorizing (male) war machine, human beings ceased to exist. What seems to be a critique of a fairly obscure text by Matties had important implications to which the *Metropolitan Women* only alluded in a footnote on the rhizome, which they described as a return to an age of 'pure biology'. And while the French might dispense with the subject, the Germans could not, lest 'we [Germans] become fascists'.[149]

Other leftists criticized 'French theorists' in less polemical terms, but for similar reasons. Günter Pütz, author of the Frankfurt *diskus*, for example, claimed that the theories of Foucault, Deleuze and Guattari were popular within the West German left because their thoughts encountered a milieu that had effectively accepted the 'violent loss of personality'.[150] The theoretical attack against the 'bourgeois subject' thus matched, as Alex Schubert put it in *diskus* as well, the real dissolution of subjectivities in the alternative left.[151] Yet, whereas Foucault and Deleuze sanctioned this dissolution, according to Pütz at least, he himself bemoaned it. Without memories that are structured by reason, subjects (in the emphatic, bourgeois sense) dissolve and are no longer able to ground their resistance on actual experience, Pütz claimed. In this scenario, language loses its power because everything it has to say resembles 'the consternation [*Betroffenheit*] of the precursor and the shit of the latecomer'.[152] Röttgen and Rabe, who clearly drew on Deleuze and Guattari, faced similar criticisms. In a review for the *Blatt*, G. Rossi remarked that only myths 'below or above any critique' remained. But given that there were no grounds for any genuine

---

[149] Metropolitan Women, 'Last Picture Show einer "Feministin"', in *Autonomie: Materialien gegen die Fabrikgesellschaft* 13, January 1979, 60–63.

[150] Günter Pütz, 'Die Puppe zerschlägt die Puppe, um endlich ihre Vorrechte als ein Ding unter Dingen in Anspruch nehmen zu können', in *Diskus* 3/4, 1978, 10–14.

[151] Alex Schubert, 'Identität ist die Urform der Ideologie', in *Diskus* 5/6, 1978, 32–35.

[152] Pütz, 'Die Puppe'.

critique, it became impossible to really distinguish – a critique that was, as we have seen, not entirely adequate.[153] Whereas many alternative leftists hoped that feelings, desires, and dreams might disrupt the monotony of reason and thus yield a more diverse and colourful world, these critics saw the opposite happening: instead of colourful dreams, the dispensation of rationality and the dissolution of stable subjects would only result in indistinguishable amoebae.

Rather than undermining power, critics argued that the one-sided celebration of feelings would only consolidate it. Whereas most alternative leftists associated the capitalist system with rationality and hoped for the emancipatory power of feelings, critics argued that the very separation of rationality and emotionality was part of the system. In a debate in *Pflasterstrand* about the TUNIX Congress of February 1978, to be ana-lysed in more detail in Chapter 5, an anonymous discussant argued that 'simple antinomies' had replaced any theory: 'norms – transgressions, normality – insanity'. In this way of thinking, the 'existing system' was declared 'rational', which is why 'irrationality' seemed to be 'the only possible grounding for a revolt'. From the discussant's perspective, this 'unquestioning focus on irrationality' was extremely dangerous, as it failed to see that both the 'alienated rationality and the chaotic irrationality' were connected and part of a system. Thus, not only rationality, but also irrationality needed to be questioned.[154] The feminist *Panthertanten*, who polemicized against the anti-intellectualism and the norms of emotionality in the women's movement, similarly argued that the 'duality [of rationality and emotionality] is itself the result of social relations [*gesellschaftlicher Verhältnisse*]' that are characterized, on the one hand, by a 'scientific pro-duction hostile to experience [*erfahrungsfeindliche Wissenschaftsproduktion*] that contains an independent concept of rationality [*verselbstständigten Rationalitätsbegriff*]', and on the other hand by an understanding of emotionality as an 'irrational structure of desires, subject to mere feelings [*eine unrationale, dem bloßen Gefühl ergebene Bedürfnisstruktur*]'. Without further defining it, they thus called for a 'female intellectuality', which, however, did not yet exist as a 'social practice'. It would require 'overcoming [*Aufhebung*]' the 'duality of rationality and emotionality' in a way that would not perpetuate it, that is, by prescribing people how they should be. By 'willingly disposing of the mind', women, the *Panthertanten* charged, were

---

[153] G. Rossi, 'Der Tanz um einen erloschenen Vulkan', in *Das Blatt* 123, 23 June–6 July 1978, 25.
[154] 'Diskussion über TUNIX'.

ultimately just following men's ideas of emancipation.[155] And in *Schwarze Botin*, a feminist magazine that was one of the first to critically discuss the work of Michel Foucault in Germany, Gabriele Goettle criticized the 'separation of reason and feelings and their attribution as "male" and "female"' within the women's movement.[156] Critics like Goettle, the *Panthertanten*, or the anonymous discussant in *Pflasterstrand*, were certainly a minority in the alternative left. Yet they noticed an important paradox: while leftists typically wanted to overcome strict boundaries and categories, they effectively introduced new antinomies and separations.

This separation was not only problematic, leftists argued, because it reproduced a duality that was fundamental for the existing social order, but also because it split individuals and prevented them from being 'whole'. Questioning the fascination with psychotherapies, an issue to be discussed in more detail in Chapter 4, Jörg Bopp, a social psychologist in Heidelberg, remarked that 'emotional outbreaks gain the dignity of religious conversion experiences'. What was missing amidst all the 'dazzling and contradictory' emotionality, however, was a 'rational working-through' of the emotional experiences. 'Emotionality and intellect are not integrated.' Ultimately, Bopp worried, this 'aversion to criticism' might lead to new authoritarian and even fascist characters.[157] Helmuth Loeven, editor of one of the earliest alternative magazines *Der Metzger*, saw a similar problem in the women's movement. When a woman told him during a discussion of his articles criticizing the woman's movement that he had apparently 'thought about all this very thoroughly', it dawned on him that this was a critique. What mattered, from her perspective, was 'her (female) emotionality', and not rationality. But this separation of thinking and feeling was exactly, Loeven argued, the basis for social domination. Loeven insisted, 'I exist only once, and completely. I don't exist once as head, and once as rump, once as reason and once as feeling. [*Ich existiere nur einmal, und zwar vollständig. Ich existiere nicht einmal als Kopf und einmal als Rumpf, nicht einmal als Verstand und einmal als Gefühl.*]'[158] A year later, he reiterated the point in *Ulcus Molle*: 'All aspects of human life, that is the intellect

[155] Die Panthertanten, 'Neue Weiblichkeit in der Frauenbewegung?'
[156] Gabriele Goettle, 'Gedanken über mögliche Formen feministischer Anarchie', in *Schwarze Botin* 7, April 1978, 31–34.
[157] Jörg Bopp, 'Auf der Jagd nach dem kleinen Glück', in *Carlo Sponti* 32/33, probably spring 1977, 13.
[158] Helmut Loeven, 'Editorial', in *Der Metzger* 30, January 1979, 13–14.

(=intelligence) *and* reason (=ratio) *and* feeling (=emotion) definitely have to be complete. Only as a wholeness are humans alive, feeling, and happy.'[159] Interestingly, these critics shared the goal with those who celebrated feelings: they all wanted to overcome categorical separations. But for critics like Bopp and Loeven, this meant emotions and the intellect had to be integrated, rather than played off against each other.

Critics of the one-sided celebration of feelings and irrationality were, it seems (there are, of course, no statistics in this matter), a minority within the alternative left. Yet they deserve our attention. For once, any discussion of the alternative left that does not emphasize how contested the 'politics of feelings' were, would remain incomplete and inadequate. It would provide a monolithic and simplified portrayal of the alternative left. More importantly, such criticisms from within the alternative left indicate an acute awareness of the blind spots in the search for a transgressive diversity. The sharp and sophisticated arguments by the *Metropolitan Women* and the *Panthertanten* are particularly revealing in this regard, since they shared a longing for a 'diversity of feelings and thoughts', but understood that the 'domesticated emotionality' only yielded a different kind of one-dimensionality. And this was not only of theoretical importance. Leftists understood that 'spontaneity and collective fondness [*Zärtlichkeit*]' could not be 'prescribed', as happened all too often.[160] The search for individual emancipation produced (internalized) norms and prescriptions, as Sven Reichardt stresses;[161] remarkably, alternative leftists frequently knew this. Throughout this book, we can observe this simultaneity of internalized restrictions, and critiques of those. Indeed, the very longing for spontaneity, for genuine feelings and their free expression made it imperative to be constantly aware of new restrictions that might limit this freedom, of the separations that needed to be questioned. Far from being a coherent program, the 'new politics' of the alternative left was, both in its theoretical and practical dimensions, contested and full of potential contradictions.

---

[159] Helmut Loeven, 'Der ideale Mensch wäre das Thermometer', in *Ulcus Molle* 5/6, 1980, 77–79. See also Lina Ganowski, 'Ausfallserscheinungen: Vulgärfeminismus und Vulgärpazifismus', in *Ulcus Molle* 7/8, 1981, 20–21.

[160] Redaktionskollektiv, 'Die Angst, die aus der Ware kam: Persönliche Emanzipation und politische Arbeit', in *Politikon* 45, probably fall 1974, 3–9, esp. 5. See also Mad, 'Kunscht, Kultur und die Linken'.

[161] Reichardt, *Authentizität*, 71.

Conclusion

Alternative leftists developed an understanding of politics that can hardly be grasped in terms of conventional assumptions about democracy. Their 'new politics' was a struggle against the categorizing and hence restrictive powers of rationality. Feelings, dreams, and desires that had the potential to disrupt these categories were the weapons of choice for alternative leftists in this struggle against a rational world. Conceiving of alternative politics as a struggle for 'participatory democracy' and 'radical egalitarianism' in all spheres of life thus misses the crucial shift in leftist thinking about power and challenges to power.[162] Alternative leftists did not simply struggle against all kinds of authority, but very specifically against the authority of rationality. Understanding this political project of the alternative left helps us making sense of some crucial developments within the radical left. Intimate relations, for example, gained political significance because they were a central place where new feelings could be developed to challenge the domination of rationality. This perspective also sheds a different light on radical leftists' turn against terrorist violence in the late 1970s. Texts that indicate such a shift, such as Joschka Fischer's *Vorstoß in 'primitivere' Zeiten*, the Frankfurt women's *Manifesto for the Invention of Happiness*, or the invitation to the TUNIX Congress, must be read against this background.[163] Fischer renounced violence not because he had turned into a pacifist. Rather, he identified with the children and women who had the fantasy that male militants lacked; to develop this fantasy, overcoming one's 'internalized fascism', or violence, was first and foremost necessary. Similarly, the women's call for the invention of happiness makes sense only as part of a broader discourse that celebrated feelings and disorder.

Beneath the project of a 'new politics' was an understanding of power that dramatically differed from the understandings of power in the 'old' left. Whereas the 'old' left had thought about power in terms of capitalist exploitation of the working class, alternative leftists turned their gaze on how capitalism and capitalist rationality shaped and deformed the subject and its feelings. For alternative leftists, power manifested itself in the most intimate situations. Developing different, more emotional and sensual relations to themselves and their own bodies, to others and the world thus became a central *political* goal for leftists. Leftists, as it were, internalized

---

[162] For such an argument, see Brown, *West Germany*, 371.
[163] For a different reading of these texts, see Hanshew, *Terror and Democracy in West Germany*, 203–204, 239–240.

the political struggle, a move perhaps best exemplified by Joschka Fischer's critique of violence. But by internalizing the political struggle in an attempt to 'liberate' feelings and desires, leftists also produced new, internalized norms and regulations – something leftists were remarkably well aware (and critical) of, as the following chapters discuss. Leftists' search for ever-new destabilizations ultimately also required the questioning of those newly self-imposed boundaries. This concern with internalized power puts contemporary scholarship on the radical left in a noteworthy position. The Foucauldian argument that the 'freely chosen self-thematization culture' of the left was not only liberating, but also forced activists to problematize the self, builds on the very understanding of power that radical leftists of the 1970s, themselves referring to Foucault, developed. Indeed, leftists' search for authenticity had, as Reichardt notes, 'romantic, nostalgic, totalitarian or illusionary' effects; but leftists knew that.[164]

---

[164] Reichardt, *Authentizität*, 71.

CHAPTER 3

The Emotional Misery of Capitalism

In February 1980, the West Berlin magazine *radikal* published a lengthy article about 'thoughts before and while staying at a bar', written by an anonymous male author who signed his article simply as '6(ma)'.[1] The man was apparently deeply involved in the alternative scene. He worked in a 'self-managed' company and lived in a communal apartment (*Wohngemeinschaft*). But life was bad. Even 'self-organized work is not always fun', he wrote. There were days with nothing but 'frustration, stress, trouble.' And the situation at his *Wohngemeinschaft* wasn't any better. He longed for meaningful relationships with his roommates, but his hopes were in vain; after all, he had already decided to move out. One night, he finally told his roommates. It made him feel relieved, but that feeling lasted only for a short moment. Usually, he went to a bar around the corner in such moments of misery, he wrote, no matter whether he hoped to meet some acquaintances or not: it couldn't get worse than staying at home. But that day, he wanted to stay home and write about this feeling of 'big emptiness', or to read a psychological text. The situation reminded him of Dieter Duhm and his work on fear, which had been widely discussed in the radical left during the early 1970s. But 6(ma) hadn't even read the book ('Fear in Capitalism'), as he freely admitted. Nor had he read another popular book, Horst-Eberhardt Richter's 'Escaping or Resisting'. 'I know little, but I sense everything.'[2]

Going to a bar for a drink, which is what 6(ma) usually did in such miserable situations, did not solve his problems either. For some brief ten minutes, the open atmosphere at the bar could cheer him up, but soon enough the openness revealed itself to be nothing but a 'psychological

---

[1] 6(ma), 'Gedanken vor und während eines Kneipenbesuchs', in *radikal* 75, 2–21 February 1980, 14.

[2] Dieter Duhm, *Angst im Kapitalismus: Zweiter Versuch der gesellschaftlichen Begründung zwischenmenschlicher Angst in der kapitalistischen Warengesellschaft* (Lampertheim: Kübler, 1973); Horst-Eberhardt Richter, *Flüchten oder Standhalten* (Reinbek bei Hamburg: Rowohlt, 1976).

setting'. 'Everyone, or at least the majority of those present don't show themselves as they really are.' Since he didn't show his true self either, it was easy for him to read the 'coolness in the faces and acting'. 'Behind the masks hides either immodestly consumed alcohol, or the fear and incapability to communicate.' Under the influence of 'one or two beers', he fell into an even deeper hole, and now his personal armour was completely dismantled. Sometimes, it happened in such situations that someone came and looked behind the 'thin façade'. Once a woman had asked him why he looked so sad, and he had told her about how damaged (*kaputt*) he felt. The woman could sympathize with him, she said, but that day, she was in a cheery mood, talking to her friends about a play they had seen. She invited the author to join, but he refused, even though he had seen the play as well. 'I would have liked going on talking to her about myself', he wrote sadly. On the night he had announced that he would move out of the commune, he had first wished to stay home. But eventually, he went to the bar, where he even enjoyed letting himself fall into the deep hole. To distract himself, he then looked at the people around him, young men trying to get some young women drunk and hitting on them. First he felt sympathetic to the women, but when he realized how drunk the women were, all that solidarity was gone. Even being drunk, these youngsters failed to overcome their loneliness and isolation.

And so the author went on describing the emotional misery of his life. Of course, he was not alone in this misery. Most customers in the bar, at least according to his account, just acted cool, but were in reality either afraid or incapable of communicating, or they were simply drunk, which would not result in meaningful exchange either. Even the brief moment when he had an opportunity to talk to a woman about his misery was quickly cut short. The article presented a world in which emotional suffering was the norm. Fear seems to have been the basic emotional condition, people felt 'damaged', and personal relations were meaningless. This was a common rhetoric in the radical left. Left-wing magazines abound with discussions of fear in all situations of social and political life, and countless texts describe both individual personalities and interpersonal relations as deeply 'damaged'. If at all, the text by 6(ma) was only insofar exceptional in that it did not engage in a discussion of the social sources of the emotional misery it is describing, except for the brief allusion to Dieter Duhm's work. Leftists, however, would have understood that it was capitalist modernity that was to be held responsible for the fear, loneliness, and incapability of communicating the author expressed.

Analysing capitalism in such emotional terms, leftist authors like 6(ma) produced an emotional knowledge about capitalism. Leftists *knew* about the emotional consequences of capitalism – that it produced fear, damaged personalities, and personal relations, isolated people from each other. Using a term coined by historian William Reddy, we might argue that leftists developed an analysis of the emotional regime of capitalism. In Reddy's words, an 'emotional regime' is a 'set of normative emotions and the official rituals, practices and emotives that express and inculcate them'; for him, any stable political regime needs such an 'emotional regime'.[3] An emotional regime sets norms for emotions and their expression, but also limits how and where other emotions can be expressed and experienced. An emotional regime, that is, shapes and restricts 'legitimate' emotions. It may grant, as Reddy argues, more or less emotional freedom, it may generate more or less (unnecessary) emotional suffering by restricting how people can express their feelings. We might expand on this understanding of an emotional regime by adding that it not only restricts what emotions can be expressed, but also generates certain feelings, perhaps normally in the form of emotional suffering because it bans the expression of other feelings. In this sense, I propose that leftists developed an analysis of what they considered the emotional regime of capitalism: they analysed how capitalism shapes emotions, how it prohibits certain positive feelings and generates certain negative feelings. For leftists, who, as we have seen, regarded feelings and desires as inherently subversive, the regulation and restriction of feelings were a central aspect of capitalism's oppressive power.

Whether leftists were 'correct' with their analysis of emotions under capitalism is not the issue here. Yet the emotional regime leftists described was not a mere fiction. It was, for leftists at least, a powerful regime, precisely because leftists analysed capitalism in such terms. The multiplicity of texts that discussed and described what capitalism did to feelings, how it damaged personalities and intimate relations, that is, should not be misread as a mere analysis of emotions under capitalism. Rather, these texts had a productive function, as they themselves created an emotional regime.[4] The text by 6(ma), for example, not only described how the

---

[3] William M. Reddy, *The Navigation of Feeling: A Framework for the History of Emotions* (Cambridge: Cambridge University Press, 2001), 124–126, quote 129.

[4] Though Reddy does not engage in a discussion of how emotional regimes are created, my argument here resembles Reddy's about 'emotives', that is speech acts, such as saying 'I love you', that both explore one's feelings *and* give shape to them. Like Reddy, I emphasize the productive function of such speech acts, though in this case with regards to emotional norms. On emotives, see ibid., 96–110, 129.

author felt going to the bar, but in doing so also posited how one *should* feel in that place: afraid and lonely, feelings merely concealed by an expression of coolness. This was, to be sure, not a strictly formulated emotional rule; yet, by describing the lone and fearsome drinking behind a curtain of coolness as an emotional normalcy, he effectively (re)created a peculiar emotional style that others were to emulate.[5] Studying texts like that by 6(ma) thus allows us to understand the practical creation and implementation of an emotional regime and the emotions it produced. At the same time, however, the knowledge about the emotional regime of capitalism leftists created also provided them with ideas of how to overcome this regime. The brief conversation with the woman 6(ma) described was, for example, both a way of practising his 'brokenness [*Kaputtheit*]', and an opportunity for overcoming his loneliness and, therefore, his brokenness – if only the conversation had lasted a bit longer. The emotional knowledge of capitalism leftists produced thus created an emotional regime that made negative feelings like fear and loneliness the norm; simultaneously, leftists could draw on this knowledge to overcome these very feelings.

The first three sections of the chapter discuss the emotional knowledge of capitalism leftists created, and how this shaped an emotional regime. The chapter first turns to fear, an emotion that was ubiquitous in left-wing emotional discourse. The chapter then explores leftists' 'damaged personalities', their damaged feelings and bodies, and their equally damaged personal relations. Following the approach outlined in this section, it proposes that leftists, by describing how capitalism 'damaged' their personalities and personal relations, effectively practised a 'damaged' subjectivity, though they created, at the same time, the potential for a different form of subjectivity. Third, the chapter turns to the importance of space for leftists' understanding of feelings by exploring how leftists criticized modern cities for fostering specific feelings, like fear and isolation, and depriving people of sensual experiences. The final section then moves away from the emotional knowledge leftists created to discuss the emotional regime that reigned within the radical left itself.

A Regime of Fear

Any cursory look into leftist publications of the 1970s and early 1980s reveals the centrality of fear in left-wing discourse. A 'general precautionary

---

[5] See Benno Gammerl, 'Emotional Styles: Concepts and Challenges', *Rethinking History* 16 (2012).

sense of fear' characterized modern life, an author of *Autonomie* claimed in 1978.[6] According to leftists, there were many reasons to be afraid, ranging from seemingly small and personal fears, such as the fear of failure to perform sexually, or of exams at university, to large-scale, even existential fears caused by the destruction of the environment or the danger of nuclear disaster. From Dieter Duhm's *Angst im Kapitalismus* (1972), to Gudrun Pausewang's children's novels *Die letzten Kinder von Scheweborn* (1983) and *Die Wolke* (1987), which depicted the horrifying consequences of nuclear warfare and catastrophe and were mandatory reading in numerous German elementary schools, it is clear that fear was pervasive in leftist discourse.[7]

The most important point of reference for leftist discourse about fear was arguably Dieter Duhm's book. First published in 1972, it quickly became a bestseller in the post-1968 left. By 1975, the 11th edition was in print. All over West German university cities, students held workshops to discuss the book.[8] Written in a simplistic manner, which should make the argument accessible to apprentices and young workers, Duhm sought to show that capitalist society by necessity produces fear. Drawing on a Marxist understanding of capitalism, Duhm identified five core elements of a capitalist society that together make 'humans afraid of each other'. First, Duhm analysed capitalism as a system that relies on authority. Personal relations at school or at work are all structured hierarchically. But authorities rarely have to rely on direct violence or the threat of violence to enforce their power. Rather, people have, from childhood onwards, internalized fear of parental or other authorities. How much the subconscious is dominated by fear becomes evident, Duhm claimed, by people's reactions to confrontations with figures of authority, for example when students go to a professor's office hours or apprentices have to talk to their boss: 'in most cases, they break into sweat, have strong heartbeats, tremble'.[9] Importantly, this fear is, for Duhm, deeply

---

[6] Anon., 'Die Sprache von Baeumen [sic] und Voegeln [sic]', in *Autonomie: Materialien gegen die Fabrikgesellschaft* 10, January 1978, 70–73.

[7] Duhm, *Angst*, Gudrun Pausewang, *Die letzten Kinder von Schewenborn oder … sieht so unsere Zukunft aus?* (Ravensburg: Maier, 1983); Gudrun Pausewang, *Die Wolke* (Ravensburg: Maier, 1987).

[8] See for example Anon., 'Das Seminar zum Buch! (Angst im Kapitalismus v. D. Duhm, Kübler)', in *Hundert Blumen* 8, n.d., probably spring 1973, 5. See also the positive review of Duhm's book in *ABBLDIBABBLDIBIBBLDIBABBLDIBU. Schülerzeitung der HCO* 2, December 1973, 22. On the reception, see Maik Tändler, *Das therapeutische Jahrzehnt: Der Psychoboom in den siebziger Jahren* (Göttingen: Wallstein, 2016), 298–301.

[9] Duhm, *Angst*, 34.

irrational, as it stands in no proportion to the original 'real fear' of actual punishment.

Second in his list of core elements of capitalism was the commodification of human relations. Summarizing Marx, Duhm wrote that as people sell their commodified labour, and buy other commodities in return, they interact merely as commodities. People, in other words, have to put on 'character masks'.[10] Not only does this result in loneliness and isolation, but in fear, as people are constantly afraid of letting their masks down, lest they are fleeced in economic or psychological matters. In Duhm's analysis, life in capitalism consists of constant examining. Accordingly, 'all our fears are exam fears, including the fear of sexuality, the fear of bosses, the fear of the future'.[11] People have to constantly ask themselves 'Am I doing this right?', 'What might the other think about me?', 'How much does he appreciate me?'[12] If priests talked about an 'existential fear', they were thus utterly mistaken, because they did not recognize the social conditions of this fear, even though they were right that fear indeed 'shapes the entire life of capitalist humans'.[13] Third, Duhm turned to how alienation results in fear, an issue closely related to the commodification of human relations. As people cannot realize themselves in their work, but only produce commodities for a market, they feel subjected to the anonymous forces of the market. 'The feeling of being at someone's mercy [*ausgeliefert sein*] is becoming the basic feeling of alienated life. Being subjected means fear', Duhm posited.[14] Once again, he stressed that any rhetoric of an 'existential fear' independent of social conditions only conceals the social relations of capitalism that produce this general fear.

The fourth element of capitalism Duhm discussed was the 'performance principle [*Leistungsprinzip*]'. Constantly improving performance is a question of survival for companies, and hence workers. But the performance principle extends to all human relations, Duhm claimed. In all situations of life, people are confronted with 'fear-inducing tests of their capabilities [*angsterregenden Bewährungssituationen*]'. 'The performance principle inevitably leads to fear of failing', and the more the performance principle structures life, the more pervasive fear becomes.[15] To make matters worse, one's success is often another's failure, and hence the performance principle also isolates people from each other and makes them feel lonely. This already points to the final core principle of capitalism, competition (*Konkurrenz*), which appears to be a natural law in capitalism (and thus in contrast to socialist competition [*Wettbewerb*]). In capitalism, people have

[10] Ibid., 40.   [11] Ibid., 41.   [12] Ibid.   [13] Ibid.   [14] Ibid., 47.   [15] Ibid., 50.

to compete with each other incessantly, and are thus always afraid of losing this competition, be it in professional or in personal matters. Since much of this competition and the concomitant fear happens unconsciously, people lose their appetite, develop depressions or 'neurotic unfitness to work'.[16] All these emotional conditions are a result of capitalism, Duhm claimed.

Fear, Duhm summarized his argument, is a 'basic feeling' in capitalism; hence people have to develop strategies that allow them to cope with fear. Indeed, capitalist society is able, he wrote, to 'program individual fears' and to channel them in a way that is useful for capitalism.[17] Following an ideology that supports the existing social and political order, for example, lessens the emotional burden of fear, Duhm argued, as it strengthens people's self-esteem and makes them part of a community, rendering the prospect of isolation less threatening. Furthermore, finding a common enemy elevates people to the role of a powerful judge, which means that they themselves can be less afraid of others' judgment. Pop culture and consumer industry, too, according to Duhm, help people cope with fear without solving the actual problem. Buying specific brands, for example, helps people to be more self-confident. The capitalist system not only 'cripples' individual personalities, but even profits from these crippled personalities by selling 'ersatz personalities' and using them to stabilize its power.[18] And finally, pursuing a career or behaving in an authoritarian manner at the workplace is nothing, in Duhm's mind, but an attempt to compensate for personal fears, notably feelings of sexual inferiority. For Duhm, these are all compensation mechanisms that leave the fundamental problem, that is, the fear capitalism necessarily produces, unaddressed.

Following Duhm, leftists regarded fear as an essential 'means of domination [*Herrschaftsinstrument*]' in capitalist society. Of course, the state's repressive forces were terrifying. Activists often reported about the horrendous moments of deep anxiety and feelings of helplessness they went through in confrontations with the police.[19] The state constantly expanded its apparatus of oppression, leftists from West Berlin argued, which in fact indicated that 'those in power [*die Herrschenden*]' were themselves afraid. Yet the new means of oppression also resulted in 'retreat, distancing, disengagement, fantasies of emigration' within the left, the authors worried. And thus, the repressive measures had already

---

[16] Ibid., 54.   [17] Ibid., 117.   [18] Ibid., 120.

[19] See, e.g., Inge und Gisela, 'Die gehen über Leichen: Polizeieinsatz Brokdof', in *Andere Zeitung* 10, December 1976, 4–6.

accomplished their goal.[20] Indeed, fear of being victimized by the police was not even the worst fear, Bernhard Jost and Gerhardt Stecker explained in the aftermath of a demonstration in reaction to Ulrike Meinhof's death that had turned extremely violent. Even more frightening was the sense of losing one's identity in the process of escalating violence, and the prospect of separation from one's comrades, not only due to arrest and imprisonment, but because comrades might distance themselves from the violence in reaction to press campaigns and would hence be incapable of understanding the rage and desperation that had motivated the violence.[21] Given these internalized fears, making use of actual violence had become mostly unnecessary for maintaining order, an author for the *Blatt* noted; threatening with guns was sufficient. People remained conformist and friendly (sic) out of pure fear of social consequences. Having lost all hope for future change, the writer bemoaned, activists became wearily (*resigniert*) and hopeless.[22] And another group from Munich admitted that 'late capitalism' constantly invented new means of oppression, but nevertheless stressed the importance of 'recognizing the mechanisms in ourselves that are in accordance with these means of oppression: the repression against ourselves. Self-repression is, after all, fear, the incapability of doing what we want . . .'[23] Fear was, in other words, such an effective means of oppression because it internalized oppression and squashed the very spirit of resistance.

The state and its forces of oppression were, of course, not the only sources of fear that leftists criticized. Following Dieter Duhm, leftists identified numerous sources of 'examination fears' in capitalism. Unsurprisingly, the educational system provided leftists with plenty of examples of this socially caused examination fear. For example, in an interview with secondary school students who 'dropped out', fifteen-year-old Nina said about her classmates: 'The folks in our class, they're totally afraid of life, that's at least how I see it. First of all, the fear of not graduating from school, the fear for their marks, if they have a bad mark, they go crazy, you know, they get pure existential fear, and that's why they always bow to teachers, especially if they are authoritarian and threaten them to put stones in their way . . . and later, it's the foreman or the boss, they'll

[20] Anon., 'Wer hat Angst vor wem?', in *Info BUG* 102, 12 April 1976, 2.
[21] Bernhard Jost and Gerhard Strecker, 'Persönlicher Brief eines Frankfurters über seine Erfahrungen mit der Staatsgewalt', in *Info BUG* 116, 2 August 1976, 16–17.
[22] BLATT-Redaktion, 'Psychoserie, Teil II', in *Das Blatt* 50, 18 July–7 August 1975, 8–9.
[23] Pamphlet by 'Leute vom Schwarzmarkt', quoted in Herbert Röttgen, 'Liebe, Angst und Terror', in *Das Blatt* 73, 2–15 July 1976, 4–6.

brown-nose [them] just out of fear.'[24] In *Klenkes*, a left-wing magazine from Aachen, children would complain about the fears that not doing their homework caused, something that frequently, they alleged, resulted in physical violence from the parents, and at times even in children committing suicide.[25] Three students from Charlottenburg and Siemensstadt in West Berlin similarly described fear as a normal feeling at school: fear of being caught without homework, and of course fears before exams. Students were afraid, they claimed, of parents who might reduce their pocket money, or of feeling embarrassed in front of the teacher or classmates. According to them, instilling fear by threatening students with bad marks was a 'means of domination' for teachers. But even if teachers tried to avoid scaring students, there were still sources of fear beyond the teacher's powers, such as the marks one needed to go to university (*numerus clausus*), or the general fear of unemployment. Fear was thus, they wrote drawing on Duhm's work, a necessary consequence of capitalism. In individual students, this fear caused a lack of self-confidence and an increasing feeling of not being accepted and appreciated. All too easily, students became mere followers (*Mitläufer*); they simply did what they were expected to do at school, at work, or in a group of friends. And such docile students – and, later on, workers – were exactly what capitalists needed, the students wrote.[26] At university level, not much changed. Already in 1968, a pamphlet by students from Munich had claimed: 'We are all afraid and suffer from psychic pressure.'[27] Eight years later, an author for the Heidelberg *Carlo Sponti* wrote that 'every exam renews old, laboriously suppressed [*mühsam verdrängte*] fears and adds news fears. Thus, tensions between the apathetic incapability of standing up against exams and the increasing antipathy against exams emerge.'[28] In an educational system that was based on constant examination, leftists argued, fear was a necessary consequence.

---

[24] 'Interview mit Schülerinnen / Schülern, die aussteigen', in *Info BUG* 193, 2 June 1978, 14–16.

[25] Anon., 'Sind wir wirklich die Bekloppten?', in *Klenkes: Zeitung Aachener Bürgerinitiativen* 6, June 1976, 4.

[26] Michael, Andreas, Henry, 'Haben wir in der Schule Angst', in *Schüler Info Charlottenburg. Schülerzeitung der Gruppe unabhängiger sozialistischer Schüler (GUSS) für Charlottenburg und Siemensstadt*, n.d., 5–7, Ordner Schulkämpfe, Papiertiger Archiv Berlin.

[27] Ad-hoc-Gruppe Sozialisation, 'Prüfungen, ein Instrument der Anpassung' (Flugblatt), kept at Archiv der Münchner Arbeiterbewegung, Sammlung Christine Dombrowsky (Archiv 451), cited in Pilzweger, *Männlichkeit*, 240.

[28] Lili (=Linke Liste), 'Gesellschaftliche Fabrik und Studenten-Bewegung', in *Carlo Sponti* 18/19, April 1976, 13–18.

The pervasiveness of fear in capitalist society had, according to leftist analyses, further emotional repercussions. Fear affected other feelings. The constant competition under capitalism and the 'fear of loss [*Verlustangst*]' it induced made it imperative, leftists argued, not to show any weakness and to stay rational at all times. A men's group from Frankfurt for example claimed that men were still loved not due to their 'sensibility or emotionality', or even because of their body, but only because of what they earned. For this reason, men had to at least present themselves as successful and, crucially, compete with other men in their striving for success. The permanent competition caused two 'emotional processes in the male psyche': first, an incapability amongst men of forming 'really caring relationships [*wirklich liebevolle Unterstützungsbeziehungen*]', because true solidarity was impossible amongst competitors. This resulted in 'distrust amongst men', which – the second emotional process – led to men's 'catastrophic fixation on women'. 'Good feelings of trust and being understood' are to be found only in relations with a woman; '[man] lives at the expense of her feelings, without discovering his own feelings and being able to experience them with other men.'[29] A true man had to be afraid of nothing, a cartoon in the men's magazine *Mannsbild* suggested: Asked by his son 'And you think a man has no fears at all', the father confirms, and adds: 'Well, one fear! Not being a real man!'[30] Admitting fears was, these leftists believed, a sign of weakness in capitalist society that amounted, for men, to an act of emasculation.

But men were not alone with their fears. Girls and women, too, suffered under the capitalist regime of fear. For example, an activist from the *Frauenzentrum* (women's centre) in Hamburg noted that women knew all too well how to compete with each other, which was why they were afraid of other women rather than men. Women, she argued, had only learned to 'conceive of themselves as substandard, weak and inferior', but lacked self-confidence. Just as men, but for different reasons, women were afraid of themselves and other women, which was, she claimed, why they were reluctant to visit the *Frauenzentrum*.[31] And a teenage girl from Berlin noted that she was permanently afraid of doing something wrong when she was with boys, not because, as some of her friends told her, of mental

---

[29] Männergruppe Frankfurt, 'Tod dem Patriarschismus [sic]: Es lebe der Mann!', in *diskus* 3, November 1975, 26–28.
[30] 'Ein Mann und sein Profil (Cartoon)', in *Mannsbild* ,1976, 26. See also Olaf Stüben, 'Ich liebe Jungs', in *Große Freiheit* 24/25, August 1979, 10–12.
[31] Anon., 'An eine Freundin, die mir vorwirft, dass ich männerfeindlich bin . . .', in *Lesbenpresse* 2, June 1975, 10–11.

issues, but because she was not able to talk openly about her sexuality.[32] According to leftist analyses, these texts suggest, men and women were equally suffering under constant fear, not least because they lived in a world that was hostile to feelings and did not allow for the expression of them. The omnipresence of fear created an emotionally void world, precisely because fear prevented people from talking openly about their feelings.

Intimate and sexual relations were similarly affected by the capitalist regime of fear, leftists argued. In their mind, the capitalist performance principle also extended to sexual relations, which is why people had to be constantly afraid of failing sexually or doing something wrong. Sexual therapists Ulli and Martin from Munich for example explained that the social taboo of sexuality created 'insecurity and a lack of knowledge about the anatomy of the other sex', which in turn resulted in fear. 'Fear of finishing early – or not at the same time – or to fail – etc.'[33] More to the point, a man from Heidelberg exclaimed in *Carlo Sponti*: 'I want to sleep with my girlfriend *now*, without being afraid of screwing up [*ich könnt's nicht bringen*].'[34] Unsurprisingly, leftists held the upbringing in childhood responsible for this fear of sexuality. For example, the men's group in Frankfurt mentioned earlier in the section posited that boys were trained 'to use' their body when playing, but not to experience it in a pleasurable way. Thus, boys, and eventually men, had an alienated relation to both their feelings and their bodies.[35] And, being alienated from their bodies and feelings, they were also afraid of them, the argument went. In Pforzheim in southwest Germany, a group of youngsters (they were, in fact, all teenagers) had formed a 'children's liberation front [*Kinderbefreiungsfront*]' that called for the liberation of children's sexuality. Traditional sex education had turned them, they claimed, into 'cold consumption-humans [*Konsumermenschen*], who are afraid of their own wishes for fondness'.[36] Creating an 'atmosphere of [sexual] deadlock, fear, and suppression' was indeed necessary for maintaining the capitalist social order, an author for the *Blatt* argued, as the hostile reaction demonstrated in the conservative

[32] Anon., 'Schneekönigin', in *Schülerforum* (Berlin) 3, October 1976, in Papiertiger Archiv Berlin, Ordner Schulkämpfe. First published in *Auseinandersetzung* (Kassel).

[33] Uta, 'Die Sache mit der Sexualität', in *Das Blatt* 67, 2–15 April 1976, 15–16.

[34] W. S., 'Ich scheiß auf die Gesellschaft … aber sie gibt's mir ganz schön zurück', in *Carlo Sponti* 4, May 1974, 1.

[35] Männergruppe Frankfurt, 'Tod dem Patriarchismus'.

[36] Pamphlet by 'Kinderbefreiungsfront', quoted in Peter Schult, 'Aufstand der Kinder', in *Das Blatt*, 27 July–9 August 1979, 26.

Bayernkurier newspaper to the left-wing children's play *Darüber spricht man nicht*, which sought to convey a more positive attitude towards sexuality to children. But the *Bayernkurier*'s reaction – it had depicted the play as 'crude class war with the means of pornography' – only indicated how effective the play might be, the author noted.[37] What might seem like two mutually exclusive critiques of capitalism – that it simultaneously produces fear and a general emotional void – were only two sides of the same coin: in capitalism, people have to be afraid of showing emotions; and the general hostility towards feelings in capitalism makes them afraid of their potentially uncontrollable feelings, leftists argued.

The 1970s and early 1980s were an 'age of fear', as *Ulcus Molle* put it in 1982.[38] Indeed, this sense of living in times of fear was nothing specific to the alternative left. Writing for the Catholic monthly *Herder Korrespondenz*, D. A. Seeber also claimed that fear had become a 'civilizational disease' that included fears of diseases, fears of the destruction of the environment, social fears, a general fear of the future amongst the youth, and fear of the 'superpowers of technical and administrative apparatuses'.[39] But whereas Seeber hoped that a sense of being protected by 'God's hand' would cure this disease and thus foster hope rather than fear, leftists held capitalism responsible for the omnipresence of fear. Under the constant pressure to compete against each other and to outperform competitors, people could not help but feel afraid. Hence, only abolishing capitalism might create a society without, or at least with less, fear. But while capitalism created fear, expressing this as well as other feelings was deemed impossible in a capitalist society. The omnipresent fear *created* the emotionally void world leftists bemoaned. Admitting and showing feelings, enjoying bodies and sexuality, forming tender relations based on solidarity – all this was impossible, according to left-wing thinking, in a world governed by permanent competition and the fear of losing out in this competition. Analysing capitalism in such terms, leftists produced an emotional knowledge about capitalism that was itself emotionally

---

[37] Oppodeldok-Peter, 'Theater: Darüber spricht man nicht', in *Das Blatt* 67, 2–15 April 1976, 18. See my discussion of the play in Joachim C. Häberlen, 'Ingrid's Boredom', in *Learning How to Feel: Children's Literature and Emotional Socialization, 1870–1970*, ed. Ute Frevert et al. (Oxford: Oxford University Press, 2014).

[38] Anon., 'Sehnsucht nach dem Paradies (Book Review), in *Ulcus Molle* 7/8, 1982, 2–4. See also Matthias Horx, 'Es geht voran. (Excerpts of a Novel)', in *Das Blatt* 219, 26 March–8 April 1982, 16–19.

[39] D. A. Seeber, 'Angst als Zivilisationskrankheit?', *Herder Korrespondenz* 31 (1977): 165–168, quoted in Frank Biess, 'Die Sensibilisierung des Subjekts: Angst und "neue Subjektivität" in den 1970er Jahren', *WerkstattGeschichte* 49 (2008): 51.

productive as it shaped how leftists would feel. If fear was a 'basic feeling' in capitalism, then it would also be normal for leftists to feel afraid; and indeed they did. And yet it would be misleading to think of leftists as being permanently afraid and thus paralyzed. Fear motivated political and personal activism, not least to overcome fear. Describing alternative leftists as 'fearful subjects' would thus be, despite the constant talk about within the left, one-sided.[40] The analysis of fear in capitalism also enabled leftists to develop practices that would help them to overcome fear, as Chapter 4 shows. Paradoxically, then, the 1970s and early 1980s were not only an era of fear, but also of being free of fear.

Damaged Personalities & Personal Relations

By inducing fear and fostering a general hostility towards emotions and the body, capitalism 'damaged' and 'crippled', as leftists put it, personalities and personal relations. The categorizing and separating forces of capitalist rationality fragmented wholesome humane beings, they argued, notably their feelings and bodies. People would never experience their body as a whole, but use only those parts they needed for a specific task, be it at work or when having sex.[41] And since people were not able to genuinely relate to themselves, to their bodies and feelings, they were not able to relate to others either, not least, as we have seen, because they were incapable and afraid of showing their emotions. Above all, of course, leftists claimed to suffer themselves from this fragmentation capitalism imposed on them. They practised, we might say, a 'damaged' subjectivity. Yet such an analysis would be as one-sided and misleading as arguing that leftists were 'fearful subjects', since leftists developed a plethora of practices that served to help them 'heal' or 'fix' their 'damaged' selves. To make sense of these attempts to fix a fragmented self and to recuperate feelings as a political project, we first need to understand precisely how leftists thought about capitalism as damaging personalities and personal relations.

The rhetoric of being damaged emerged quickly in the aftermath of the euphoria of 1968. Already during the years of revolt in the late 1960s, both student activists and professional therapists frequently worried about the emotional and sexual suffering of (usually male) students.[42] By early 1972,

---

[40] See ibid. Though Biess notes new 'technologies of security', these are not quite part of his analysis of the 'fearful [*angestbesetztes*] subject'.
[41] This is also a point left-wing children's books tried to make. See Häberlen, 'Ingrid's Boredom'.
[42] See Tändler, *Therapeutische Jahrzehnt*, 282–295.

the Berlin magazine *Fizz*, an antiauthoritarian magazine that emerged in the environment of the anarchist terrorist group Movement 2nd June, proclaimed on its cover page: 'We are damaged, completely damaged, not some other folks – they too!!! We cannot love, we cannot be solidaristic. We are afraid. We pass on the oppression we're suffering from. We go crazy, we have no ground under our feet.'[43] Being damaged, the brief lines that lacked any further explanation implied, meant being incapable of forming meaningful, intimate relations, be they personal (love) or political (solidarity). Some three years later, the successor magazine *Hundert Blumen* described 'Our Self' as 'weakened, damaged, depressive, fearful [*angstbesetzt*], neurotic, fixated on authorities, dependent, intolerant, dogmatic, aggressive against those who are themselves oppressed, oriented towards consumption, dominated by constant frustration and existential fears'. The symptoms of these damages included, to name but some: 'Difficulties to work', 'competitive behaviour', 'isolation', 'psychoses', 'functional diseases (circulatory, digestive and nerve systems)', or 'lack of fantasies'. All this was a result of the 'psychic misery' capitalism produced by ignoring real 'desires', a misery that damaged the self, crucially, also in bodily ways.[44] By 1977, simply 'nothing' seemed to be 'alright' for an alternative leftist who called for the foundation of communes: 'Our bodies, emotions, sexuality are just as damaged as our mind, rationality [*Verstand*], intellect.'[45] Capitalism, it seems, damaged human beings in their entirety.

Leftists traced the origins of these damages to childhood when boys and girls learned to play the appropriate roles. Children who were brought up in state institutions or by bourgeois families where a 'hygienic-undercooled atmosphere' reigned for the purpose of 'income and status' suffered particularly, the left-wing magazine *Heim-Erzieher Zeitung* wrote. Whereas other children, especially those who received 'emotional support' in families, developed a 'social mask [*soziale Hülle*]' that protected them from the 'social cold', children raised in state institutions lacked this cover, and thus '[froze] internally and mentally [*friert innermenschlich und seelisch*]'. Being damaged in such a way, these children, soon to become adults, were unable of conceiving 'human warmth', only 'cold', a condition that made it impossible to form genuine social relations.[46] And while boys suffered particularly because they 'had to subordinate their feelings to their

[43] Coverpage, in *Fizz* 10, n.d., early 1972.
[44] Anon., 'Psychisches Elend und Politische Praxis' in *Hundert Blumen* 9, n.d., probably summer 1973, 6–7.
[45] Anon., 'The Time Is Right for Communes', in *Info BUG* 160, 13 June 1977, 17.
[46] Hand-Dietrich Wedephl, 'Leserbrief', in *Heim und Erzieher Zeitung* 2, December 1972, 1–4.

mind',[47] girls did not remain unaffected. The Hamburg magazine *Revolte* for example published a series of letters French men and women had written 'against' their parents. One of the women, named Aurore, noted sadly that her parents had ridiculed her as 'retarded' when she showed, at the age of six or eight, too much affection for father, hugged him (*hängte sich um seinen Hals*), or said nice things. Feeling ashamed, she had been incapable of showing her love for anyone ever since. 'Later, I felt that I was suffocating, that my self, my ability to love, to be loved, to hope, to enjoy life, would die and suffocate.'[48] Without using the term, Aurore, too, described how her parents had 'damaged' her by oppressing her emotional side and the ability to express feelings.

Left-leaning parents might try to keep children's emotionality and 'liveliness' alive, but schooling would surely quell these qualities, as a woman from Heidelberg explained when she enrolled her daughter in school. 'Being imprisoned, incapacitation, being subordinated to the future [*verzukunftet werden*]', the 'cold bureaucracy and tradition' will 'destroy everything that is lovable about her', she predicted.[49] And as grown-ups, both men and women had learned to play their self-damaging roles. Indeed, conforming to societal norms of masculinity that required emotional self-restraint was, a gay group from West Berlin claimed, deeply exhausting for men. In this situation, women had to 'maintain men's emotional stability', the group argued. Their emotionality was utterly subordinated to men's emotional needs that resulted from the suppression of feelings.[50] Thus, while boys might be particularly 'crippled' by the demand to not show their feelings, girls and women were no less 'damaged' by an emotional regime that prohibited the free expression of feelings, leftists argued.

As the previous chapter has shown, leftists criticized capitalist rationality for its categorizing and dissecting powers. In their mind, capitalism imposes a set of functionalist distinctions upon human beings that frag-ments their personalities and bodies. Indeed, the very distinction between 'body and soul', as Lucy Körner, an otherwise unknown author, put it in *Ulcus Molle*, is something children have to learn as they become adults. Children still experience their feelings with their entire body. When they feel joyous, they bounce and jump around, they laugh, Körner noted.

---

[47] Anon., 'Gedanken zur Männerfete', in *Info BUG* 10, 13 May 1974, 2.
[48] Aurore et al., 'Briefe gegen die Familie', in *Revolte* 13, May 1975, 22–29.
[49] Ute and Theo, 'WG-Nachrichten', in *Carlo Sponti* 18/19, April 1976, 12.
[50] Anon., 'Zum Rosa Winkel', in *Info BUG* 64, 30 June 1975, 11–13.

As they grow up, however, they restrain their feelings, lest they lose their parents' approval, they stop 'living their natural joy of life' and begin to 'cramp'. By the time they had become adults, they have learned to conceal their feelings. If adults would bounce and jump around like children, they would be considered insane. But of course, this suppression of feelings, the separation of soul and body does not work, Körner argued. Feelings were not the proverbial 'sleeping dogs', but were well awake and resisting their incarceration. Physical pain and constantly cramped muscles were the bodily result of this suppression, according to Körner. For her, it was thus no surprise that an increasing number of people 'complain that they feel empty and unfulfilled, that they live an obtuse and passionless life [*abgestumpft vor sich hinleben*], and try to use drugs and other stimuli to feel life at all, because they cannot otherwise'.[51]

Along similar lines, leftists bemoaned the fragmentation of sexuality under capitalism, where sexuality would be limited to specific times and spaces, to specific personal relations, and to specific regions of the body, namely genitalia.[52] In *Carla Sponti*, an anonymous author analysed sex under capitalism in a text entitled *The Exchange Value is Gay*. For men, he wrote, sexual activity is part and parcel of a 'daily schedule organized according to the principle of the division of labour [*arbeitsteilig organisierter Tagesablauf*]'. 'Just as activities of the head or hand, activities of the dick are arbitrarily available events that are subject to the demands of value abstraction, that recognizes labour only as abstract and time only as ahistorical unit of measurement.' Men might purchase 'sensual satisfaction' from prostitutes, and 'tender affections' at home – the division of labour at work. This 'adaption of male sexuality to [the principles of] commodity exchange' requires 'sacrificing men's female sexuality' (sic). So-called female characteristics that men have, too, such as 'tenderness, kindness [*Güte*], capability of sexual satisfaction [*sexuelle Befriedigungsfähigkeit*], warmth' have to be eliminated from men as disrupting 'the social movement of commodity and labour owners'.[53] The capitalist mode of production, the somewhat confusing article suggested, reduces specifically male sexuality to an activity next to other tasks, like work, that simply needs to be done.

---

[51] Lucy Körner, 'Bioenergetik', in *Ulcus Molle* 9/10, 1979, 21–23.
[52] For an elaboration of the argument, see Joachim C. Häberlen, 'Feeling Like a Child: Visions and Practices of Sexuality in the West German Alternative Left during the Long 1970s', *Journal for the History of Sexuality* 25 (2016).
[53] Hans, 'Der Tauschwert ist schwul, oder: Frauengruppe', in *Carla Sponti* 7, October 1974, 4–7.

A central aspect of leftists' critique of sexuality under capitalism addressed the limitation of sex to genitalia. For example, the Frankfurt men's group mentioned in the previous section claimed that boys learn to masturbate during puberty, but 'not to caress their entire body', a form of sexuality that 'by necessity results in a fixation on genitals. The rest of the body remains dead.' For the male authors, this form of sexuality is entirely 'goal-oriented', that is, fixated on ejaculation, which they considered not to be the same as an orgasm. In sexual relations with women, such men are usually utterly fixated on their own orgasm, and if they learn to move beyond their egotism, they start to measure their 'success' according to 'their ability to make women climax as often and as intensely as possible'. Hence, the fixation on genital orgasms remained as much alive as the capitalist goal orientation and the pressure to perform well.[54] This reduction of sexuality to genitalia was not limited to men, leftists believed. Women's bodies, too, were fragmented into 'breast, cunt, ass', Brigitte Reuß from Munich wrote, until women learned in the women's movement how to masturbate and enjoy their entire bodies.[55] But even in the women's movement, the fixation on the clitoral orgasm ('rub, rub, rub') had merely replaced male penetrative sexuality ('in and out'), another woman from Aachen worried.[56] Women in the lesbian scene noted a sexual 'pressure to perform [*Leistungszwang*]' that prohibited genuine communication and left women 'frustrated, empty and alone' after such sexual adventures.[57] Heterosexual relations equally suffered. After a night that 'belonged to our genitalia', a man noted sadly (even though 'mechanical' sex was better than no sex at all, he added) that they had been incapable of 'giving each other an all-encompassing corporality [*Körperlichkeit*]'. His ideal of sexuality was a form of bodily communication. But how should any genuine communication happen, if 'only our genitals "talk", while the people to whom they belong do not find any common ground', he wondered.[58] The fixation on genitals and genital orgasms, itself a result of the capitalist 'performance principle', 'damaged' both personalities by limiting the parts of the body people could enjoy, and personal relations by preventing people from engaging in full, bodily communication.

---

[54] Männergruppe Frankfurt, 'Tod dem Patriarschismus'.
[55] Brigritte Reuß, 'Frau und Verhütung', in *Das Blatt* 83, 10–22 December 1976, 15–16.
[56] Sylvia, 'Die Last meiner Lust', in *Erotik und Umbruch. Zeitung zu Sexualität*, Mittsommer 1978, 32–33.
[57] Anon., '"Potente" Lesbe', in *Lesbenpresse* 4, November 1976, 7–8.
[58] rms, 'Rauswerfen will ich sie natürlich nicht', in *Andere Zeitung* 1, February 1976, 6.

Leftists equally criticized labour under capitalist conditions for fragmenting bodies. Some authors even drew an explicit parallel between the reification of sexual bodies and the reification of working bodies. Writing for *Autonomie*, Matthias Beltz for example suggested to expand 'the critique of economy with the concepts of sexual pathology: the struggle against labour as a rejection of the genital seriousness that turned into labour'. In his mind, 'the existence of this factory society destroys [*zerstört*] human beings into parts of the machine, into head, stomach and sex'. And yet, he added, 'as perversely as it might sound, labour keeps erotic alive', because at work, bodies come close to each other, and people can talk to each other thereby disrupting the isolation of modern cities.[59] Leftist children's books made a similar point. In his 1977 novel *Der Job*, Gerd Gustl Müller described a teenager named Manne who had, after a period of unemployment, found a job producing cupboards and towel rails. But the job was anything but a fulfilling experience, since it required that he use only a part of his body. 'Ass, stomach, noggin, cock, and feet – none of that was necessary. Ready to be amputated. All you needed was your thumb and two fingers.'[60] A young, presumably working-class leftist man from Frankfurt even compared his situation at work with the situation of prostitutes (he had just seen one and tried to talk to her, but without success). The prostitute's vagina was, he claimed, the pimp's tool, and the prostitute herself his machine, just as his own 'weak self' was the tool for his foreman, and his body the foreman's machine.[61] In that sense, he resembled the prostitute, because his body was reduced to its functionality. Under the capitalist regime of the performance principle, then, leftists argued, bodies were reduced to the function necessary for the task at hand: achieving the best and maximal number of genital orgasms, or producing most effectively for capitalism. The body in its entirety, including its feelings, however, did not matter.

Finally, leftists saw a similar process of reductive fragmentation at work with regards to capitalist consumption. The leftist music and cabaret group Checkpoint Charlie tried to make this point in a controversial play, suggesting that capitalists are interested in human beings only as objects that might buy goods. To turn human beings into objects, the group argued, it is necessary to isolate them and alienate them from their bodies.

[59] Matthias Beltz, 'Abenteuer aus der Fabrik: Geschichten aus der Beziehung zwischen Linksradikalen und Arbeiterbewegung', in *Autonomie: Materialien gegen die Fabrikgesellschaft* 9, October 1977, 9–22: 17.

[60] Gerd-Gustl Müller, *Der Job: Roman* (Munich: Weismann Verlag, 1977), 74.

[61] Anon., 'Soziale Kommunikation', in *Andere Zeitung* 6, July 1976, 4–6.

The vagina, for example, is typically presented as something disgusting, something that smells and tastes bad, which prevents any communication (according to capitalist sales strategies), and that hence has to be cleaned and made 'pure'.[62] Going a step further, an author for the *Info Nürnberger Undogmatischer Gruppen* argued that the 'spectacle of commodities' restricts people's sensuality. Smells are, he claimed, largely eliminated in this sterile world, with the exception the 'non-smell' of purity, which can be sold by the cosmetics industry. Tactile sensations are equally irrelevant for the spectacle of commodities; only seeing and hearing matter as senses of consumption. For the author, this amounts to a 'monologic sensuality', as people only listen passively, or look actively, but without anyone being looked at.[63] In particular the space of modern cities, which is discussed in the next section, was deemed to be sensually depriving. Modern machinery as well as the consumer goods produced by this machinery, *Pflasterstrand* claimed in April 1977, 'replace concrete activities, relations, human problems and their solutions – and thus [machinery] replaces a piece of life. Life impoverishes.'[64]

According to leftist analyses, capitalist relations of production, namely the division of labour and the commodity form, damaged people's personalities and fragmented their bodies; they also alienated people from each other, prohibited meaningful communication, and thus damaged intimate relations. An anonymous author for the magazine *Schwarze Protokolle* explained in July 1973 that there are two interrelated forms of communication in capitalist society: The '*reified* mediation of society through the net of exchange communication', which interacts with the second form of communication, the '*personal* mediation through the hierarchies of the state and companies'. But 'direct, nonhierarchical personal communication between societal individuals', which leftists tried to establish since the movement of 1968, has no place in capitalism, the argument went, as it threatens the reified and hierarchical communication on which capitalism relies.[65] Nearly a decade later, the *Info Bremer Undogmatischer Gruppen* made a similar argument about the lack of '"real", "original", "direct", "meaningful" experiences with nature and above all human beings' in modern society. Under conditions of capitalism, the 'existential need' to form reliable personal relations has been destroyed and

---

[62] Anon., 'Checkpoint Charly', in *Pflasterstrand* 15, 8–21 September 1977, 14–15.

[63] Anon., 'Monlogische und Dialogische Sinnlichkeit', in *Info Nürnberg* 8, October 1976, 18–20.

[64] Anon., 'Technologie und Bedrüfnisse', in *Pflasterstrand* special issue, April 1977, 8–12.

[65] Anon., 'Gesellschaftliche Vermittlung und Bewegung der Autonomen Gruppen', in *Schwarze Protokolle* 5, July 1973, 1–16, esp. 11–12. Emphasis in the original.

'retained [*aufgehoben*] in insurance systems'. As people no longer have to form personal relations out of pure existential need, they have become 'apathetic [*gleichgültig*]' vis-à-vis most other human beings. 'Love relations, that is, erotic relations, are usually rather fleeting relations, burdened by the hope to ideally tie together [*ideell zusammenzuhalten*] something does not hold together with material necessity (to fend off misery).' Capitalism has made meaningful relations unnecessary, they proposed. In these circumstances, people longed to break with their 'mummified relations'. But unfortunately, from the authors' perspective, they simply tried to escape into the 'Third World', where they hoped to find 'real' relations, but utterly ignored the very material hardships people in the Third World had to endure.[66] Finding better alternatives for forming meaningful intimate relations that would help people overcome the isolation of capitalism thus became a central agenda for the alternative left, as the *Schwarze Protokolle* had remarked already in 1973.

Leftist authors frequently described the social isolation modern society suffered from in drastic terms. *Ulcus Molle* for example published a poem by a man writing as Richard L. Wagner that described the loneliness and boredom of an ordinary Saturday evening. 'It's panicking, sitting alone in the apartment / sweating your shirt yellow out of pure boredom / no one calls me tonight / no one rings at the door . . .'[67] In *Carlo Sponti*, a young, presumably male student from Heidelberg wrote about the painful loneliness of student life. Living in a single room in the suburbs, he had no one to talk to through the entire weekend. Thus, he went to a bar in the inner city and got drunk, but even though the bar was crowded, there was no one he could talk to. Fortunately, the entire 'charade' ended at midnight, when he had to catch the last tram home. At university, the situation was not much better. Lecture halls were overcrowded with 'strange anonymous beings one does not know and one will never get to know under these circumstances'. When he accidentally touched someone, he even apologized. Why, he wondered, was it impossible for him to start talking to his neighbour in a lecture hall – perhaps his classmate was just as bored by the 'same dumb palaver', perhaps he would like to watch the same movie in the evening, but, alas, he remained silent and could not even cry: 'you must not do this either'.[68] Once again, showing feelings, in particular in a

---

[66] Anon., 'Anders leben, aber wie?', in *Info Bremer Undogmatischer Gruppen* 65, n.d., September 1981, 36–37.
[67] Richard L. Wagner, 'Samstagabend', in *Ulcus Molle* 3/4, 1979, 66.
[68] W. S., 'Ich scheiß auf die Gesellschaft'.

bodily way through crying, had no place in this society, the author claimed. But expressing feelings of joy and sympathy that might overcome the social isolation was not possible either. A man from Frankfurt (he apparently went through some rough times after breaking up with his girlfriend) complained that 'I cannot dance in the streets when I want to. I cannot hug women I like. Totally unknown women.' And thus he was on the verge of having himself hospitalized. In a mental institution, after all, he would have the 'jester's license', and might dance and hug strangers.[69] But also men who were not on the verge of insanity felt they could not simply start talking to women, as the women would feel afraid of their aggressive male sexuality.[70] A teenage boy from Pforzheim for example complained: 'Everywhere I am afraid (and surely not only I) to simply approach people I like, without fear or making a big show.'[71] Loneliness was, these texts suggest, a basic condition both in capitalist society and in the leftist scene itself.

The lack of social communication seems to have been a particularly concerning issue for teenagers. Left-wing school magazines frequently addressed this problem and sought to explain its social origins. A pamphlet by the *Liberale Schüleraktion der Jungdemokraten* from the early 1970s noted that the 'struggle of everyone against everyone' destroys 'relations between us students'. Feelings at school, they claimed, 'have to be suppressed lest the idea of competition is not questioned'. Showing feelings might, after all, result in relations based on solidarity and trust rather than on selfish competition, the argument implied. Furthermore, sexual relations between students, who would for example kiss in the school's courtyard, were subject to punishment, while gay and lesbian students had to face discrimination, and biology teachers taught 'wrong and outdated approaches' to homosexuality.[72] It was not only the school as an institution that suppressed relations and made communication about feelings impossible. Discos, where lonesome teenagers desperately hoped to break through their isolation and to 'establish sexual contacts', a student complained, were effectively designed to 'foster speechlessness': 'loud music does not allow for any conversation'. But most teenagers were, the author claimed, quite happy about this, as it gave them 'a reason for

---

[69] jk, 'Soziale Kommunikation: Ich ... Angst', in *Andere Zeitung* 10, December 1976, 38.
[70] Detlef Klein, 'Mann, Männer, Männe-Käng', in *Andere Zeitung* 15, May 1977, 15–16.
[71] *Kinderbefreiungsfront*, summer 1979, 3.
[72] Pamphlet by *Liberale Schüleraktion der deutschen Jungdemokraten*, probably early 1970s, Ordner Schulkämpfe, Papiertiger Archiv Berlin.

snoozing away and keeping silent'.[73] Since communication was rendered impossible by loud music, a similar article in *Sexpol* noted, teenagers were drawn to the dance floor. But dancing, teenagers would soon realize, did not satisfy the desire for communication that had brought them to the disco in the first place.[74] And if they finally met someone they liked, they had to go home due to parental curfews, the *Kinderbefreiungsfront* complained:

> And another nice experience: I'm together with a boy from my school, a lot of things happen between us, we lie together, fondle us (in the youth club, lots of shitty people around us, cigarette smoke, disco lights, totally loud music, but still better than being at home), I get sleepy, somehow we dream together, a large meadow, wind, I want to fall asleep, with him, and I want to wake up with him . . . but it doesn't work, because both of us have to get 'home', each in his own bed – and then we see each other another day at school, already a bit estranged.

For that reason, teenagers demanded to be allowed to move out from their parents' home into communes, where they might be free.[75] In this situation of social isolation, a group of students worried, an increasing number of teenagers took drugs – alcohol, marihuana, trips, or other things – because they believed it might produce a more communicative atmosphere. But this belief was misguided, the authors assured their readers, not least because taking drugs did not help changing the general situation of social isolation.[76] Teenagers' everyday life – at home, where they could not talk to their parents about feelings,[77] at school, at work, or when going out to discos – was, these texts suggest, deeply lonely. Yet this was not their fault, but the result of a social environment that isolated people from each other.

---

[73] Anon., 'Torschlusspanik um 10 (Discotheken)', in *ABBLDIBABBLDIBIBBLDIBABBLDIBU. Schülerzeitung der HCO* 2, December 1973, 8–10. See similarly Patricia von Böckmann, 'Traumfabrik', in *Rumpelstielzchen*, May 1974. See also Albrecht Herrenknecht, Wolfgang Hätscher, and Stefan Koospal, *Träume, Hoffnungen, Kämpfe ... Ein Lesebuch zur Jugendzentrumsbewegung* (Frankfurt a.M.: Verlag Jugend und Politik, 1977), 64–65; Alexa Geisthövel, 'Anpassung: Disco und Jugendbeobachtung in Westdeutschland, 1975–1981', in *Zeitgeschichte des Selbst: Therapeutisierung – Politisierung – Emotionalisierung*, ed. Pascal Eitler and Jens Elberfeld (Bielefeld: transcript, 2015), 251.

[74] Anon., 'Hoffnung auf Kommunikation', in *Sexpol* 2, September 1972, 8–16.

[75] *Kinderbefreiungsfront*, 8.

[76] Anon., 'Drogen: Schlüssel zu einem neuen Bewusstsein', in *ABBLDIBABBLDIBIBB LDIBABBLDIBU. Schülerzeitung der HCO* 2, December 1973, 17–21.

[77] See for example *Kinderbefreiungsfront*, 16–20, and Helma Fehrmann and Peter Weismann, *Und plötzlich willste mehr: Die Geschichte von Paul und Paulas erster Liebe* (Munich: Weismann, 1979), 20–21, 99–106, 131. See also my discussion in Häberlen, 'Ingrid's Boredom', 235–236.

Leftists in the 1970s formulated, this discussion has shown, a peculiar critique of capitalism's destructive potential: capitalism damages and, indeed, destroys personalities, it fragments bodies and feelings, and it disrupts social relations and produces isolated individuals, they argued. In capitalism, feelings, including bodily feelings, and their expression are marginalized and prohibited. For successfully competing, showing any genuine feelings is detrimental. In this sense, we can read leftist discourse as a description and analysis of an 'emotional regime of capitalism', that is, how capitalism regulates feelings and their expression. Yet leftist discourse about damaged personalities and personal relations was more than merely descriptive. It provided leftists with 'scripts' how to practise their 'damaged personalities'. In this sense, their personalities really were 'damaged'. Criticizing capitalism for damaging personality also implied that struggling against the destructive forces of capitalism required 'fixing' or 'healing' personalities. The struggle against capitalism would be, as it were, a collective therapeutic process that might restore some original uncrippled and unfragmented personality. As authors for *Info BUG* noted in the context of a discussion about heroin: 'It is necessary to resist this total system with one's entire suppressed will to live [*Lebenswillen*], one's ability to still feel, to love, to give anything of oneself [*irgendetwas von sich geben zu können*].'[78]

The Loneliness of Modern Cities

As we have seen in Chapter 2, leftists claimed that rationally and functionally planed cities had turned into boring places that isolated people from each other and fragmented urban space. The critique of modern urbanity, the 'deserts of concrete' or 'concrete silos', as leftists called modern cities, was a central aspect of leftist critiques of capitalism in the 1970s. Time and again, left-wing magazines reprinted images depicting the destruction of old, beautiful buildings and their replacement with 'modern', monotone housing blocs.[79] Indeed, leftist critiques of the boredom of suburban life were part and parcel of a much broader discourse that reached beyond the left. Contemporary sociologists suggested that newly built neighbourhoods like the Märkische Viertel in West Berlin isolated people from each other. Given the lack of social interaction in these neighbourhoods, inhabitants preferred travelling to their former old working-class neighbourhoods, like

[78] Anon., 'Fortsetzung der Junk Diskussion', in *Info BUG* 191, 4 May 1978, 21.
[79] For left-wing children's books making similar arguments, see Häberlen, 'Ingrid's Boredom'.

Figure 5   'Ten Years of Progress in Frankfurt'.
(*Rumpelstilzchen*, May 1974.)

Wedding or Kreuzberg in Berlin, to go shopping, since this allowed them to maintain old contacts. According to urban sociologist Hermann Fischer-Harriehausen, the 'primary isolation' of new suburban neighbourhoods contrasted with the 'dense social contacts' that had existed in the neighbourhoods where people had previously lived.[80]

For alternative leftists, the makeup of modern cities played a pivotal role in the 'emotional regime' of capitalism. Alienation was, the *Blatt* argued, no longer solely rooted in work relations, but in the 'concrete silos of suburbia'.[81] Just as with the 'dying rivers and forests', the 'breathlessness in the concrete [*im Beton*]' was 'an expression of mummified souls', argued Rädli in his critique of technological thinking.[82] The very way in which cities were planned, the very architecture of modern apartment buildings and consumer temples, leftists claimed, created the conditions for the feelings that capitalism, as an oppressive economic system, needed. According to leftist thought, space, or, more adequately, the production and arrangement of space, was critical for shaping and limiting emotions. Scholars have often noted how important questions of space became for leftist activism in the years after 1968, for example in the fight against

[80] Christiane Reinecke, 'Am Rande der Gesellschaft? Das Märkische Viertel – eine West-Berliner Großsiedlung und ihre Darstellung als urbane Problemzone', *Zeithistorische Forschungen* 11 (2014): 222.
[81] Anon., 'Nicht wählen, sondern wühlen', in *Das Blatt* 78, 1–10 October 1976, 4–5.
[82] Rädli, 'Verdorrte Seelen', in *Das Blatt* 128, 1–14 September 1978, 24–27.

urban renewal and for collective living projects.[83] To fully make sense of this concern with space, however, we need understand how leftists related space and feelings in their analyses of capitalism.

According to leftist critiques, modern cities encapsulated the problems of capitalism. Writing about Jack Kerouac's *On the Road*, Wolfgang Dorsch and Gisela Hellinger claimed that 'all fundamental elements of western-capitalist societies are concentrated in the city [of New York]: the predetermined channels, the hierarchical structures, the centralized organization'.[84] Detlef Hartmann, a prolific left-wing author and activist engaged in the struggle against urban renewal in Cologne, developed this point further in an article that compared modern cities to prisons. In his mind, cities and their facilities like shopping centres aim at suppressing spontaneity in order to 'dissect and fragment complex, all-encompassing areas of life into exactly predetermined places, where it is exactly prescribed what is the matter there, what has to be done there. Those individually predefined places are chained and put next to each other, so that people have no inch of space [*kein Quentchen Platz*] anymore where they can do what they want.' Unlike ancient or medieval cities, which were centred around the market square where everything was possible, even a 'critique of sexuality', Hartmann posited, modern cities are 'functionalized', that is, separate areas of a city fulfil different functions like living, working, or shopping. Residential areas, for example, were consciously made 'dull', so that their inhabitants would be driven to the city centre with its shopping areas.[85]

This urban fragmentation resulted, as the Situationist-inspired magazine *Revolte* had argued in 1974, in 'neighbourhoods like the Märkische Viertel in Berlin, the Osdorfer Born in Hamburg', but also in 'growing suicide rates, psycho-pharmacological medication for six-year-olds, the domination of concrete over the needs of human beings. Asphalt and concrete, objectivity [*Sachlichkeit*] next to irrationality, motorways, pedestrian zones through the trauma of the commodity, concrete cells without bars, but

---

[83] See only most recently Alexander Vasudevan, *Metropolitan Preoccupations: The Spatial Politics of Squatting in Berlin* (Chichester, UK: John Wiley and Sons, 2015); Moritz Föllmer, 'Cities of Choice: Elective Affinities and the Transformation of Western European Urbanity from the mid-1950s to the early 1980s', *Contemporary European History* 24 (2015). On West Berlin, see Belinda Davis, 'The City as Theater of Protest: West Berlin and West Germany, 1962–1983', in *The Spaces of the Modern City: Imaginaries, Politics and Everyday Life*, ed. Gyan Prakash and Kevin M. Kruse (Princeton: Princeton University Press, 2008).

[84] Wolfgang Dorsch and Gisela Hellinger, 'Zen und die Kunst ein Motorrad zu warten', in *Autonomie: Materialien gegen die Fabrikgesellschaft* 8, August 1977, 44–52, quote 44.

[85] Detlef Hartmann, 'Stadtknast – Knaststadt', in *Große Freiheit* 43, March 1981, 10–13.

filled with always the same loneliness of a prison cell.' The emotional consequences of this built environment were dramatic, the author suggested: 'At the margin of the chaos man [*der Mensch*] stands. He leaves for work in the morning, and in the evening, he returns back to the same misery of isolation, alienation and reification.' Importantly, the author concluded, this was not simply a matter of architecture. Rather, the 'environment of glass and concrete' was a 'real expression of life in its entirety. Power, violence no longer needs the letter of the law to be enforced, but develops and reveals itself in the lines of streets that dictate us the ways we can go, how we can move; or through the verticals and horizontals of concrete silos that also prescribe to everybody where to place the TV, how large the cabinet and the entire furniture of their living-toilets [*Wohnklos*] may be.'[86] Fragmented and functionalized, modern cities in this leftist interpretation enforced the rules of capitalism and subordinated everything to efficiency, but left no space for spontaneity and genuine communication. Isolated and emotionally deprived, people committed suicide or had to take psychological medication. Not only did the regime of capitalism prohibit the expression of feelings, but capitalism as it manifested itself in the built environment *produced* negative feelings like boredom and frustration.

With a somewhat nostalgic perspective, leftists bemoaned the destruction of old and less functionalized cities that had allowed for a more spontaneous and communicative life in the process of urban renewal. An ever-growing number of old, 'grown' cities, Hartmann argued, were 'dissected and fragmented'. Full of pathos, the small magazine *Anschläge* from Nuremberg observed that 'the neighbourhood [the author referred to an unnamed neighbourhood in Paris] where one might lead the most moving and most daring life without ever leaving it is destroyed'. Under its rubbish, only 'fragments of a lost poetry' might be found. 'With the progress of technology that what dreamers had hoped for was destroyed: the subterranean city is buried and with it all the reservoirs of love and firestorms.'[87] Old houses, the Stuttgart *'s Blättle* noted, might look miserable, and were nevertheless remarkable, at least more remarkable than monotone modern office buildings whose windows and doors looked all the same. But old and miserable-looking houses yield no profits, and hence they can be torn down, according to capitalist logic. For the *'s Blättle*

---

[86] Anon., 'Beton und Asphalt', in *Revolte* 9, January 1973, 6.
[87] Anon., 'Widerstand und Aneignung in der urbanen Geometrie', in *Anschläge* 6, December 1983, 21–40, esp. 23.

authors, this was an 'attack against our sensuality to make profits rise.' And tearing down old buildings was not the only way sensuality was under attack. 'At the work place, work place designers come and tell us how it has to look.' For the authors, the defence of old houses was thus nothing less than a defence of happiness in the city, a happiness that required 'human contacts', 'collectively organizing our life, and the sensual qualities that we wish'.[88]

The Brunnengasse in the inner city of Heidelberg, a small street that city planners wanted to (and eventually did) subject to an urban renewal project, provided leftist students with an example of what might be possible in such an 'old' and not yet functionalized space. 'Rarely did I see something like the convoluted back- and intermediate houses [*verschachtelten Hinter- und Zwischenhäuser*] in the Brunnengasse', an author for *Carlo Sponti* wrote. 'Student dorms, the Free Clinic, and other inhabitants of the Brunnengasse look each other into the window, molest each other with music; and still, barely any curtains or closed windows. Whenever I see this, my heart opens, and when I imagine that it's all gone in a year, then I'm full of cold rage.'[89] Leftists' struggles against urban renewal projects were, these examples indicate, not simply about a fight for affordable housing, for keeping inner cities 'beautiful', or for defending local autonomy.[90] Rather, by defending old and decaying neighbourhoods, leftists aimed to protect spaces that were, in their understanding, not yet subdued to the functionalist logic of capitalism and that hence allowed for feelings they otherwise missed in modern housing.

From leftists' point of view, the functionalization of modern cities destroyed personal relations as it isolated people from each other and prohibited spontaneous communication. 'Gigantic street constructions', '*s Blättle* argued, 'cut' neighbourhoods into pieces, 'destroy social contacts' and make neighbouring areas 'uninhabitable due to noise and exhausts'. Such city planning pursued a clear goal, the authors believed: 'Communication between people is to be made more difficult, everything is made anonymous, everyone for himself and against everyone else, everything is

---

[88] Anon., 'Neues vom Bohnenviertel', in *'s Blättle* 11, October 1976, 5.
[89] Anon., 'Heidelberg: Die Stadt mit Herz', in *Carlo Sponti* 24/25, December 1976, 12.
[90] See for example Alexander Sedlmaier, *Consumption and Violence: Radical Protest in Cold-War West Germany* (Ann Arbor, MI: University of Michigan Press, 2014), 205–232; Carla MacDougall, 'In the Shadow of the Wall: Urban Space and Everyday life in Berlin Kreuzberg', in *Between the Avant-Garde and the Everyday: Subversive Politics in Europe from 1957 to the Present*, ed. Timothy Brown and Lorena Anton (New York: Berghahn, 2011).

easier to control and to monitor.'[91] In Kreuzberg, the urban renewal process had pushed families into suburbia, where they now lived 'isolated and usually without any contact to their neighbours', a member of the neighbourhood initiatve *Stadtteilzentrum Kreuzberg* argued. In the meanwhile, 'modern life' in the form of 'Lego multi-storey buildings' conquered Kreuzberg.[92] The traffic that authorities envisioned for the streets of modern cities was limited, leftist critics alleged, to 'moving from one department store to the next'. Leftists longed for a kind of traffic that would be a form of unrestricted communication, but for the authorities, this was a 'special usage [*Sondernutzung*]' of streets that required an official permission. After all, communication was potentially dangerous for the capitalist system, since it might result in solidarity and was not exploitable for profit (in contrast to the desire for communication, though).[93] In modern streets, nothing of the 'folk festivals, street fights, public mass dances, barricades and open air bars' that had characterized old cities remained, but only 'purchasing and profiting zones of the capitalist conspiracy', only 'vacuum-strawberries, paper pants and freshness seals, and depending on the season plastic sausages or water milk'.[94] Even sexual encounters were made impossible in this built environment, a certain Klaus argued in a stunningly sexist way in 1982 in the *Blatt*. In earlier times, men might have looked at girls washing themselves in a river; as late as 1950, lonely men could watch a sales girl climb a ladder to reach for some merchandise and see 'where her nylons ended', Klaus claimed. But by 1982, supermarkets had replaced small shops, and men had nothing to look at. People lived in 'clairaudient, slippery, squarishly normed concrete blocks, all fitted with large windows', where even the lift 'shields them from frequent encounters'. Sometimes, men might observe how a woman undresses in front of a 'hastily closed curtain', but that was all. 'Men feel lonely in the evening', Klaus concluded, 'because they have so little opportunities to establish contacts.'[95]

Leftists also argued that the monotony of cities damaged individual personalities and bodies. They typically described cities as grey, monotone, and full of poisoned air. Colours, at least natural colours, had no place in these cities: 'the dull death-grey of concrete devours living green',

[91] Anon., 'Häuserkampf', in *'s Blättle* 70, June 1982, 6.
[92] 'Gespräch mit einem Vertrer des Stadtteilzentrums Kreuzberg', in *Traumstadt* 3, May 1978, 6–11.
[93] Anon., 'Straße und Straßenmusik', in *Großstadtpflaster: Eine Zeitung für Asphaltaktivisten* 1, n.d., probably winter 1976/77, 1–4.
[94] Anon., 'Wer hat uns die Straße geklaut', in *Pflasterstrand* 5, 2–15 March 1977, 22.
[95] Klaus, 'Piep', in *Das Blatt* 217, 26 February–11 March 1982, 16–17.

according to an article in the Nuremberg-based *Info Nürnberg*.[96] In those cities, a 'sensorial deprivation' reigned that was, as Detlef Hartmann argued, tied to capitalist interests. The absence of anything pleasurable in the 'concrete silos', the 'dearth [*Öde*], feelings of monotony, apathy and lethargy are meant to make people look for recovery [*Erholung*] in the city centres, to shop in the city centre and to consider, as it were, the act of buying as central for their life'.[97] Senses, such as 'tasting, smelling, listening, seeing, feeling', were all crippled, a 'women's collective' from Frankfurt argued, by living in and with 'concrete, noise, exhausts, smog, canteen food, phosphorous sausages, rubber bread'. Whenever they (and others) returned from vacation to Frankfurt, they had 'stabbing headaches' for a couple of days, until their body had again gotten used to 'a lack of oxygen and cell-poisons'. In the struggle against this world of sensual deprivation, a 'new sensibility' was necessary, the women declared, that defined their understanding of politics. 'Doing politics means for us women concretely that we insist on our subjectivity and want to make it visible as a positive aspect of our understanding of politics and life – a sensuality that most men have lost somewhere on the thorny way of their male socialization.'[98] The sensual monotony of cities, that is, required a new form of political struggling based on their understanding of a specific female subjectivity.

But leftists also criticized cities that were overflowing with artificial sensual stimuli. Reviewing Martin Scorsese's 1976 film *Taxi Driver* under the headline 'The Loneliness in Cities', an author for the *Blatt* described how the film depicted New York as a symbol for any city: 'Reflexes on the retina: the red of traffic lights, the flashy white of headlights and neon bills. Signals that blind and threaten.' In this urban life, Travis Bickle, the film's main protagonist, feels sick, has headaches and stomach aches, takes medication. He feels threatened, enclosed, and lonely in this city.[99] The members of a rural commune from Kucha, near Nuremberg, made a similar point to explain why they had fled to the countryside. The city, with its 'aggressiveness', its 'high-rise buildings, streets full of cars, noise, stench, lighting bills, hectic, neurotics, artificial nature', had simply become unbearable. In the countryside, they found happiness 'running

---

[96] 'Back Side', in *Info Nürnberg* 7, September 1976.   [97] Hardtmann, 'Stadtknast'.

[98] Frauenkollektiv, 'So, so, einen Frauenasta habt ihr – Ach ja, einen Frauenasta?', in *diskus* 5, 20 October 1976, 18–27.

[99] Ingolf Bonset, 'Die Einsamkeit in den Städten', in *Das Blatt* 84, 24 December 1976–13 January 1977, 22–23.

barefoot over the grass, drinking fresh milk from healthy cows'.[100] The concrete of cities, by contrast, made them literally sick, as it violated the electrical 'so-called equality field' that human beings would need for their physical health, according to a newspaper article the commune reproduced in its magazine.[101] Whether the sensual monotony of modern cities resulted in the degeneration of human senses, or a sensual overflow made people nervous and sick: modern cities damaged personalities and bodies.

Leftists did not limit their critique to urban planning and living in high-rise apartment buildings. They similarly criticized places such as schools or universities as isolating. A female teacher described the desperate situation at her school, where touching students, hence establishing personal relations with them, was strictly forbidden. The school's rooms were, she wrote, 'sterile (allegedly for the janitors – as if any high school teacher would give a damn about janitors!), bald, miserable, to make them really appropriate for the school-reality, that is to make the last colourful dreams go away'.[102] University buildings looked similarly sterile, according to leftists. Entering the university of Kassel, an author writing as Dragana claimed that the 'concrete bloc' induced her with fear. 'This concrete bloc with its long floors, reminiscent of a parking house, with its aluminium windows and bluely shining [blauschimmernden] panes. From every corner, from every white, shiningly cleaned table, a sterility yells at you that is only insufficiently covered [überplastert] with posters.' Looking at all the 'intel-lectuals' with their serious faces and the briefcases, the author realized that she would always need to wear a mask in these rooms.[103] In such sterile buildings, it was neither possible to dream of a better life in which something other than capitalist efficiency mattered, nor was it possible to express one's feelings and 'authentic' personality.

Leftists were keen to point out the very real damages that this urban environment caused. For example, the *Blatt* reported about the death of Ernst Hemm, who died at age twenty-three in a motorcycle accident. 'Ernst had grown up in the outskirts of Munich, in the shadows of concrete silos. At day, there is no life between those concrete silos, and at night, in the cold neon light, they resemble a spooky city of the dead. In these soulless suburbs [trostlosen Trabantenstädten], there is only one kind

---

[100] Raymond, 'Das Land ist frei', in *Päng* 4, n.d., probably spring 1971, 6–7.
[101] Anon., 'Wer in Beton lebt, wird krank', newspaper notice of unknown origin, reprinted in *Päng* 7, Spring/Summer 1973, 2.
[102] Anonyme Lehrerin, '"Wer hier eingeht, Des Nam und Sein ist ausgelöscht – er ist verweht"', in *Das Blatt* 147, 1–14 June 1979, 12.
[103] Dragana, 'Erfahrungen im ersten Semester GH Kassel', in *Kassler Kursblatt*, October 1976, 3–4.

of leisure activity for teenagers: stealing mopeds and breaking vending machines [*Automatenknacken*].' At age fourteen, Hemm was first convicted and sent to prison. Ever since, he stayed in trouble. When he tried to evade a police search and fled with a motorcycle, he smashed against a tree and died.[104] Quite literally, the 'soulless suburbs' had destroyed his life. Leftists themselves equally suffered. *Pflasterstrand* exclaimed, 'The systematic isolation of human beings by living silos [*Wohnsilos*] and satellite towns [*Trabantenstädte*], by consumption that markets every inch of the body and that claims to provide sense and self-estimation, the senselessness and monotony and the hence necessary organization of leisure time with the help of a industry of stultification, and so on, those are not only the problems of a normal citizen, but also ours! [*Die systematische Isolierung der Menschen untereinander durch Wohnsilos und Trabantenstädte, der jeden Körperwinkel vermarkende Konsum als Sinn- und Selbstwertspender, die Sinnentleerung und Monotonie und dadurch notwendig gewordene Organisierung der Freizeit mittels einer Verdummungsindustrie usw. sind eben nicht nur die Probleme des normalen Bürgers, sondern auch die unseren!*]'[105] And in partnership ads, which were common in left-wing magazines such as the *Blatt* or *Pflasterstrand,*[106] usually men referred to their living situation as a reason for why they were searching for (female) contact. As a man named Thomas wrote: 'After living for one year alone (high-rise building), I observe beginning symptoms of an inner devastation [*seelischer Verödung*].'[107]

Children were particularly affected by this urban regime, leftists argued. In the eyes of one author for the *Stadtzeitung für Freiburg*, the new suburbs created an environment 'hostile to children'.[108] An anonymous letter to the *Heim- und Erzieherzeitung* from West Berlin in 1972 even stated that these suburbs were the result of a 'general hatred against children' amongst those 'brain-dead architects'.[109] Quietness was the order of the day, and thus parents issued numerous bans for children, fearing for their safety, or

[104] PS (Peter Schult), '. . . ne hübsche Leiche', in *Das Blatt* 130, 28 September–12 October 1979, 4.
[105] Anon., 'Die Fahrradguerilla geht um', in *Pflasterstrand* 66, 3–16 November 1979, 30–31.
[106] On personal ads in left-wing magazines, see Sven Reichardt, 'Von "Beziehungskisten" und "offener Sexualität"', in *Das Alternative Milieu: Antibürgerlicher Lebensstil und linke Politik in der Bundesrepublik Deutschland und Europa 1968–1983*, ed. Sven Reichardt and Detlef Siegfried (Göttingen: Wallstein, 2010); Sven Reichardt, *Authentizität und Gemeinschaft: Linksalternatives Leben in den siebziger und frühen achtziger Jahren* (Berlin: Suhrkamp, 2014), 659–674.
[107] Kleinanzeige by Thomas, in *Das Blatt* 57, 14–27 November 1975, 47.
[108] Anon., 'Weingarten zwischen Beton und Abenteuer', in *Stadtzeitung für Freiburg* 12, May 1977, 3–6.
[109] Anon., 'Die Kriminellen . . . sind ganz woanders', in *Heim und Erzieher Zeitung* 2, December 1972, 7–10.

that they might cause conflicts with local authorities or landlords.[110] Above all, those places lacked any opportunities for children to play. What were meant as playgrounds for the children were rarely more than 'brain damages made of steel pipes and a bit of dry sand'.[111] The 'unchangeable equipment of steel and concrete' are in no ways adequate to 'stimulate children's fantasies', Claudius Habbich and Pit Möller charged in the *Heim-Erzieher Zeitung*.[112] Children, the author from Freiburg wrote, lack a 'space for experience that does not remain limited to pouring of concrete and asphalt [*Betonierung und Asphaltierung*]'.[113] Such unimaginative equipment disciplines children by telling them how to play, ultimately 'to prescribe them what should be, what is allowed and what is not', Habbich and Möller claimed. No matter how elaborate a conventional playground might be, its equipment 'can be used and consumed, but it cannot be shaped and changed creatively'. These restrictions imposed upon children 'deform [them], if not openly and directly visibly, then all the more reliably and profoundly'.[114] Playgrounds thus resembled the 'totally planned' cities, Detlef Hartmann argued. Even some parents realized spontaneously that 'children are turned into conveyor-belt workers for slides'. But children, Hartmann noted, disliked such playgrounds, and in fact frequently vandalized them. 'The issue is immediately political', he emphasized, because it was an indication that a 'spontaneous collectivity' emerged in the suburban neighbourhoods that was able to 'reappropriate the diffuse spaces', something city planners were deeply afraid of.[115]

The built environment of modern cities, the 'concrete silos' of 'satellite towns', played a fundamental role in leftist analyses of the emotional regime of capitalism. According to leftists, the physical layout of cities was entirely subject to the interests of capital and consumption. Streets cut neighbourhoods apart and organized cities in a rational and efficient manner, but made it impossible for people to form personal relations based on trust and solidarity and left no space for dreams and fantasies. People in these cities lived isolated lives, leftists believed; they were deeply bored by the sensual monotony of greyish concrete buildings, lacked opportunities for (sexual) encounters, and children were nothing but passive consumers of playgrounds that failed to facilitate experimentation and exploration. Analysing cities in such terms, leftists established an

---

[110] Anon., 'Weingarten'.   [111] Anon., 'Die Kriminellen'.
[112] Claudius Habbich and Pit Möller, 'Abenteuerspielplätze', in *Heim und Erzieher Zeitung* 9/10, July/August 1973, 45–49.
[113] Anon., 'Weingarten'.   [114] Habbich and Möller, 'Abenteuerspielplätze'.
[115] Hardtmann, 'Stadtknast'.

emotional knowledge that explained how the built environment 'damaged' personalities, feelings, and bodies. Leftists knew how living in the city would feel. And the grey of concrete, the broad streets that dissected old neighbourhoods, could indeed evoke feelings, precisely because leftists had an understanding of how cities would shape emotions. When leftists described how lonely they felt in modern high-rise buildings, they not only (re)produced a knowledge about the relation between space and feelings, but also practised the very feelings they were describing. At the same time, their analysis of urban feelings gave them a sense of how to change the built environment in order to produce better emotions.

The Emotional Regime of the Left

So far, this chapter has discussed how leftists produced knowledge about feelings in a capitalist society: how capitalism induces fear, how it damages personalities and personal relations, and how modern cities evoke feelings of boredom and loneliness. To conclude the chapter, I shift the focus from the production of an emotional knowledge to an investigation of how leftists enacted this regime practically within their own scene. Not surprisingly, leftists claimed to suffer themselves under the emotional restrictions of capitalism. They, too, felt afraid, socially isolated and were incapable to communicate; their personalities, bodies, and personal relations were just as 'damaged' as anybody else's. The leftist scene was no island, as it were, exempted from the emotional regime of capitalism, leftists would argue. But leftists also tried to challenge this regime in their search for the feelings they missed in capitalism. In doing so, they created new emotional norms, something leftists were remarkably well aware of. Not least, expressing one's feelings and damages became a requirement within the left. Leftists, to put it pointedly, had to constantly talk about being incapable of communicating about their feelings and problems. Emphasizing the difficulties of communicating in capitalism, leftists both enacted the emotional regime of capitalism, *and* transgressed it. Leftists, that is, simultaneously enforced the emotional regime of capitalism amongst themselves, and created a counter-regime for the left.

The critique of technological rationality Rädli published in the *Blatt* provides an idea of the emotional situation in the leftist scene. In December 1977, the band The Embryos played a concert in the Olympiamensa. At least for Rädli, it was as much a frustrating experience as it was a revelation.

The rhythm only trickles into the inside, or it doesn't. Barely any external movement of the bodies. Barely anyone who dances, who lets the revolving stanzas into himself. Uncommunicative, caved, sitting there, boiling, waiting. At most, a daring shaking. Back and forth. Has anyone seen it, me being out of control? Nevertheless, I've danced and realized how rarely an eye makes contact with another eye. The stream of feelings is blocked. Isolated. It's more likely that a dead rat will fuck a bicycle lamp than that two strangers will pierce holes into their armour.

[*Der Rhythmus versickert nurmehr im Innersten oder auch nicht. Kaum eine äußerliche Bewegung der Körper. Kaum jemand der tanzt; der die aufwühlenden Takte in sich kommen lässt. Unkommunikativ, in sich zusammengefallen, dasitzen, kochend, warten. Wenn's hochkommt ein gewagtes Wippen. Hin und her. Hats jemand gesehen, meine Unkontrolliertheit? Trotzdem habe ich getanzt und gemerkt, wie selten ein Auge sich mit einem anderen berührt. Der Strom der Gefühle blockiert. Vereinsamt. Noch eher fickt eine tote Ratte mit einer Fahrradlampe, als dass zwei Fremde ihre Panzer durchlöchern.*]

The experience at the concert gave him reason to think about the prospects of the left, its search for freedom, the 'experiment with the body, the liberation of desires, pleasures and perceptions, the dismantling of the armour with which life protects itself against orgasms'. The 'logic of the present', he claimed, 'is the logic of the body'. And hence capital 'has created countless methods to control, to discipline, to poison, to geometrize, to block, to saw, to break apart, to nail bodies'. Indeed, bodily practices that alternative leftists had developed, like bioenergetic exercises, had already been commercialized. Rädli presented a desperate analysis of the left's state of mind: the 'armours' of capitalism were intact, and even the 'most shrill chants of the guitarist' had failed to break the armour apart. Total isolation seemed to reign in the Munich radical left.[116]

Many leftists shared Rädli's analysis. Nearly five years earlier, in January 1973, a rather bizarre text by a 'Necrophilia Liberation Front' that was published in the West Berlin magazine *Hundert Blumen* had made a similar point. Why would sex with dead women be preferable to having sex with living women, the text asked. 'How often has a living (female) partner ruined an erotic evening by opening her mouth at an inappropriate moment? How often did you go after frustrated girls, just because you hoped that you might get laid by them? Screwing dead women is very different; you don't need to, for example, if you're not in the mood, and you can avoid those stupid compliments, like "Hey, you're looking great

---

[116] Rädli, '[Title illegible]', in *Das Blatt* 111, 23 December 1977–12 January 1978, 24.

tonight!" . . . In fact, you don't need to say anything unless you really want to."[117] Not surprisingly, Berlin's leftist scene was outraged. But two issues later, the editorial team explained their intentions for publishing the text. It was meant as a critique of the leftist scene that treated women as if they were dead objects and avoided genuinely communicating with women; thus, dead women would be perfect.[118] Whereas leftists in Munich remained isolated in a bodily sense, if we are to believe Rädli, the social isolation in Berlin was due to a lack of communication, especially between men and women, the text suggests.

A year later, in Berlin's *Info BUG*, a woman named Claudia complained about a lack of communication. Having had sex with her regular sex-companion, but certainly not partner, she wanted to ask him many questions, for example if he knew where women could be stimulated, and if their 'being-together [*Zusammensein*]' would be more intense if he knew; yet she remained silent. After a second round of sex, which was apparently better, since she came at least close to an orgasm, she continued thinking, while her partner Christian just fell asleep. Once, they had been a couple, but now, all the feeling was gone; attempts to re-create these feelings by having sex of course failed. 'I've only got to know Christian's body. I don't know anything about your feelings, your sadness, your desires. That's not a way to understand someone!', she exclaimed. It was, it seems, a purely physical 'object relation', devoid of any communication.[119]

This was not an individual experience, as a reaction to her account pointed out a few weeks later. 'Each and every one of us could have written this text', the author claimed. The lack of communication in the scene 'increasingly damages us'. This 'speechlessness [*Sprachlosigkeit*]' was not limited to sexuality, according to the anonymous author. Leftist bookshops just functioned like the large department store *Kaufhaus des Westens* (*KaDeWe*). 'You look for a book, march to the cashier, pay and leave without saying a single word.' Usually, nothing beyond the 'mere act of purchasing (exchange) happens'. At leftist parties, bars, teach-ins, and movie theatres, it was the same: 'speechlessness and disinterest in others', because 'we pretend psychic stability that does not exist'.[120] And in Frankfurt, the situation was not much better. 'We talk like strangers to

[117] Necrophilia Liberation Front, 'Es lebe die Necropholie! Die sexuelle Befreiung der Leichen ist kein Privileg der Reichen', in *Hundert Blumen* 6, January 1973, 6.

[118] Anon., 'Wir über uns', in *Hundert Blumen* 8, n.d., probably spring 1973, 6–7.

[119] Claudia, 'Gedanken, die du ohne Worte nicht verstehst', in *Info BUG* 30, 29 October 1974, 7.

[120] Anon., 'Gedanken zu Gedanken', in *Info BUG* 32, 11 November 1974, 9, 12.

each other and create an atmosphere of cruelty that allows only somewhat stable marathon speakers [*Dauerredner*], who are usually a caricature of themselves, to discuss like representatives, stuck, blocked, and usually unproductive. [*Wir reden wie Fremde zueinander und bringen eine Grausamkeit auf, in der nur noch einigermaßen stabile Dauerredner, die meistens nur die Karikatur ihrer selbst sind, repräsentativ sich streiten können, eingefahren, blockiert, meist unproduktiv.*][121] Loneliness was, it seems, a common feeling in the West German left.

Even events that were meant to disrupt the general isolation, like parties or group meetings, often failed to accomplish these goals. In the *Blatt*, Wolfgang Thempel claimed that he felt 'totally incapable of making contact' at parties or other events and hence retreated into the circles he already knew, not least because he was too worried that women might consider his behaviour 'manly-aggressive' when he expressed his desire for 'mutual caressing [*gegenseitige Streicheleinheiten*]'.[122] But this was not an exclusively male problem. In West Berlin, female activists organized women's-only parties to facilitate communication amongst women. But that failed, as a woman complained in February 1976. With two thousand guests, the party was simply too large, which made women nervous and hence resulted in an 'inability to communicate'.[123] Political groups like the editorial teams of leftist periodicals faced the same problem. Newcomers typically felt uneasy [*beklommen*], remained shy and restrained, being too afraid of other's opinion to show themselves the way they wanted to.[124] Despite all the critique of the 'capitalist' isolation and communicative void, it was the leftist scene itself, these texts indicate, that suffered most from a general 'speechlessness'. Just as in a capitalist regime, it was imperative not to show any weakness. Leftists could rationally talk about alienation, but suppressed their 'fears, rage, tenderness, tears, joy, sorrow . . . feelings', as a member of a Munich men's group wrote.[125] Leftists, such texts show, adhered to the emotional style that capitalism seemed to prescribe, according to their own analyses. They knew how to feel in capitalism, and they felt that way. In that sense, the emotional regime of capitalism was indeed powerful – at least within the left.

[121] Drei aus der Redaktion, 'Von Feen und Faunen', in *Pflasterstrand* 23a, 9–22 February 1978, 4–5.
[122] Wolfgang Thempel, 'Gedanken zum Pfingstkongress', in *Das Blatt* 73, 2–15 July 1976, 20.
[123] Anon., 'Heiße Luft und die Erinnerung: Nachlese Frauenfest', in *Info BUG* 95, 24 February 1976, 3.
[124] Cartoon of the Editorial Team, in *Hundert Blumen* 8, n.d. probably spring 1973, 3.
[125] Lothar, 'Ich freue mich, angefangen zu haben . . .', in *Das Blatt* 60, 19 December 1975–8 January 1976, 11–12.

But the analysis of the emotional misery under capitalism also called for dealing differently with feelings. If people only pretended to be psychically stable, then of course admitting one's problems and 'damages' was imperative. The author who responded to Claudia's letter for example claimed that 'we all know that we're working through some problems which are of a social nature. Because we know that our difficulties (jealousies, sexual problems, loneliness, etc.) are not individual [difficulties], but an expression of our psychic deformation by the commodity-exchanging society, we should not be afraid of making them public.' Claudia's letter had set an example in that regard that was for other leftists to emulate.[126] In *Carlo Sponti*, a woman named Bea complained about men's 'incessant coolness', and demanded that they would be able to talk about their feelings, their 'fears and insecurities'. 'I want to know what's going on with you, how you feel, if you feel shitty, where that comes from and what you do about it.' After all, she alleged, 'you [men] are emotionally quite crippled and still behind'.[127] It was, a woman from Berlin wrote, necessary for men to break with their rationalism and to start feeling.[128] Here, leftists formulated quite explicit emotional expectations based on a knowledge about the feelings that capitalism was supposed to produce (fears, insecurities, emotional damages, etc.), and instructions how to deal with those difficulties: admit them and talk about them.

These demands to talk about 'damaged' feelings did not fall on deaf ears. As we have seen, leftists frequently described themselves, both individually and as a collective, as emotionally crippled and unable to communicate. In partnership ads, alternative men (and sometimes women) presented themselves as 'lacking contacts', 'shy' or 'damned sensible', looking for someone to 'help me get over my general disgust [*Daseinsekel*]'.[129] Participants of groups emphasized how 'shitty' they felt.[130] In Munich's scene, Evi K. claimed in the *Blatt* that people 'just live and try to act out their being damaged and are even mighty proud of it. People are armoured, and they need it, otherwise they would just collapse. They can't afford feelings, they are tough against the outside ...' Of course, she

---

[126] Anon., 'Gedanken zu Gedanken'.

[127] Bea, 'Zur Situation des weiblichen Entwicklungsdienstes in der BRD', in *Carlo Sponti* 36/37, October 1977, 3.

[128] Bettina, 'Antworten einer schönen und sonderbaren Sumpfblüte (Leserbrief)', in *radikal* 6, 21 October 1976, 11.

[129] See the personal ads in *Das Blatt* 51, 8–28 August 1975, 40, and *Das Blatt* 74, 16–29 July 1976, 44.

[130] See for example Lothar, 'Ich freue mich, angefangen zu haben ...'. See also Micha, 'Warum ich in die Männergruppe gegangen bin', in *Mann-o-Mann*, February 1975, 11–12.

herself was damaged by her parents, too. Her mother had just said 'Yes' to everything, and her father, 'that tough guy, he could never show his feelings'.[131] And autobiographical accounts like Verena Stefan's widely read *Häutungen*, or Dieter's 'men's diary', *Was wird aus mir werden? Ich hoffe ein Mensch*, reported extensively about emotional and sexual suffering.[132] Leftists, these texts suggest, not only described and analysed the emotional misery of capitalism, but they felt that misery themselves: they *practised* being 'emotionally crippled'.

These emotional norms that called for spontaneously expressing one's damaged feelings were, however, not unproblematic, as leftists recognized. In a letter to *Schwarze Protokolle*, a man named Mario quite perceptively described the paradox *Spontis* faced. The main elements of being *Sponti* – 'spontaneity, emotionality, satisfying needs here and now, antiauthoritarianism, revolutionizing interpersonal relations, collectivity' – turned into 'new norms' within the *Sponti* scene, he argued, that competed with old norms. 'The fear of not acting like a *Sponti*, the permanent pretence [*Anspruch*] not to come across as authoritarian, "abstract-theoretical" or even openly bourgeois, the constant pressure of "emancipation guardians" [*Emanzipationsbeobachtern*] that you feel everywhere not only lets us fall back behind the difficulties of the antiauthoritarian revolt, but prevents exactly what *Spontis* want to achieve . . . You always have to *pretend*, you never can simply *be*.'[133] Therapy groups, where leftists tried to speak openly about their feelings, as the next chapter discusses, only created new norms: 'Openness, authenticity, showing feelings. A new pressure to conform emerges.' Critical discussions had no place in this world of expressing one's personal feelings, a writer for *Carlo Sponti* noted.[134] And in *Kursbuch*, Michael Schneider remarked that thirty years old critics, 'who effectively remained bourgeois critics despite Marx, Lenin and Mao', lived by the 'new imperative: "be sensible!" As if an asthmatic could be healed by the command "Take a deep breath!"'[135]

The emotional regime leftists created within their own scene could be as restrictive as the regime of capitalism they sought to criticize. Certain emotions and bodily feelings were simply not accepted in the left, some

---

[131] Evi K., 'Peter Schult Prozess, in *Das Blatt* 146, 18–31 May 1979, 6.
[132] Verena Stefan, *Häutungen* (Munich: Verlag Frauenoffensive, 1975); Dieter, *Was wird aus mir werden? Ich hoffe ein Mensch. Ein Männertagebuch* (Berlin [West]: Parallel Verlag, 1978).
[133] Mario, 'Leserbrief', in *Schwarze Protokolle* 10, January 1975, 64–66.
[134] Gerda, 'Gestalttherapie', in *Carlo Sponti* 26/27, January 1977, 5–7.
[135] Michael Schneider, 'Von der alten Radikalität zur neuen Sensibilität', in *Kursbuch* 49, 147–187: 183.

activists complained. The critique of a sexuality that was limited to genitalia, for example, made it impossible to enjoy genital sex without feeling a lack of solidarity with the women's movement, a woman from Heidelberg wrote.[136] In a leftist scene that condemned stable, monogamous relations as bourgeois, expressing love became impossible, Gabi from Kiel worried. Even though she fell in love and wanted to say so, she did not, out of fear of a 'rational analysis' of her supposedly bourgeois feelings. Expressing such feelings, she alleged, would be considered an expression of 'demands [*Ansprüche*]'. Perhaps she had not yet learned how to express her demands in a non-bourgeois way, she mused. 'I want to conquer limitations, restraints, fears; I don't want to create new ones. Lovers used to pledge eternal love – today, I . . . pledge never to have any demands. One is just as absurd as the other.'[137] A man named Edi complained that in the leftist gay scene that propagated promiscuity, monogamous relations were similarly outcast.[138] Beyond these rather intimate feelings, the 'comforting wave of general depression, frustration and sadness' was infuriating, as it destroyed any hope for creating something better, Bernd from Heidelberg noted. 'It just turns into a huge pile of shit.' Being called a (male) 'retarded psycho-cripple' was simply not true, and just prolonged the general frustration, he wrote. He at least did not want to join this general frustration; rather, he wanted to 'bounce around being high and turned on, be happy that I live . . . live like an insane, hungry, curious, drunk, completely'.[139]

Perhaps the most important opportunity to discuss new emotional norms and the problems those entailed were debates about 'new guys' in various cities. In Berlin, the republication of an article about 'softie' men from the feminist *Frauenoffensive* in the local *Info BUG* in early 1976 resulted in a debate about new ideals of masculinity that continued over several weeks.[140] In 1979, the Munich *Blatt* published a series about

---

[136] Anon., 'Zeit, Verbindlichkeit, Sexualität', in *Carlo Sponti* 30/31, March 1977, 4.

[137] Gabi, 'Eine "anspruchs"-lose Tagebucheintragung', in *Kieler Fresse* 15, n.d. (probably February 1978), 18.

[138] Eldi, 'Promiskuität – Flucht vor der Verantwortung', in *Emanzipation* 3, 1975, 3–9.

[139] Bernd, 'Frustig, Frustig, Trallala! Geschichten, die die Szene schreibt', in *Carlo Sponti* 36/37, October 1977, 3.

[140] Claudia Rößler, 'Der Mythos von der Ausnahme, oder: Auch der "softe Mann" ist keine Alternative", in *Info BUG* 90, 19 January 1976, 2–5, first published in *Frauenoffensive* 3, January 1976; Annie C., 'Abschiedsbrief an einen Softie', in *Info BUG* 91, 26 January 1976, 7; Eine Frau, die denkt, dass Männer auch Menschen sind, 'Leserbrief', in *Info BUG* 91, 6 January 1976, 8; Patrick, 'Zaghafte Antwort eines "Softies"', in *Info BUG* 92, 2 February 1976, 7–8; Anon., 'Leserinnenbriefe', in *Info BUG* 92, 2 February 1976, 9; Patrick, 'Zaghafte Antwort eines "Softies" (Fortsetzung)', in *Info BUG* 93, 9 February 1976, 2–3; Patrick, 'Zaghafte Antwort eines

the 'new type', though it remains somewhat unclear whether it was meant ironically or not.[141] In *Ulcus Molle*, Michael Hiltl discussed the 'Steppen-wolf' type of the new, alternative man, a man who remained lonely but longed for contact.[142] And in Frankfurt, a gay comedy group mocked the women's, men's, and gay movements' ideals of nongenital sexuality and 'tenderness'.[143]

In all these debates, leftists formulated, mocked, and criticized new emotional ideals, mostly for men, but at times also for women. At the heart of this new ideal was the notion of 'tenderness [*Zärtlichkeit*]'. The *Blatt* described the 'New Guy' as someone who had discovered his 'tender [*sanfte*]' side, whereas women (*die Typin*) had discovered their active sides; in fact, both simply became human beings who 'lost their fears of tender-ness'.[144] In Berlin, a man emphasized that he 'practised tenderness', which meant that his 'entire human-goal-oriented [*menschenzielgerichtet*] behav-iour is full of tenderness';[145] others, though, criticized this idea of a man 'practising tenderness' without explaining why as 'utterly superficial'.[146] In general, the 'softie' type became 'softer, more feminine', Patrick from Berlin noted.[147] The 'new tenderness' called for emotionally and bodily more intimate relations. The twenty-two-year-old 'softie' man Claudia Rößler had described in *Frauenoffensive* (the text that *Info BUG* repro-duced and that started the debate in West Berlin), a strong, athletic man of 1.90 meters, was indeed so afraid of his strong, male body, she claimed, that he did not dare touch her. If women refused to have penetrative sex, 'softie' men would accept this and just cuddle with them until they fell asleep.[148] These men were ready to admit that they 'suffered from

"Softies" (Ende)', in *Info BUG* 94, 16 February 1976, 3–4; Ein Mann, 'Sowohl Regel als auch Ausnahme', in *Info BUG* 94, 16 February 1976, 5. Anon., 'Antwort auf den "Softie"', in *Info BUG* 95, 24 February 1976, 4; Anon., 'Gedanken: Erinnerungen eines Hetero-Mannes', in *Info BUG* 95, 24 February 1976, 4–5; Micha, 'Seele ←→ Kampf', in *Info BUG* 95, 24 February 1976, 6; Zwei Kreuzbergschwule, 'Warnung vor den Softies', in *Info BUG* 97, 8 March 1976; Anon., 'Bravo, Bravo, Bravo', in *Info BUG* 98, 15 March 1976, 7.

[141] Reimar Lenz, 'Der neue Typ I: Religiöse Subkultur, Ökobewegung und neue Linke finden zueinander', in *Das Blatt* 136, 22 December 1978–14 January 1979; Reimar Lenz, 'Der neue Typ II', in *Das Blatt* 137, 12–25 January 1979; Werner, 'Der neue Typ III: Zur Erklärung', in *Das Blatt* 138, 26 January–8 February 1979, 26–27; Rudolf Kuhr, 'Leserbrief', in *Das Blatt* 138, 26 January–8 February 1979, 55; Anon., 'Leserbriefe', in *Das Blatt* 138, 9–22 February 1979; Reimar Lenz, 'Leserbrief', in *Das Blatt* 139, 23 February–8 March 1979, 54.

[142] Michael Hiltl, 'Steppenwolf: Ein Männerbild aus der "Alternativ"-Szene', in *Ulcus Molle* 7/8, 1979, 20–24.

[143] Anon., 'Das Bewegungsgericht', in *Andere Zeitung* 13, March 1977, 28–29.

[144] Lenz, 'Der neue Typ I'.   [145] Patrick., 'Zaghafte Antwort (Ende)'.

[146] Micha, 'Seele ←→ Kampf'.   [147] Patrick, 'Zaghafte Antwort'.   [148] Rößler, 'Mythos'.

speechlessness and orgasm-orientation'.[149] But they were able to deal with these problems. They listened to others, especially to women,[150] they questioned their role as 'tough men', understood that women's struggles were important, and were 'sensible' and open for tender relations with other men.[151] Their sexuality was not restricted to penetrative genital sex, but included more 'tender' actions; for them, cuddling and fondling was just as important.[152] Ideally, Reimar Lenz wrote in the *Blatt*, the 'new guys' (both male and female) 'integrate body, soul and spirit'. They are no longer willing to 'divide Eros and Agape, Sexus and Solidarity, Amor and Caritas'.[153] The 'new guys', in other words, knew about their 'crippled emotionality', were willing to admit it, and, above all, wanted to 'heal' these 'damages'.

Healing a 'damaged personality' principally required overcoming the internalized domination of rationality. The 'new guys and gals are more interested in sensations [*Empfindungen*] than in clear concepts', Lenz wrote. 'He often doubts that the occidental crisis can be solved with occidental concepts.' The 'new guy' reads Buddha and Lao Tse, and 'expands the critique of capitalism to a critique of civilization ... Arm in arm, the new guy and his gal call for limits to the instrumental reason. They recuperate the split-off capabilities of the listening reason [*vernehmende Vernunft*] from the underground, whereto they had been repressed, in the light of everyday: intuition, fantasy, creativity. Democracy succeeds the dictatorship of the autocratic ratio: body and soul participate in the household of life. [*Der neue Typ und seine Typin fordern, Arm in Arm, die bloße instrumentelle Vernunft in die Schranken. Sie holen die abgespaltenen Vermögen der vernehmenden Vernunft zurück aus dem Underground, wohin sie verdrängt sind, ans Alltagslicht: Intuition, Phantasie, Kreativität. Auf das Diktat der selbstherrlichen Ratio folgt Demokratie: Mitbestimmung von Leib und Seele im Lebenshaushalt.*]'[154] The 'new guy' thus turned to mysticism, understanding that rationality might construe relations between separate entities and establish a structure, but that, under its gaze, the 'whole remains puzzling'. He perceived those 'new teachings' not intellectually, but with his heart.[155] Travelling to a small Native American settlement on the Rio Grande, Patrick, a 'softie' man from Berlin, realized a 'deficit in my spiritual life' and how limited his 'politics and gay trip' had been.[156]

[149] Patrick, 'Zaghafte Antwort'.   [150] Patrick, 'Zaghafte Antwort'.
[151] Annie C., 'Abschiedsbief'; Anon., 'Bravo'.
[152] See, with a critical perspective, Hiltl, 'Steppenwolf'; Anon., 'Das Bewegungsgericht'.
[153] Lenz, 'Der neue Typ I'.   [154] Lenz, 'Der neue Typ I'.   [155] Lenz, 'Der neue Typ II'.
[156] Patrick, 'Zaghafte Antwort (Fortsetzung)'.

The ultimate point of any religion for the 'new guy' was, Lenz pointed out, 'therapy, healing, sacralization. Its goal and measure: the liberated, entirely loving [*liebevolle*] human being. Its caricature [*Zerrbild*]: a new incapacitation, and human beings can also be incapacitated by subordinating them to a new messiah.'[157]

These ideals of a 'new', more emotional masculinity, of tenderness, and of integrating body, soul, and mind, were by no means universally shared within the alternative left. On the one hand, an enthusiastic reader of the *Blatt* thought that the series 'pointed towards the future'.[158] The editors, by contrast, seemed to regard the series as a satire mocking the 'new type'. While blaming the articles for 'fighting something that is not that powerful after all', they still admitted that the tendency that the articles expressed was a problem. The 'new type' it described simply played in the sandbox that capitalism provided, they argued, but did not really fight the reality of capitalism. 'That's not a refusal of the state, that's stupidity.'[159] For them, the search for feelings and a unity of body and soul had replaced political struggles – an argument we have encountered already in the previous chapter.

The main critique that leftists formulated about the 'softie' type, however, concerned the new forms of coercion the ideals of communication and tenderness produced. For example, former 'softie' Patrick, who had found spiritual inspiration at the Rio Grande, described the coercive forces of constantly talking about personal relations in his communal apartment. Debates evolved around his roommate Karl-Heinz, a 'superb example of the sensible man', and his girlfriend, Sonja, a 'spontaneous, relaxed' sports student who initially would not quite understand why her roommates, five pedagogically trained men, were so eager to constantly discuss personal relations. But they forced her to address her 'problems'. The subject was of course sexuality. Making use of his psychological skills – 'psycho-terror', as Patrick wrote – Karl-Heinz succeeded in securing support in the group for his desire to sleep more often with Sonja. Being able to listen and understand, he pressured her to have sex with him. The general expectation, also for women, to talk about emotional problems had effectively created a context in which he could make use of these emotional skills.[160] In another contribution to the 'softie' debate, a man named Micha wrote that he had tried to become 'more feminine and that', but that he happened to be 'edged and coarse [*kantig und ungeschliffen*]'. Just

---

[157] Lenz, 'Der neue Typ II'.   [158] Kuhr, 'Leserbrief'.   [159] Werner, 'Der neue Typ III'.
[160] Patrick, 'Zaghafte Antwort (Ende)'.

submitting to an ideal would not make him 'nobler [*edler*]'. Even though he knew how to act like a 'softie', he felt exploited and unloved, and thus he started acting 'coarse' again.[161]

The ideals of a 'tender', nongenital sexuality were equally criticized. The 'cuddling-tenderness', Michael Hiltl charged in *Ulcus Molle*, had 'frozen' into a 'superficial greeting-ritual' that prevented a further-reaching sexuality (primarily amongst men), that is, actually sleeping with each other. The 'new sexual taboos', he wondered, might well be an 'alternatively embellished [*verbrämte*] hostility to the body, an utterly internalized backlash into bourgeois-tabooized sexual behaviour'.[162] Similarly, gay men charged heterosexual men that their 'perennial pre-lust' would not lead anywhere; even if it could not be expressed, desires for genital sexuality remained alive and well.[163] The ideals of a 'tender' sexuality created, they argued, only new restrictions that equally suppressed sexual desires. Leftist activists, these debates indicate, were highly aware of the new forms of coercion that their attempts to free themselves from the constraints of capitalist and rational society had created. Merely submitting to new norms of tenderness was neither liberating nor a sign of authenticity.

Conclusion

During the 1970s, alternative leftists created a detailed knowledge about how capitalism shaped and restricted feelings. In their mind, capitalist society necessarily produced fear, damaged personalities, fragmented bodies, and disrupted social relations by isolating people from each other and subjecting them to constant competition. In modern, functional cities, people felt alone and isolated, leftists argued, and lacked sensually diverse experiences. Alternative leftists were not alone in formulating such emotional analyses. Both conservative and left-leaning urban sociologists bemoaned the alleged lack of interpersonal communication in supposedly anonymous suburban neighbourhoods, and fear of social decline, of environmental destruction or of diseases, notably cancer, were broadly discussed issues.[164] Amongst leftists, these discourses took a decisively political and anti-capitalist turn. It might be tempting to assess the adequacy of leftist critiques: Did (and does) capitalism really produce fear? Did people in new suburban neighbourhoods like Märkisches Viertel in Berlin really live an

---

[161] Micha, 'Seele ⟵⟶ Kampf'.   [162] Hiltl, 'Steppenwolf'.
[163] Anon., 'Das Bewegungsgericht'.
[164] See Biess, 'Sensibilisierung'; Reinecke, 'Am Rande'; Föllmer, 'Cities of Choice', 587–595.

isolated and boring life, longing for an interpersonal intimacy that had once existed in 'old' working-class neighbourhoods? However, such questions would be beside the point. Instead, we need to grasp the productive quality of the emotional knowledge leftists and others formulated. By analysing capitalism in emotional terms, leftists learned how they would normally feel living in a capitalist society: afraid, lonely, bored, 'damaged' and 'crippled', and so on. And leftists indeed did feel that way, not necessarily because capitalism created these feelings, but because they knew that capitalism would do this. Discussing how capitalism shaped and restricted feelings, leftists effectively created an emotional regime for the alternative scene itself. In that sense, the emotional knowledge leftists developed was highly productive. But it was also productive by suggesting how the emotional constraints of capitalism might be disrupted, how different feelings might be produced, and damaged personalities might be 'fixed'. The emotional discourse amongst leftists should thus not be read as evidence for a peculiar emotional culture characterized by feelings like fear and loneliness. Rather, the critical emotional analysis of capitalism created opportunities for a variety of emotional and bodily experiments that were to yield the feelings leftists missed under capitalism. The following chapter turns to these emotional experiments and explores how they sometimes failed, but sometimes also succeeded.

CHAPTER 4

Searching for Intimacy

'I want to learn to be myself': under this title, five seventeen-year-old secondary school students wrote about themselves in a March 1977 article for the widely read magazine *Kursbuch*.[1] Ulla, Birgit, Susan, Sabine, and Barbara, as the girls were called, had all participated in a women's group that a female teacher in training (*Referendarin*) had initiated. In addition to the young teacher, two more *Referendarinnen*, and between six and eight students, had joined the group. Participating in the women's group was a transformative experience for the girls as it helped them overcome loneliness and isolation. Indeed, Ulla wrote, meeting other women and breaking through her isolation was the very motivation to join the group. And while talking about personal issues in front of the entire group was difficult, she emphasized, it became much easier in informal settings after the actual meeting was over. 'We talked about our sexual problems, masturbating, sleeping together, and it was a really great experience for me to say things in that area that I was thinking about. It was all very much free of fear.' Susan, too, emphasized that she could say whatever she was thinking without being afraid of being judged by the other group members. Instead of criticizing her, fellow group members usually described similar experiences, and as a result she often felt relieved that she was not alone with her difficulties. For Birgit, understanding that others had similar difficulties sleeping with their boyfriends was an important experience. Talking about 'our feelings, our sexuality, our bodies' helped them, Susan stressed, to 'concern ourselves with ourselves [*sich mit sich selbst zu beschäftigen*]'.

The girls also began to think differently about their sexuality, though it took them a while to draw practical consequences from their discussions. Barbara emphasized that she now tried to affirm (*bejahen*) and 'act out' her 'feelings of tenderness' towards women. In theory, she also wanted to stop

---

[1] Ulla, Birgit, Susan, Sabine, and Barbara, '"Ich möchte lernen, ich selbst zu sein." Siebzehnjährige Oberschülerinnen schreiben über sich', in *Kursbuch* 47, March 1977, 143–158.

oppressing her sexual feelings for women, but that was still very difficult for her. At least, talking about masturbating helped her develop a more positive relation to her own body, which she could now enjoy. Birgit on the other hand no longer thought about sexuality 'as something absolute that could only take place between me and my boyfriend', but regarded 'sexuality as a form of communication'. It would only be natural to show feelings for others, men and women, through 'tenderness [*Zärtlichkeiten*], kissing, and so on.' But reaching this ideal was a difficult process that she had not yet entirely completed. For Sabine, who had initially been a bit sceptical about the group, talking about bodies and sexuality had important consequences as it made her stop taking the pill, which changed her and her boyfriend's sexual practices dramatically. They stopped sleeping with each other, a change they both liked, she claimed, because it helped them 'getting to know each other in a different, more intense way. Tenderness can no longer focus on the genitalia, we experience every bit of skin, and I'm not under this horrible pressure to sleep with him, whether I want or not, something I could never tell him.' All in all, the girls developed a desire to interact more with other women; it became easier for them to talk to other women about personal problems, an experience Ulla characterized as a 'great liberation'.

But by no means did the girls uncritically idealize the group and what they learned in it. Especially Sabine stressed that participating in the group discussions was not always easy. It took her a while to talk about her sexuality, but then it felt as if the others were not really interested in what she was going through, 'they just liked hearing themselves talk, to finally express [*endlich mal loswerden*] what is usually kept for oneself.' Sharing experiences created connections, but these connections remained superficial and weak. 'I've felt a group pressure, that is, everyone has to talk about herself, and that means that everyone has to have made certain experiences to be able to keep up in these conversations.' Feelings of sympathy were a mere illusion, Sabine felt, created by a cosy atmosphere. 'You talk about very intimate issues you wouldn't even tell your boyfriend, but if you meet someone [from the group] at school or in the city, you have nothing to say ...' In an 'organized women's group', Sabine noted, she could rarely express herself. It was necessary to have a firm opinion in such groups that could be defended with arguments, but she did not consist only of 'opinions and standpoints.' Hence she preferred talking to female friends, since she and her friends could express their 'true thoughts' that 'anonymous women' might simply make fun of. Sharing her 'rape fantasies or dreams of a great guy, who is very self-confident or looks really good' in a women's group was, it seems, impossible. A remarkable statement, given all the emphasis on dreams and desires in the radical left: apparently, it was still important to have the *right* dreams that could be expressed.[2]

And talking was not enough if it did not have practical consequences. Ulla for example noted that they discussed her sexual problems in the women's group – she had slept with her boyfriend even though she did not want to, except when she was drunk, and often cried afterwards – which was 'very relieving and liberating, but that was it'. She never managed, at least while she was in the group, to actually change her sexual behaviour. Talking about problems and experiencing other women's solidarity might in fact have perpetuated the situation, Sabine worried. Nor did talking about 'tender' bodily feelings towards women simply produce such feelings. After a year or so, the group had discussed all sexual problems and did not quite know what to do next. One girl then had the idea of an 'experiment', that is to 'just try how one reacts to being touched or fondled by another woman.' But the experiment went quite wrong. For Susan, who usually 'incredibly liked physical contact with other people', this had to happen spontaneously. 'I just can't do this on command, fondling someone.' To make things easier, they thought of games to initiate the touching. But they were all equally 'insecure', as Birgit stressed, not least because it was unclear how far one should go. 'We had long discussions, and when we touched each other, it was all cramped and compelled.' In the end, they decided they rather wanted to continue talking about women's problems, like being afraid of loneliness later in life. But soon enough, the group simply disbanded. The girls did not convey the impression that they would like to join another women's group after these experiences. For Barbara, focusing on her body, thinking about 'bioenergetics' and yoga and using them to 'delve further into my psyche' was more important. 'I don't pursue big political goals, because I don't believe in positive social changes and because my personal development is more important to me.'

Participating in a women's group was, the girls' testimony shows, an ambivalent experience. It could be both transformative and liberating, and restraining and frustrating. Women groups provided an opportunity for the liberating experience of talking about personal problems, and they forced girls and women to talk about themselves. It provided them with an opportunity to develop 'tender' feelings towards women, but attempts to

---

[2] See also Barbara Sichtermann, 'Der Tanz des sich Vorwagens: Gewalt und Lust', in *Courage* 6, December 1981, 6–9.

enforce such (physical) tenderness ended rather quickly and unsuccessfully. And finally, the women's group allowed girls to overcome their isolation and to understand their seemingly individual problems as social and political, but it could also push them towards merely focusing on their personal development without engaging in politics.

In many ways, the group the girls had participated in was typical for the numerous consciousness-raising groups, or, as they were called in German, 'self-experience groups' (*Selbsterfahrungsgruppen*) that flourished in the alternative left during the 1970s. These groups, no matter whether they were designed as women's, men's, gays' or just general self-experience groups, provided leftists with a space for experimenting with feelings, to try out communicative and bodily practices that would help them, they hoped, to 'fix' their damaged personalities, to overcome their isolation and to develop personal relations based on tenderness and solidarity. Sometimes, those experiments worked very well, and helped participants to change their feelings in a way they had hoped for, but sometimes, they also went terribly wrong and left participants feeling lonely and frustrated. The account of the teenage girls encapsulates these ambivalences.

The preceding chapters have explored how leftists reimagined politics as a struggle against the domination of rationality – a capitalist rationality that induced fear, caused loneliness, and 'damaged' personalities and personal relations. The struggle against this emotionally damaging society called for developing and expressing feelings, for 'fixing' damaged personalities, overcoming isolation, and for disrupting the fear-inducing emotional regime of capitalism. In that sense, politics became a kind of self-therapeutization that required constantly working on the self. This chapter discusses how leftists tried to accomplish their therapeutic goals, for example in consciousness-raising groups, in communes, or during moments of collective activism, such as festivals and demonstrations. The chapter, in other words, explores the practical side of the alternative left's political project of emotional transformation, moving away from more or less theoretical discussions within the alternative left. Building on Monique Scheer's conceptualization of emotions as practices, it analyzes what leftists *did* in order to have the feelings of intimacy and intensity they longed for. Verbalizing one's feelings, most prominently in consciousness-raising groups, was an important aspect of this endeavour. But frequently, as the earlier example has indicated, leftists considered merely talking about feelings to be insufficient. They wanted to feel the body, and to feel *with* the body. Leftists touched each other, tried to develop a more inclusive sexuality, and sought to intervene in the built environment to create the conditions for overcoming loneliness and isolation. Bodily and spatial practices thus figure prominently in this chapter.

The practices this chapter discusses could be analyzed as what Michel Foucault called 'technologies of the self', that is, in Foucault's famous formulation, as practices 'which permit individuals to effect by their own means or with the help of others a certain number of operations on their own bodies and souls, thoughts, conduct, and way of being, so as to transform themselves in order to attain a certain state of happiness, purity, wisdom, perfection, or immortality.'[3] Scholars have indeed, as the introduction has noted, turned to Foucault to make sense of such practices, arguing that a culture of subjectivity emerged in the alternative left that called for constantly expressing one's 'authentic' feelings. Whereas leftists proclaimed to 'liberate' feelings, they effectively created a new regime of subjectivity with its own rules and demands that anticipated the contemporary 'neoliberal' self. There is much to be said for such a perspective. Yet it tends to result in rather static images of a peculiar regime of subjectivity. What is lost is the productive dynamics of experimenting with feelings. Based on an understanding of how emotions work, leftists tried to produce feelings, sometimes successfully, sometimes not, by engaging in a variety of emotional and bodily experiments. Studying these experiments with a microhistorical perspective that pays attention to the often-unintended emotional dynamics, the chapter seeks to restore a sense of contingency and openness to our understanding of the 1970s. It offers a perspective on the 1970s that explicitly refuses to integrate those years into a prehistory of the present.

The chapter begins with a discussion of the world of groups, arguably the most prominent place where leftists could try out bodily and communicative practices that would help them to develop feelings of intimacy. Moving beyond the world of groups, the second section then takes a closer look at how leftists tried to feel their bodies, individually and collectively. Third, the chapter investigates various contexts in which leftists tried to overcome loneliness and practise intimacy, such as communes or alternative youth centres. Not least, activists tried to intervene into the built environment in order to create the spatial conditions that might yield feelings. In all these instances, leftists pursued a therapeutic politics that was meant to 'fix' the 'damaged' self. However, as the fourth part shows,

---

[3] Michel Foucault, 'Technologies of the Self', in *Technologies of the Self: A Seminar with Michel Foucault*, ed. Luther H. Martin, Huck Gutman, and Patrick H. Hutton (London: University of Massachusetts Press, 1988), 18.

they also tried to disrupt the seemingly oppressive and boring normalcy of life in the Federal Republic in order to yield feelings of intensity – consider, for example, the report of the bicyclists' demonstration in Munich discussed in Chapter 2. Even if such moments proved transformative, they can hardly be described as 'therapeutic' politics in the sense that they required people to work on themselves. Given the chapter's interest in exploring the practical trying out of feelings, detailed descriptions of leftists' emotional and bodily practices are necessary to understand the micro-dynamics of emotional experiments. To conclude, the chapter addresses leftist critics of the politics of therapeutization who charged their comrades for effectively contributing to a new regime of power that relied on psychologists as experts.

Trying Intimacy: The World of Groups

In the 1970s, West Germany saw what contemporaries already called a 'psychoboom', and what scholars have since described as the emergence of a 'therapeutic society'.[4] Psychology as an academic subject boomed with an ever-increasing number of students, and subsequently psychotherapists, a development not least facilitated by the inclusion of psychoanalytical therapy into the catalogue of benefits covered by health insurances. 'Therapeutic interventions', and individual guidance for people in need of help, became tremendously important within the Catholic Church.[5] Particularly therapy groups of all kinds flourished massively.[6] According to

[4] Frank Biess, 'Die Sensibilisierung des Subjekts: Angst und "neue Subjektivität" in den 1970er Jahren', *WerkstattGeschichte* 49 (2008): 68–69. For a contemporary critical perspective on the 'therapeutic society', see the contributions in *Kursbuch* 82, November 1985.

[5] Maik Tändler, *Das therapeutische Jahrzehnt: Der Psychoboom in den siebziger Jahren* (Göttingen: Wallstein, 2016), 95–138; Benjamin Ziemann, 'Zwischen sozialer Bewegung und Dienstleistung am Individuum: Katholiken und katholische Kirche im therapeutischen Jahrzehnt', *Archiv für Sozialgeschichte* 44 (2004): 379–382.

[6] On the leftist psychoboom and groups, see, with further references, Barbara Sutter, '"Selbstveränderung und Sozialveränderung": Von der Selbsthilfegruppe und ihren Verheißungen zum Bürgerschaftlichen Engagement und seinen Zumutungen', in *Das beratene Selbst: Zur Genealogie der Therapeutisierung in den 'langen' Siebzigern*, ed. Sabine Maasen et al. (Bielefeld: transcript, 2011); Maik Tändler, 'Therapeutische Vergemeinschaftung: Demokratie, Emanzipation und Emotionalisierung in der "Gruppe", 1963–1976', in *Das Selbst zwischen Anpassung und Befreiung: Psychowissen und Politik im 20. Jahrhundert*, ed. Maik Tändler and Uffa Jensen (Göttingen: Wallstein, 2012); Maik Tändler, '"Psychoboom": Therapeutisierungsprozesse in Westdeutschland in den späten 1960er und 1970er Jahren', in *Das beratene Selbst: Zur Genealogie der Therapeutisierung in den 'langen' Siebzigern*, ed. Sabine Maasen et al. (Bielefeld: transcript, 2011); Tändler, *Therapeutische Jahrzehnt*, 158–166; Sven Reichardt, *Authentizität und Gemeinschaft: Linksalternatives Leben in den siebziger und frühen achtziger Jahren* (Berlin: Suhrkamp, 2014), 782–806. On women's groups, see Eva-Maria Silies, *Liebe, Lust und Last: Die Pille als weibliche*

an estimate from 1983, some five hundred thousand people had participated in group therapy activities of some kind.[7] Groups were particularly popular in leftist milieus, where the idea that groups provided individuals with an opportunity to 'give new meaning to their deformed and emptied relations', as left-leaning psychoanalyst Horst Eberhardt Richter put it, resonated.[8] These groups would usually meet in private places, though some chose more 'neutral' environments, to talk about personal issues and problems. The informal nature of these groups makes it impossible to provide any exact statistics about how widespread they were, but anecdotal evidence suggests that groups were a common phenomenon in the alternative left. In February 1975, for example, some hundred members of men's groups from cities such as West Berlin, Munich, Frankfurt, Hanover, Freiburg, Tübingen, Aachen, and Vienna gathered in Berlin to discuss their experiences,[9] and in Heidelberg, a veritable 'psycho scene' emerged, a writer for *Carlo Sponti* noted.[10] While groups differed with regards to their composition and designation, they all created spaces for trying out new feelings.

Expectations what participating in groups might yield ran high. At first sight, it might appear that participants joined these groups mostly for personal reasons. In a call to form a men's group, Martin Defren from Freiburg for example expressed his longing for solidarity and 'strengthening feelings'.[11] Men from Berlin who joined such a group declared that they

Generationserfahrung in der Bundesrepublik 1960–1980 (Göttingen: Wallstein Verlag, 2010), 395–397; Andrea Bührmann, *Das authentische Geschlecht: Die Sexualitätsdebatte der neuen Frauenbewegung und die Foucaultsche Machtanalyse* (Münster: Westfälisches Dampfboot, 1995), 134–152; Ursula Krechel, *Selbsterfahrung und Fremdbestimmung: Bericht aus der neuen Frauenbewegung* (Darmstadt, Neuwied: Luchterhand, 1975), 43–48.

[7] Tändler, 'Vergemeinschaftung', 143. On self-help groups, see also Tändler, *Therapeutische Jahrzehnt*, 158–166.

[8] Horst-Eberhardt Richter, *Die Gruppe: Hoffnung auf einen neuen Weg, sich selbst und andere zu befreien. Psychoanalyse in Kooperation mit Gruppeninitiativen* (Reinbek bei Hamburg: Rowohlt, 1972), 33, quoted by Tändler, 'Vergemeinschaftung', 142.

[9] 'Sind Männergruppen ein Sicherheitsrisiko? Protokoll im ersten deutschen Männergruppentreffen am 22. Februar 1975', in Autorengruppe, *Männerbilder: Geschichten und Protokolle von Männern* (Munich: Trikont Verlag, 1976), 49–79. On men's groups, see also Helmut Rödner, *Männergruppen: Versuche einer Veränderung der traditionellen Männerrolle. Ursachen, Wege, Schwierigkeiten* (Berlin: Editora Queimada, 1978); Till Kadritzke, 'Bewegte Männer. Men's Liberation und Autonome Männergruppen in den USA und Deutschland, 1970–1995', in *Feminismus in historischer Perspektive. Eine Reaktualisierung*, ed. Feminismus Seminar (Bielefeld: transcript, 2014); Klaus Mecking and Heino Stöver, *Männersexualität: Gespräche, Bilder, Notizen* (Bremen: Verlag Roter Funke, 1980).

[10] K., 'Transaktionsanalyse – Solidarisches Handeln', in *Carlo Sponti* 26/27, January 1977, 7–8.

[11] Martin Defren, 'Männer-Gruppen in Freiburg, gibt's die?', in *Stadtzeitung für Freiburg* 53, December 1980, 37.

were 'dissatisfied with their role as men', which required them to be tough, not to show feelings, to compete with other men, and to 'have a sexuality of the hard dick'.[12] By joining men's groups, participants wanted show that they were different; they wanted to learn how to express their feelings not only in front of women, but also amongst men.[13] In some cases, men joined groups to deal with the aporias of political activism. A man from Munich for example noted that he had understood how 'social coercions' worked and that he fought them. But nevertheless, he claimed that he had failed to change his personal behaviour. In the men's group, he wanted to move beyond merely theoretical insights and start changing his own personality.[14] Women, who discussed their seemingly personal problems as political problems in consciousness-raising groups, hoped to 'erase not only the wall between us and our bodies, but also the wall between us women.' Joining a women's group would help them to explore and understand their body, and to develop intimate relations with other women.[15] Praising the potential benefits of therapy groups more generally, Lucy Körner argued in *Ulcus Molle* that, in a society that deemed expressing feelings freely embarrassing, groups provided an opportunity to 'let go and let the body run free'. With the help of a therapist, people might learn not being afraid of their feelings. But even without a therapist, they could do 'bioenergetic exercises' alone or with a partner that would have a 'liberating and relaxing effect', at least if one practised them long enough and did not give up after experiencing anger and fear at the beginning.[16] By participating in groups, these examples suggest, leftists hoped to accomplish a personal self-transformation.

But leftists also saw an immense political potential in therapy groups. Blaming capitalism for 'damaging' their personalities, any attempt to 'fix' these personalities was inherently an act of resistance. Heidelberg's *Carlo Sponti* made this argument most explicitly in a January 1977 special issue of therapies. Capitalism, the authors argued, reduces 'the senses, characteristics, drives and desires' to a focus on 'property, power, labour power, character masks, surplus-value production, and so on'. Human beings, with their 'five senses, countless characteristics, nonhierarchical desires,

[12] Micha, 'Warum ich in die Männergruppe gegangen bin'.
[13] Anon., 'Männergruppen', in *Mannsbild*, 1976, 12–13; Shirley, 'Das Ende eines Traumes', in *Mann-o-Mann*, February 1975, 1.
[14] Lothar, 'Ich freue mich, angefangen zu haben', in *Das Blatt* 60, 19 December 1975–8 January 1976, 11–12.
[15] See 'Körperbewusstsein: Erfahrungen einer Selbsthilfe-Gruppe', in *Frauenjahrbuch* 1976, 135–151. See also the translated text by a women group from Sweden, 'Was sollen Männer in Frauengruppen', in *Hundert Blumen* 5, n.d., probably early 1973, 7.
[16] Lucy Körner, 'Bioenergetik', in *Ulcus Molle* 9/10, 1979, 21–23.

abilities that go beyond individuals, and so on', revolt against this reduction. In this situation, therapeutic theories and 'techniques' have an emancipative potential if they 'help us to discover this multiplicity inside us'; such techniques 'should support us in our struggle against abstractions and the reductions of our five senses, for the multiplicity of our characteristics and capabilities.' Ideally, therapeutic practices would enable people to see both their own and others' diverse capabilities and desires that are trapped in capitalism. An emancipatory sexual therapy, for example, grasps the 'contradictive aspects of sexuality' and 'reassembles them' in a holistic way. The magazine from Heidelberg thus sought to examine different therapeutic approaches, asking whether or not these approaches were genuinely doing something about the 'capitalist fragmentation of identity' and helping to overcome the bourgeois distinction between private and public. It was therefore essential to find the 'right' form of therapy, which is why *Carlo Sponti* published a discussion of different therapeutic approaches.[17] In the *Blatt*, Rädli made a similar point: 'We need to learn distinguishing between forms of therapy that enable individuals to find their centre in themselves, and those that destroy their previous identity in order to integrate it into a terrorist mass formation [*Massengebilde*].'[18] While therapies had, according to leftists, an immense emancipatory potential, they could also be extremely dangerous.

Finding the right form of therapy could be challenging, with regards both to the therapeutic approach and to practical questions. How many people should participate in groups? What should be done in groups to facilitate genuine communication? To solve these questions, leftist activists developed more or less strict guidelines. Rules a women's group from Freiburg formulated included, for example, that between five and seven women should be in a group, that they should meet without a group leader once a week for two to three hours, but also that participants should say 'I' instead of the general 'one' [the German *man*], that women should not give advice but just listen, or that they should not interrupt each other when talking about their experiences. Potentially difficult themes like sexuality should be avoided at the beginning.[19] Since the presence of a 'coach' would make working in a group more productive, some groups explicitly encouraged psychologists or psychology students to work with

---

[17] *Carlo Sponti* 26/27, January 1977.
[18] Rädli, 'Verdorrte Seelen', in *Das Blatt* 128, 1–14 September 1978, 24–27.
[19] Frauen aus der Frauengruppe Freiburg, 'Kleingruppen – Erfahrungen und Regeln', in *Frauenjahrbuch* 1975, 184–198.

them.[20] Others relied on guidance literature. A gay group from Berlin for example made use of psychoanalytical concepts, but read anti-psychiatrists David Cooper and Ronald D. Laing, as well as American communication theorists Gregory Bateson and Jay Haley.[21] A particularly popular book was *Anleitung zum sozialen Lernen für Paare, Gruppen und Erzieher*, by Lutz Schwäbisch and Martin Siems, which was used by several self-experience groups. Schwäbisch and Siems had developed a detailed program for eleven multiple-hours sessions. Each session would be devoted to a specific theme. At the beginning of every meeting, there would usually be a 'flashlight' round, during which everyone would say how they felt or what they wanted to talk about, while entering any discussion was strictly forbidden until everyone had spoken. In a session that focused on 'dealing with feelings', participants would sit in a circle and touch their neighbours' hands, trying to express feelings like fear, anger, or tenderness with their hands.[22] At the end of the sessions, the authors promised, participants would have learned to deal with feelings, for example, how to be 'free of fear'. Participants would also have reduced their own 'blind spots' by learning about themselves, and they would have learned how to communicate effectively without a leader.[23]

Such guidance books provided leftists with clear models of how to 'do' self-experience groups. What happened in practice was, however, another matter. A gay self-experience group from Hamburg for example noted that they did everything according to Schwäbisch and Siems, but private conflicts were still carried out behind the group's back.[24] We thus need to shift attention from the more or less instructive guidance literature to the detailed reports that activists produced about their experience in groups. These reports show how groups became spaces for experimenting and 'trying out' feelings of intimacy. A close reading of these reports allows us to see how alternative leftists tried, failed, and succeeded at 'doing' emotions in a different way.

For many groups, talking about personal problems and experiences, about the pressures and expectations they faced as men and women, and

---

[20] Anon., 'Selbsterfahrungsgruppen', in *Das Blatt* 61, n.d., probably January 1976, 3.

[21] Anon., 'SE-Panik', in *HAW Info* 21, March/April 1976, 15–56.

[22] Lutz Schwäbisch and Martin Siems, *Anleitung zum sozialen Lernen für Paare, Gruppen und Erzieheher: Kommunikations- und Verhaltenstraining* (Reinbek bei Hamburg: Rowohlt, 1974), 293. By 1995, this book had seen multiple editions with a print run of close to four hundred thousand.

[23] Ibid., 256–257.

[24] Dieter, 'Selbsterfahrungsgruppe am Rande der HAH [=Homosexuellen Aktion Hamburg]', in *Rosa* 4, May 1976, 3–6.

not least about their (genital) sexuality, was a first step towards challenging their rational self and breaking through the isolation so common in capitalism. Participants of men's groups hoped that discussing these issues with other men would help them overcome the rational, anti-emotional, and isolated male roles they had internalized. It would make them capable of showing feelings not only to women, but also to other men. In the process, they might develop both a 'new consciousness' and 'new feelings', as a member of a Dutch men's group put it at a meeting in Berlin.[25] Indeed, the very act of 'honestly' talking about themselves was something that produced 'very good feelings', as one member of a Berlin-based men's group wrote.[26] Talking about feelings was thus both a way of practising emotional intimacy, and creating a more emotional male subjectivity. Members of a women's group from Munich, too, felt that talking about such issues in the group was 'free of fear, exhilarating, liberating, strengthening'; it was something new, something they had never experienced before. Talking about feelings was an emotional practice that helped them overcome fear. Interestingly, when they tried to analyze their communication, they turned again to words like 'role structures, dominating hierarchy' and others, words that had bored them so much in previous groups because they were 'evaluating, abstract, crushing the seed, not allowing for any light.' Such concepts were incapable of describing what they experienced, the women argued, and hence they simply stopped their analysis.[27]

But talking about feelings was not necessarily enough, nor was it unproblematic. The Heidelberg men's group reported that the intention to talk openly resulted in a 'performance and competition pressure ... Verbal power does not create emotionality, verbal orgasms still don't yield emotional climaxes.'[28] To experience genuinely the feelings they longed for, it would be necessary to act out feelings with the body. Lothar, a member of a Munich men's group, noted how some of the group members 'censored' '"dangerous" feelings or experiences'. 'The group lacked immediacy.' When they decided to address relations in the group, two of the 'big theoreticians' quit, afraid of having to show their feelings, Lothar claimed. 'But we [that is, the rest of the group] dared the attempt [to show feelings].' For Lothar, it seems, something changed. He left 'ways of

---

[25] Autorengruppe, *Männerbilder*, 65.

[26] Manfred et al., 'Hickhack', in *Mannsbild*, 1976, 5–9 (remarks by Manfred).

[27] 'Körperbewusstsein', 149.

[28] Die verbliebenen fünf aus der Männergruppe, 'Männer – ohne Männlichkeit ratlos?', in *Carlo Sponti* 20/21, May 1976, 8–9.

understanding and rationalizing' behind him, or so he claimed; he was able to 'simply write from within [*aus mir herausschreiben*, literally 'to write out of myself'], unarticulated, uncensored, without caring about coherence. Suddenly, a sobbing broke out of me – I felt that a chunk had started moving inside me.' His fellow group members first reacted helplessly, not knowing how to deal with this emotional outbreak, but then approached him, cuddled and hugged him. 'It was the first time that I allowed men to do this, without a conscious rejection.'[29] Expressing his feelings in a bodily way, by sobbing, triggered his fellow group members to also engage with him in a bodily manner. It resulted in a bodily intimacy Lothar had longed for.

In a Berlin group, talking about feelings and personal problems did not result in frustrations, but made the men feel closer to each other. One day, this sense of intimacy translated into bodily closeness, as they 'all piled up and cuddled with each other.'[30] Another group from Munich went a step further during a weekend in the Alps. Taking turns, members got undressed and then gave each other massages. At first, a man named Hans noted, he was 'insanely afraid' of having an erection, a fear he himself described as a 'shitty story'. But afterwards, when he had not had an erection, he realized that it was a pleasurable experience, even an erotic experience, 'though it did not work at this level', meaning that it was not erotic in a genital way. The experience apparently changed how the men related to each other in a bodily way. Hugging each other was no longer a formality amongst friends, but 'real tenderness', they claimed.[31] Practising a bodily intimacy, touching each other, though usually in a nongenital manner, was deemed essential for breaking through the 'body armour' of 'rational' men, these examples indicate. It helped men both overcome their isolation amongst each other, and to be oneself: to practise, in other words, an 'authentic' self.

For members of women's groups, exploring their own bodies was at least as important as learning how to touch other women.[32] Reproductive issues played a crucial role in this regard, as many women were deeply

[29] Lothar, 'Ich freue mich'.   [30] Manfred et al., 'Hickhack' (remarks by Manfred).
[31] Autorengruppe, *Männerbilder*, 56–58.
[32] On the exploration of bodies in the women's movement, see Bührmann, *Geschlecht*, 175–176; Andrea Trumann, *Feministische Theorie: Frauenbewegung und weibliche Subjektbildung im Spätkapitalismus* (Stuttgart: Schmetterlingsverlag, 2002), 88–91; Krechel, *Selbsterfahrung*, 55–59; Imke Schmincke, 'Von der Befreiung der Frau zur Befreiung des Selbst: Eine kritische Analyse der Befreiungssemantik in der neuen Frauenbewegung', in *Zeitgeschichte des Selbst: Therapeutisierung – Politisierung – Emotionalisierung*, ed. Pascal Eitler and Jens Elberfeld (Bielefeld: transcript, 2015).

sceptical about contraceptive pills due to the damage it could do to the body.[33] Looking for an alternative, women sought to understand their menstrual cycle, not only to determine during which days they would be fertile, but to 're-include our body into our life (sensing – finding), and to consciously live (love) with it (us) in an emotional way'. Thinking about the body and 'feeling and experiencing ourselves in a sensual way (with eyes, ears, noses, hands, fingers, breasts, bellies, mouths, flanks, cheeks and lips of all kinds)' was, they claimed, difficult, due to the 'hostility against the body' that they had already developed at the moments of conception and birth, and that had subsequently been strengthened by gynaecologists and the pharmaceutical industry. Against those enemies, women tried to recuperate a feeling for their body. To feel their body, however, they needed to understand and know their body. Temperature curves to determine their cycle should help them doing so. Women not only measured their temperature, but added up to thirty criteria, like 'feeling good or bad, dreamed, active, depressive, cried, thunder storm, thirsty, hungry, nervous, sad, and so on.' Some even added an 'emotional curve' to their temperature curve. But the initial euphoria disappeared quickly. Their expectations of a 'normal', twenty-eight-day cycle were not fulfilled. Soon enough, the detailed self-observation became a burden. Having hectic days ahead of them, they forgot about measuring their temperature. Thinking for ten minutes every day about the body proved surprisingly difficult, an issue they discussed in the group as the project did not yield the expected results. Observing their mood was equally challenging. 'Every day hectic, depressive, sad, disrupted, relationship troubles. That's something we can only suppress [*verdrängen*].' Eventually the women reduced the complexity of their daily observation forms, focused on the really essential criteria, and summarized their emotional situation every couple of days. The experiment of feeling their bodies through understanding them had, despite the initial enthusiasm, failed at first. But the women adjusted the experiment, and in the end it seems that they succeeded in developing a more positive relation towards menstruation. While they previously thought about the bad smell or sickness, they now felt that it was 'pleasant, despite the pain and psychic instability, to feel, to experience his, I mean of course her, that is, my period.'[34]

---

[33] On discussions about the pill and its impact on the female body in the women's movement, see Silies, *Liebe*, 385–412.

[34] 'Körperbewusstsein', 140–142. The German plays with differently gendered pronouns: 'seine, ich meine natürliche ihre, d.h. meine, Periode zu spüren'.

Producing bodily feelings proved to be a difficult endeavour for both women's and men's groups. Cuddling in a group made one man wonder if 'one can focus on one person without hurting the others, or whether one should give the same amount of cuddling units [*das gleiche Maß an Streicheleinheiten* – note the quantifying language!] to everyone.'[35] Being simply spontaneous was obviously impossible. Collective cuddling remained an exceptional experience that did not necessarily shatter the internalized domination of rationality in a long-term perspective. In line with many other reports, a gay group from Berlin reported that the permanent conversations frustrated them, that they perpetuated relations of power rather than yielding 'mutual understanding'. Group members yelled at each other, but did not find access to the 'most inner emotional world'. One day, however, that changed. After a 'very chaotic group meeting, we experienced long desired group feeling.' 'Physically and psychically exhausted', group members tried to relax on the floor, listening to classical music. Some began cuddling, and soon enough, most group members moved closer to the bed, where 'the most intimate hugs and caresses were exchanged'. Some group members touched each other for the first time, while two other group members 'euphorically fucked' in another room. 'The group had unlocked a tiny bit [*Zipfelchen*] of warmth that was necessary for an emotional opening.' One evening, the attempt to produce intense bodily feelings had suddenly and unpredictably worked. But it was a singular event that quickly gained a reputation as something 'forbidden and extravagant', and the group quickly returned to the stiff 'rational discussions'. 'The fear of the envisioned [*erahnten*] new dimension of communication grew.' In the end, some members even worried that they might commit suicide.[36]

Another experience of the same group, which by then had been joined by two women, shows how the attempt to practise different feelings could fail. The group discussed nudity. They had realized that 'sensual experience of the own body in the group public was still fear-laden [*angstbesetzt*]'. Even though they had fantasized about seeing each other naked, the 'real' fear of losing the clothes that 'helped us, if in doubt, to maintain our identity' was larger. But at some point, 'curiosity about the other's body broke the taboo of obscene nudity'. Men worried that their penis might be too short, that their midsections might be too large, or that they might not have enough chest hair; women worried that their breasts might be too saggy, or that people might look at their vagina if they spread

---

[35] Manfred et al. 'Männergruppe Hickhack' (remarks by Leo).   [36] Anon., 'SE-Panik'.

their legs. After verbalizing these fears for a long time, group members started, albeit reluctantly, to undress. Suddenly, a latecomer stepped into the 'pent-up group atmosphere'; 'spontaneously', he undressed, which made it easier for others to follow his example. But this did not help to relax the atmosphere. Now, the group members sat 'cramped' on their matrasses, but did not dare touch each other; eventually, they fondled arms and legs, but left genitalia untouched. 'Nudity was there, but the fear of not being accepted remained.' For one woman, the report claimed, the 'idea of mass fucking' was even worse than the 'fear of her body being rejected.' She kept her legs closed and tried to hide behind a man's back. 'Very obviously, despite our intentions and better knowledge, bourgeois morality was so strongly anchored in our feelings that we still had to negate our corporality and sexuality', the group wrote in its report. Members began talking about fears from childhood, but soon stopped and talked about the function of clothing; eventually, they dressed again. Nudity turned out to be a 'bluff'. 'We were naked and still had not really undressed. Instead of touching, smelling or fondling each other, we hold tight to our external shells by talking about clothing.' The experiment to produce feelings of intimacy by doing something with their bodies – getting undressed – had failed, in their own understanding because they had failed to do something else with their bodies: physically touching each other. Only later on, when going to the sauna as a group, did they learn how to deal with nudity.[37]

Developing a more emotional personality, ultimately one of the goals of groups, proved similarly difficult. Despite their hard work, men and women often seemed incapable of transforming their emotional selves. The men's group from Heidelberg provides perhaps the most drastic, and somewhat absurd, example. Doing 'self-experience' produced 'difficult conflicts'; the men seem to have constantly yelled at each other or struggled for power inside and outside the group. Ultimately, the group broke apart due to a conflict between two members who were in love with the same woman. The group realized that the most traditional conflict – courting a woman – threatened to undo a year and a half of work. And that is what happened: the group disbanded. In their concluding remarks, the remaining members who wrote about the group's experiences worried about the dangers of 'naiveté, superficiality and striking [*plakativ*] emotionality'. Reducing 'masculinity' to problems of sexuality, at the expense of issues such as private life, the job, or political activism, would be a

---

[37] Ibid.

mistake, they argued. While they saw the necessity to strengthen their 'emotional basis', they wanted to become more political, more radical, and, not least, question the idea of exclusive men's groups.[38] Though the Heidelberg group was exceptional, other groups, too, encountered tensions and conflicts they could not solve. When discussions turned too emotional, individual members often withdraw, and instead of making progress, group meetings ended with participants simply yelling at each other.[39]

Given these frustrations, it is hardly surprising that participants rarely described their experiences as stories of complete liberation. They understood and worried that they created new norms, pressures, and constraints, not least to 'know as much possible about others', as one man wrote.[40] In a somewhat farcical way, the (initially male) homosexual group from Berlin that eventually also included two women institutionalized these pressures. Group members suspected that one of the women had fallen in love with another member, but was not willing to 'confess'. Since she refused the group's demands to open herself in a 'fairy-tale game', in which she would be the princess and pick her chosen one, the group held 'court' over her. They 'played like children "court in session"'. In the end, the group acquitted the woman, but required her to address the problem again. Apparently, the group liked the procedure, since they continued using it for 'aggression rebuff [*Aggressionsabfuhr*] or the canalization of fear'.[41] A participant of another men's group from Berlin was much more critical about the pressures a group created. 'We were not allowed any aggressions (it's all socially conditioned, one has to get rid of all of this)'; if he wanted to get closer with someone he liked, he was criticized as a 'total sleaze [*schlimmer Anmacher*]'. And when he told someone who was 'wallowing in his suffering to deal with the causes and not to drown in it (oh, I'm sooo weak and soft), then I was the bloke [*Macker*] and pressured him to perform and acted in a competitive manner [*übte Leistungsdruck und Konkurrenzverhalten aus*]'. Paradoxically, this implied for him that 'emotionality, wants towards other men were not allowed, first the intellect had to speak'.[42]

---

[38] Die verbliebenen fünf, 'Männer'. On the Heidelberg group, see Reichardt, *Authentizität*, 707–709.

[39] Lothar, 'Ich freue mich'. For another example, see Anon., '[No title]', in *Info BUG* 111, 28 June 1976, 8.

[40] Jockel and Heinz, 'Protokoll einer Selbsterfahrungsgruppe', in *Mann-o-Mann*, February 1975, 13.

[41] Anon., 'SE-Panik'.

[42] Anon., 'Heiße Schokolade: Einer über sich als Mann', in *Info BUG* 112, 5 July 1976, 11.

Given these accounts, it would be easy to write a 'critical' history of leftist attempts to develop an authentic, emotional, and nonrational subjectivity in these groups that debunks any myth about those groups' emancipatory accomplishments. Rejecting the notion that the 'emotional regime' of the 'therapeutic milieu' was particularly liberal, Maik Tändler for example notes that 'the therapeutic search for authenticity required the submission under a strict system of emotional rules' that could only be ignored at the price of social exclusion.[43] After all, activists themselves wrote that history. Yet this would be a simplification of all that such groups did and accomplished. Despite all frustrations, participants also reported how the group helped them change their personal relations, solve conflicts, and relate differently to their bodies. In an obituary for a comrade who had committed suicide, leftists from Stuttgart for example claimed that he had rediscovered his 'buried feeling', including his anger, in a therapy group, a feeling he then made productive use of in a local citizen's initiative.[44] Lothar from Munich found his expectations in a men's group fulfilled, even though it was a difficult process. He had learned how to show 'feelings of affection, tenderness, vulnerability, jealousy – but also directly expressed anger and aggressiveness' vis-à-vis other men, thus 'extending' his feelings, which had hitherto been 'reserved for women'. In the group, 'well-oiled argumentation robots' turned, meeting by meeting, into 'humans-men [*Menschen-Männer*]'. In his case, the emotional self-transformation seems to have worked.[45] Experiences in men's groups also changed men's relations with their girlfriends. Manfred from Berlin noted that his girlfriend no longer had to force him to talk about personal issues. He became 'more sensitive', paid attention to 'human feelings and problems', and tried not to 'drag a conflict [with his girlfriend] to a rational level, where she doesn't get along.' Even though he was still not flexible and open enough for his own taste, conflicts with his girlfriend were now easier to solve. Leo, a man in the same group, emphasized that his sexuality had changed, meaning that he paid more attention to his girlfriend's desires as a result of the men's group.[46] Of course, one might argue that these men simply acted according to the requirements of an 'authentic' and emotional subjectivity. Yet such a perspective would miss the *emotional* productivity of groups. In their

---

[43] Tändler, *Therapeutische Jahrzehnt*, 349. Tändler adds, however, that the 'subcultural pluralization' of possible emotional expressions also led to a generally less strict emotional regime of West German society as a whole.

[44] Ulli, 'Zu Christoph Junck', in *'s Blättle* 38, May 1979, 8.   [45] Lothar, 'Ich freue mich'.

[46] Manfred et al., 'Männergruppe Hickhack' (remarks by Leo).

groups, these men had learned how to 'do' feelings differently, how to practise intimacy with their wives and girlfriends. Focusing solely on the requirements and constraints the search for an authentic self imposed upon people would not do justice to this production of (bodily) feelings.

Experiments with the body could be scary, but they could also yield extraordinarily intense feelings and help people feel more self-confident. In the gay magazine *Schwuchtel*, Peter Schmittinger from Stuttgart reported about a weekend seminar of a self-experience group. Towards the end of the weekend, Schmittinger got undressed except for his underpants. The others then carried him through the room, placed him on a mattress, and caressed him. 'I become only body, sensation [*Empfindung*], my head is turned off. Every inch of my body lives, prickles, breaths. I'm like a wave, I flow, I swarm. I try to describe how and where I feel what. But then I stop, I don't want to reflect, being passive and active at the same time.' Others in the group did not have the courage to engage in this exercise; they did not know what they missed, Schmittinger claimed. For him it was a special experience, as if there was 'no yesterday, no tomorrow'. It was, certainly, an 'island', but how should he know how the island, the 'concrete utopia', might look like if he had never tried it?[47] For Schmittinger and his fellow men, this was a one-time experience. Members of a women's group from Munich went through a more profound and long-lasting transformation. When they examined their vaginas during group meetings, they were at first afraid of their own bodies, the women wrote. But when the actual self-examination was rather 'easy and unproblematic', they explored their body and felt more secure about it, not least when talking to their gynaecologists.[48] Exploring the body could be, despite all pressures, liberating.

A final episode may indicate how closely intertwined the creation of new constraints and the liberation from (self-imposed) constraints could be. In the spring of 1976, the gay group from Berlin that we have already encountered several times had arranged a meeting with another group called 'men's council'. Both groups had rather different approaches to 'finding' emotions. Whereas the men's council believed in 'verbal, emotionally charged conflicts [*verbale, gefühlsbetonte Auseinandersetzung*]', the gay group wanted to act out their feelings in a bodily way. For the men of the gay group, 'merely discussing the role of men in a heterosexual society'

---

[47] Peter Schmittinger, 'Gruppendynamik', in *Schwuchtel* 7, Spring 1977, 18.

[48] 'Körperbewusstsein: Erfahrungen einer Selbsthilfe-Gruppe', in *Frauenjahrbuch* 1976, 135–151, here 144–145.

seemed to be a 'rationalization' that protected them from 'actually desiring men in a tender way.' Discussing would not 'burst the real fears, but only conceal them'. The discussion of these differences forced the gay men's group's hand, given their claims that only acting out feelings in a bodily way would really affect men. Facing the men's council's critical eyes, the group remained silent. 'Full of fear, we remained tensed and waited for the transformation of our pretence [*Anspruch*].' One man (apparently belonging to the gay group) charged that the situation was utterly artificial, whereupon a member of the men's council replied sarcastically, asking what he was afraid of. But both turned silent when a third man suddenly hugged yet another man named Uli. This was the decisive moment. 'The other group members slowly free themselves from their state of being cramped and approach Uli, who drowns somewhat bashfully in a mop of caressing hands.' Afterwards, the men's council members 'smiled mildly, but did not ask any questions', nor did they formulate a critique.[49] The gay group acted under pressure, which they had, after all, produced themselves with their claim that only physical contact would break the normal rationalization apart. And yet, acting according to these self-imposed pressures, under the watchful eyes of other, critical men, could be liberating, precisely because it showed, to those men, that their approach to creating feelings worked.

There are thus good reasons to highlight both the liberating moments of self-experience groups, and the practical constraints that came with this 'liberation'. Yet, rather than trying to balance or mediate such perspectives, it might be more productive to think about such groups as spaces for experimentation with feelings and bodies. Participants *tried* to practise and experience feelings of 'tenderness', intimacy, solidarity, or freedom of fear, shame, and pressures to perform. They developed and reflected on techniques that, they hoped, might yield such feelings. Sometimes they failed; sometimes they succeeded in producing feelings. No doubt, new norms and expectations emerged in the process. Indeed, these norms and expectations were crucial for the successful production of feelings. But those rules were subject to critiques as well, pending new emotionally productive experiments. What is historically remarkable, and indeed perhaps characteristic of the alternative left of the 1970s, is this constant search for new experiments by learning from what went wrong in previous experiments.

[49] Anon., 'SE-Panik'.

Feeling the Body

Feeling the body played a central role for leftist emotional practices, within and beyond groups. As previous chapters have discussed, leftists believed that bodily feelings and desires have to place in the capitalist world. In capitalist society, they argued, only those parts of the body matter that might be used most efficiently for production or, in the case of sex, reproduction. Capitalism, they charged, fragments bodies according to the logic of efficiency, and restricts the desires of bodies. To challenge this oppressive logic, leftists deemed it necessary to feel the body, ideally in its entirety, without dividing it into parts with specific functions. Feeling the body was a way to put the program of 'unchaining desires' discussed in Chapter 2 into practice. Drawing on this knowledge of the body and its oppressed desires, leftists devised a variety of practices that would allow them to feel their bodies, as well as other bodies, in unfragmented and intense ways. By analyzing these practices, we can understand how leftists tried to feel intensively. At the same time, bodily encounters with others, with friends and comrades, would disrupt the feeling of isolation that characterized capitalism, and create a sense of intimacy that leftists longed for.

Most prominently, leftists sought to develop a different form of sexuality. Leftist sexual politics have, of course, received tremendous attention from scholars. Scholars have primarily focused on how left-wing students, especially during the revolts of 1968, challenged the sexual norms that they blamed for the emergence of fascism – even though a process of sexual liberalization had, scholars now argue, been well underway by 1968. For women active in the movement, the so-called sexual revolution often meant, as female activists were quick to note, that they should always be available for men wishing to have sex. Not least, the 1970s also saw the emergence of homosexual movements.[50] What is missing in this scholarship, however, is an account of how leftists during 1970s developed a more

---

[50] For leftist sexual politics, see only Peter-Paul Bänziger et al., eds., *Sexuelle Revolution? Zur Geschichte der Sexualität im deutschsprachigen Raum seit den 1960er Jahren* (Bielefeld: transcript, 2015); Gert Hekma and Alain Giami, eds., *Sexual Revolutions* (Basingstoke, UK: Palgrave Macmillan, 2014); Massimo Perinelli, 'Longing, Lust, Violence, Liberation: Discourses on Sexuality on the Radical Left in West Germany, 1969–1972', in *After the History of Sexuality: German Interventions*, ed. Dagmar Herzog, Helmut Puff, and Spector Scott (New York: Berghahn Books, 2011); Pascal Eitler, 'Die "sexuelle Revolution" – Körperpolitik um 1968', in *1968: Handbuch zur Kultur- und Mediengeschichte der Studentenbewegung*, ed. Martin Klimke and Joachim Scharloth (Stuttgart: Metzler, 2007); Dagmar Herzog, *Sex after Fascism: Memory and Morality in Twentieth-Century Germany* (Princeton: Princeton University Press, 2005).

specific critique of sexuality under capitalism which is, in their view, limited to genitalia, as Chapter 3 has discussed – a limitation that is part and parcel of the fragmentation of the body in capitalism. Leftists thus called for a sexuality that would involve the entire body. Unrestricted desires might undermine the categorizing powers of capitalist rationality. Clearly resonating Deleuze and Guattari's celebration of desires, 'a couple of women' from Munich for example argued in the context of debates about paedophilia that 'living an illegality of desire', a desire that 'knows no roles, no boundaries', is itself 'a rebellion, it is the repeatedly occurring revolutionary event that turns our everyday life on its head, that lets feelings break out and that shatters the foundation of our thinking'.[51] In *Autonomie*, Matthias Beltz similarly called for legitimizing 'forbidden dreams'. Waiting in line in a supermarket, he had mistaken an under-aged boy's buttock for a 'insanely cute girl's ass', a mistake that shocked him, not least because he had only seen the buttock, but not the entire human being. But it also made him admit secret, and in his view subversive, desires. 'Feeling ecstasy, being sexually besides myself, losing myself in the infinity of debauchery – it is still an alien dream.' As of yet, his self-discipline worked and kept his armour intact, but the forbidden dreams – an implicit admission of paedophile desires – signalled 'how the armour might be violently exploded'.[52] For leftists, these examples show, sexual desires had a deeply subversive potential.

Yet this does not mean that leftists were on the hunt for a 'super-orgasm', or regarded genital orgasms as panacea for all political problems.[53] Rather, leftists challenged the focus on orgasms and genital sexuality more generally, arguing for the sexualization of the entire body in an attempt to break down the division of the body into sexual and nonsexual parts.[54]

---

[51] Ein paar Frauen, 'Frauen und Päderastie – das gabs noch nie', in *Das Blatt* 81, 12–25 November 1976, 10. On pedophilia in the left, see Joachim S. Hohmann, ed., *Pädophilie Heute: Berichte, Meinungen und Interviews zur sexuellen Befreiung des Kindes* (Frankfurt a.M.: Foerster Verlag, 1980); Franz Walter, Stephan Klecha, and Alexander Hensel, eds., *Die Grünen und die Pädosexualität: Eine bundesdeutsche Geschichte* (Göttingen: Vandenhoeck & Ruprecht, 2015); Jens Elberfeld, 'Von der Sünde zur Selbstbestimmung: Zum Diskurs "kindlicher Sexualität" (Bundesrepublik Deutschland 1960–1990)', in *Sexuelle Revolution? Zur Geschichte der Sexualität im deutschsprachigen Raum seit den 1960er Jahren*, ed. Peter-Paul Bänziger et al. (Bielefeld: transcript, 2015). See also, with further references, Joachim C. Häberlen, 'Feeling Like a Child: Visions and Practices of Sexuality in the West German Alternative Left during the Long 1970s', *Journal for the History of Sexuality* 25 (2016).

[52] Matthias Beltz, 'Trotz der Zensur der Träume', in *Autonomie: Materialien gegen die Fabrikgesellschaft* 5, February 1977, 65–67.

[53] Reichardt, *Authentizität*, 652, 658. See also Trumann, *Theorie*, 37–49, 174–179.

[54] For a full elaboration of this argument, see Häberlen, 'Feeling Like a Child'.

For that reason, they also admired children's sexuality. They believed, in Herbert Röttgen's words, that children have a 'multidimensional and splendid erotic life'. 'It's just total – it reaches from shitting to fondling, kissing, grabbing, and glances. For children, the dick and pussy are [two] organs of lust among many, many others. In their sexual personality structure, they have long overcome our one-sidedness and narrowness.'[55] Taking this understanding of children's sexuality as an ideal, leftists tried to develop a sexuality that would not be fixated on 'dick-fucking', as genital heterosexuality was called in the left, but treated the entire body as an object of sexual desires. A woman from Aachen for example reported excitedly how she had caressed her entire body, which was a much better experience than achieving an orgasm. Happiness, she wrote, was something she achieved through 'quiet, affectionate cuddling'.[56] Another woman celebrated 'snuggling, quietly, relaxed, extensively, goalless ... smelling bodies, tasting, feeling them, sinking into each other countless times' as bodily practices that were more fulfilling than having genital sex.[57] Men who participated in men's groups also noted that they had less genital sex, but cuddled more often, which allowed them to feel their entire body.[58] At times, men took quite radical bodily measures, such as undergoing a sterilization to break the 'dick-fixation', an act that indeed resulted, some men claimed, in being less focused on genital sexuality.[59] For leftists, practising a sexuality that involved the entire body and did not remain limited to genitalia was one way to undo the functionalist fragmentation of the body under capitalism. It allowed them, or so they hoped, to feel the whole body, and not only specific parts of it.

The prominence of sexuality notwithstanding, leftists also tried to feel their body in other contexts. We have already encountered how women examined their bodies, notably their genitalia, in women groups, hoping to relate more positively to their own body. But women not only paid attention to their genitalia. In Frankfurt, women drew nude paintings of each other attempting to 'achieve a better relation with our female bodies and a better understanding amongst us'.[60] This desire to explore the body

---

[55] Herbert Röttgen, 'Kinderrevolution', in *Das Blatt* 92, 22 April–5 May 1977, 14–16.
[56] Anon., 'Orgasmus ... Zweifel und Verunsicherung', in *Erotik und Umbruch. Zeitung zu Sexualität*, Midsummer 1978, 35–37.
[57] Anon., 'Oh, Orgasmus', in *Erotik und Umbruch. Zeitung zu Sexualität*, Midsummer 1978, 34.
[58] Manfred et al., 'Männergruppe Hickhack' (remarks by Manfred).
[59] Rainer, Jürgen, Joachim, 'Sterilisationsgruppe', in *Mannsbild*, 1976, 53. For a critique, see Juppi, 'Sterilisation ist auch keine Alternative', in *Mannsbild*, 1976, 49.
[60] Gisela S., 'Frauen malen Frauen', in *Andere Zeitung* 8, October 1976, 15.

was not limited to women. In Bremen, a male activist demanded, somewhat against the usual trend to criticize a 'fixation' on genitalia, that men should take women as a role model and examine their penises. 'I don't think of dicks as particularly beautiful. I have no particular relation to my genitalia, and I know that I'm not alone in this regard. How can we men turn to [other] men, if we don't know anything about us and don't get a (bodily) feeling for us?', he wondered.[61] Learning about one's own body and perceiving it as beautiful was then one way to develop the '(bodily) feeling' he longed for.[62]

Feeling the body was also considered an important part of therapeutic processes. Two women from Heidelberg who attended a 'feminist therapy congress' in Cologne in the spring of 1977 knew exactly what they wanted: 'dancing, ranting, making hectic, yelling, feeling energy, feeling our bodies'. And after they had found six other women with similar interests, they collectively felt their bodies in an 'explosion-like dynamic':

> Pantomimic dancing, wild yelling, making grimaces, smirking until it reverts into aggressive blustering ... playing birth, collective dancing that suddenly turns rhythmic due to a woman snapping with her fingers; by and by, everyone else joins her, then clapping with the hands, stomping with the feet, drumming against the walls: all in the same rhythm, related to each other, but still, everyone for herself = autonomous.[63]

Other women learned to feel their body by practising karate. Knowing karate would not only help her defending herself against potential rapists, one woman from Hamburg wrote, but it also helped her 'developing a body feeling'. It contributed to her 'growing self-consciousness', because she finally 'learned to like something' about herself, 'namely, my own body!'[64] Those practices – and yoga, autogenic training, and mediation, which became popular at the esoteric fringes of the alternative milieu, could be added to the list[65] – permitted leftists to feel their body; by

---

[61] Anon., 'Männer', in *Info Bremer Undogmatischer Gruppen* 15, 17 February 1978, 12.

[62] See also my discussion of the leftist theatre play for children *Darüber spricht man nicht*, in Joachim C. Häberlen, 'Ingrid's Boredom', in *Learning How to Feel: Children's Literature and Emotional Socialization, 1870–1970*, ed. Ute Frevert et al. (Oxford: Oxford University Press, 2014). See Kinder- und Jugendtheater Rote Grütze, *Darüber spricht man nicht. Ein Spiel zur Sexualaufklärung* (Munich: Weismann, 1973).

[63] Elisabeth, 'Weck die Kraft, die in dir steckt: Feministischer Therapiekongress in Köln, 20–22. Mai', in *Carlo Sponti* 34/35, June 1977, 12.

[64] Anon., 'Karate', in *Lesbenpresse* 2, June 1975, 6.

[65] See for example Eva Goldmund, 'Nachwuchs', in *Frankfurter Frauenblatt*, September 1980, 22. See, with further references, Pascal Eitler, '"Alternative" Religion: Subjektivierungspraktiken und Politisierungsstrategien im "New Age" (Westdeutschland 1970–1990)', in *Das alternative Milieu: Antibürgerlicher Lebensstil und linke Politik in der Bundesrepublik Deutschland und Europa,*

writing about those practices, leftists developed a knowledge about how feeling the body might function upon which others could draw.

Debates about giving birth in the women's movement provide an excellent case to show how much feeling the body in a pleasurable way was conceived of as part and parcel of a struggle against the domination of (male) rationality, in this case in the form of medical science. Giving birth in a hospital is, Frauke Lippens argued in *Courage*, traumatic for both mother and child. The infant is 'thrown into a hostile environment: glistening light in the delivery room, relative cold, loud voices of doctors and midwives'. Prospective mothers have to face 'an impersonal, hectic apparatus. She is kept ignorant. Ignorance causes fear, fear prevents relaxing, and that means more pain.' All this makes giving birth a 'traumatic experience' for women in which they do not actively participate. The alternative Lippens and other women propagated was 'soft childbirth' or giving birth at home.[66] 'The young human being is born into a friendly environment that does not immediately take him away from the mother.' This experience of childbirth is simply 'fantastic, splendid, great', it is feeling, even 'too much feeling', a woman reported in the *Blatt*. Giving birth at home keeps the young child 'warm' and traumatizes neither mother nor child.[67] If women had to go to the hospital for giving birth, another article advised them to remain confident and to know their rights. Women should remain in charge of their body, the text proposed, and refuse unnecessary medical equipment like foetal monitoring, a cardiograph for the child's heartbeat, or that a doctor would put an electrode on the child's head. If women would follow the author's advise and keep their 'faith in their body', without giving in to doctors and midwives, then giving birth could be an 'ecstatic experience only women could have', the author wrote.[68] Such texts conveyed a specific knowledge about the female and infant body. Making use of that knowledge would allow women to stay in charge of their own bodies and to feel the body in a pleasurable way. Submitting to the scientific knowledge and the technical apparatus of

---

1968–1983, ed. Sven Reichardt and Detlef Siegfried (Göttingen: Wallstein, 2010); Reichardt, *Authentizität*, 807–831; Michael Mildenberger, *Die religiöse Revolte: Jugend zwischen Flucht und Aufbruch* (Frankfurt a.M.: Fischer Verlag, 1979).

[66] Frauke Lippens, 'Die sanfte Geburt', in *Courage* 4, February 1979, 46–47. See also Trude Berlin and Barbara Straeten, 'Hausgeburt – eine Alternative?', in *Courage* 2, January 1977, 30–32; 'Brief über Geburt und Schwangerschaft', in *Frauenjahrbuch*, 1976, 151–153.

[67] Sonja, 'Hausgeburt', in *Das Blatt* 88a, 18 February–3 March 1977, 11. See also Mo., 'Internationaler Frauenkongress, in *Info BUG* 161, 20 June 1977, 16.

[68] Ein Medizinstudent, 'An alle Frauen, die nicht die Möglichkeit haben, eine Hausgeburt zu machen', in *Das Blatt* 98, 1–14 July 1977, 19.

modern medicine, by contrast, deprived women of that autonomy and caused only fear, pain, and trauma. To really feel their bodies, the argument implied, women needed to develop a knowledge about their bodies based on self-observation rather than on science.

While these practices would allow leftists to feel their own bodies, they also sought to feel others' bodies hoping to break down the boundaries that isolated people from each other. A 'holiday alternative for communes' that took place in Kamp-Lintfort near Duisburg in the summer of 1976 and that attracted about one hundred leftists provides an example for how this might work.[69] Not everything was great and harmonious at the camp. While some believed to be in the know, but failed to act accordingly, others condemned any kind of thinking and just wanted to 'enjoy life blindly, live just according to feelings.' Predictably, conflicts emerged, and people yelled at each other, sometimes even resorted to violence; some charged that those who were aggressive simply did not have enough sex, others upheld ideals of a 'tender' sexuality. But by and large, reports were positive. It was an 'island', an 'chamber for experimenting', as one author put it, where 'people lived intensively, doing damaged things as well as beautiful things'.[70] Feeling the body was central for this intensity, both because people perceived their bodies intensely and because they could build new relations with other bodies.[71] Participants organized massaging workshops, meditated, did bioenergetics exercises and practised Tai Chi. Less-organized bodily experiences were perhaps even more important for creating intense feelings of intimacy: running in a long chain into the ice-cold water of a lake, washing each other with 'bio-soap', sitting in a row and oiling the back of the person in front, which turned into massaging and fondling, or being naked in the rain;[72] dancing around the campfire, painting each other's bodies, sitting in a circle and laughing at each other, in short, 'all the wonderful moments, when competitiveness and performance pressure, fear disappeared, when we felt free, when we could be the way we really were and did not have to be the way we believed others would expect us to be'.[73] By practising a bodily intimacy, people felt they could be 'authentic' without playing roles. It was, it seems, an experiment that went well.

---

[69] Anon., 'FAK '76', in *Info BUG* 129, 24 October 1976, 2; Anon., 'FAK '76, Teil II', in *Info BUG* 130, 1 November 1976, 3–4. See also Thommi, 'FAK '76: Freizeitalternative für Kommunen', and Elisabeth, '10 Tage Alternativismus FAK '76: Liebe – Freude – Shit – u. Freiheit', both in *Carlo Sponti* 22/23, October 1976, 15–16.
[70] Anon., 'FAK '76, Teil II'.   [71] Anon., 'FAK '76'.
[72] Elisabeth, '10 Tage Alternativismus FAK '76'.   [73] Anon., 'FAK '76, Teil II'.

Visitors of the camp also reflected on the 'significance of these [bodily] techniques'. Such techniques, they claimed, could only be a 'means to make us aware of how damaged we are emotionally and bodily, a means to give us the energy to do something against this damagedness'.[74] Even though it might be difficult, the authors of another report hoped that the experiences they had made at the camp would help them fight against the 'interpersonal damagednesses [*Kaputtheiten* – an odd word in German!], against competition (against, not with each other), un-openness, being stuck, that distance (just don't let anyone get close to you), escapes into dyadic relations or into any ideology (political or religious), isolation (separation), alienation (from our body, and so on), the open and concealed oppression of the system (consumption and norming terror, rushing at work, censorship, police terror, and so on)'.[75] The bodily and emotional intensity of the camp, that is, would only be meaningful if it supported a long-term personal transformation that would ultimately challenge the 'oppression of the system'. In that sense, massaging, dancing in the rain, or collectively jumping into a lake could gain political meaning.

Leftists, these examples suggest, turned their bodies into political weapons. Scholars have explored this weaponization of the body in the radical left, though mostly focusing on terrorists and particularly on how imprisoned terrorists made use of their body as a weapon in hunger strikes.[76] For alternative leftists, the body's subversive powers lay elsewhere. In their perspective, the (nude) body as a source of sensual pleasures could be subversive. A seemingly trivial incident that happened in Stuttgart in the summer of 1977 may exemplify the point: A group of some fifty leftists went nude swimming in a local open-air swimming pool. Unlike other local leftists, presumably with more communist leanings, who criticized the event as 'mocking workers' or a 'waste of energies', guests at the swimming pool seem to have liked it. They were eager to read the pamphlets activists distributed and threatened to throw the intervening forces of order into the pool. For the activists, going nude swimming in a

---

[74] Anon., 'FAK '76'.   [75] Anon., 'FAK'76, Teil II'.

[76] On terrorists, especially the RAF, using the body as a weapon, see Marcel Streng, 'Der Körper im Ausnahmezustand: Hungern als politische Praxis im westdeutschen Strafvollzug (1973–1985)', in *Ausnahmezustände: Entgrenzungen und Regulierungen in Europa während des Kalten Krieges*, ed. Dirk Schumann and Cornelia Rauh (Göttingen: Wallstein, 2015); Martin Jander, 'Isolation oder Isolationsfolter: Die Auseinandersetzung um die Haftbedingungen der RAF-Häftlinge', in *Der 'Deutsche Herbst' und die RAF in Politik, Medien und Kunst: nationale und internationale Perspektiven*, ed. Nicole Colin et al. (Bielefeld: transcript, 2008); Christoph Riederer, *Die RAF und die Folterdebatte der 1970er Jahre* (Wiesbaden: Springer, 2014), 158–269; Leith Passmore, 'The Art of Hunger: Self-Starvation in the Red Army Faction', *German History* 27 (2009).

public pool was an act of realizing a 'desire that is usually ignored by those in power [*die Herrschenden*]', an act that anticipated a 'concrete social utopia', and that was simply fun. It was one example how the struggle for 'resurrecting paradise', as the pamphlet said, could be fought with 'fantasy, creativity, sensuality, and humour'.[77] Collective nudity realized, at least for the moment, a utopia of sensual, bodily pleasures that ordinary people enjoyed, but the forces of orders tried to end.

By the end of the 1970s, learning how to feel the body in karate and therapy groups had become a major issue in the alternative left. A personal text by Walter Güntherot, published in *Autonomie*, may show what it took to 'accept the body' and thereby to begin 'a new life'. Güntherot started his article, written in the wake of the German Autumn, with a discussion of the Red Army Faction, but then turned to his personal situation. After all, he trusted his 'self-experience [*Selbsterfahrung*]' more than he did theoretical treatises. Hence he recounted his relationship with Hilga, presumably his girlfriend at the time. During a 'depressive phase' he spent a morning with her. They 'played in a very sensual [*lustvoll*] way, showed each other [their] karate skills, were bodily very close, but without having an ecstatic orgasm'. He would have liked being similarly close with his other roommates, but the 'moral codex' prohibited that. Then they went to the indoor swimming pool:

> The contact with water has never before been as intense as that morning. I could have grunted loudly all the time and recalled bathing with gays at a lake in southern France. That morning, I spontaneously did a header from the one-meter-board, which I haven't done for ages; it must have been some inner force [*innerer Zwang*]. I took a long shower and the bodily experiences culminated in a sense of complete timelessness. The imagination was enough: I didn't need my body any longer for reproduction, I could gamble with my body and yield to the body what is for the body [*dem Körper lassen, was des Körpers ist*]. By now, I have more faith in such self-experience than in library-long treatises about physical and intellectual labour.[78]

Practising karate, doing a header, taking a long shower – these might seem to be trivial experiences. Yet they provided Güntherot with opportunities for intense feelings. What created this intensity that made it worth writing about them in a leading magazine of the radical left? Three aspects seem noteworthy. First, the bodily intimacy with Hilga that was, however, not

---

[77] Anon., 'Nacktbadeaktion', in *'s Blättle* 20, September 1977, 16–17.
[78] Walter Güntherot, 'Augenblicke', in *Autonomie: Materialien gegen die Fabrikgesellschaft* 10, January 1978, 106–115.

focused on achieving an orgasm, but rather was playful, which implies that it was not goal-oriented. Second, the feeling of timelessness, the utter focus on the here and now, which also implies that no future goal mattered. This, finally, freed the body from the demands of reproduction, which allowed him to 'gamble' with the body. In the moment of intensely feeling the body, nothing but the body mattered.

In their attempts to feel the body, these examples show, leftists devised a great variety of practices, reaching from a nongenital sexuality to karate, painting each other, and simply taking a long shower. Intense bodily feelings might satisfy the 'hunger for experience' – for concrete, bodily experiences – that characterized the alternative left, as a widely read essay by Michael Rutschky put it.[79] Leftists never formulated any clear rules for how to feel the body. Certain tendencies are visible, however. Ideally, the entire body would be involved, and ideally, any social or intellectual restraints imposed upon the body would loosen; thus the emphasis on not being 'cramped' and on the fluidity of practices: oiling backs could turn into massaging and fondling, collective dancing could become rhythmic and turn into drumming against the walls. Reports about bodily experiences provided examples how to feel the body, but they left ample space for experimenting with the body in a search for new ways of feeling the body. Even with regards to sexuality, where perhaps the strongest, antigenital norms existed, the ideal of an all-embracing and boundary-transgressing sexuality called for new attempts how to transgress such boundaries. Politically speaking, we can interpret such seemingly trivial bodily practices as attempt to put the politics of desire Chapter 2 has discussed into practice. In a capitalist world dominated by rationality, producing feelings of bodily intensity was inherently subversive.

Overcoming Loneliness, Practising Intimacy

In 1973, *Schwarze Protokolle*, a leftist magazine for theoretical discussions, claimed that the current revolution was nothing but 'the creation of universal, direct, humane communication'.[80] The very purpose of the 'underground' press, *Ulcus Molle* argued in the same year, was to 'show how it is possible to break out of this isolation, how one can and should

---

[79] Michael Rutschky, *Erfahrungshunger: Ein Essay über die siebziger Jahre* (Cologne: Kiepenheuer und Witsch, 1980).

[80] Anon., 'Gesellschaftliche Vermittlung und Bewegung der Autonomen Gruppen', in *Schwarze Protokolle* 5, July 1973, 1–16.

and has to liberate oneself.[81] Numerous articles about individual relations and the problems couples encountered in their communication can be read as case studies for the alternative scene to demonstrate how difficult, but also how rewarding breaking out of isolation could be. The *Andere Zeitung* from Frankfurt published an entire rubric called 'social communication', documenting how beneficial talking to each other about feelings and sexuality, to therapists, in groups or amongst friends, could be. Teenage girls discussing the 'performance pressure' they faced in their relations with boys, for example, realized that they were not alone facing these problems, which helped them become more self-confident.[82] Which kind of desires, however, could be articulated in the alternative press was heavily contested, as heated debates about personal ads show.[83] When a man named Alfred published a personal ad in *'s Blättle* from Stuttgart expressing his desire to be hugged [*in die Arme genommen*] by a woman, female members of the editorial collective were outraged, charging Alfred for reducing women to their body. Interestingly, not only male members of the editorial collective, but also female readers defended him. They appreciated that Alfred, if somewhat clumsily, had expressed his desire for fondness [*Zärtlichkeit*] and his loneliness, which happened all too rarely; another female writer charged the women's movement for having demonized men and their sexuality. Alfred's admission was only 'honest and courageous', while the women reacted 'hysterically'.[84]

Scholars have often noted the importance of talking about one's personal problems within the leftist scene, emphasizing that leftists not only could, but indeed had to talk about their personal issues.[85] Telling the truth about oneself was a crucial aspect of being 'authentic'. Groups

---

[81] Anon., 'Editorial', in *Ulcus Molle* 11/12, 1973, 2.

[82] Anon, 'Soziale Kommunikation: Was er von mir will und ich von ihm (aus: Roter Kalender 1976)', in *Andere Zeitung* 1, February 1976, 5. See also later issues (esp. issues 5 and 9–12) for more examples of the 'Soziale Kommunikation' series.

[83] See the discussion in Sven Reichardt, 'Von "Beziehungskisten" und "offener Sexualität"', in *Das Alternative Milieu: Antibürgerlicher Lebensstil und linke Politik in der Bundesrepublik Deutschland und Europa 1968–1983*, ed. Sven Reichardt and Detlef Siegfried (Göttingen: Wallstein, 2010).

[84] See the original ad in *'s Blättle* 41, August/September 1979, 27. The editorial team commented on this in *'s Blättle* 42, October 1979, 2, and asked for readers' reactions; for those, see *'s Blättle* 43, November 1979, 3–5, and *'s Blättle* 44, December 1979/January 1980, 3–4 (quote from here).

[85] See, in addition to the work by Reichardt, Nina Verheyen, 'Der ausdiskutierte Orgasmus: Beziehungsgespräche als kommunikative Praxis in der Geschichte des Intimen seit den 1960er Jahren', in *Sexuelle Revolution? Zur Geschichte der Sexualität im deutschsprachigen Raum seit den 1960er Jahren*, ed. Peter-Paul Bänziger et al. (Bielefeld: transcript, 2015); Bührmann, *Geschlecht*. On communes, see Rudi H.P. Damme, *Zur Stabilität von Wohngruppen: Ein Modell aktivierender Sozialforschung zur Theorie und Praxis des kollektiven Alltags* (Bonn: Projektbereich 'Hochschul- und Studentische Sozialpolitik', 1980), 19.

forcing their members to speak about their most intimate feelings often unleashed, as observers were well aware of, a 'psycho-terror' on their members. As much as this is true, the focus on the requirement to talk about oneself is one-sided. From the perspective this chapter has suggested, it is more productive to consider communication as an emotional practice that might, or might not, yield feelings, specifically feelings of intimacy leftists desperately longed for. Leftists created a multitude of spaces for feelings that would allow them to overcome loneliness and fear and to practise intimacy, including not only various self-experiences groups, but also communes and youth centres.

In the situation of general isolation that was, according to leftist diagnosis, typical for capitalism, simply talking to strangers could amount to an act of personal liberation. A woman from Berlin for example wrote about how she had started talking to another woman in a pizzeria. After seeing a movie with people whom she was not particularly fond of, she had gone to the pizzeria for a glass of red wine and had remained all on her own. When another woman entered the place alone as well, she wanted to talk to her, but it required a great effort. What if the other woman would prefer being alone? What should she say? But then, showing insecurity should not be a bad thing, and if the other woman wanted to be alone, it was not a personal issue, she told herself. 'It is up to me whether I retreat tonight, succumbing to my fear, or if I make the step to stand up for my needs.' She took another sip from her glass of wine, was afraid of herself, the 'tension increased', and finally, she asked the other woman if she could sit with her. It turned out to be very easy; she did not stammer or collapse. 'I get my stuff, I feel incredibly liberated ... I think all my face is gleaming.' And then they simply talked nicely.[86] All it took to communicate was the courage to overcome her fear. She tried to feel not alone, not to be afraid, and she succeeded. Showing that it was possible to overcome the general isolation made this seemingly trivial everyday story politically meaningful worth being published in a leftist magazine.

Much of what alternative leftists did to shape their everyday lives can be read as an attempt to create conditions that would allow them to overcome isolation and loneliness. They moved into communes, hoping to build spaces where 'new intimate relations' might develop that would break through the isolation of 'concrete desserts' and the nuclear family, and where 'competitiveness and rivalry' might be

---

[86] Anon., 'Ich hab's gebracht', in *Info BUG* 106, 17 May 1975, 16–17.

abolished.[87] Communes should, as the authors of a study on *Children in Communes* (as the book is titled) wrote, 'revolutionize' the 'psychic constellation' of 'bourgeois individuals', that is, submissiveness vis-à-vis authorities and an 'individualistic way of thinking', and thereby anticipate 'the principles of a new society'.[88] For alternative leftists, collective living had thus an inherently political quality. Squatting houses to 'do politics without being disturbed' was, the Frankfurt group *Revolutionärer Kampf* for example argued, not sufficient. Living collectively, they realized, was itself political, as it helped them change their personal relations.[89] In West Berlin, authors for *Info BUG* argued for campaigning for large apartments in social housing projects that would allow young workers to live collectively as well.[90] Even if communes were not 'the great salvation', as a *Wohngruppenzentrum* from Frankfurt acknowledged, they nevertheless offered an opportunity to 'dissolve irrational authorities' and to 'reduce inhibitions'. To result in societal change, however, they had to make an impact beyond the collective itself.[91] Somewhat similarly, Frankfurt's *Andere Zeitung* claimed that a complete emancipation would require a 'political struggle with the system of production', but until this would happen, communes could help individuals to 'overcome their bourgeois structures of socialization'.[92]

Expectations for what communes should personally and politically achieve ran high in the leftist scene. In *Ulcus Molle*, Michael Hiltl summarized the 'obvious benefits' of living collectively:

> Fear of loneliness is replaced by the stability of the group; everyone can retreat whenever he wants, without being forced into loneliness. This also deprives the clenching dyadic relation [*umklammernde Zweierbeziehung*] and jealousy of their social basis, voluntaristic and individualist strategies are replaced by changing social structures. Generally speaking, the number and intensity of social contacts can be increased, the temporal formation of closer dyadic relations is possible, but also their loosening/separation is easier in the group.[93]

---

[87] Reichardt, *Authentizität*, 351–459; Detlef Siegfried, '"Einstürzende Neubauten": Wohngemeinschaften, Jugendzentren und private Präferenzen kommunistischer "Kader" als Formen jugendlicher Subkultur', *Archiv für Sozialgeschichte* 44 (2004).

[88] Ute Straub and Barbara Schröder, *Kinder in Wohngemeinschaften* (Herford: Zündhölzchen, 1978), 35–36.

[89] Anon., 'Wenn nachts in Frankfurt die Glocken läuten', in *Wir Wollen Alles* 10, November 1973, 10–13.

[90] Anon., 'Theorie über die Stadtteilarbeit', in *Info BUG* 9, 6 May 1974, 14–18.

[91] Wohnungruppenzentrum im Studentenwerk, 'Wohngruppenzentrum in Frankfurt', in *Pflasterstrand* 28, 20 April–3 May 1978, 35.

[92] rms, 'In der Privathölle untertauchen', in *Andere Zeitung* 1, February 1976, 28.

[93] Michael Hiltl, 'Soziale Beziehungen in der Alternativbewegung', in *Ulcus Molle*, January 1981, 4–20.

Other activists shared these hopes. Three men from West Berlin who wanted to form a *Wohngemeinschaft* and looked for other men to join them, planned on working on their 'personal difficulties' and 'group conflicts', not only through talking about problems, but also 'with the help of body exercises (breathing, role plays, meditation)'. For them, this was not an end in itself, but a 'necessary part of our political labour'.[94] Other people had less explicit political ambitions, but nevertheless emotional expectations. One twenty years old man from Munich for example stated in his personal ad that he wanted to move into a collective with the 'general willingness to openly show feelings and to listen to problems'.[95] Gudrun Cyprian, who interviewed members of nearly one hundred communes, cites similar desires as rationales for moving in: 'Individual development', 'search for emotional backing [*Rückhalt*], safety and security', 'rejection of bourgeois life', 'overcoming isolation and a desire for contacts', or 'political motives'. People living in communes longed for 'openness and trust, without the necessity of permanent reassurance', but also hoped to develop their own 'personality structure, but not in a separate room [*im stillen Kämmerlein*], but in the midst of a social entity, characterized by communication and interaction'. They 'control and correct' their personal behaviour, to 'solve personal problems', to learn to speak freely and to 'intensify my ability to experience [*Intensivierung meiner Erlebnisfähigkeit*]'.[96] In the leftist scene, such personal goals were usually regarded as inherently political.

It would be easy to note that such expectations were too high, that the 'ideals of liberation' did not survive the test of reality.[97] Activists were well aware of the problems they faced. As early as 1973, the magazine *Bambule* complained that communes were reduced to 'economic utility associations [*Zweckverbände*]', where people resided, but did not live together.[98] In his sympathetic study of communes, Johann August Schülein noted that after an initial period of euphoria, problems typically developed and a process of (collective) learning had to start that required patience and hard labour to solve conflicts about all kinds of problems a collective might encounter,

[94] Anon., 'Auf der Suche ...', in *Info BUG* 111, 28 June 1977, 2 and 11.
[95] Kleinanzeige, in *Das Blatt* 60, 19 December 1975–8 January 1976, 52.
[96] Gudrun Cyprian, *Sozialisation in Wohngemeinschaften: Eine empirische Untersuchung ihrer strukturellen Bedingungen* (Stuttgart: Ferdinand Enke Verlag, 1978), 29, 32–33. Quoted in Reichardt, *Authentizität*, 375–376.
[97] Reichardt, *Authentizität*, 457.
[98] Anon., 'Wohngemienschaften', in *Bambule* 8/9, June 1973, 14. (The magazine is in Apo-Archiv FU, S 058–060.)

ranging from personal relations to different expectations regarding chaos and order.[99] Leftists indeed developed a variety of techniques to make the program of overcoming isolation and fostering communication work. 'Role- and psycho-games', a participant at a meeting to discuss the situation of communes remarked, had proven useful for some communes. 'Supervision', the author added, should not be regarded as a sign of weakness.[100] Steve Peinemann similarly noted in his 1975 book on communes that having a few outside observers participate in a debate might help to solve problems and to show new solutions.[101] Sympathetic observers like Schülein and Peinemann were well aware that communes developed their own rules and norms, and that high expectations often prevented personal liberation rather than fostering it.[102] Yet merely noting that 'technologies of the self' – such as group discussions or psychological role-playing games – 'produced norms and regulated behaviour' would miss the point.[103] Just like groups, communes constituted a space where activists could try out new forms of social interaction that might, or might not, yield the feelings of personal intimacy they longed for. Certainly, activists created new norms and regulations in the process; but they also found solutions for the problems they encountered, and they produced emotions.

The detailed report of a commune published in a volume edited by Johann Schülein may illustrate the point. The group refrained from giving the exact location of their commune, instead locating it in the fictional small town of 'Posemuckel', a term used to designate small, provincial towns out of touch with urban life.[104] Three women and three men lived in the commune, all of whom had previously participated in women's and men's groups, which is also how they got to know each other. While this

[99] Johann August Schülein, 'Einige Bemerkungen zur Entwicklung der Wohngemeinschaftsbewegung', in *Vor uns die Mühen der Ebenen: Alltagsprobleme und Perspektiven von Wohngemeinschaften*, ed. Johannes August Schülein (Giessen: Focus-Verlag, 1980).

[100] Ute, Elisabeth, Jens, and Peter, 'Seminar zu Wohngemeinschaften auf Burg Rothenfels', in *Carlo Sponti* 18/19, n.d., probably April 1976, 9.

[101] Steve Peinemann, *Wohngemeinschaft: Problem oder Lösung?* (Frankfurt a.M.: Verlag Rieta Hau, 1975), 5–6. See also Schülein, 'Bemerkungen', 28–29.

[102] Steve Peinemann, 'Beziehungsprobleme', in *Vor uns die Mühen der Ebenen: Alltagsprobleme und Perspektiven von Wohngemeinschaften*, ed. Johann August Schülein (Giessen: Focus-Verlag, 1980); Peinemann, *Wohngemeinschaft*, 18–25.

[103] Reichardt, *Authentizität*, 458.

[104] 'Bericht der Wohngemeinschaft aus Posemuckel', in *Vor uns die Mühen der Ebenen: Alltagsprobleme und Perspektiven von Wohngemeinschaften*, ed. Johann August Schülein (Giessen: Focus-Verlag, 1980). On the group and its therapeutic experiences, see also Tändler, *Therapeutische Jahrzehnt*, 346–348.

might be exceptional, it makes the commune all the more interesting as a case study for understanding emotional dynamics within a leftist *Wohngemeinschaft*. At least for some of them, the longing for 'strong emotional ties', the desire to live with people 'who are close to me' was a crucial motivation to move into the commune. The beginning went well, full of 'curiosity' and 'euphoria' about living together. 'It's a great feeling not to be alone', one of them wrote into the group's diary. But conflicts emerged soon, though it remains unclear why. The group had to learn how to deal with them; this was, after all, their goal. Most importantly, they emphasized communicating about their feelings as a way of solving conflicts. Women were, at least initially, better at expressing their feelings, but ultimately, also men learned to voice their needs. This included, as the group emphasized, expressing aggressions without being afraid to do so, resulting in the commune's collapse. In this sense, the group successfully learned to deal with fears and aggressions, not least in a collective Gestalt therapy they did with the explicit aim of learning how to deal 'efficiently with situations of conflict'.

Bodily intimacy played an important role for the group's feelings as well. For a while, they slept in the same room, but without getting close to each other physically. One night, however, three of them, two women and a man, fell asleep after having talked about their fears and hopes. When they woke up, they cuddled and fondled each other. Soon enough, the other group members joined them. Cuddling with each other and drinking wine, the members of the commune practically, and successfully, created a feeling of safeness (*Geborgenheit*). It remains unclear whether this remained a unique experience. The men in the group, however, emphasized that they had overcome their 'fears of contact [*Berührungsängste*]' and were now able to cuddle or hug each other. But limitations remained, and men had no 'erotic' relations with each other, a situation that at least one of them experienced as problematic as he felt the pressure to overcome his sexual fixation on women. But forcing him to have 'the same relation to men' as he had to women would just be another form of 'rape', he argued. 'I'm myself, and my needs and possibilities, which have grown with me (or shrivelled), they can't be straightened out with some "emancipatory" intentions. I'm not smooth.' The group, or at least its male members, had to learn to deal with expectations they could not and would not fulfil. And indeed, they learned that lesson. Other group members realized that they could not have the same intense relation with all group members all the time; there were ups and downs, but this should not endanger the group as a whole. The group's experimenting with creating intimacy in communicative and bodily ways thus seems to have succeeded, not by producing perfect harmony or maintaining the initial euphoria, but by finding sustainable ways of dealing with feelings.

Other communes were, not surprisingly, less successful with their attempts to overcome isolation. *Montagsnotizen*, a magazine devoted to communes, described the situation in the Hamburg neighbourhood of Steilshoop, a suburb with multi-storey apartment buildings: 'The atmosphere of tenement houses [*Mietskasernen*], despite playgrounds and gardening and somewhat cumbersome house-paintings'. This environment prevented any interaction and communication between different communes. And though the layout of individual apartments looked somewhat better as it was likely to foster communication, the situation was not. There was no political activism; only students lived there for a short while, and there were neither elderly people nor children. Isolation prevailed. This was not a space for alternative living; probably, it was not even intended as such.[105] Even those communes that had started as alternative projects often lost their enthusiasm. In the *Andere Zeitung*, a man complained that, despite proclamations to raise children collectively, his two young children were effectively raised exclusively by their parents, while the other members lived as singles, always looking for potential partners. The situation escalated when their housemates asked the young family to move out and thus wanted to deprive the children of their home and garden.[106] A woman living in another commune in Frankfurt charged that her roommates, who had all declared their desire to 'live collectively', had no interest in creating a community, and that they mistook their egotism for personal freedom.[107] Members of these communes, the charges imply, were not willing to engage in the labour necessary to produce the desired feelings of solidarity and intimacy. Shared apartments and communes might be a place for experimenting with feelings and practising intimacy. But for these experiments to work, the built environment had to be adequate, as in the case of Hamburg, and members needed to be actively engaged, which was often not the case.

Alternative attempts to facilitate opportunities to practise intimacy in their everyday lives did not remain limited to collective forms of living. Reflecting the perceived lack of opportunities to build meaningful relations

---

[105] Erwin, 'Nochmals Steilshoop. Nichts Alternatives', in *Montagsnotizen* 25, August 1977, 12–13.

[106] Wildfried Goldhorn, 'Bürgerkrieg Arndtstr. 30, 1. Stock, oder: wie verschlafe ich die Revolution!', in *Andere Zeitung* 11, January 1977, 4.

[107] Hans and Ellen, 'Positionen', in *Andere Zeitung* 14, March 1977, 26–27.

with neighbours, friends, or schoolmates, leftists campaigned for neighbourhood, contact, and especially youth centres that would allow people to
form 'contacts'. 'Community centres' in the 'concrete deserts of suburbia',
the *Blatt* argued, might help create a 'feeling of community amongst lonely
and isolated people'. Struggling against the urban 'Moloch', groups and
communes could develop 'a feeling of belonging [*Geborgenheit*], manage-
ability [*Überschaubarkeit*] and solidarity'.[108] Normal leisure time activities
for teenagers, the Cologne-based magazine *Befreiung* alleged, like buying
expensive records or clothes, or going to bars or discos, would yield
nothing but 'boredom and frustration'. Leisure time was thus no more
'free' than the time they had to spend at school or work.[109] In the same
magazine, teenagers complained that they lacked a place to 'meet, get to
know each other, to love and talk'. The independent youth centres, for
which numerous initiatives campaigned throughout West Germany, were
conceived to provide a solution for this problem.[110] They would offer
teenagers an opportunity to communicate and to develop a sense of
solidarity beyond alienated labour and leisure-time activities, an issue that
made them, leftists charged, politically dangerous for the establishment.[111]
In a less politicized tone, a youth centre initiative from Hanover argued in
1976 that teenagers should 'learn under professional guidance to talk about
their personal problems and to manage the youth centre themselves'. But
even without an explicitly political agenda, local politicians were hesitant
to support such initiatives.[112]

Like communes, youth centres were spaces for trying out feelings, in
particular for practising intimacy. But practical experiences were ambivalent. On the one hand, engaged leftist social workers successfully encouraged the foundation of girls' groups, where girls talked about their

---

[108] Anon., 'Nicht wählen, sondern wühlen', in *Das Blatt* 78, 1–14 October 1976, 4–5.
[109] Anon., 'Selbstverwaltete Jugendzentren', in *Befreiung*, May 1975, 7–8.
[110] On the history of youth centre movement, see David Templin, *Freizeit ohne Kontrollen: Die
Jugendzentrumsbewegung in der Bundesrepublik der 1970er Jahre* (Göttingen: Wallstein, 2015). On
leftwing pedagogics, see also Imbke Behnken and Jürgen Zinnecker, '"Hi ha ho, die Bonzen
komm'n ins Klo!" Sozialpädagogische Studentenbewegung und Modernisierung Sozialer Arbeit in
Deutschland', *Westfälische Forschungen* 48 (1998); Sven Steinacker, '"... daß die
Arbeitsbedingungen im Interesse aller verändert werden müssen !!!" Alternative Pädagogik und
linke Politik in der Sozialen Arbeiten der sechziger und siebziger Jahre', in *Das Alternative Milieu:
Antibürgerlicher Lebensstil und linke Politik in der Bundesrepublik Deutschland und Europa
1968–1983*, ed. Sven Reichardt and Detlef Siegfried (Göttingen: Wallstein, 2010).
[111] Anon., 'Für ein selbstverwaltetes Jugendzentrum in Alsdorf', in *Befreiung*, January 1975, 6. See
also Albrecht Herrenknecht, Wolfgang Hätscher, and Stefan Koospal, *Träume, Hoffnungen,
Kämpfe ... Ein Lesebuch zur Jugendzentrumsbewegung* (Frankfurt a.M.: Verlag Jugend und
Politik, 1977), 13–22, 64.
[112] 'Gespräch über das Jugendzentrum', in *Rundschlag* 4, 1976, 3–14.

sexuality and relations, built trust, learned 'to solve problems collectively', and developed 'mutual fondness [*Zärtlichkeit*]'. In one case, boys formed a group in response to the girls' group; in another case, the girls succeeded in convincing their male friends to meet with them every other week to talk about 'women's questions and sexuality'.[113] Talking about seemingly individual problems concerning drugs, sexuality, or depression, teenagers realized that these problems were 'socially mediated', activists claimed. This was an insight that might provide the basis for overcoming the capitalist system.[114] And one group that had squatted a building for an independent youth centre reported: 'The most positive thing about the occupation was that one established contact to people with whom one had previously no relation at all.' Despite problems, 'there was, at least emotionally, an atmosphere that was fundamentally different from everyday life. For a long time, we were just sitting around, doing nothing, but never did it get boring.'[115]

On the other hand, left-wing and student magazines are full of complaints about the lack of commitment by teenagers; most teenagers, it seems, were just drinking alcohol, which, as one student magazine emphasized, did not foster any communication either.[116] Intended as places where teenagers might overcome loneliness and learn how to organize their leisure time according to their 'creative and social needs and possibilities',[117] some youth clubs achieved this, while others struggled with teenagers' preference for cheap alcohol.

Finally, leftists sought to intervene into the urban space to engender communication amongst ordinary people. According to the magazine *Großstadtpflaster. Eine Zeitung für Asphaltaktivisten*, communication cannot be used for profit, but isolation and the desire for communication can be marketed. Hence it is in the interest of the capitalist system to prevent people from communicating with each other, but to stir a desire for communication. The 'asphalt activists' thus looked for a way to disrupt

[113] Anon., 'Mädchengruppen im Jugendfreizeitheim', in *Heim- und Erzieher Zeitung*, July/August 1976, 21–23.
[114] 'Bericht vom ersten Bundesseminar der JZ-Bewegung vom 27.12.1973 bis 4.1.1974 in Vlotho', in Herrenknecht, Hätscher, and Koospal, *Träume*, 61–63.
[115] 'Dokumentation der Aktion Jugendhaus Wertheim', 9, cited in 'Phantasie gegen die Macht – Aktionen sind der Kern der JZ-Bewegung', in Herrenknecht, Hätscher, and Koospal, *Träume*, 69–73, quote 70.
[116] See for example Claudia Neubert, 'Jugendzentrum Hofheim', in *Rumpelstielzchen*, December 1973; 'Interview mit Rainer Schandeera, 26 Jahre alt, Heimleiter im Jugendzentrum', 'Interview mit Jugendlichen', and Sönke Halbeck, 'Eindrücke vom Jugendzentrum', all in *Rundschlag*, January 1977, 37–39, 40, 43, and Herrenknecht, Hätscher, and Koospal, *Träume*, 17.
[117] Anon., 'Selbstverwaltete Jugendzentren', in *Befreiung*, May 1975, 7–8.

the isolation and to facilitate genuine communication. Performing street music would achieve this aim, they believed. Every street performance is a form of 'street occupation' that appropriates the street for 'our needs', they wrote.[118] In the winter of 1976–77, for example, a crowd of some two hundred people listened to street musicians in Bremen. Eventually the police tried to stop the performance. When the musicians refused to follow the orders, 'a liberating spark of approval and solidarity' spread. 'The people – housewives, bummers, office workers, tourists, unemployed, who, in this dull stone dessert, usually only walk past each other, full of boredom – suddenly start, facing the police forces, to clap rhythmically and to jump. We play like the devil and the police doesn't look good in the end.'[119] A band from Frankfurt similarly argued that new relations between people in their audience and between the audience and them-selves emerged during a street performance. 'All the grey passersby, who usually pass each other silently and isolated, suddenly start to move, they smile, giggle, clap, express themselves. A counter-public emerges, from very below, a rhythm against the world of commodities around us that everyone can understand.'[120]

Whereas music would engender communication, painting walls and streets would disrupt the aesthetic monotony and boredom of urban life. 'Trees and sun on concrete, colour against grey, dragons on brick walls in bleak neighbourhoods and playing children under the sun of a lawn, where no sun gets through, where no grass grows', *Ulcus Molle* wrote in a review of a book about wall paintings.[121] The book itself discussed not only the practical challenges and potential legal ramifications wall painters had to face, but also how much fun collectively decorating walls could be, and how this could facilitate communication amongst neighbours that was otherwise unlikely. In Berlin-Gropiusstadt, antinuclear power activists for example picked a 'dull and dirty wall of a parking lot' to paint a colourful image. Sunday strollers stopped and talked about the image, and children wanted to join the painting crew.[122] Tenants of a house in Berlin-Kreuzberg used a 'painting action' as a 'first step to break out of the isolation and anonymity of our one-to-two-bedroom apartments'. When

---

[118] Peter Blum, 'Straße und Straßenmusik', in *Großstadtpflaster* 1, n.d., probably winter 1976/77, 1–4. The text was also published in *Andere Zeitung* 10, November 1977, 40–41.
[119] Anon., 'Die Bremer Stadtmuskanten [sic]: Ein Märchen aus unserer Zeit', in *Großstadtpflaster* 1, n. d., probably winter 1976/77, 23.
[120] Anon., 'Wer hat uns die Straße geklaut?', in *Pflasterstrand* 5, 2–15 March 1977, 22.
[121] Klaus Bernd Vollmar, 'Wandmalereien', in *Ulcus Molle* 1/2, 1980, 20.
[122] *Wandmalereien & Texte: Nehmt der Langeweile ihren Sinn*, (Berlin: Kramer, 1979), 71.

they painted walls in the backyard, children immediately joined them. In the aftermath, they reported, communication amongst the tenants improved.[123] Tenants of another house in the same neighbourhood combined the painting of walls in the backyard with organizing a small festival that, of course, included free beer. Despite initial worries that tenants not involved in the plan would react in a hostile manner, reactions were 'incredibly positive'. Some neighbours even suggested that they should paint the entire house. After the festival, there was more personal contact and less anonymity amongst tenants.[124] Along similar lines, a group from Frankfurt noted that the very act of spontaneously blocking and painting streets was simply fun and could, once again, overcome the lack of communication amongst citizens.[125]

Living in communes, being active in self-organized youth centres, organizing street festivals, or painting the grey walls of parking lots and apartment buildings – in all these instances leftists tried to overcome the isolation and loneliness they deemed typical of capitalism. Facilitating opportunities for communication was crucial for this purpose. Only by talking with each other, not only but also about personal problems, would it be possible to create the feeling of personal intimacy leftists longed for. To make this happen, leftists created spaces – some, like festivals, more temporal, some, like communes, more long-lasting – that would make communication possible. Here, leftists hoped to engage with roommates, as well as strangers and passersby, to overcome the boundaries that separated them from each other. Just like groups, these were spaces for experimenting with communication in a way that would, if the experiment worked, yield feelings; and, just like groups, these experiments could work or fail.

Moments of Rupture

Wall paintings did more than beautify monotone grey cities. Some made rather opaque political statements. 'Experiment without knowing where you end up!' – 'Long live the short-lived, revolutionary pessimistic youth!' – 'Only moments matter.' – 'Let your senses burn!', read some slogans on Munich walls. The *Blatt* provided a characterization of the (arguably fictitious) teenager who had sprayed them: 'The teenager is someone who loses himself, pounding his head around [*beim Hinundherschlagen des Kopfes*], who uses radio- and disco music in a way that differs from the way the

---

[123] Ibid., 92–93.   [124] Ibid., 102–103.
[125] Anon., 'Die Fahrradguerilla geht um', in *Pflasterstrand* 66, 3–16 November 1979, 30–31.

producers of the spectacle intend it . . . He vibrates, just as the scripture he leaves behind on the walls when he resurfaces from the urban underground and goes home. The constant running away makes his head explode, intensifies his perception, changes the thinking, he gives a shit about school or his future . . . he hangs around.' Being caught by the police did not deter him. He continued, stealing big advertisement posters, and thereby creating new, 'surprising' works of art. Coherent thought did not matter for his slogans. 'He doesn't care about his external attitude, but only about his rebellious individuality. He loves his way of unlimited expression, because he can throw it away, wipe it away, expand it, paste it over, just like his life.'[126] The call for experimenting, the desire for 'unlimited expression', the disregard of the future – all this resonates with the ideal of permanent transgressions in the alternative left discussed in Chapter 2. Yet interpreting this as part of the therapeutic politics of the alternative left discussed in this chapter does not quite work. Neither the slogans nor the article are calls for working on the self, for fixing 'damaged' personalities or personal relations. Rather than aiming at any long-term personal or political transformation, which was ultimately the goal of self-experience groups and *Wohngemeinschaften*, the slogans celebrated the moment; rather than colourfully beautifying the city, the teenager's graffiti disrupted urban space.

Disrupting the emotional normalcy of boredom, loneliness, and fear was a central element of leftist emotional politics. Consider the street musicians who tried to create a situation that would break through the usual monotony and that would help themselves and their audience to break through their isolation. Perhaps this contributed to a long-term personal transformation; primarily, however, it was a momentary spark. Producing feelings of solidarity and joy was still central in such situations, but they did not require people to work on themselves and their personal relations as they did in therapy groups. The often painful, though nevertheless productive introspection in self-experience groups or *Wohngemeinschaften* played no role in these disruptive moments, which might explain the sense of exuberance activists often described. The production of feelings, that is, worked differently in those situations. Perhaps most intriguingly, the temporality of feelings and, ultimately, politics changed. The aim was no longer to heal, as it were, damaged personalities, but to experience momentary and intense feelings. This focus on the moment also constituted a radicalization of the politics of the 'here and now', as the 'now' was not simply the 'present', as opposed to a distant future, but the radical

---

[126] Hihi, 'Wandmalereien', in *Das Blatt* 115, 24 February–9 March 1978, 20.

moment. For our purposes it also implies that leftist politics of emotions cannot be reduced to a project of therapeutic self-transformation. Leftists not only tried to express their 'true' and 'authentic' feelings (they did that, too); they also tried (and frequently succeeded, it seems) to produce exuberant feelings of joy and fearlessness.

Carnivals and festivals played, as Chapter 2 has discussed, a central role in the political imagination of the radical left. For leftists, these were moments when social boundaries collapsed and people could overcome their isolation, a quality that made festivals inherently subversive. The street musicians discussed previously created a miniature version of this. Larger festivals fulfilled a similar function. The Munich group *Revolutionärer Kampf*, for example, noted in March 1973 that organizing festivals for foreign workers had been much more successful than agitating among them in front of factories. 'It was a first opportunity for them to escape from their isolation and boredom and to make contact with other nationalities', the group wrote. Tellingly, it was a lesson the group had learned from their Italian comrades, who had achieved more with their 'spontaneity, emotionality and collectivity, with their songs, festivals and collective feasts' than they had with agitating in front of factories for months.[127] Neighbourhood festivals celebrating Mayday in West Berlin similarly helped activists to overcome the distance between them and the local population, or so they claimed.[128] Breaking through 'daily isolation' at festivals also empowered leftists themselves, perhaps even more so than public protest, as the *Blatt* noted after the Pentecost meeting in June 1976 in Frankfurt.[129] During festivals after successful 'actions', the 'everyday fear is partied down [*die Alltagsangst wird niedergefeiert*]', a group of youth centre activists claimed.[130] Bodily practices were, once again, of crucial importance during such festive moments. Collective dancing, laughing, and singing at an exclusively female party in Berlin created a 'feeling of loosening up [*Gelöstsein*], of relaxation as well as one's own power that was shared with everyone'.[131] Without the presence of men, another woman wrote, regarding a women's-only party, the atmosphere was 'much warmer, much freer'. Though it was by no means easy to 'demolish the barricades between us women without reproducing heterosexual shit',

[127] Anon., 'Wir wollen leben', in *Wir Wollen Alles* 2, 19 March 1973, 6–8.
[128] Anon., '1. Mai-Feste', in *Info BUG* 5, 31 March 1974, 7–8.
[129] Anon., 'Bericht über den Pfingstkongress', in *Das Blatt* 72, 18 June–1 July 1976, 4–5.
[130] Herrenknecht, Hätscher, and Koospal, *Träume*, 72.
[131] Anon., 'ML-Genossin auf der Frauenfete', in *Info BUG* 10, 13 May 1974, 3–4.

dancing together was nevertheless 'insane, in a way liberating, feeling the body and all that'.[132]

The event that came perhaps closest to the carnivalesque ecstasy Rabe and Röttgen had described in *Vulkantänze* was a party after a gay liberation demonstration – not in West Berlin or Frankfurt, but in provincial Tübingen. 'At midnight, the Barn [the location of the party] was a volcano, I haven't seen something like that before, everything curls topsy-turvy, women, men, leather folks, tranny chicks [*Fummeltrinen*], heteros, lesbians, nearly naked and completely naked, half-orgies on the stage – the festival is immensely gay, immensely perverse, no inhibitions, and immensely affectionate', an anonymous participant wrote. The pressure to find to find someone for the night, so common at parties, was gone. 'It's just this feeling of emotional security [*Geborgenheit*], of community, of getting lost [*Aufgehen*] in the music, the dancing, the people, the atmosphere.' Even during breakfast the next morning, people were 'cuddling, relaxed, caring [*verschmust, gelöst, lieb*]'.[133] The party as an emotional experiment seems to have worked, at least for this participant. Boundaries collapsed in the sense that Röttgen and Rabe had imagined, which allowed partygoers to overcome loneliness, and facilitated intensely exuberant feelings.

While feelings of exuberance were exceptional, and in that sense indeed disrupting an emotional normalcy, they did not simply emerge spontaneously. Leftists organized such festivities at least implicitly hoping to facilitate intense bodily and communal feelings. When leftist partygoers went to such events, they knew what to expect: that excessive dancing would be bodily liberating and would help them overcome social isolation. But this did not always happen as expected; emotional experiments could always fail. In the first place, however, it was necessary to create spaces for such experiments. The women's movement that had established dance bars had succeeded in this, an activist from Berlin claimed, whereas men lacked similar places to 'flip around bodily'.[134] But even where spaces for such emotional experiments existed, their success was never certain. For example, the woman from Berlin praising the warm and free atmosphere at a women's-only party stressed that it was difficult to erase barriers between women. Theoretically, she wanted to be able to fall in love with any woman who did not act utterly unacceptably, but the reality, deeply

---

[132] Anon., 'Ein kleines Stück auf dem Weg zur Begreiung!! Von 'ner Frau für Frauen', in *Info BUG* 87, December 1977, 4–5.
[133] Toni/Magnus, 'Schwuler Befreiungstag in Stuttgart', in '*s Blättle* 41, August/September 1979, 8–9.
[134] Anon., 'Berliner Subkultur', in *Info BUG* 111, 28 June 1976, 17. The author identified himself as 'a man who would rather not be a man [*ein Mann, der lieber keiner wäre*]'.

worrying for her, was that external features determined whether she actually could. Apparently she had not been able to distance herself from these 'shitty commodity aesthetics'. And, despite her longing to be affectionate with women, she realized that she could not, and ended up going home alone, as always.[135] The wrong kind of music and the wrong kind of dancing could be equally problematic. Women from Göttingen who attended a women's congress in Stuttgart for example complained about 'slow gooey music' that made women dance stereotypically in a 'cutely female, gracefully, charming' way, but kept them from letting out their 'energies (and aggressions)'.[136] At this party at least, the hope for acting out exciting and 'aggressive' feelings was disappointed.

It is perhaps not surprising that parties provided people with an opportunity to experiment with their feelings and bodies. In the alternative left, this experimenting with feelings gained a political meaning as it allowed people break through the isolation that characterized, or so they claimed, their daily life. Reports about parties provide us with a glimpse into how people tried to achieve this: they danced, cuddled, dressed up, or got undressed. Just as the other emotional practices discussed in this chapter, these experiments sometimes worked and produced exuberant feelings of getting lost in a community, of personal and bodily intimacy and affection, but also failed and, in doing so, made leftists feel frustrated and lonely again.

According to leftists, demonstrations and riots resembled festivals in this regard. An article about Walpurgis Nights in the Hamburg magazine *Große Freiheit* from May 1981 made this connection most explicitly. Drawing on Hans-Peter Duerr's *Traumzeit*, the author described Walpurgis Nights as 'dream times [*Traumzeit*]'. 'Between the ages, when the old age is gone and the new age has not yet started, things stand outside of normality, the order is reversed and at the same time its continued existence is threatened', he quoted Duerr. This is what happened during Walpurgis Nights, when the normal (gender) order was reversed because only women and men dressed as women were allowed to participate. In such topsy-turvy moments, human beings might accept their 'nature' and could 'experience themselves', he wrote. Capitalism, he claimed, in line with alternative thinking, 'represses' the 'sensual'. In capitalism, anything that cannot 'be grasped with rational concepts' remains 'alien' to people, the author charged. To 'destroy the factory society' and to 'reclaim our

[135] Anon., 'Bericht von einer Frauenfete', in *Info BUG* 87, December 1977, 4–5.
[136] Anon., 'Bericht über das nationale Frauenhaustreffen', in *Frauenzeitung* 2, December 1977, 17–23.

autonomy, in all parts of our lives', including that what become 'alien' in capitalism, it would be necessary to revive the tradition of Walpurgis Nights, he argued, a tradition that lives on, if not always consciously, 'at every demonstration that does not traipse on like a funeral march, at every festival that blows up its boundaries [*den Rahmen sprengt*]'. From this perspective, events such demonstrations and festivals were a 'threat for the factory society' not because of their expressed political goals, but because 'we claim our right for what is uncontrollable and irrational in our lives. [*Die Walpurgisnacht und ähnliche Ereignisse sind genau das: sich ein Recht nehmen auf das, was in unserem Leben unkontrollierbar und irrational abläuft.*]'[137] This somewhat esoteric understanding of demonstrations and festivals as remnants of the topsy-turvy celebrations of Walpurgis Nights resonated with earlier calls for making demonstrations less boring and more joyful events. In 1974, an author for *Info BUG* had complained that the 'bloodily idle, unimaginative, traipsing-demonstrations [*lahm-arschige, einfallslose Latschdemos*]' under the aegis of the Communist Party had turned into a mere 'matter of duty' for the arduous task (*Fleißaufgabe*) of abolishing capitalism.[138] Once again, Italian and Portuguese comrades did it better, *radikal* wrote four years later. Their demonstrations were more 'casual [*locker*]'; they had bands and played theatre, which showed that politics was much more than 'chanting slogans, but life that is fun'.[139] Just like festivals, demonstrations were, or at least were meant to be, emotional experiments that should produce joy and recuperate the 'irrational'. For leftists, these emotional aspects could be as important as the explicit political goals of a demonstration. And just like festivals, demonstrations could succeed or fail as emotional experiments.

For the emotional experiments to work, something extraordinary and unexpected had to happen. Consider the bicyclist demonstration against nuclear power in Munich in the summer of 1977.[140] Chapter 2 has already discussed a somewhat surreal report about the event. A more realistic text suggests that the demonstration was indeed quite a joyous event. Some activists, Rädli reported, had decorated their bikes with windmills and banners, while others had built bike trailers to drag music boxes along. The demonstration thus became an intervention into the monotony of urban space. 'For a few hours, the streets were illuminated by a colourfully mixed

---

[137] Anon., 'Walpurgisnacht', in *Große Freiheit* 45, May 1981, 3.
[138] Anon., 'Zur Demonstrationsinflation', in *Info BUG* 21, 18 August 1974, 2–3.
[139] V., 'Politik und Rummsdada', in *radikal* 23, 9–23 June 1977, 8.
[140] See Chapter 2 for a somewhat surrealist report about the event.

[*zusammengewürfelt*] trail of wheels that proved that even in this city, so close to the abyss, bolts of light are possible.' For a brief moment, they beautified the city by decorating cars with flowers and planted a strip of grass in the middle of a street, used acetone to destroy a 'concrete monument' in front of a construction company, and left a crest of beef bones in front of the ministry of the interior. Singing, laughing, and 'howling like Indians', they biked through the Munich's streets. 'I've learned', Rädli wrote, 'that a demo doesn't have to look like this, that we march with grim faces through the streets, yell our slogans and go home full with frustration. No, it's possible to make a demonstration where we can have fun, where we can love and rejoice.'[141] At least according to this account, the bicycle demonstration disrupted both the urban monotony by making the city, if only for a moment, a more colourful place, and the monotony of normal demonstrations – biking and rollerblading rather than marching, and singing, laughing, and howling rather than chanting slogans. All this created what I suggest to describe as a moment of emotional rupture: a temporarily limited moment of extraordinary, exuberant feelings that broke through the constraints of the emotional regime of capitalism as leftists saw it.

Riots could be similar moments of emotional intensity. In his 1977 article, *Vorstoß in primitivere Zeiten*, famous for its critique of violence, Joschka Fischer admitted that he had experienced 'spontaneous solidarity, really emotional flipping-into-each other [*Aufeinandereinflippen*] ... in the streets, when it really nicely banged [*gebollert hatte*] ...'; Fischer, though, then criticized how 'we and I had dealt with all of this in our Sponti-cadre-heads'.[142] His critical voice was certainly a prominent one in the alternative left, yet we should not read his critique as evidence for a general turn against violence in the left.[143] Other leftists still celebrated militant actions. For example, an antinuclear power activist from Freiburg wrote that he and his comrades blew up utility poles 'because our subjectivity survives [in those actions], because it is a possibility to "live" rage and hatred, energies and fantasies, rather than swallowing them [*und nicht in sich rein zu fressen*]'.[144] Riots during an anti-neo-Nazi demonstration in June

---

[141] Rädli, 'Achtung, Achtung: Hier spricht der Atomtod – Huiiihhh, Oder: Wie wir uns für ein paar Stunden die Straße zurückerobert haben', in *Das Blatt* 99, 15–28 July 1977, 4.

[142] Joschka Fischer, 'Vorstoß in primitivere Zeiten', in *Autonomie: Materialien gegen die Fabrikgesellschaft* 5, February 1977, 52–64, esp. 56.

[143] For such an argument, see Karrin Hanshew, *Terror and Democracy in West Germany* (Cambridge: Cambridge University Press, 2012), 203.

[144] Anon., [No Title], in *Stadtzeitung für Freiburg* 42/43, December 1979/January 1980, 9–10.

1978 in Frankfurt provide a telling example how an emotional intensity could be created. Neither had anyone expected the 'offensive escalation' of the protests, nor had anyone prepared for it, an author of *Pflasterstrand* assured. 'It is the fantasy of resistance that creates such situations in shortest time, seemingly out of nothing, which the participants in the street-fighting experience as intensive moments of coming alive [*Aufleben*] – even if it's only for the ten minutes that the barricade stands.' Not surprisingly, the 'new experiences' were the theme for evening discussions in bars, whereas others danced listening to The Rolling Stones' 'Street Fighting Man', the article claimed.[145] The riots in Frankfurt created, the account suggests, a brief moment of emotional intensity, which activists cherished. Crucial for this feeling of intensity was, first, that the riot happened rather unexpectedly, and contrasted with the normalcy of peaceful demonstrations, and, second, that the normal order, that is, the superiority of the forces of orders, was reversed, if only for ten minutes during which a barricade was successfully defended.

But should we trust this rhetoric of spontaneity? If we interpret riots, as I have suggested, as emotional practices that were *meant* to yield intense feelings, then the rhetoric of spontaneity and unexpectedness is puzzling. The idea of emotional practices implies a sense of intentionality that contradicts any suddenness and spontaneity. Paradoxically, I would suggest, activists knew, and indeed expected, that *unexpected* situations like riots (or, for that matter, excessive festivities) would yield intense feelings. In other words, neither the riots, nor the momentary reversal of orders, when, for example, a barricade was successfully defended for a few minutes and the police had to run, was part of a script; but how one would feel in such situations was part of an emotional script. The extraordinary feelings of intensity and jubilation during unexpected riots were, then, both and at the same time unexpected, as the riot as the event that facilitated these feelings indeed 'emerged out of nothing', and expected, as people had an understanding of how this unexpected riot might feel. Neither taking the rhetoric of spontaneity at face value, nor considering such descriptions of spontaneous emotional intensity as merely part of an emotional script, would grasp the emotional contingency of those situations.

---

[145] Mickey, 'Römerberggespräche', in *Pflasterstrand* 33, 1–14 July 1978, 23–24; Anon., 'Frankfurt: Wut macht Mut', in *Info BUG* 1026, 26 June 1978, 6. On the demonstration and the 'euphoric feeling', see also Wolf Wetzel, 'Die Besetzung der Siesmayerstraße', in *Häuserkampf: Teil 1. Der Beginn einer Bewegung* (Hamburg: LAIKA Verlag, 2012), 101–102.

Riots and demonstrations also provided activists with an opportunity to momentarily overcome the allegedly omnipresent fear in capitalist cities.[146] Writing about a demonstration that resulted in heavy riots after the death of Ulrike Meinhof in May 1976, the *Andere Zeitung* for example claimed that, contrary to what 'perennial sceptics' had predicted, the demonstration did not result in more frustration and 'individual fear', but in 'collective overcoming of individual fears'.[147] Similarly, activists noted after violent confrontations at an antinuclear power demonstration in March 1977 in Grohnde that marching past the police in a calm manner was 'an incredible feeling', which made the previous fears go away, even though the author also noted that the 'feeling of strength' eventually resulted in numerous casualties as protestors were beaten up by the police.[148] Overcoming fear was a particularly important issue for the 'Reclaim the Night' demonstrations organized by the women's movement in various German cities around May 1977 and May 1978. A woman from Stuttgart, where some two hundred fifty women joined a women's demonstration, for example noted how 'in the midst of so many women' the 'mist of fear of the night turned finally into joy and strength'.[149] In Hamburg, women had organized a nightly demonstration with the explicit aim of marching through the streets 'without fear'.[150] Only a few individual men tried to assault women here, but they failed due to the number demonstrators. 'Nobody is afraid. But an ungovernable [*unbändige*] joy amongst us. How can we bring trouble [*Trubel*] in the dark, abandoned streets?'[151] In Frankfurt, women painted their bodies and dressed up in an effort to look like witches. They marched with flashlights, torches, whistles, and firecrackers through the city, and emptied flour-bags over the heads of 'smirking pub-folks'. That way, women reconquered the nightly city.[152] In Munich, finally, women dressed like witches, too, and covered their faces behind gypsum masks, which made it easier to react freely to harassing men. Collectively singing, they not only expressed their desire to overcome fear and loneliness, but also achieved their goal through the very act of singing: 'But we are women, we want to live, an end to fear

---

[146] See, e.g., Anon., 'Die Sprache von Baeumen und Voegeln', in *Autonomie: Materialien gegen die Fabrikgesellschaft* 10, January 1978, 70–73.

[147] Anon., 'Wer sich nicht wehr, lebt verkehrt', in *Andere Zeitung* 5, June 1976, 14–15.

[148] See, e.g., Anon., 'Bedeutet jede Niederlage unseren nächsten Sieg?', in *Info BUG* 149, 28 March 1977, 5.

[149] Anon., 'Wir holen uns die Nacht zurück', in *'s Blättle* 17, May 1977, 10–11.

[150] Anon., 'Bullenterror in der Walpurgisnacht', in *Info BUG* 1020, 15 May 1978, 8.

[151] Angelika, 'Frauennacht', in *Große Freiheit* 4, June 1977, 12.

[152] Anon., 'Walpurgisnacht', in *Pflasterstrand* 9, 4–15 May 1977, 13.

and loneliness, we want to give [this] to us, hey, women, it's our time!'[153] Demonstrating at night, dressing up like witches or singing together were all, these reports suggest, emotional practices that yielded feelings of collective strength, free from fear.

Rioting and demonstrating, dancing wildly, and dressing up like witches: these could all be therapeutic acts insofar as they had an emotionally transformative impact by helping activists to lose their fears and overcome their isolation. Yet these therapeutic acts differed from the therapeutic practices discussed in the chapter's previous sections. Unlike talking about feelings in a self-experience group or practising intimacy in a *Wohngemeinschaft*, the practices discussed here would not help activists to build or 'fix' a stable self; they did not require a patient learning process of new emotional styles. Rather, they were transgressive and disruptive acts that might, or might not, yield brief but intense and exuberant feelings. Rioting and excessive dancing were not 'technologies of the self' that helped activists transform their selves, but were acts of 'self-dissolution', as the rhetoric of 'flipping apart [*auseinanderflippen*]', 'throwing out [*herauswerfen*]' and of 'loosening up [*gelöst sein*]' suggests. Leftists longed for such moments when their stable and rational selves dissolved, believing that only then intense and otherwise oppressed feelings might surface. Rioting and dancing excessively could be emotionally productive practices, precisely because leftists expected them to be so.

Therapeutic Politics and Its Critics

In a world in which fear was common, where people lived isolated and boring lives, devoid of meaningful communication and constantly suppressing their real feelings, learning to express feelings in therapy groups, to communicate with others in communes, or to feel the body in karate or yoga sessions, became an inherently subversive political activity. A women's collective writing in the Frankfurt magazine *diskus* adequately summarized this approach to politics: 'Alternative projects reawaken a consciousness of long forgotten desires', they 'show possibilities of a more humane life', but without confronting the 'global destruction'. They praised a 'new sensuality [*Sinnlichkeit*]' that 'enables us to translate sorrow and rage about the destructive system into new forms of activism'. Sensuality, they wrote, 'means an unbroken desire [*ungebrochene Lust*] for using

---

[153] Anon., 'Walpurgisnacht', in *Das Blatt* 94, 10 May–2 June 1977, 6. For a critical discussion of Walpurgis Night demonstrations, see also 'Walpurgisnacht', in *Courage*, June 1978, 4–5.

all human senses in our relations amongst each other, to nature, to the city, to our body. It means the conscious insistence on this desire vis-à-vis and despite all the hostility towards desire, such as cops, jails, bureaucracy, factory, seminar and the structures we ourselves have in our body.' Resistance then meant to 'develop this lust for life'; 'infecting ourselves [with this lust for life], we will learn how to go on the offensive'.[154] This was, as Chapter 2 has argued, a radical redefinition of politics and political practices. For alternative leftists, exuberant dancing, rioting, setting up communes, or meeting in dance bars or simply groups to talk about feelings and to cuddle were all ways of diffusing the 'lust for life' that would undermine the antisensual and rational world of capitalism.

But not everyone agreed with this understanding of politics. Herbert Röttgen, though he did consider 'exercises of Zen Buddhism and mutual massaging' as ways of trying out alternative forms of living an important development, asked critically if 'macrobiotic food will solve social problems'.[155] In the *Blatt*, Lothar Hildebrandt wrote laconically that 'every political movement turns into a mere self-experience group'.[156] Along similar lines, Gaby Weber worried in the *Andere Zeitung* that the exclusive concern with personal 'needs [*Bedürfnisse*]', the focus on individual problems and 'self experience' made comrades turn away from political activism. Many political groups, Weber noted, desisted from engaging in any political activism, but simply convened for 'mutual and self-experience [*um sich gegenseitig zu erleben, um sich selbst zu erfahren*]'. Political activism or theoretical discussions were no longer part of the agenda, she bemoaned, but only how damaged individuals were, or what happened with 'personal relations.' The imperative to personally 'understand' everyone else had replaced political judgment; under the premise of 'understanding', any possibility of (solidaristic) critique disappeared. This 'pandemic' became most apparent in the 'self-experience groups', she argued, that took 'individual frustrations' as their starting point, but ultimately only provided an 'outlet for their shitty situation' without changing anything, since participants would rarely draw practical consequences. These groups made the 'frustrated SELF the basis for any individual actions', and considered only 'immediately lived experiences', without recognizing that 'society deforms lived experience [*Erlebniss und*

---

[154] Frauenkollektiv, 'So, so, einen Frauenasta habt ihr – Ach ja, einen Frauenasta?', in *Diskus* 5, 20 October 1976, 18–27.

[155] Herbert Röttgen, 'Politik und Leben', in *Autonomie: Materialien gegen die Fabrikgesellschaft* 4, October 1976, 8–11.

[156] Lothar Hildebrandt, 'Liebe allein genügt nicht', in *Das Blatt* 75, 30 July–19 August 1976, 18.

Erfahrungen]' and thus creates a 'false consciousness'. Where only the self mattered, the 'suppressed class' became irrelevant. In the end, then, such groups only helped stabilize the capitalist regime, Weber charged.[157] Considering that one of the members of the girls' group discussed at the beginning of the chapter turned away from politics after the group disbanded, and instead wanted to focus more on her body and psyche, such criticisms do not seem to be totally unfounded.

Criticizing therapy groups but also rural communes as forms of escaping from social and political problems was not uncommon.[158] Yet there was also another line of criticism that placed leftist therapeutic politics in the context of the broader therapy boom during the 1970s. From the perspective of critical authors such as Jörg Bopp or Herbert Nagel, the leftist idea that 'psychoanalytical practice is emancipatory'[159] had effectively contributed to the emergence of a new form of political power based on expert knowledge. These and other critical authors saw remarkably clearly that the effects of leftist therapeutic politics were, despite proclamations to the contrary, by no means emancipatory. Their critical perspective is still instructive for historians sceptical of the enthusiastic promises of personal liberation or claims of genuine authenticity. In the preface of an entire issue devoted to therapies, the editorial team of *Autonomie* for example argued that the longing for an 'original self unstained by history' is at the core of the 'totally uncritical consumption expectation for therapies of all kinds as cornucopia of happiness and salvation'. Rather than really changing the self in a way that might facilitate changing the world, therapies that abstract from history only result in a 'phylogenetic return to an amoebae-like state of being', the authors wrote. Therapies that might genuinely transform the self in an emancipatory way, then, would not try to excavate, as it were, an immaculate original self, but support individuals in 'appropriating their own history with all its contradictions and thus to increase the inner space of freedom vis-à-vis history, and always "in relation to it"'.[160]

---

[157] Gaby Weber, 'Der Tanz der Bedürfnisse', in *Die Andere Zeitung* 12, February 1977, 4–5.

[158] See the critical discussions of different therapy forms in the special issue of *Carlo Sponti* on therapies, January 1977.

[159] Herbert Nagel, 'Psychologie als Elend der Politik, oder: Ich, der letzte Mensch', in *Autonomie: Materialien gegen die Fabrikgesellschaft* 13, January 1979, 8–28. He quoted from a lecture 'Klinische Psychologie und Psychoanalyse' by Günter Ammon, 15 June 1971. See also Tändler, *Therapeutische Jahrzehnt*, 155.

[160] Anon., 'Editorial', in *Autonomie: Materialien gegen die Fabrikgesellschaft* 13, January 1979, 1–2.

Elaborating on this point, Herbert Nagel argued in the same issue of *Autonomie* that therapeutic experts did not help uncover any authentic self, but played a crucial role in shaping the self: 'The subject that has no knowledge of itself in our society anymore can *construct* [*erarbeiten*] a shape of itself *only* in cooperation with experts.' Therapeutic experts, that is, shaped, and had to shape, the subject that would otherwise remain without contours. When they claimed to 'uncover' their clients' most private, unspoken wishes, they effectively formed their clients' consciousness in a way that cemented their own power as experts, Nagel charged. His point was thus not to bemoan the 'depoliticization through therapy', but to understand 'the formation of a new form of politics: the construction of reality through therapy as a social form of power', to which, in his mind, the post-1968 left, with its emphasis on therapy as a form of emancipation, had greatly contributed. Therapeutic knowledge, he argued, construed (personal) problems in a specific way, and offered solutions for these problems. Neither stress nor illness 'as a form of resistance of the body or simple exhaustion' was acceptable any longer; both required therapists. Even idleness (*Untätigkeit*) was regarded as something that required 'interpretation, advice, support'. 'People are unhappy, but nobody really knows what causes this unhappiness. Dealing with oneself and with others seems not to work (anymore?).' Thus the demand for experts that could guide their clients to '"meaningful" activities', ranging from yoga to group therapies, was high, Nagel concluded.[161]

Whereas left-wing psychologists had believed in the emancipatory potential of therapy, Nagel regarded the formulation and solution of individual problems in therapeutic settings as part of the 'finishing of a social productive force [*Zurichtung einer gesellschaftlichen Produktivkraft*], that is the individual and collective [*gruppenmäßige*] attention (as selective perception of social complexity), to which different possibilities of action [*Handlungsmöglichkeiten*] correspond. Exactly this process of power-political contention is systemically concealed by the fiction of voluntariness (autonomy), with which an individual submits to treatment and works on the solution of problems in different ways by discarding other options.'[162] More crudely (and without analyzing a specific knowledge as a form of social power), *Carlo Sponti* wrote: 'Therapy is class war from above.'[163] A bit more cautiously, Helga Bilden worried in *Beiträge zur feministischen*

---

[161] Nagel, 'Psychologie'.   [162] Ibid.
[163] M., 'Primärtherapie: neuer Weg ins Heil? oder: Wie der befreiende Anstoß der Gefühlstherapien zur Fessel der Befreiung wird', in *Carlo Sponti* 26/27, January 1977, 11–13.

Theorie und Praxis that women 'too easily seek help from experts, authorities; made insecure by the psychologization wave and generally having a low self-esteem and prejudices against women, they have little confidence in themselves and other women to understand and solve their own psychosocial ("personal") problems'. After an initial enthusiasm for feminist therapy, Bilden thus became sceptical about the consequences of this trend. Her critical remarks at a women's congress in Cologne, however, were received rather negatively.[164] Therapeutic discourse, not least within the alternative left, these authors argued, created a knowledge that was itself a form of social power that stabilized capitalism rather than undermining it.

Along somewhat similar lines, leftist therapist Jörg Bopp criticized the idealization of 'emotional immediacy' so common in the alternative left as a 'religious desire for a fundamental rebirth'.[165] Rather than being an 'act of liberation', he considered the 'eruption of feelings', not least in the context of therapies, to be itself only a 'manifestation of a social pathodynamic that conditions feelings just as much as the mind'. Far from condemning rationality as inherently oppressive and celebrating feelings as inherently subversive, Bopp argued that only a rational analysis of feelings could succeed in emancipating those. Where this analysis lacked, therapies ended up preventing rather than facilitating the release of 'experiences from armouring [*die Erfahrung aus Verpanzerungen zu lösen*], the reduction of fierce self-control, the liberation of emotions, sensuality, fantasy and spontaneity'. Looking at therapeutic languages and practices within the left, Bopp diagnosed a ritualization of emotional expressions. In his mind, the expression of feelings had become a mere show; 'theatrical routine replaces spontaneity ... Rituals of affection and commanded erotics – "in the next five minutes, everyone may fondle whomever he likes" – turn feelings into a group of dance-bears during the therapy.'[166]

The consequences of this ritualized expression of feelings, Bopp suggested, reached far beyond the therapeutic context itself. Therapeutic language shaped how people construed their selves, and how they related to others. Within what Bopp called the 'leftist psychodrome', an 'incredible interest in one's own and – derived from that – others' problems' was

---

[164] Helga Bilden, 'Frauen und Psychotherapie, oder: Verlangt massenhaftes psychisches Leiden von Frauen nur nach Frauentherapie/feministischer Therapie?', in *Beiträge zur feministischen Theorie und Praxis* 2, November 1978, 102–113.

[165] Jörg Bopp, 'Der linke Psychodrom', in *Kursbuch* 55, March 1977, 73–94, also for the quotes that follow. See also Tändler, *Therapeutische Jahrzehnt*, 320–321.

[166] Bopp, 'Psychodrom'.

common. People celebrated their personal problems, as only these problems made them interesting and attractive; indeed, the more problems one had, the more critical and hence emancipated one was, according to the logics of the leftist 'psychodrome'. Actually solving these problems in a therapy would thus be entirely detrimental, Bopp noted. As the therapeutic language permeated everyday life, language came to lack any real 'emotional and sensual quality'. To make his point, Bopp described an 'invented but true moment' about a man who had been on vacation in Greece. 'When he returned from Greece, they asked him whether he had liked it. He responded: "It was very important for me."' Since everything was viewed from the perspective of personal problems, a genuine and pleasurable experience (in this case of visiting Greece) was impossible; the fictitious trip mattered only insofar as it helped transform the fictive man's personality. In that sense, the 'crippled' therapeutic language with its restrictive focus on the self 'reduced experience', which ultimately also reduced the possibility of spontaneous emotional expression. Not surprisingly, Bopp too complained about the depoliticization of psychotherapy; more interestingly, however, Bopp also saw, and criticized, how a therapeutic language shaped a new subjectivity that was based on the formulation and constant reformulation of individual problems and the ritualized expression of feelings. Far from celebrating feelings, critical writers like Herbert Nagel and Jörg Bopp understood the (leftist) 'psychoboom' as the emergence of a new, peculiar kind of power that deserved critical attention. From a historical perspective, their critique is not only interesting due to their remarkable insightfulness, but because it indicates that the development of new forms of power based on psychic knowledge was, from the very beginning, accompanied by a critique of this form of power. Critical accounts of the norms and requirements that shape the authentic self of the alternative left as well as the neoliberal self of the present draw, if implicitly, on such critical perspectives developed by leftists themselves.

Conclusion

In consciousness-raising and therapy groups, in communes and independent youth centres, at parties and in the streets: leftists tried to produce feelings of intimacy and intensity. To accomplish this, they developed a great variety of communicative and bodily practices that would allow them to feel close to their friends and comrades, to feel bodies, and to overcome the allegedly omnipresent fear in capitalism. They talked about their feelings in groups, they practised karate or yoga to feel the body, and they danced excessively at parties; they engaged in street battles with the police, and threw Molotov cocktails into department stores, in order to overcome fear. All of this shows how immensely emotionally productive the alternative left was. Leftists produced (bodily) feelings; or at least they tried to do so. After all, the practices leftists developed were meant to produce feelings of intimacy and intensity, but whether they always worked is another matter. The chapter has thus suggested interpreting those practices as emotional experiments that sometimes succeeded in yielding feelings, and sometimes failed to do so. In that sense, the alternative left can be understood as a vast space for trying out feelings.

Arguably, the alternative left and its therapeutic politics were part and parcel of a wider 'psychoboom' that resulted in a 'therapeutic society' that required people to work on themselves in a preventive way, be it by doing yoga or sports to remain physically healthy, or by managing the self with the help of psychotherapeutic experts.[167] Leftists, too, tried to manage their emotional selves and worked on their bodies. For radical leftists, working on the self was an inherently political project as they sought to 'undo' the damages capitalist society had, in their mind, inflicted on their selves. By producing feelings of intimacy, leftists hoped to foster solidarity and to challenge the isolation in capitalism; by feeling the body in its entirety, leftists sought to overcome the fragmentation of the body typical of capitalism; and by finding ways to overcome fear, they disrupted the emotional regime of capitalism that, according to a leftist understanding, made fear omnipresent. In a world that 'damaged' personalities, 'fixing' or 'healing' the emotional and bodily self was an eminently political project. Leftists, that is, were engaged in (self)-therapeutic politics that created, as scholars have suggested, a more or less restrictive regime of emotional self-management concealed under a rhetoric of personal liberation.

This chapter complicated such a perspective in two ways. First, it has emphasized that by trying out feelings in numerous emotional experiments, leftists produced feelings. Interpreting the alternative left as a space for experimenting with feelings that sometimes worked and sometimes didn't, the chapter has sought to establish a sense of contingency and openness of the 1970s that is easily missing in the ultimately teleological narratives that treat the decade as a prehistory of the present and its simultaneously neoliberal and therapeutic regime of subjectivity. Second,

---

[167] See Biess, 'Sensibilisierung', 68. From the perspective of medical history, see the contributions in Martin Lengwiler and Jeannette Madarász, eds., *Das präventive Selbst: Eine Kulturgeschichte moderner Gesundheitspolitik* (Bielefeld: transcript, 2010).

the chapter has shown how critics within the alternative left challenged such therapeutic politics. Not only did they worry that practising yoga or talking about one's feelings hardly questioned capitalist society. They also argued that the 'psychoboom' within and beyond the alternative left created a new form of power that shaped any experience in psychological terms. These critiques indicate that not only a new regime of subjectivity emerged, but also a critique of this very regime and the peculiar form of power tied to it.

CHAPTER 5

Exuberance and Intensity

As the year 1980 started, nothing hinted at a particularly tumultuous year. After a series of terrorist attacks in the autumn of 1977 had shocked the Federal Republic, the situation seemed to have calmed down. Few people had expected the wave of protests and riots that erupted across cities in the Netherlands, Switzerland, and West Germany: in Amsterdam, squatters engaged in massive street battles with the police during the spring of 1980.[1] In Germany, riots first erupted in Bremen on 6 May 1980, when

[1] On the revolts of 1980–81, see Bart van der Steen and Knud Andresen, eds., *A European Youth Revolt: European Perspectives on Youth Protest and Social Movements in the 1980s* (Basingstoke, UK: Palgrave Macmillan, 2016); Sven Reichardt, *Authentizität und Gemeinschaft: Linksalternatives Leben in den siebziger und frühen achtziger Jahren* (Berlin: Suhrkamp, 2014), 516–571; Freia Anders, 'Wohnraum, Freiraum, Widerstand: Die Formierung der Autonomen in den Konflikten um Hausbesetzungen Anfang der achtziger Jahre', in *Das alternative Milieu: Antibürgerlicher Lebensstil und linke Politik in der Bundesrepublik Deutschland und Europa, 1968–1983*, ed. Sven Reichardt and Detlef Siegfried (Göttingen: Wallstein, 2010); Hanno Balz and Jan-Henrik Friedrichs, eds., 'All we ever wanted ...': *eine Kulturgeschichte europäischer Protestbewegungen der 1980er Jahre* (Berlin: Dietz, 2012); Alex Vasudevan, *Metropolitan Preoccupations: The Spatial Politics of Squatting in Berlin* (Chichester, UK: John Wiley and Sons, 2016); Carla MacDougall, '"We too Are Berliners": Protest, Symbolism and the City in Cold War Germany', in *Changing the World, Changing Oneself: Political Protest and Collective Identities in West Germany and the U.S. in the 1960s and 1970s*, ed. Belinda Davis et al. (New York: Berghahn, 2010); Andreas Suttner, 'Beton brennt': *Hausbesetzer und Selbstverwaltung im Berlin, Wien und Zürich der 80er* (Vienna: Lit-Verlag, 2011); Sebastian Haumann, 'Schade, daß Beton nicht brennt ...' *Planung, Partizipation und Protest in Philadelphia und Köln, 1940–1990* (Stuttgart: Franz Steiner Verlag, 2011); Georgy Katsiaficas, *The Subversion of Politics: European Autonomous Social Movements and the Decolonization of Everyday Life* (Oakland: AK Press, 2006), 88–106; A. G. Grauwacke, *Autonome in Bewegung: Aus den ersten 23 Jahren* (Berlin: Assozation A, 2003), 34–86; Stefan Aust and Sabine Rosenbladt, eds., *Hausbesetzer: Wofür sie kämpfen, wie sie leben und wie sie leben wollen* (Hamburg: Hoffmann und Campe, 1981); Volkhard Brandes and Bernhard Schön, eds., *Wer sind die Instandbesetzer? Selbstzeugnisse, Dokumente, Analysen* (Bensheim: päd.-extra-Buchverlag); Lynn Owens, *Cracking under Pressure: Narrating the Decline of the Amsterdam Squatters' Movement* (University Park, PA: Pennsylvania State University Press, 2009); Eric Duivenvoorden, *Een voet tussen de deur: Geschiedenis van de kraakbeweging, 1964–1999* (Amsterdam: Arbeiderspers, 2000); Klaus-Jürgen Scherer, 'Berlin (West): Hauptstadt der Szenen. Ein Porträt kultureller und anderer Revolten Anfang der achtziger Jahre', in *Pöbelexzesse und Volkstumulte in Berlin: Zur Sozialgeschichte der Straße (1830–1980)*, ed. Manfred Gailus (Berlin: Verlag Europäische Perspektiven, 1984); *Häuserkampf I: Wir wollen alles – Der Beginn einer Bewegung.* (Hamburg: Laika Verlag, 2012). For a German-Italian perspective on urban

a demonstration against a military recruitment ceremony ended with heavy clashes between protestors and the police. Next followed Zurich in Switzerland, where a protest against the municipal policy to subsidize the local opera but not to give in to demands for an Autonomous Youth Centre resulted in two nights of rioting on 30 and 31 May 1980.[2] In June, the police evicted the occupants of the Dreisameck in Freiburg, which again led to violent protests.[3] It took a while until the West Berlin scene joined the wave of revolts, but when it finally happened in December 1980, the revolt was more intense, more violent, and more long-lasting than in any other city. For participants, it was a time of 'intoxication and ecstasy [*Rausch*]', of 'euphoric feelings of happiness', as former activists from West Berlin told me.[4]

These urban revolts, and how they are related to the alternative politics of emotions of the 1970s, are the subject of this chapter. The squatting movement of 1980–81 was one of various products of the dissolution of the alternative left by the late 1970s and early 1980s that also included social movements like the peace and environmental movements, the Green Party, and a growing esoteric scene. While the emergence of the Green Party, as well as the peace and environmental movements, signalled a return to conventional politics, the urban revolts of 1980–81 were both a radicalization of the emotional politics of the alternative left, and, as a product of this very radicalization, a turn away from alternative emotional politics. In that sense, the revolts of 1980–81 were a culmination of the story this book has been telling.

In many ways, squatters drew on critiques formulated in the alternative left during the 1970s. For example, they frequently criticized modern cities as isolating and monotone concrete deserts. For them, squatting buildings was about much more than merely 'space for living [*Wohnraum*]'. They

struggles, see the contributions in Martin Baumeister, Bruno Bonomo, and Dieter Schott, eds., *Cities Contested: Urban Politics, Heritage, and Social Movements in Italy and West Germany in the 1970s* (Frankfurt a.M.: Campus, 2017).

[2] Hanspeter Kriesi, *Die Züricher Bewegung: Bilder, Interaktionen, Zusammenhänge* (Frankfurt a.M.: Campus Verlag, 1984); Heinz Nigg, ed., *Wir wollen alles, und zwar subito! Die Achtziger Jugendunruhen in der Schweiz und ihre Folgen* (Zurich: Limmat Verlag, 2001); Thomas Stahel, *Wo-Wo-Wonige: Stadt- und wohnpolitische Bewegungen in Zürich nach 1968* (Zurich: Paranoia City, 2006); Sophie von Vogel and Lars Schultze-Kossack, eds., *Zür(e)ich brennt* (Zurich: Europa Verlag AG, 2010); Mischa Brutschin, 'Züri brännt', in *Häuserkampf I: Wir wollen alles – Der Beginn einer Bewegung* (Hamburg: Laika Verlag, 2012).

[3] On Freiburg, see Volkhart Schönberg, 'Freiburg: Bewegungen in den besetzten Häusern', in *Häuserkampf I: Wir wollen alles – Der Beginn einer Bewegung* (Hamburg: Laika Verlag, 2012).

[4] Personal conversation G. U. and the author, Berlin, October 2011, and personal conversation with U. W. and G. W., Berlin, November 2011.

longed for places where they could find 'warmth', where they could overcome the social isolation that characterized, in their minds, modern cities. Like *Wohngemeinschaften*, squats were places to practise intimacy. Activists of 1980–81 also drew on thinkers like Gilles Deleuze and Félix Guattari, discussed in Chapter 2, who had become popular in the alternative left towards the end of the 1970s. It is probably not by accident that a bar called *Rhizom* frequently advertised in *radikal*, the most widely read left-wing magazine in West Berlin during the revolts. The rhetoric of transgression and playfulness, arguably inspired by those French thinkers (though Jean Baudrillard seems to have been even more popular), we have encountered in previous chapters was pervasive during the revolts of 1980–81. Activists were, as we will see, constantly searching for new transgressions. From this perspective, it might seem as if the protests were nothing but another, perhaps particularly intensive episode in the history of the 'alternative milieu'.

However, squatters also broke with alternative politics. Berlin activists made this point explicitly, when they criticized the alternative left as a 'minor cycle [*Nebenzyklus*] of capitalism that is no danger for the system'.[5] Above all, squatters in 1980–81 radicalized the politics of the moment that we have already encountered in the alternative left. For protestors in 1980–81, the (emotional) intensity of the moment mattered, but not what came after the intense moment. But by longing for disruptive moments of exuberance, they left the therapeutic politics of the alternative left behind them. There is no evidence of therapy or consciousness-raising groups amongst radical protestors in 1980–81. For them, politics ceased to be about personal transformation as a result of hard labour. Rather, politics was about creating intense moments.

Arguably, the emergence of the Green Party and the rise of the peace and environmental movements in the early 1980s had more of a lasting impact on the political culture in Germany. The emotional culture that had developed in the alternative milieu lived on in these movements. By turning to the revolts of 1980–81, this chapter explores the radicalization of the search for intensity in the radical left. Not least, this focus on the intensity of the moment, rather than on its transformative qualities, makes the revolts of 1980–81 an interesting event to study from a theoretical perspective. Events, as William H. Sewell, Jr. has argued, disrupt (and transform – a point I will come back to) structures; and, crucially, events need to be construed by historical actors as disruptive and transformative

---

[5] Anon., '"radikal" im Bruch', in *radikal: Für d'Bewegig, von de BeWeGig* 84, November 1980, 2.

moments to become meaningful.[6] Both points hold true for the revolt of 1980–81. Participants clearly perceived them as an event that represented a disruption of normalcy. Yet, whereas Sewell has emphasized the transformative quality of events, protestors in 1980–81 were distinctly disinterested in transformation, stressing the intensity of the moment instead. In that sense, the revolts resembled the 'liminal areas of time and space' of rituals that Victor Turner has described. For Turner, rituals such as carnivals provide the space to break with the classifications and routines of the quotidian; they are moments 'open to the play of thought, feeling and will'.[7] As moments outside of the quotidian, rituals provide a sense of extraordinary (emotional) intensity.[8] Participants of the revolts of 1980–81 not only described such intense feelings, but explicitly longed for them. Yet, whereas Turner focuses on ritualized 'liminal areas' that have their fixed place in the cycle of the year and are thus legitimate reversal of orders, which implies that the temporal reversal of order is itself part of the order, the revolts of 1980–81 were distinctly not a predicted or predictable ritual, an aspect that makes them a distinct event. Indeed, once activists observed a ritualization of the demonstrations and riots, the event was over.

Discussing the revolts of 1980–81 as a liminal event, the chapter does not inquire about the impact these revolts had on West German society. Rather, it seeks to understand the emotional intensity activists described, the sense of effervescence and exceptionality. The chapter is thus neither interested in explaining the revolts, for example by asking about social causes, nor is it interested in lasting consequences of the revolts. The chapter, that is, does not ask the questions about transformations that historians usually ask, but tries to understand what created the temporary feelings of extraordinary exuberance. Building on an argument developed in the previous chapter, it proposes that activists not only knew how extraordinary situations like rioting or squatting would feel, but in fact needed this knowledge to feel intensely. Yet this is not to argue that such feelings were simply wilfully produced, even if activists at times tried to create them. Whether attempts to produce feelings of exuberance

[6] William H. Sewell, Jr., *Logics of History: Social Theory and Social Transformation* (Chicago: The University of Chicago Press, 2005), 197–224.
[7] See Victor Turner, *The Ritual Process: Structure and Anti-Structure* (Ithaca, NY: Cornell University Press, 1969), vii.
[8] See the highly illuminating discussion of romantic dates by Eva Illouz who argues that dates provide a temporarily limited and ritualized moment of intensity outside the routines of the everyday, see Eva Illouz, *Consuming the Romantic Utopia: Love and the Cultural Contradictions of Capitalism* (Berkeley: University of California Press, 1997).

succeeded was contingent. And sometimes, situations of intense feelings happened in an utterly unpredicted fashion.

The chapter begins with a brief outline of the history of the revolts, going back to the TUNIX Congress of February 1978 that created a new sense of activism, preparing the ground for the revolts that began two years later.[9] The following three sections explore different practices – aesthetic production, squatting and collective living, and rioting – and ask how those practices produced the feelings of exuberance many activists described. In all three instances, moments of transgression and disruption played a crucial role for creating feelings of intensity. Finally, the chapter considers the process of ritualization that put an end to the revolts. Unlike the previous chapters, this chapter does not remain limited to Germany, but also look at the events in Zurich, which were an essential part of the wave of revolts.

From TUNIX to Tuwat

In the autumn of 1977, a series of terrorist attacks by the Red Army Faction hit the Federal Republic: the abduction of Hanns-Martin Schleyer, president of the Employers' Federation; the hijacking of Lufthansa flight 592 to support terrorists' demands to free imprisoned comrades; the violent conclusion of the hijacking by German special police forces; and finally the murder of Schleyer when terrorists realized they would not accomplish their goal. The state reacted to this series of violent events with increasing pressure on leftist political groups, by searching houses and stopping cars of suspected terrorist supporters.[10] For leftists, these were dark months. Responding to this dire situation, and even more so to the bleak atmosphere that had taken hold of the leftist scene, activists looked to Italy, where the radical left had hosted a huge congress in Bologna in late September 1977.[11] The atmosphere in Bologna could not have been more different than in Germany during the Schleyer abduction that very same month. Contrary to what the conservative Italian

---

[9] This is an argument former activist G. U. made in a conversation with the author in October 2011.

[10] For a good account of the 'German Autumn', see Karrin Hanshew, *Terror and Democracy in West Germany* (Cambridge: Cambridge University Press, 2012), 192–261.

[11] On Italy, Angelo Ventrone, *'Vogliamo tutto': Perché due generazioni hanno creduto nella rivoluzione 1960–1988* (Rome: Editori Laterza, 2012), 348–351; Pablo Echaurren, *La casa del desiderio: '77: indiani metropolitani e altri strani* (Lecce: Manni Editore, 2005); Robert Lumley, *States of Emergency: Cultures of Revolt in Italy from 1968–1978* (London: Verso, 1990), 295–312; Phil Edwards, *More Work! Less Pay! Rebellion and Repression in Italy, 1972–7* (Manchester, UK: Manchester University Press, 2009), 71–96; Katsiaficas, *Subversion*, 61–62.

press had anticipated, there were no riots, the German alternative press reported. 'Rather, *buone vibrazioni nell'aria* [good vibrations in the air; Italian in the original]. The atmosphere was magnificent, the entire thing was a huge party. Men and women had painted themselves with insane colours, had dressed differently, and it clowned and indianed through the city like nothing [*es clownte und indianerte nur so durch die Stadt*].'[12] People played music and theatre, danced, and presented their magical skills. For West Berlin activists, the event was likely an inspiration. Soon afterwards, Berlin leftists called for a meeting themselves that would develop new perspectives of resistance. 'Come on, said the cock, we will find something better than death anywhere', the 'call for a journey to TUNIX [Do-Nothing]' read. Winter was too dull, spring too contaminated, and in the summer, 'we suffocate', the organizers wrote. And hence they invited their fellow comrades to 'sail to the beach of TUNIX'. For three days in late January 1978, the organizers wanted to discuss how they might escape from the 'model Germany', to find new forms of resistance beyond the 'helplessness of permanently reacting'.[13]

The TUNIX Congress itself was a rather odd event. According to some estimates, twenty-five thousand people gathered in Berlin, much to the organizers' surprise;[14] others give a much lower number, claiming only five thousand people were in Berlin, among them prominent visitors from abroad like Michel Foucault, who stayed in a Berlin *Wohngemeinschaft*, but remained somewhat in the background during the congress itself. Workshops discussed a variety of topics, ranging from adult education, the situation of imprisoned terrorists, the project of a radical-left-wing daily newspaper (which eventually became the *tageszeitung*), but also the work of Guattari, Deleuze, and Foucault.

Yet these discussions were arguably not the most important facet of the gathering, but the vague sense of euphoria participants described. 'At TUNIX', an author for *Pflasterstrand* wrote, 'space and time were united in one state-of-being. At Tunix, buckling downwards diagonally is celebrated as an act of desire. [*In Tunix wird das Wegsacken nach schräg unten als Lustprozess gefeiert.*]' Perhaps two-thirds of the 'travellers' to TUNIX, the author claimed, had probably missed it, despite having been in Berlin;

[12] Ruth & Ati, 'Italien: Kongress in Bologna, 23–25. September', in *Info BUG* 176, 10 October 1977, 7.

[13] The invitation to the TUNIX Congress, 'Auf nach Tunix: "Komm mit, Sprach der Hahn, etwas besseres als den Tod werden wir überall finden"', can be found, for example, in *Das Blatt* 111, 23 December 1977–12 January 1978.

[14] Rädli, 'Bericht von Tunix', in *Das Blatt* 114, 10–23 February 1978, 8–9.

the result was that TUNIX happened in unexpected situations.[15]
A woman named Heidi from Bremen noted that most discussions were
rather boring and unimportant; but she was impressed by the atmosphere.
'A product of change, pregnant with euphoria, but also a bit serious. Theatre
of all possibilities. Living of all possibilities [English in the original].'[16]
Another man from Bremen named Dirk was also disappointed by the
'bureaucratic' discussions, but enjoyed the 'atmosphere of euphoria – that
was not caused by anything'. TUNIX was, he claimed, 'like a red balloon in
the morning sky, that shows us colourfully dazzling the way to the future',
but also 'tender and fragile'.[17] Helmut Höge, writing also for *Info Bremer
Undogmatische Gruppen*, emphasized the 'vitalizing effect' of TUNIX, not
least because the normal feeling of isolation, he claimed, was suspended
there.[18] In Frankfurt, the editorial team of *Pflasterstrand* claimed that
TUNIX had created an 'illusion of warm feet – we are many, we are
colourful' amidst the impotence of the German autumn. Yet, from his
perspective at least, what remained after TUNIX was only perplexity.[19]
Illusion or not, the congress created new perspectives.

TUNIX was, as scholars have recognized, a watershed moment for the
new left. In the aftermath, the left split into different directions. A plethora
of new 'projects' developed, ranging from cafés to bookshops, self-managed
workshops, and most prominently the *tageszeitung*. The emergence of the
Green Party in the late 1970s and early 1980s, though not a topic discussed
at TUNIX, can be considered as an outcome of the dissatisfaction with
violent politics as well.[20] On the other hand, (self-)therapeutic and esoteric
ideas and practices gained further attraction within the left as part of a search
for an allegedly suppressed authenticity. In spring of 1979, Inge Heinrichs
for example claimed in the *Blatt* that 'electromagnetic fields' existed in
human bodies as well as in animals and plants. 'But today, all expressions
of life like feelings, drives, impulses have to be first examined by experts and

---

[15] Micky, '[No title]', in *Pflasterstrand* 23a, 9–22 February 1978, 44–45.
[16] Heidi, 'Komm mit, sprach der Hahn, etwas besseres als den Tod werden wir überall finden', in *Info Bremer Undogmatischer Gruppen* 15, 17 February 1978, 9.
[17] Dirk, 'Tunix hat keine Geschichte – außer meiner eigenen Geschichte', in *Info Bremer Undogmatischer Gruppen* 16, 3 March 1978, 11.
[18] Helmut Höge, 'Beautiful Looser', in *Info Bremer Undogmatischer Gruppen* 16, 3 March 1978, 12–14.
[19] Redaktion Pflasterstrand, 'Anmerkung zum Artikel von Joschka', in *Pflasterstrand* 28, 20 April – 3 May 1978, 15.
[20] On TUNIX, see Sabine von Dirke, *All Power to the Imagination! The West German Counterculture from the Student Movement to the Greens* (Lincoln, NE: University of Nebraska Press, 1997), 105–142; März, *Linker Protest*, 203–244. See also the collection at APO-Archiv, FU Berlin, Boxes 1134–1135, Tunix.

channelled correctly.' At the top of these experts were, she claimed, psychiatrists. 'Had my grandmother needed a certificate for love and wisdom, I would surely be dead today.' Her political program was thus a program of mutual self-healing, which required her fellow leftists to become 'sympathizers of life'. 'Being radical means: going to the roots, into the underground, descending into our true being, where we are all the same. That too can be a form of political struggle.'[21] Along similar lines, another text in the same issue discussed feminist books about the moon, magic, healing, and menstruation.[22]

Two years later, to give another somewhat obscure example, a short-lived magazine called *Doktorspiele: Zeitung für Körperinstandsetzung* [sic!] appeared in West Berlin, at the height of the squatting movement, charging an unspecified 'you' for still not taking care of their bodies. 'The Grey Gentlemen' – a reference to Michael Ende's children's novel *Momo* – 'still steal your time, your dreams, the laughing and crying. They take away your strength, your love, your magic. You are giving them even your body to experiment with, for money and fame.' Thus the magazine called its readers to 'return to your roots, into the world of magic, of sorcerers and witches. Bear in mind your body, the power for self-healing'.[23] Very practically, the magazine then advised its readers how to use techniques of acupuncture, providing exact prescriptions where to press the hands in order to overcome fear.[24] These admittedly obscure texts blamed society for repressing and controlling human nature in the very physical sense; the proposed solutions, however, focused entirely on the self without intervening into society.

The most prominent example of the esoteric turn that prominent leftists took during the late 1970s is the publishing house *Trikont Verlag*, which renamed itself, under Herbert Röttgen and Christiane Thurn's leadership, *Dianus Verlag*, now publishing books concerned with magic and ghosts.[25]

---

[21] Inge Heinrichs, 'Heilen kann jeder', in *Das Blatt* 142, 23 March–5 April 1979, 25–27.

[22] Meg, 'Die Träume der Geschichte – oder was können wir Frauen erforschen', in *Das Blatt* 142, 23 March–5 April 1979, 23–25. The article included reference to Elizabeth Gould Davis, *Am Anfang war die Frau*; Anne Kent Rush, *Mond, Mond*; Dr. Rosemary Rodewald, *Magie, Heilen und Menstruation*, all of which were published by the Verlag Frauenoffensive.

[23] Anon., '[No title]', in *Doktorspiele: Zeitung für Körperinstandsetzung* 2, n.d., probably spring 1981, 2.

[24] Anon., 'Erste Hilfe mit natürlichen Mitteln', in *Doktorspiele: Zeitung für Körperinstandsetzung* 3, n. d., probably spring/summer 1981, 2–5.

[25] See Uwe Sonnenberg, *Von Marx zum Maulwurf: Linker Buchhandel in Westdeutschland in den 1970er Jahren* (Göttingen: Wallstein, 2016), 313–315. A prominent publication that resulted from this turn was Christiane Thurn and Herbert Röttgen, eds., *Die Rückkehr des Imaginären: Märchen, Magie, Mystik, Mythos, Anfänge einer anderen Politik* (Munich: Trikon-Dianus Buchverlag, 1981).

Resonating with Röttgen's earlier writing, the publishers proclaimed in November 1980, when the new wave of urban revolts had already begun:

> From fascism, we wrest the myths that it has defiled, concepts like friendship, *Heimat*, nature, which it [fascism] has smirched; from the nobility [we wrest] the feeling of esteem, politeness and courtly love [*Minne*] that it has lost; from the church, its most beautiful and nevertheless most undeservingly treated daughter: mystics; from the vagabonds, their freedom and neglected creativity. From all peoples, we take back their sparkling imaged and dancing fairy-tales, to marry them with ours. In the books, we search feelings and vibrations that for being lived and jittered.

Thus the publishers wanted to accomplish a new way of perceiving the world – 'seeing, listening, tasting, feeling', that would allow them to access 'the great incessant prayer, the language of the blades of grass and the rock, the language of light blue and red, the language of growing hair and the grain of dust in the light'.[26] Whether this was a move away from politics or not was contested. For example, Uwe, who was a member of the *Blatt* editorial group, cautioned readers not to dismiss it too easily as a 'retreat into the private'.[27] Another commentator in the following issue praised the renamed *Trikont Verlag* for its step because exploring 'intuition, dream, meditation, exuberance [*Rausch*], trance, ecstasy' might be a way to prepare against the 'colonization of our subconscious'.[28]

But what happened with the sense of euphoria that participants of TUNIX described? Was the editorial team of *Pflasterstrand* correct in claiming that TUNIX created only an illusion of warm feet? One participant in the revolts of 1980–81 with whom I talked disagreed. He emphasized that the congress had shown that 'something was possible'; for him, TUNIX created new perspectives that ultimately led to the revolts. Finding such a line from TUNIX to the revolts of 1980–81 in sources is difficult. Sporadic accounts of demonstrations suggest, however, that something did change. A report about a 1978 May Day demonstration in Hamburg that resulted in brief riots and clashes with trade union stewards for example summarized: 'Finally action again. The sun is dancing too. We are still alive.

---

[26] Christiane Thurn and Herbert Röttgen, 'Die höchste Ehre der Rebellion? Trikont-Verlag nennt sich Dianus und erklärt', in *Das Blatt* 184, 7–20 November 1980, 20–21. For a somewhat similar tendency, see Margaretha Huber, *Rätsel: Ich schaue in den geheimnisvollen Raum eines verschollenen Denkens, dessen Tür die Romantik einen Spalt weit geöffnet hat* (Frankurt a.M.: Verlag Roter Stern, 1978).

[27] Uwe/Blatt, '[No title]', in *Das Blatt* 184, 7–20 November 1980, 21.

[28] Euphorius, 'Eine Utopie für Deutschland', in *Das Blatt* 185, 21 November–4 December 1980, 9–11.

Dancing, drumming, cuddling, yelling, colour eggs [*Farbeier*], slogans, rocks, police.' And even though the riots and a subsequent attempt to squat a house ended in a disaster, the author did not despair. 'Tears and blood have flown, but the past loses itself in our future. Let's stop whining, it's just the beginning.'[29]

Later that year, a demonstration in Frankfurt turned violent. Marching alongside heavily armed police had created a feeling of tension; everyone expected something to happen. And suddenly it did. According to the report, some two to three thousand militant activists charged seventy to eighty officers and a water canon in an attempt to attack the American consulate. 'The liberating moment of breaking out. The feeling of joy when fighting back. The feeling that it's finally us who can say what's happening.' While the riot was brutal, the author felt it was justified. 'Destroying telephone booths, kiosks, tram shelters – isn't that an expression of our rage against the uninhabitability [*Unbewohnbarkeit*] of our cities, a sign of impotence and despair?'[30] And by early 1980, *radikal* reported an antinuclear power demonstration in Brokdorf, where activists tried to climb over the fence protecting the construction site. But the most important aspect, *radikal* emphasized, was 'the feeling of those who were there. For a long time, I haven't seen that many jolly, laughing, cheerful, dear people around me. I had a feeling of intimacy towards the people around me that I had recently known only with the people in my commune's kitchen. [*Ich fühlte eine Vertrautheit zu den Leuten ringsum, die ich in letzter Zeit höchstens noch aus der Küche meiner Wohngemeinschaft kenne.*] For a moment I stood, for example, next to a tall, big guy in leather, who slapped me on the shoulder and was happy like a little boy.'[31] Though these riots were isolated events that took place far away from the centres of revolts of 1980–81, they point to a changing atmosphere within the radical left.

But it needed a spark from the outside to inflame the revolt in Germany. The Amsterdam *krakers* (as squatters were called in Dutch) provided this spark. In Amsterdam, a strong squatters movement had developed in the preceding years. When the police cleared a squatted house there in February 1980, it did not seem to be an extraordinary

---

[29] Anon., 'Der Mai ist gekommen – 1. Mai in Hamburg', in *Große Freiheit* 13, June 1978, 8.

[30] Die Mili TANTEN UND ONKELS, 'Saturday Afternoon Fever: Krankfurt, die Bullizei, der Schah, das BKA und viele Demonstranten', in *Das Blatt* 135, 8–21 December 1978, 12–13.

[31] Anon., 'Brokdorf: Eine schöne Bescherung, oder: Was wollte der Weihnachtsmann und seine himmliche Heerschaft', in *radikal* 74, 11 January 1980–1 February 1980, 6. The article was part of a series of reflection on militancy in the 'movement'.

event. But this time, squatters reoccupied the house, built barricades, and prepared for battle with the police using helmets, sticks, and stones. On 3 March, the Dutch police employed overwhelming force, including tanks, to evict the squatters. Massive riots ensued, and the police did not succeed in doing so. A few weeks later, on 30 April, a demonstration during the crowning celebration of Queen Beatrix resulted in further riots. German leftists were fascinated by what happened in Amsterdam. Activists from Hamburg who happened to be in Amsterdam during a riotous week described, full of excitement, how police ran panicking into their van to escape the hail of stones.[32] Thence from Amsterdam, the revolt spread to Germany. On 30 April, a women's Walpurgis Night demonstration in Bremen ended with rocks and coloured eggs flying; a week later, on 6 May, a demonstration against a military recruitment ceremony turned extremely violent.[33]

Next came, of all places, Zurich in Switzerland. On 30 May 1980, left-wing activists had protested, at first peacefully, the municipal cultural policy that supported the local opera but did not, as activists demanded, fund an Autonomous Youth Centre (*Autonomes Jugndzentrum*, AJZ). To both the protestors' and the police's surprise, the demonstration turned violent, not least because attendees of a nearby Bob Marley concert joined the protests. The following night again saw riots in Zurich's inner city; demonstrations continued throughout the summer, in Zurich and other Swiss cities. In Zurich, the 'movement', as the protests were simply called, accomplished its goals for a short while as the city provided a building for an AJZ. Yet problems soon emerged, not least due to the movement's policy of allowing drugs inside the centre. Only a year later, the AJZ was closed. Meanwhile in nearby Freiburg, the police had cleared a squatted complex of buildings called Dreisameck in June 1980. Activists responded with a massive and violent demonstration, and squatted another building, the Schwarzwaldhof, only a few days later, which remained squatted until March 1981 when it, too, was cleared by the police. Predictably, another series of demonstrations and riots ensued, with regularly more than ten thousand activists in the streets. And while Zurich, Freiburg, and, as we

---

[32] Geo., 'Und was ist hier los?', in *Große Freiheit* 32, April 1980, 9. The issue, which had the subtitle *Zeitung für Hamburg und Amsterdam*, also contained other reports about the riots in Amsterdam. See also the report, including numerous photos, in *Info Bremer Undogmatischer Gruppen* 53, 2 April 1980, 5–8.

[33] See the reports and comments in *Info Bremer Undogmatischer Gruppen* 54, 11 May 1980, 4–12. The riots in Bremen have not yet been subject to academic writing. See, however, the fictional account in Sven Regener, *Neue Vahr Süd* (Frankfurt a.M.: Eichborn, 2004).

will see in a moment, West Berlin were centres of the revolt, other German cities such as Cologne, Frankfurt, Munich and Stuttgart saw, if on a smaller scale, a squatting movement emerge too.

Compared with provincial cities like Freiburg, West Berlin, a centre of alternative scene by the late 1970s, remained surprisingly quiet during the summer of 1980. Even though some houses were already squatted, this did not cause major protests or riots. A first sign that the situation was to change occurred in October 1980, when a demonstration turned violent and police had to retreat from hailing stones.[34] Yet the date that would come to mark the beginning of the revolt was 12 December 1980, when a demonstration in Kreuzberg after the police had prevented the squatting of a house turned into riots that lasted for the entire weekend.[35] In the following weeks and months, a rapidly increasing number of houses were squatted in West Berlin; by June 1981, the number of squatted houses had reached 165. Simultaneously, squatters organized numerous demonstrations in support of imprisoned activists and protesting forced evictions. Frequently, these demonstrations resulted in heavy riots. Politicians tried to negotiate with more moderate squatters to find a legal solution of the problem. Meanwhile, the police regularly searched squatted houses, charging squatters with various crimes, notably of forming a criminal organization, which is a serious offence according to German penal law (§129). It was, by all accounts, a year full of activism and hope to conquer spaces for a different way of living.

Encouraged by the activism, squatters in Berlin decided to organize a four-week 'Tuwat Spectacle' in August 1981 (meaning 'Do Something', of course a nod to the TUNIX Congress three years earlier) that would mobilize supporters from all over West Germany and Europe to Berlin to help prevent evictions. But instead of the tens of thousands of supporters that Berlin activists, in their enthusiasm, had hoped for, only two thousand came. Tuwat might then be seen as a first indication that the movement had lost its momentum, though it was far from over yet. The mobilization could not prevent the police from evicting squatters from eight houses in late September 1981. While the police had sealed off the houses that were to be evicted, heavy riots erupted elsewhere in Berlin, notably in Schöneberg. In the course of these riots, eighteen-year-old squatter Klaus-Jürgen Rattay was run over by a bus and killed; a mourning

---

[34] See Joachim C. Häberlen and Jake Smith, 'Struggling for Feelings: The Politics of Emotions in the Radical New Left in West Germany, c. 1968–84', *Contemporary European History* 23 (2014): 634.
[35] For details, see Vasudevan, *Metropolitan Preoccupations*, 105–109.

march for Rattay that same evening ended with further riots. Rattay's death resulted in the Berlin Senate announcing a moratorium on further evictions. But by April 1982, the police started to evict squatters again, while other houses tried to negotiate a legalization of their status, sometimes with success. It became increasingly clear that the forces of order had regained the upper hand. The movement lost its enthusiasm after the summer of 1982, though activists still managed to organize a massive demonstration, including the inevitable riot, when American president Ronald Reagan visited Berlin in June. By the end of that year, only some 40 houses were still squatted, out of the original 165. In July 1984, the last strongholds of the militant wing of the squatter movement, notably the *Kunst- und Kultur Centrum Kreuzberg*, known as *KuKuCK*, famous for its mural painting of three dancing witches, were evicted; by then, only ten houses were squatted. The movement was definitely over.

Transgressive Aesthetics

'The Unchaining of Desires': under this title, a brochure from the early 1980s reproduced 'movement discussions in Babylon and elsewhere'.[36] Containing articles from left-wing magazines, most of them from Zurich, but some of them from Berlin and Freiburg, the brochure provides a good example for the aesthetics of the revolt. But making sense of its pages is a challenging endeavour. The texts tend to be surreal, they are arranged in a confusing manner, and the imagery in the background is disturbing: skulls and strangely mutilated bodies, and occasionally an erotic half-naked girl. What are we to do with these strange words and images? Their analysis helps us, I suggest, understand the production of feelings of intensity in the revolt, feelings that were not least aesthetically created. Not only did practices like rioting gain an emotional meaning through their representation in texts and imageries, but, even more importantly, those aesthetic forms were themselves a way to produce feelings of intense exuberance. Such brochures as *The Unchaining of Desires*, as well as the texts and images published in *radikal* (Berlin) and *Stilett* (Zurich) – the two most important magazines of the revolt – produced, so to speak, unchained desires. Creating aesthetic confusion and ruptures was central in this regard. It was an aesthetic protest, as it were, against any categorization of the movement.

---

[36] *Die Entfesselung des Begehrens: Bewegungsdiskussion in Babylon und Anderswo*, n.p., n.d.

Figure 6   Cover page of *The Unchaining of Desire*.

Both the rhetoric and the graphic design of the movement's publications are full of playfulness and confusion. This is how *radikal* and *Stilett* described themselves: 'Magazine for Freedom and Adventure'; 'Magazine for Uncontrolled Movement'; 'Magazine for Lighthearted Hours';

Figure 7   'A hot summer.'
(*Stilett* 56, June 1980, 2.)

'Magazine against Technocracy and Normal Time'; or 'Magazine for
Decramping [*Entkrampfung*]' (*radikal*); and 'Propaganda Machine for
Premature Alcoholics'; 'Magazine for Confusion, Distribution and
Worsening', and 'Organ of the Rising Seed of Dragons' (*Stilett*).[37] *Stilett*,
perhaps the most anarchically playful of all publications, joyfully celebrated
the riots in Zurich. An 'ABC' lexicon for protestors for example contained
an entry on 'bellow [*grölen*]': 'at the end of the riot, when the cops are
already retreating, cheering with full voice: guys, come back, we won't
knock you down. When they happily return, still knock them down.'[38] It
is only fitting that *Stilett* ceased publication by the end of 1980, when its
authors felt that a 'humorous' movement had turned into a political
movement.[39] *Subito*, another magazine from Zurich, similarly mocked
the public's longing for organization with its celebration of confusion, as

[37] See *radikal* 78, May 1980; 85, December 1980; 114, March 1983; 117, June 1983; and *Stilett* 54,
February/March 1980; 55, April/May 1980; 56, June/July 1980.
[38] 'Kleines ABC für Demonstranten, Praktikanten und militante Panthertanten', in *Stilett: Organ der
aufgehenden Drachensaat* 56, June/July 1980, unpaginated.
[39] Interview with *Stilett*, Mappe 'Fernsehbeitrag Jugendbewegung 80', 17–18, Schweizersches
Sozialarchiv, Ar 201.83.3.

a 'plan' for the riots it had found after 'extensive research' shows.[40] Graphically rearranging fragments of texts into collages was a central way to achieve this sense of confusion and disruption. We can interpret a page taken from the *Stadtzeitung für Freiburg*, which assembles text fragments about graffiti without creating a coherent text, along these lines: there was no clear argument, only disruptive fragments (see Figure 9). Indeed, one of those fragments, apparently taken from a text by Jean Baudrillard, made this very point about graffiti: Graffiti, it claimed, 'defiles and forgets' architecture; it simply runs from wall to wall, over doors, windows, even onto subway trains. 'Its graphism is like the polymorph perversion of children that ignores gender boundaries and the limitation of erogenous zones.'[41] The text-image collages and the fragmentation of texts did, or at least tried to do, something similar: ignore boundaries and conventional forms.

Using a Deleuzian vocabulary, radical and theoretically minded activists described their revolt as a liberating act of all the 'forces of desire' that were suppressed in the rational world. Consider the opening scene of the documentary *Züri brännt* (*Zurich Burns*), which, as a voiceover announces, depicts a bureaucratic world of grey concrete 'that would not burn', of 'plastified playgrounds', in short, a world in which only cleanliness and hygiene mattered, whose parking lots were as 'empty and free of desires [*wunschlos*]' as the heads of family fathers. But in the stinking canalization, 'the rats live', who 'speak a new language', and when this 'new language comes to the light of day', 'then it will be said and no longer be done, black and white will no longer be clear, and old and new will be one thing'. And then follows a list of future rebels that resembles the lists we encountered in Chapter 2: 'Cripples, fags, drunkards, junkies, eyeties [*Spaghettifresser*], negroes, bomb planters, arsonists, vagabonds, lags, women, and all dream-dancers will flock together to burn the fathers.'[42] This was not only the rhetoric of artistic filmmakers. Other youthful activists declared that 'autonomy means simply life, and for us: realizing our wishes, and it's no experiment for us'. Taking up a conservative rhetoric that denounced the youth movement as 'purulence' and 'rats', they continued: 'And it's perhaps clear that purulence doesn't have much brain; that's logical. There are many feelings; there is love; there is the searching for tenderness, for a new life; there's a new beginning ... so, we fight for a better life and for

---

[40] 'Der Plan', in *Subito* 1, n.d., unpaginated.
[41] Reprinted in *Die Entfesselung des Begehrens*, unpaginated.
[42] Videoladen Zürich, 'Züri brännt' (Switzerland: 1980).

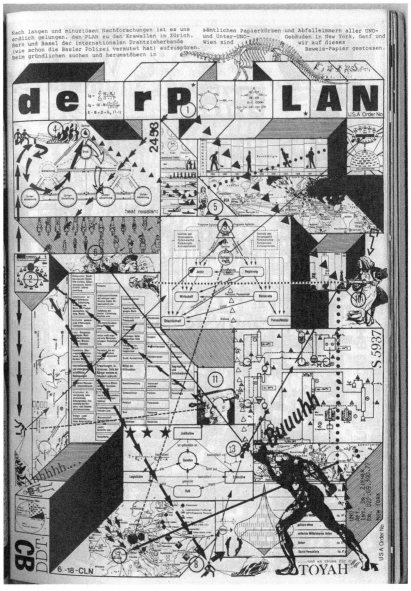

Figure 8   'The Plan'.
(*Subito* 1, ca. May 1980, 10.)

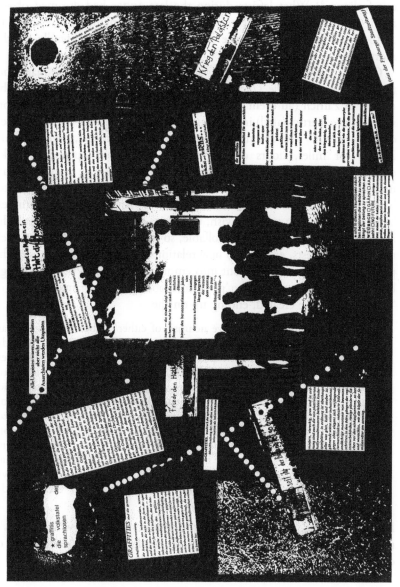

Figure 9   'Graffiti'.
(*Stadtzeitung für Freiburg* 55, March 1981, 41.)

our feelings.'[43] What leftists during the late 1970s had dreamed of – a revolt against rationality – seemed to happen in Zurich (and elsewhere) in 1980–81, if we are to take the activists' self-description literally for the moment.

Consider an article from *Jabberwocky*, an otherwise obscure magazine, that the brochure *The Unchaining of Desire* reprinted. It describes the rioting in Zurich (an event in which only some three hundred protestors seem to have participated) in jubilant terms that can hardly be summarized or paraphrased: 'The desert's dust swirls beneath our feet, horses remain behind for miles, doors of unimagined nature are opened, the sky explodes . . . The armouries of power have been inadequate to our immeasurable desire for a long time, new machineries of war are tried out, water begins to burn, cities burst, *burn Babylon burn.* ' And so the text continues. 'And then, and then asks the wish, the desire pushes us further ahead, the autonomy, so beautiful, uncontrollable, so stunned [*fassungslos*], eats itself through the forests, enters into new relations, sucks up the poisons of the processing plants and pours out into empty clichés, pours out and lets go burst . . .' But never would the 'game turn boring'. Ever again discourses of 'catastrophe' were created, ending up on the

> tracks of manorial compulsive neurosis of either/or, but we laugh, catastrophe? So what! I don't know [any catastrophe], the extortion with the objective conditions of the social and technological catastrophe, the alternative discourses of social control burst like soap bubbles, we fly and leave the do-gooders and caretakers snoring with rage behind, who should they improve after all, the final goals crepitate, the rigid discourse builds thrombosis, the body slumps down, the order suffocates . . . Autonomous schizo-boats drift meaninglessly, dock somewhere, drop the anchors whose connective lines are capped, capped for light years, infiltrate, sow hatred and contradictions, let the courage explode and unchain the theatre of rationality to turn it into a festival of humming spinners, the end of the world will be meaningless, after all, we have the cosmos – and then still the nothingness!'[44]

In surreal images, the text celebrates the summer of 1980 – which events it refers to exactly remains elusive – as the prelude to the 'unchaining of desires'. Was this what happened in Zurich?

---

[43] Statement by the Gruppe Werkstatt 'Halbmon', in Mappe 'Fernsehbeitrag Jugendbewegung 80', 19, Schweizersches Sozialarchiv, Ar 201.83.3.

[44] Anon., 'Auftakt', in *Jabberwocky* 7, n.d., unpaginated, reprinted in *Die Entfesslung des Begehrens*, unpaginated. I have not been able to locate *Jabberwocky* anywhere else.

Another Zurich-based magazine called *Eisbrecher* indeed described the revolt as an 'aesthetic' rebellion, a rebellion desperately necessary given the aesthetic plight Zurich suffered in the author's view. 'The shop windows and the decorators, their bosses and their superiors at the southern hill-sides, plastered with villas, of Pfannenstil, Zürichberg, Üetliberg and whatever those "good" neighbourhoods are called: They all disperse an omnipresent aesthetics amongst us, they put their ideas of beauty like a blanket of foam rubber (a well-proven packing material) over the entire city, they terrorize the streetscapes with mannequins, they fill the advertisement columns with cheap meat, their images look tantalizingly upon us from the hoardings of construction sites.' But rioting had introduced a new aesthetic: 'The rattling of panes, some bigger edges remain in the frame and unexpectedly, eighteen tenths of a second after the breakthrough, these too dissolve and fall out of the frame, into the alley, RATTLE, SPLINTER, CRACK, KAPUTT, JUHU (out of the deepest heart, in still night, when the Christ Child laughs, because the pane cracks). Down with the barricades that separate us from each other, down with the cut-off wheels of all quality classes, down with the decorators of shop windows and the promotional designer-nuisance [*verkaufsförderndes Grafikerunwesen*]. To new horizons: to Bellevue [the central shopping street in Zurich], to reduced street lightening, to freedom.'[45]

And, remarkably, the forces of order were included into this new aesthetic: 'Bizarrely formed, riveted giant things, ghostly cruising around the traffic refuges of our era, move like over-dimensional insects from Bellevueplatz to the Quai Bridge, direct their splashing trunks wildly through the area, und splash as much as they can. Immense fountains demonstrate the basic laws of artillery and Newton in the light of an amazed crowd: a beautiful spectacle. The rattling of panes, the burning of wood, the splashing of water canons: these are new approaches of a deeply liberating aesthetic: AGAINST THE DECORATORS, FOR AN ACTIVE FORMING OF THE ENVIRONMENT!'[46]

We find a similar rhetoric of 'unchained desires' amongst activists from Berlin, even though the language was perhaps less joyful than in Zurich. This is how activists of the magazine *Die Plünderer* describe the situation in Berlin, a city that 'did not become, but will become': 'A death rattling [*Röcheln*] weaves through the vault, indefinable the whining far away, the

---

[45] Anon., 'Wider die Dekorateure und ihren Terror', in *Eisbrecher 3*, n.d., reprinted in *Die Entfesslung des Begehrens*, unpaginated.
[46] Ibid.

disgusting smell of a sewer spreads, gets increasingly dense and tries to tear down this curtain that, drenched in blood, drags on through the houses, the city, behind which we – hysterical fags, lesbians, cannibals and looters – are longing for the moment when the storm's howling, the bursting of a store window, a sharp braking, a hysterical cry that unchains us the insane.' Berlin activists, too, invoked a rhetoric that longed for movement as an inherently subversive power: 'Reason, conviction, morality and duties – that's what they are called, all that what turns movements into a dead trickle, like in a sandglass, grain by grain fall onto this slippery ground, this DEMOCRATIC RULE OF THE GAME, which is NOT MADE BY US, not wanted by us, to drown with nightmarish wrenches.' In this nightmarish order, schizophrenia – a term activists might well have taken up from Deleuze and Guattari – created a subversive disorder: 'But we schizophrenics have long recognized them and turn away full of disgust, put IT on, the cloak of invisibility of orgasmic lust, that makes us unassailable; we appear here and there, throw bolts of the unchaining of our desire into the metropolises, make the earth tremble with a thousand quakes . . .'[47] On the opposite page, the authors mocked the 'managers of Tuwat' and instead called for 'do everything [*tu alles*]': 'Do everything is the joy of destruction that does not express itself but plays, defiles, deforms, kills.'[48]

What are we to do with these surrealist texts celebrating confusion, destruction, and desires? We might place them into intellectual and artistic traditions, which might not only point to Deleuze and Guattari, but also to the Beat Poets and the Situationist International, discussed in Chapter 1. We might also note the aesthetic critique of urbanity that reflected earlier critiques of boring and monotone cities. While this is all true, it would little help us to understand the situation of revolt in which these texts were written. After all, are these texts doing anything more than providing us with an impressionistic account of the 'atmosphere' of the revolts (and are thus perhaps of little relevance for understanding the revolts)? To the contrary, I propose that the aesthetic of the revolt, which includes its visual imagery as well as texts like those quoted here, played a crucial part in creating the intensity of the moment – not for the 'unchaining of desires', but for the creation of unchained desires. Textually and visually (and, as a look at punk music as the sound of the revolt might show,

[47] Anon., 'Berlin wurde nicht, aber es wird werden (Nero)', in *Die Plünderer*, n.d., 2, Papiertiger Archiv Berlin, Schuber Häuserkämpfe West Berlin.

[48] Anon., 'Tuwat? Tu alles!', in *Die Plünderer*, n.d., 3. Papiertiger Archiv Berlin, Schuber Häuserkämpfe West Berlin.

sonically), activists created disruptions and 'movements', attempting to destabilize an aesthetic order. This aesthetic destabilization, the manifold transgression of boundaries in texts and images, helped creating 'unchained desire', joy and laughter – not because desires are inherently unstable and fluid, as affect theorists might argue, but because activists imagined and produced desires *as unchained desires*.[49]

Living Intensely: Squatting and Urban Activism

Aesthetic production, which was, after all, the product of a fairly small group, was not the only form of transgression and disruption that produced feelings of intensity. To understand the intensity of the revolts, we need to look at other practices as well. Particularly in West Berlin, but also in Freiburg (less so in Zurich), the movement was above all known as a squatting movement. Especially in Kreuzberg 36, a part of West Berlin right next to the Wall, numerous decaying houses were squatted. In Naunynstraße in central Kreuzberg alone, eight houses were squatted, more than thirty in adjacent streets like Waldemarstraße, Adalbertstraße, and Manteuffelstraße. Other hotspots of squatting were in the area around Fidicinstraße and Willibald-Alexis-Straße in Kreuzberg and Winterfeld-platz in Schöneberg, though squatters living in these areas were less well known for their militant activism.[50] Some squatters started renovating houses hoping to halt a process of urban renewal and looking for opportunities to live cheaply and collectively, while other, more radical squatters regarded the houses only as a basis for further struggles and cautioned the movement not to retreat into the houses. By no means was this a unified squatting movement. Some activists were keen to negotiate with the Berlin authorities to legalize their situation, while others demanded that all imprisoned protestors should be freed in order for negotiations to start. Reconstructing these conflicts and negotiations is, however, not the goal of this chapter, nor does it interpret squatting as part of a struggle against urban renewal and what became known as gentrification.[51] Rather, what

---

[49] For a discussion of affect theory and a case of making use of it for understanding social movements, see for example Deborah Gould, *Moving Politics: Emotion and ACT UP's Fight against AIDS* (Chicago: University of Chicago Press, 2009), 22–42. A classical text on the politics of affect is Nigel Thrift, *Non-Representational Theory: Space, Politics, Affect* (London: Routledge, 2007). See also from a feminist perspective Eve Kosofsky Sedgwick, *Touching Feeling: Affect, Pedagogy, Performativity* (Durham, NC: Duke University Press, 2003).

[50] For a map of squatted houses in Berlin, see www.berlin-besetzt.de/#.

[51] On gentrification and the role of squatting movements, see Andrej Holm, *Wir bleiben alle! Gentrifizierung – Städtische Konflikte um Aufwertung und Verdrängung* (Münster: Unrast Verlag,

follows is an attempt to understand how squatting and living in squatted houses contributed to the feeling of intensity during the revolt.

Squatters themselves described their movement as a struggle against the monotony of urban life discussed in Chapter 3. The West Berlin *Besetzer-Rat* (squatters council) for example noted in July 1980 that 'concrete silos are built from the ground, square and grey; separated into small living cabins they are the building blocs of a machinery that, at first, does not want to break us physically, but that aims at affecting our psychic sensations. Fragmentation [*Vereinzel(l)ung* – an allusion to prison cells] and hopelessness are stirred, they are meant to create an atmosphere of fear that deprives people of their strength and confidence to act in solidarity with others.'[52] Squatting was thus more than a struggle for 'cheap spaces of living [*Wohnraum*]', but part and parcel of the left's struggle for feelings in a world devoid of emotions. 'We wanted to live and work together', the Schöneberg Squatters Council declared. 'We wanted to put an end to isolation and the destruction of collective living. Who in this city doesn't know the agonizing loneliness and emptiness of everyday life that resulted from the ever increasing destruction of old relations, through restoration and other forms of urban destruction?'[53] For the squatters of *KuKuCK*, a stronghold of the radical faction amongst the squatters, the goal was the 'recuperation of all areas of living vis-à-vis a farcical bureaucracy and state',[54] while *radikal*, putting it most drastically, regarded squatting as 'resistance against the totally administrated world in the form of modern concrete cities with its administrative buildings'.[55] Just like the forms of communal living discussed in the previous chapter, squatting gained political meaning by disrupting the presumed isolation of modern cities. These, at least, were the proclaimed goals of squatters.

It is much more difficult to establish what happened in the squatted houses themselves and how this contributed to the sense of emotional intensity in throughout the spring and summer of 1981.[56] For example,

---

2010); Andrej Holm and Armin Kuhn, 'Squatting and Urban Renewal: The Interaction of Squatter Movements and Strategies of Urban Restructuring in Berlin', *International Journal of Urban and Regional Research* 35 (2011).

[52] Besetzer-Rat, 'Widerstand gegen die Maschine', in *Besetzer-Rat Info* 2, July 1980, found in *Ordner Häuserkämpfe*, Papiertiger Archiv Berlin.

[53] Schöneberger Besetzerrat, 'Offener Brief an die Bürger Berlins', 8 December 1981, found in *Ordner Häuserkämpfe*, Papiertiger Archiv Berlin.

[54] 'Presseerklärung des KuKuCK', in *Instandbesetzerzeitung* 12, 29 May 1981, 7.

[55] Anon., 'Eingemachtes', in *radikal: Zeitung für unbeschwerte Stunden* 103, April 1982, 6.

[56] See Benny Härlin, 'Von Haus zu Haus – Berliner Bewegungsstudien', in *Kursbuch* 65, October 1981, 1–28.

the authors of *Autonome in Bewegung*, a book about the *Autonomen* movement that emerged out of the squatting movement, who had participated in the squatting, note that many squatters tried to stay away from often painful discussions and negotiations in order to enjoy the hot summer in the squatted houses, but do not elaborate what made this summer so special.[57] Reactions by evicted squatters that often turned into violent street protests are indicative of people's intense emotional attachment to 'their' houses. One squatter even compared the 'loss' of their house with the death of a good friend. Smashing windows after such a loss then felt 'insanely good', as another squatter put it, because every destroyed window had a personal meaning.[58] An eviction not only deprived people of their home, but destroyed intimate relations between people, which created an 'immense anger'.[59] Living in a squatted house for nine months had been, a squatter from Freiburg named Chris said at a demonstration, 'as intense as never before. Not always good, never quiet.' It was a life between extremes, both highs and lows, with difficult conflicts between squatters that had profoundly changed him.[60]

What created this sense of intensity? What did squatters do that made life so intense, that created the 'euphoric feeling of happiness' former squatters talked about? Sources remain mostly silent and vague in that regard; only a somewhat impressionistic picture can be given. Creating a sense of community and personal intimacy was probably a crucial element for the feeling of intensity many activists described. A squatter from Freiburg for example noted sadly that, after the eviction, it had become impossible to simply cross the street to meet people he knew, to go out and eat in the backyard of a squatted building.[61] Surely, life in squats was not without problems and conflicts, especially under the permanent threat of eviction; yet, as one squatter from Berlin wrote, the petty problems of communal living, like who would be doing the dishes, lost their importance in that situation.[62]

---

[57] Grauwacke, *Autonome*, 51.

[58] 'Gespräch mit ehemaligen Besetzern eines Hauses in der Mittenwalder 45: "Da gibt's keinen Weg zurück."', in *taz*, 3 July 1981, 20, found in *Ordner Häuserkämpfe West Berlin 7/81*, Papiertiger Archiv Berlin.

[59] mb, 'Ein von Räumung bedrohtes Haus: "Zwischen Kampfstimmung und Resignation"', in *taz*, 4 August 1981, found in *Ordner Häuserkämpfe West Berlin 8/81*, Papiertiger Archiv Berlin.

[60] Chris, 'Heute wäre der Schwarzwaldhof genau 9 Monate besetzt', in *Stadtzeitung für Freiburg*, Sondernummer April 1981, 11. See also Anon., 'Morgengedanken', in *Instandbesetzerpost 13*, 5 June 1981, 23.

[61] Chris, 'Schwarzwaldhof genau 9 Monate besetzt'.

[62] 'Berliner Häuserkampf aus Kreuzberger Sicht', July 1983, found in *Ordner Häuserkämpfe West Berlin 6/83 – 12/83*, Papiertiger Archiv Berlin. The source of the text is unclear, but it was apparently written by activists.

Squatters also changed the layout of squatted houses to overcome the personal isolation: they abolished private rooms and established 'functional rooms', such as sleeping rooms, eating rooms, living rooms, that were used collectively, and at times a 'love rooms' for couples to retreat to have sex.[63] These were all efforts to radically break through the isolation of normal everyday life activists bemoaned. Arguably, the lack of privacy, and uniterrupted contact with friends and comrades, was essential for creating the sense of intensity that characterized life in squatted houses.

Communal living was not the only source of the feeling of intensity. Though it is difficult to trace it in the sources, squatted houses also provided the space for bodily intensity. One former squatter for example recalled the endless nights of partying and dancing in squatted buildings that made the floors tremble.[64] Another squatter, who had described the revolt as a moment of ecstasy [*Rausch*], emphasized the summer days of 1981 he had spent sunbathing on the roofs of a squatted house – though a female squatter recalled that she and other women were not too fond of this.[65] And finally, collectively renovating houses and preparing them for a defence against the police created moments of both intimacy and bodily intensity. One former squatter for example told me how she got to know her long-term boyfriend staying awake on night watches to warn comrades when the police would attack.[66] Whether one stayed up all night to dance or to be ready for a police assault, it was an intense bodily and emotional experience.

Squatters also tried to overcome the isolation that separated them from ordinary neighbours. They sought to establish contacts, especially with Turkish immigrants, many of whom had settled in the decaying but cheap neighbourhood of Kreuzberg. The *Instandbesetzerpost* for example reported on an unspecified 'house in the neighbourhood' in which Turkish families lived next to squatters who had moved into empty apartments. While there were tensions with some neighbours, the author also claimed that some Turkish neighbours preferred spending their time in the squatted apartments rather than at home. Squatters and Turkish neighbours celebrated together, invited each other for dinner or tea, discussed family

---

[63] Personal conversation with D. Z., Berlin, December 2011.

[64] Personal conversation with U. W. and G. W., Berlin, November 2011. For a personal account, see also Johann Christoph Wartenberg, *Kreuzberg, K36, Leben in (der) Bewegung: Kreuzberg inside bis zum Fall der Mauer* (Bockenem: Lühmann, 2003).

[65] Personal conversation with G. U., Berlin, October 2011, and personal conversation with D. Z., Berlin, December 2011.

[66] Personal conversation with D. Z., Berlin, December 2011.

problems together; squatters even learned Turkish and helped more reserved families with renovations.[67] They also helped elderly neighbours by repairing radios and offering to steal electricity (something squatters quite commonly did), though not all neighbours were happy with this form of support.[68]

Klaus Pokatzky, reporter for the liberal German weekly *Die Zeit* who had spent a week in a squatted house, explicitly contrasted the 'warmth' of a 'housing community' with the 'isolation' of living alone. If the community worked, the house could become a true home [*Heimat*], where one did not walk pass doors of estranged neighbours who only yelled and gossiped, but the doors of good Turkish families or friendly communes, who would help out with food or with whom one might sit down for a Saturday afternoon chat in the backyard.[69] Along somewhat similar lines, a former squatter recalled nostalgically how old ladies had yelled at an unfriendly janitor [*Hausmeister*] who had tried to chase the squatters away when those were having dinner in the backyard.[70] And Benny Härlin, a former activist from Zurich who had moved to Berlin, reported in *Kursbuch* that neighbours reacted in a mostly friendly manner to a newly squatted house (and the sparkling wine the squatters offered). Crossing boundaries was not a one-way road, according to Härlin's report: one afternoon, five 'grannies' from a nearby retirement home took 'all their courage' and visited their new neighbours to celebrate with two home-made cakes.[71] No doubt, there were also problems and conflicts with neighbours, and any rosy, nostalgic depiction of squatters and 'ordinary' citizens harmoniously living door to door with each other would be misleading. Yet squatters did interact with neighbours. Arguably, this sense of breaking through (self-created) social boundaries also helped create a feeling of social intensity.

Finally, squatters' interventions into urban space did not remain confined to the squatted houses. The squatter who had so much enjoyed sunbathing on the rooftop for example told me somewhat nostalgically how he and his comrades had breakfast for the entire day on a big table in

---

[67] Anon., 'Ein Haus in der Nachbarschaft', in *Instandbesetzerpost* 1, 11 March 1981, 4.

[68] Anon., 'Nachbarschaftshilfe', in *Instandbesetzerpost* 1, 11 March 1981, 5.

[69] Klaus Pokatzky, 'Hausbesetzen ist ein Full-time-Job. Der schöne Traum der jungen Leute von einer Idylle inmitten der Großstadt Berlin', in *Die ZEIT* 13, 20 March 1981, 66, found in *Ordner Häuserkämpfe*, Papiertiger Archiv Berlin.

[70] Personal conversation with G. U., Berlin, October 2011.

[71] Härlin, 'Von Haus zu Haus', 5–6, 8.

the middle of a street.[72] Using public space for an activity usually confined to private space and openly disregarding the 'normal' rhythm of eating and working created a topsy-turvy situation in which the normal rules of everyday life seemed to be dispended. Such joyous events made the spring of 1981– at least in the squatters' eyes – a time of street festivals. An author for *radikal* described this festive atmosphere in vivid terms. Whereas 'petrified souls and concreted hearts' populated West Berlin's shopping street Kurfürstendamm, trying to exchange 'coins and bills' for 'adventure and life', an 'assemblage of impostors, who don't become rich, militants whose fear of imprisonment is consoled by sunshine', of junkies, freaks, and punks, of 'chauvis [chauvinistic men] who feel great and women who hate chauvis' gathered in Kreuzberg to enjoy the sun, the author claimed.[73] A similar atmosphere reigned at a festival of a children's farm that activists had built in the middle of Kreuzberg (and which still exists in Görlitzer Park) to provide an alternative to the usual 'storage' of children in kindergartens and schools that resembled life in 'prison and concrete silos'.[74] 'Love is huge. Children of any age walk into each other in the festivity's turbulences and hug each other. What if that encroaches upon adults.'[75]

By the summer of 1981, West Berlin, with its more than one hundred 'attacked, squatted or defended houses', had become an 'obscure object of newly developed desires', an author for *Traumstadt* wrote.[76] His account of 'one or two days' of living in a Berlin-specific way of 'joyful sagging' may provide a final depiction of the peculiar feeling in Berlin that summer. Sunny days were rare, the author declared, which was why a 'blue sky and sun' were in themselves enough of a reason to become 'a producer of warmth in mutual relations'. But whether the 'production of warmth' actually happened was never certain, and hence days retained their 'peculiar frustrating character', interrupted only by brief sparks of joy, he claimed. On a typical day, he got up late, between eleven and half one,

---

[72] Personal conversation with G. U., Berlin, October 2011.

[73] 'Die Nacht der Steine', in *radikal* 92, May 1981, 23.

[74] Anon., 'Aktion Kinderbauernhof Mauerplatz in Kreuzberg SO 36', in *Instandbesetzerpost* 0, 2 March 1981, 2.

[75] Anon., '21.3. Samstag: Drei tolle Instandbesetzungstage mit Sonnenschein, viel Spaß + Wein', in *Instandbesetzerpost* 3, 25 March 1981, 10–11.

[76] Anon., 'Liebe zur Stadt', in *Traumstadt* 7, n.d., probably summer 1981, 5–11. On the lure of West Berlin as a site of protesting from the late 1960s to the early 1980s, see also Belinda Davis, 'The City as Theater of Protest: West Berlin and West Germany, 1962–1983', in *The Spaces of the Modern City: Imaginaries, Politics and Everyday Life*, ed. Gyan Prakash and Kevin M. Kruse (Princeton: Princeton University Press, 2008).

had a long breakfast, strolled through the Hasenheide park with a 'dear woman', where he could 'deliver himself to a spectrum of wild-green colours'. In that situation, the usual inhibitions seemed to be gone, and people exchanged looks and words more easily. Later on, he spent some hours in Wedding working with teenagers who were at risk with drugs; then he decided to join a demonstration. Politically, the demonstration was meaningless, as 'the articulation of protest remains limited to the social-democratic-socialist orthodoxy'. But he met many old friends who were mostly trying to invent absurd slogans and to disrupt the demonstration's marching order. 'Under these circumstances, the entire thing turned into a joyous urban excursion.' The next day, he woke up around noon. Time had ceased to play a role in his life, and he considered founding an initiative for the abolishment of clocks.

If somewhat idealizing life in West Berlin, the account nevertheless captures the atmosphere in parts of city in the summer of 1981: the squatted houses in a decaying neighbourhood; the overcoming of social inhibitions; an everyday life for which time no longer played a role; and the mocking of serious politics by turning boring demonstrations into joyful events. All the conflicts and tensions notwithstanding, life for squatters in West Berlin seemed to have been somewhat akin to the 'cornucopia of feelings' Röttgen and Rabe had imagined. Unlike communes in the 1970s, squatted houses were hardly therapeutic communities. Tellingly, there is little evidence that squatters and protestors joined any consciousness-raising or therapy group that were so common in the 1970s. Rather, communal living in squatted houses, the festivals within houses and outside in the streets, and the dissolution of the temporal order of everyday life, created a sense of extreme (and often joyous) intensity that did not require laboriously working on the self.

Rioting

One defining aspect of the revolts of 1980–81, however, remains unaddressed in the *Traumstadt* account: violence and rioting. Throughout these years of revolting, cities like Zurich, Freiburg, and most notably West Berlin, but also Bremen and Hanover, saw at times heavy clashes between protestors and the police. When comrades were convicted and had to serve time in prison, squatters often reacted by smashing windows and committing arson attacks. When squatted houses at Fraenkelufer were evicted in March 1981, heavy riots ensued at a later demonstration. In May that year, rumours of an imminent eviction sufficed to cause squatters to build barricades that took the police three attempts to clear. A month later, hundreds of people rioted after a squatted house was cleared by the police.[77] The list could be continued into 1982, but my interest here is not to provide a full account of the numerous riots, nor is it to provide a social analysis of these riots by inquiring about the social background, gender, or age of the participants. Rather, I seek to understand how these riots helped to produce the feeling of exuberance during the revolt. Indeed, scholars have frequently noted how protestors celebrated and even 'mystified' violence.[78] Yet, all too often, the analysis stops there. From a history of emotions perspective, it is necessary to understand more precisely how violence could produce 'orgiastic' and exuberant feelings of intensity. To that end, it is necessary to closely examine how and why activists celebrated violence – and, as the next section discusses, when they did not celebrate violence. For radical activists, riots – which is, importantly, not the same as acts of violence – were disruptive events that could, if only briefly, suspend the normal order of things and thereby create a moment of intensity.

Days of rioting like 30 May 1980 in Zurich and 12 December 1980 in Berlin marked a rupture for activists. They were distinct moments of change. *Stilett* expressed this sense that something unexpected and new had happened on 30 May most clearly. 'Spending ten years in immersion [*Versenkung*], we have gained a nice little rage- and frustration-package [*Wut- und Frustpäcklein*] by constantly running against the walls.' Activists had talked to administrators about the possibilities of an autonomous youth centre, but to no avail. 'Nothing happened [*Nichts ging mehr*] until now, Thirtieth May: holy mackerel! How the eyes were glowing, but not full of hatred, no fanaticism – no, one could feel oneself, for once.' For both the authorities and the activists themselves, *Stilett* claimed, the events were utterly unexpected. 'Nobody, including we ourselves, could imagine that this might ever happen, but it happened, like a thunderstorm on a bright day.'[79]

In Berlin, 12 December 1980 marked a similar rupture. A reporter writing for the left-wing daily *tageszeitung*, certainly not one of the most

---

[77] For a chronology, see www.berlin-besetzt.de/#.

[78] For a rather superficial and highly moralizing analysis of violence amongst the *Autonomen*, see Sebastian Haunss, *Identität in Bewegung: Prozesse kollektiver Identität bei den Autonomen und in der Schwulenbewegung* (Wiesbaden: Verlag für Sozialwissenschaften, 2004), 122. Somewhat more substantial, but still problematic, are Anders, 'Wohnraum', 494–496; Reichardt, *Authentizität*, 562–563.

[79] Anon., 'En heissa Summer, aber subito', in *Stilett: Organ der aufgehenden Drachensaat* 56, June/July 1980, unpaginated.

radical publications of the leftist scene, noted how he had not believed rumours about rioting in Kreuzberg and had been rather reluctant to even go there. But when he arrived at Kottbusser Tor, the subway station at the centre of the riots, it dawned on him that 'this time, the powder keg had really exploded [*dass es diesmal tatsächlich gefunkt hat*]. The long pent-up aggression, the result of a permanent meandering [*Wechselbad*] between threats and negotiations, the daily pinpricks have created a situation that nobody can control.' Within a moment of looking at the scenery around Kottbusser Tor, he entered a 'different reality'. 'A feeling of euphoria spreads, collectivization is well under way.'[80] *Radikal*, the magazine that would become most closely associated with the revolt, noted in a special edition after the riots that they had created a 'hole in the wall' behind which the contours of something else became visible.[81] Indeed, the sentiment seems to have been widespread that 12 December – 'God bless it', as a *radikal* author remarked somewhat sarcastically in December 1983[82] – constituted a turning point. It was a night, Klaus Pokatzky wrote in the liberal weekly *Die Zeit*, that nobody would quickly forget. The police had not acted so brutally for a long time, but, for once, people did not silently suffer, but reacted and fought back.[83] Events, as William H. Sewell, Jr. has argued, have to be recognized by contemporaries as such, and indeed have to be construed in such terms, to become events. This is exactly what protestors did in 1980. They conceived of the riots on specific dates as marking the beginning of something significantly new.

But the riots did not start a political or social transformation in any meaningful way. For sure, protestors had specific demands, such as an Autonomous Youth Centre in Zurich, defending squatted houses, or freeing imprisoned comrades in West Berlin. But whether rioting made political sense, that is, whether it helped the movement accomplish its goals, and whether this should be the case, after all, was heavily contested. Only a few weeks after the 30 May riots in Zurich, *Stilett* mocked those activists who claimed that violence would only hurt the movement. 'It might be unreasonable [*sinnlos*] to throw rocks, but, at last, STOP BEING REASONABLE, because reasonable [*sinnvoll*] is a word of the others. It is

[80] Jürgen, 'Kreuzberg lebt', in *taz* 51, 15 December 1980, 5, found in *Ordner Häuserkämpfe*, Papiertiger Archiv Berlin.) See also Härlin, 'Von Haus zu Haus', 1–5.

[81] Themrock, 'Die Kunst der Provokation, den Staat der Lächerlichkeit preisgeben, die Ebene der nackten Konfrontation meiden, das Unabsehbare genießen', in *radikal: Zeitung für schöne Bescherung*, Extrablatt, December 1980, 4.

[82] Bazillus Optmistikuß, 'RZ und radi – kritisch betrachtet', in *radikal: Zeitung für Brigaden nach Europa* 123, December 1983, 15.

[83] Pokatzky, 'Hausbesetzen'.

only according to THEIR reason if we remain silent, it is THEIR order that we have to obey . . .' Instead of being reasonable, *Stilett* urged its readers to 'only act according to your feelings. And if you are feeling enough hatred, then just smash the windows of the opera house, the NZZ [the local Zurich newspaper], the Odeon [a fancy coffee shop in Zurich], plunder, pillage [*brandschatzt*], but don't discuss forever whether this is reasonable or whether it hurts the "movement".'[84] Radical left-wing commentators outside of Zurich were also fascinated by the 'rebellion of desire', as an author signing as Musidora wrote in the Nuremberg magazine *Anschläge*. In the riot, 'stones of indignation' learned to fly, the 'delight of encounters was rediscovered, outside of normed coordinate-movements, outside of vertical or horizontal direction-guidelines, outside of the prescribed directions one can take within the pathetic range of commodities'. The riot seemed to be an aesthetic event: 'Poetry became the poetry of cobblestones, who left behind a poem of shards that painted the grey scenery of everyday life with many colours [*bunten Farben*].' The authorities, Musidora claimed, were left utterly confused by this, trying to figure out the motivations of the revolt, but incapable of understanding that it was a pure 'lust for destruction'.[85]

Activists in West Berlin similarly described the rioting, and indeed the entire revolt, as an act of playfulness. A group signing as 'commando smoking bulldozers of Alaska' laconically noted that the integration of the 'alternative movement' into capitalist society was a done deal; the next point on their agenda was simply 'the desire to eat tons of ice cream'. Theirs was not a struggle for a perfect world. 'We are no longer preparing for our liberation or world revolution, we were never "slaves" or "not-yet-human-beings", we just play . . . just so . . . no, no! Nothing else, really just so . . . no ideology, dad or anyone else stands behind us, we are the Indians in the streets of Hanover and Zurich, just take the stereo we always lusted after, take it to bed due to its erotic silver, beautiful and horny and . . .'[86] The most drastic example for celebrating riots as a game was provided by the 'Fighters of the Erupting Sado-Marxist International' after heavy rioting against the visit of American Secretary of State Alexander Haig.[87]

---

[84] 'En heissä Summer'.

[85] Musidora, 'Züricher Nächte. Der Potlatch der Zerstörung', in *Anschläge* 2, Februar 1981, 3–16. Parts of the article are reprinted in *radikal: Zeitung für den großen Abriss* 93, June 1981, 18.

[86] rAuChEnDeN buLLdooZer alaskAS, 'Unterm Pflaster liegt der Asphalt', in *radikal: Zeitung für unkontollierte Bewegung* 85, December 1980, 17.

[87] Die Kämpfer der aufbrechenden sado-marxistischen Internationale, 'Nicht stehenbleiben', Pamphlet, June 1982, found in Ordner Anti-Nato Bewegung, Papiertiger Archiv Berlin. See also for following quotes.

Both anti-imperialist and alternative groups had called for a serious, 'dignified' demonstration, the fighters remarked, but people simply came to meet some old friends, to 'experience some real moments, in short: to have some fun'. And indeed, fun it was, if we are to believe the pamphlet:

> The crowd soon broke through the barriers to kill time for some eight hours with some stones and joyous fires, and without any chefs or prior agreements ... Beyond any categorical belonging, the proletarianized met during this game with fire. [*Jenseits einer kategorialen Zugehörigkeit trafen sich bei dem Spiel mit dem Feuer die Proletarisierten.*] ... It was (and is) not about a fight against the symbol of the police or NATO, but about a play for the sake of playing, about the delight of playfully destroying, not only with the cops, but also with and against the urbanism, the commodity, the cars, the traffic, the concrete, the fragmented time. The vandals created a zone that was partially liberated of any control, of any power and law, where encounters could develop, complicities, multifarious games against a world that controls all wishes and redirects them into production and consumption. The pleasure just to be there, to militantly [*kämpferisch*] and passionately reconquer a space and time that escaped at this moment from any political or other manoeuvre. One settled scores with the accumulated grey of work and the daily boredom.

Clearly, the group celebrated rioting. Their text, however, deserves closer attention as it helps us understand precisely how rioting could yield joyous feelings of exuberance. According to the 'fighters', the riot created a situation in which the normal rules of law and power did not apply. Not only did this facilitate unexpected encounters, it also allowed for acting outside the normal logic of politics by (only?) playing, which is why the authors were equally critical of left-wing political strategists. But the riot was not in itself an exuberant event of playfulness; rather, it needed to be interpreted in such terms, I argue. In other words, the riots felt so joyous because activists knew that riots would, and indeed should, suspend the normal logic of politics and 'liberate' desires. The 'unchaining of desires' in riots, that is, worked only through the language of desires. The fact, however, that unchained desires were in that sense produced, not least through language, makes them no less unchained, and makes the emotional experience no less intense.

While the fighters of the Sado-Marxist International were perhaps exceptionally explicit in their celebration of the riot as a game, the sense of joy during the riot appears to have been rather widespread. Acts of transgression were central for creating feelings of exuberance. In a rather surrealist text published in *Subito*, a 'diary of a cobblestone' described the riots from a cobblestone's perspective. These were sad times for cobblestones. Old roads, paved with cobblestones, were replaced by modern tarred roads, and cobblestones ended up on a big pile of stones, deprived of sunlight. But then came the riots of 30 May, and another night of rioting on 31 May. 'What a day! Gone is the frustration, the boredom and futility ... Music, music! The windows burst clatteringly into a thousand shards. Shards bring luck – to you and me.' The cobblestone had finally ended up on pile of stones itself, but then stones were picked up, it could 'sense the liberating feeling of no longer lying beneath the others. A tender, youthful hand reached for me, together we bounded towards the Limmatquai – and there they were: Cops ... The hand that was holding me hauled off. Rage clenched me and with a cry of joy I catapulted myself into the air, broke through the vapours of gas and threw myself into the midst of the enemy lines. I landed softly, a scream followed, and I was redeemed for all the previous days.'[88] In *radikal*, an anonymous author similarly described the rioting during President Ronald Reagan's visit in West Berlin on 11 June 1982 as transgressive, though in less artistic terms. Before the demonstration, there had been worries that a riot might be utterly ritualized and hence anything but liberating, an issue the final section returns to. Yet, at least for this author, the worries turned out to be false: there was action, and 'holy fuck, what an action [*sie geht geil ab*]'. It did not matter where, 'our rags [*Klamotten*] weightlessly fly over the borders of order, the law is in flames. The situations in which I succeed in freeing myself from the constraints of the usual impotence resemble each other [*Die Augenblicke, in denen es mir gelingt, aus den Fesseln der gewohnten Ohnmacht zu springen, gleichen sich*]: no matter whether it's 12 December, Goltz-Street, Haig or another occasion – the feeling is the same.'[89] In both accounts, the bodily act of throwing something is presented as a moment of transgression that disrupted the established order and thereby created a liberating and exuberant feeling.

But if violence was ritualized, it became part of the normal order, as the final section argues. Hence, evading violence when everyone, both protestors and the forces of order, expected it, could be another way of turning the normal order on its head. One demonstration in the summer of 1981 (the exact date remains, unfortunately, unclear, as both the participant who told me about the event and a book mentioning this story do not provide it) stands out as an example. Both the police and protestors had

---

[88] Anon., 'Aus dem Tagebuch eines Pflastersteins', in *Subito* 1, n.d., unpaginated.

[89] K. Ätzer, 'Rhythmuswechsel, oder: Wenn wir alle unser revolutionäres Über-Ich mitbringen, dann sind wir schon doppelt so viele', in *radikal: Zeitung für den reißenden Absatz* 106, July 1982, 8–9.

prepared for battle, police with heavy riot gear, protestors with leather jackets and helmets. But when the demonstration passed the lake Halensee, protestors decided against the riot, got undressed, and jumped into the lake, while policemen had to sweat in their riot gear.[90] It was another way of playfully disrupting the order. In Freiburg, protestors also confronted the police in a nonviolent way during a demonstration in the summer of 1980. Protestors had already thrown rocks against police vehicles, but when policemen formed a line, facing the protestors 'paralyzed and silently [*starr und schweigend*]', the situation, it seems, did not turn violent. Instead, residents of a neighbouring house provided protestors with buckets of water and music. '*Our* music. Dancing in front of the paralyzed power', an author for the *Stadtzeitung für Freiburg* wrote.[91] Here, the police were not part of the game, as it were, but instead became the 'paralyzed' other. Nevertheless, protestors unchained their desires, so to speak, in a nonviolent manner through dancing and joyous movement in front of the 'stiff' forces of order.

Similarly to what we have seen in the previous chapter, confrontations with the police also provided protestors with an opportunity to actively overcome fear. An author for *radikal* for example wrote in a text criticizing the peace movement for its nonviolent tactics: 'And then the liberating feeling when you lose your fear and fight back, and the pigs run away from you, and not the other way round.'[92] Along those lines, after the 11 June 1982 riots an activist argued that they had been a 'bodily act. A liberation of the fear, the hatred that had accumulated in the preceding weeks.'[93] Activists did not simply describe a feeling of empowerment. Rather, it was the overcoming of impotence and thus the reversal of the normal situation that felt liberating, as a comment from Freiburg shows. The weeks before the eviction of a squatted house had been full of 'gruelling waiting', but now, the situation had changed and the police had to react. 'Time is again on our side. We can determine, when and where we attack.' When police reinforcements from other cities arrived, they were soon attacked; police vans were hit by stones and windows broke. Now the young police officers' faces were full of fear.[94] A rioter from Berlin made a similar argument in

---

[90] Personal conversation with G. U., Berlin, October 2011. See also Katsiaficas, *Subversion*, 136.

[91] joseff, 'Freiburg im Juli', in *Stadtzeitung für Freiburg* 49, July 1980, 3–4.

[92] C. M., 'Frieden schaffen, oder: Sie wollen nur unser Bestes – aber das kriegen sie nicht', in *radikal: Zeitung für Anarchie und Wohlstand* 98, October 1981, 10–11.

[93] Anon., 'Blut und Spiele: Versuch einer autonomen Logig', in *Der Schwarze Kanal* 5, July/August 1982, 18.

[94] joseff, 'Freiburg im Juli'.

the mainstream magazine *Stern*. For him, the riot was a moment to liberate long-pent-up rage: 'It is simply so that all that rage, all that impotence gets out of you when the stone flies and you see how it hits a police van. And the sound, that liberates you. You know what you have done, even if it didn't do any good. At least you haven't remained a spectator. It a sign of rage, a rage that comes directly from the stomach and totally goes into the arm.'[95] Rioting could also provide a way out of isolation. Interviewed by the German news magazine *Der Spiegel*, Andrea from Zurich for example declared that they had felt 'eerily connected' during the riot. A man named Jan agreed: 'The evening [of 30 May] gave me an immensely liberating feeling: suddenly you realize how hundreds feel the same way as you and want the same thing.' And Andrea elaborated: 'We all felt liberated from the pressure weighing on us from the conformism in everyday life, at home, at school ...'[96] Rioting, all these statements suggest, was an emotional practice that helped people to overcome unwanted feelings of fear, isolation and impotence.

Interestingly, activists also frequently recounted how normal bystanders, that is, people not involved with the movement, had sometimes hesitantly, but ultimately joyfully joined the rioting and pillaging. *Stilett* for example noted that the 'Alcis [alcoholics] from the village [*Alkis aus dem Dorf*]' had chanted 'hooray' and joined the melee. 'Just ordinary people, and you could see how good it was for them to let the usually firmly encaged inner pig run free.'[97] In Berlin, the leftwing daily *taz*, while criticizing the 12 December riots as 'being without prospects, apolitical and destructive', nevertheless emphasized the 'liberating laughter of a dungarees-freak when a Turkish boy handed him a box of gummy-bears through the window, saying "That's fun, right?"'[98] Three years later, *Der Spiegel* interviewed young activists who claimed that rioting created brief moments of liberty that ordinary people had likely never experienced. But sometimes, the spark might leap over, an activist named Artur explained. For weeks, he had discussed with a saleswoman in a nearby shop about violence. And then, the day after the demonstrator Klaus-Jürgen Rattay died, he had seen her with a stone in her hand. 'And then an old gramps, he was absolutely

---

[95] 'Interview mit Hausbesetzern', in *Stern* 41, 1 October 1981, 34, found in *Ordner Häuserkämpfe*, Papiertiger Archiv Berlin.

[96] 'SPIEGEL-Gespräch: "Ich hab' ein unheimlich befreiendes Gefühl"', in *Der Spiegel* 52, 22 December 1980, 33–52, quotes 33, 36.

[97] 'En heissä Summer'.

[98] Albrecht Salamander, '6 Strumpfhosen gegen 10 Smarties – ein Freudengeplünder', in *taz*, 15 December 1980, found in *Ordner Häuserkämpfe*, Papiertiger Archiv Berlin.

over seventy, he stood there, and then he went over to the corner, lurking and lost [*heimlich und verloren*], and finally he picked up a rock – and he laughed doing it.'[99] Whether and why these ordinary citizens, if the stories are true, joyfully joined the riots (perhaps overcoming inhibitions against confronting the forces of order was indeed liberating and joyful) is difficult to answer. More importantly, such incidents arguably contributed to the sense of joy amongst protestors. From an activist perspective, new encounters between activists and non-activists had become possible. Similarly to what happened in May 1968 in France, as Kristin Ross has argued, the social categorization that separated protestors and ordinary citizens from each other was suspended in the riot.[100]

The emphasis that activists placed on acts of transgression also implied a different temporality of politics. What a riot might achieve in the long run, whether it helped or damaged the movement, became irrelevant as the momentary feelings of exuberance became central. A seventeen-year-old rioter who went by the name of Keule (meaning club) explained to a *Spiegel* interviewer that he had a 'feeling of freedom' when he saw the police running away, even if it lasted only for fifteen minutes. It was a freedom, another female activist by the name of Eva v. Zoff [*Zoff* meaning trouble] emphasized, that they had achieved themselves. And when the interviewer critically asked about what happened after those fifteen minutes, a man named Artur stressed how valuable these fifteen minutes were, 'when you are, for once, free of fear'.[101] Activist Tomas Lecorte, who wrote an autobiographical novel that was widely read in the leftist scene, described how he felt during the many riots of spring 1981 in similar terms: 'Why would I care for risk and strategy, gains or material damages given this feeling that the armoured power is at the whim of my ridiculous stones! [*Was interessierten mich Risiko und Strategien, Nutzen oder Sachschaden bei diesem Gefühl der gepanzerten Macht als Spielball meiner lächerlichen Steine!*] It should go on like this forever. It was better than any revolution.'[102]

In *radikal*, a couple of authors who formulated a program for 'anarchy as minimum requirement' attempted to theorize the radical focus on the moment. The idea of revolution as the point 'where the realm of freedom

---

[99] 'SPIEGEL-Gespräch: "Tränengas ist der dritte Bildungsweg"', in *Der Spiegel* 43, 24 October 1983, 108–126, quotes 115–116.

[100] Kristin Ross, *May '68 and Its Afterlives* (Chicago: University of Chicago Press, 2002).

[101] 'SPIEGEL-Gespräch: "Tränengas ist der dritte Bildungsweg"', 115–116.

[102] Tomas Lecorte, *Wir tanzen bis zum Ende: die Geschichte eines Autonomen* (Hamburg: Galgenberg, 1992), 81.

is supposed to start' was, they argued, nothing but a 'consolidation for a distant paradise, but we live here, now and today. Perhaps freedom is only the brief moment, from the point when the cobblestone is picked up until it hits, that is, the moment of change, of transgression, of movement.'[103] Radicalizing the politics of the present, these activists went beyond the alternative movement of the 1970s that had attempted to start building a better future in the present. For them, only the brief moment of transgression mattered, but what came after this moment remained irrelevant. After all, the perspectives for the future were bleak anyway. If there was 'no future', as a popular slogan put it, because the future meant only destruction anyway, then only today mattered, without hope but also without fear about the future.[104]

It would be stating the obvious to note that squatters celebrated rioting. It is, however, more complicated to understand exactly how riots could produce feelings of exuberance and intensity. For protestors, rioting and confronting the forces of order was one and perhaps the most important way to practise the carnivalesque revolt of desires against the powers of reasons. During the riot, as a squatter from Frankfurt put it, it was possible to be 'unreasonable'.[105] The explicitly stated purposelessness of riots turned them into games of multiple transgressions: activists overcame the boundaries that separated and isolated people from each other as well as the boundaries of law and order that flying rocks quite literally overflew. This suspension of the normal order was essential for creating the feelings of exuberance activists celebrated. However, to become an enjoyable game, protestors had to interpret the rioting in such terms. In other words, the knowledge that riotous revolts should be like carnivals, that they could and should be cornucopias of feelings, as Röttgen and Rabe had put it, turned them into such carnivals, once the revolts occurred. The heroic and joyous anecdotes were not necessarily true, as an author for *radikal* remarked, but that did not quite matter: 'If we believe in having beaten the cops, then we will face them differently the next time. When we tell each other our heroic deeds after the street battle is over, they [these heroic deeds] become reality.'[106]

---

[103] Anon., 'Anarchie als Minimalforderung', in *radikal: Lieber explosives Chaos als kontrollierte Hochspannung* 97, August 1981, 10.

[104] See for example 'Interview with "Freizeit 81"', in *radikal: Zeitung für Anarchie und Wohlstand* 98, October 1981, 17; and Anon., 'Die Ereignisse werfen Schatten', in *radikal: Zeitung für schöne Bescherung*, Extrablatt, December 1980, 2.

[105] Migro, 'Römerberg: Ein besetztes Haus wurde geräumt', in *Vollautonom* 200, [n.d., January / February 1981], 6–7.

[106] Anon., 'Mythos, Realität und Obelix-Feeling', in *radikal: Lieber explosives Chaos als kontrollierte Hochspannung* 97, August 1981, 4–5.

Ritualization and the End of the Revolt

While it is possible to identify dates that clearly marked the beginning of the revolt in such cities as Zurich and West Berlin, identifying the moment when the revolts ended is much more difficult. In Zurich, the movement came to a definite end when the Autonomous Youth Centre (AJZ) was closed and demolished in March 1982; in West Berlin, the death of Klaus-Jürgen Rattay during a demonstration against the forced eviction of several squatted houses on 22 September 1981 marked the end of a hot summer, even though the movement lived on for another few years. Later on, the eviction of the so-called Turm, a squatted house in Kreuzberg that was known for its particular radicalism, in June 1983, and then the change of the editorial team of *radikal* in spring 1984 (the new team worked underground to evade police pressure) marked the definite end of the revolt. Yet these dates only mark the final point of a process of stagnation. The end of the revolt was a slow process that began right after the famous days of rioting that had marked the revolt's beginning.

If the revolt was, as I have proposed here, a moment of peculiar emotional intensity and exuberance, then the question is how this intensity came to an end. Issues like the increasing pressure as police forces learned how to deal with riots, or, in Zurich, the troubling question of how to deal with drug dealers and users that had moved into the AJZ, certainly played a crucial role in this regard.[107] These problems were an essential part of the history of the respective local movements, as were conflicts within the movements – notably, in West Berlin, the argument between squatters willing to negotiate with the authorities in order to achieve a legalization of their status and those unwilling to do so unless all imprisoned comrades were set free.[108] For the purposes of this chapter, however, I focus on a different aspect, namely, the processes of stagnation and ritualization, in which police pressure was certainly important, that put an end to the constant searching for transgressions and fluidity.

Soon after the euphoric days at the beginning of the revolt, activists began to worry about stagnation inside the movement. As early as the second issue of *Subito* from Zurich, published in the summer of 1980 after

[107] On drug problems, see Jan-Henrik Friedrichs, 'Revolt or Transgression? Squatted Houses and Meeting Places of the Heroin Scene in Zurich and Berlin as Spaces of Transgressive Youth', in *A European Youth Revolt: European Perspectives on Youth Protest and Social Movements in the 1980s*, ed. Bart van der Steen and Knud Andresen (Basingstoke, UK: Palgrave Macmillan, 2016).

[108] On Berlin, see Katsiaficas, *Subversion*, 88–106; Grauwacke, *Autonome*, 34–86; Vasudevan, *Metropolitan Preoccupations*, 123–129.

the AJZ had opened for the first time, an author worried about 'pack-ice' (a term the movement used to describe Swiss normality) spread inside the AJZ. 'Every day into the same den [*Bude*], the same people, the same work – pack-ice.' Every Saturday, there was a disco with the same music; every Saturday, people sat in front of the TV; every Saturday 'a demonstration for which the cops could prepare as they all followed the same pattern – pack-ice? Can't you really think about anything new to realize your desires [*um eure Bedürfnisse durchzusetzen*]?'[109] In West Berlin in April 1981, *radikal* worried that the movement was 'broken [*kaputt*]'. Nostalgically, an author signing as Woll-Lust remembered the 'insane laughing with wild blue-green carnival-illumination, always with a harlequin's cape'; the 'insane and sick, clowns and niggers were on the run, ranging through the metropolis, the stones knew they were on our side. [*die Irren und Kranken, Clowns und Nigger waren los, durchstreiften die Metropole, die Steine wussten sich auf unsere Seite.*]' But then things changed. 'I turn around and search – search for the quick-change artists, the agents provocateurs [*Provokateure*] and harlequins, search for the dreamers and militants [*Phantasten und Militante*]. I comb through the old magic chest, looking for the wondrous magic cap and find only on old, tasteless [*abgeschmackt*] helmet', a 'metaphor of a lack of imagination [*Phantasielosigkeit*]'. The 'diversity of wishes' had turned into a 'controllable ritual of a labour assignment'.[110] When radical activism, whether in the Zurich AJZ or during demonstrations and riots in the streets, became predictable and a mere repetition of previous events, it lost its potential for the uncontrollable and unpredictable change that had characterized the beginning of the revolt, these authors worried.

Within squatted houses, the initial euphoria of the 'prickling adventure', when it was fun to get to know new housemates, gave way to frustrations. Squatters who had moved into squatted houses, an author for the *Schwarze Kanal* wrote, 'to accomplish a different form of living for themselves and others and to change their behaviour vis-à-vis others, recall[ed] their old strengths', and became 'tough guys' again. Participating in 'actions' became a means to brush over one's own problems and frustrations, the author argued. Even though they lived with others in a house, they remained lonely and isolated.[111] In Freiburg, where activists

---

[109] Anon., 'Chopflaschtig: Es paar Gedanke vomene nöd Tränegassüchtige', in *Subito* 2, n.d., unpaginated.
[110] Woll-Lust, 'Auf der Suche nach der militanten Kreativität', in *radikal: Bewegung kaput?* 90/91, April 1981, 8.
[111] Anon., 'Ein Jahr Glück und Anarchie', in *Der Schwarze Kanal* 2, March 1982, 26.

had successfully squatted a building and established an autonomous youth centre in 1981, the situation in the AJZ turned increasingly violent, culminating in a stabbing in 1982. For old activists, the AJZ looked 'grey, cold and dirty'.[112] It was not a place, as activists sadly noted in the summer of 1982, for 'new, changing experiences', but only for 'personal relations frozen into a show'.[113] Activists from other cities that had not been centres of the revolt voiced similar sentiments. An author for the Frankfurt *Vollautonom* wondered: 'You talk about warmth, about affection and solidarity, what did we do wrong so that it remains cold amongst us? You tell me about your arrest, the hours you spent in a cell, what did we do wrong so that your face remains unmoved?'[114] The goal to create spaces for 'warm' and 'affectionate' feelings in squatted houses or autonomous youth centres seems to have failed quickly, if we are to believe these sources (though informal conversations with former squatters suggest that collectively living in squatted houses could also be a much more positive experience).[115]

Debates in *radikal* about protests against Ronald Reagan's visit to Berlin in June 1982 may provide a final example for how activists increasingly came to perceive riots as mere rituals that lost their transgressive and subversive potential. Already after riots in the wake of a forced eviction in April 1982, *radikal* had remarked that, while 'the volcano's most recent eruption had proved those wrong who had already proclaimed the volcano being extinguished, the new steams of lava cannot hide the fact that the climate has changed'.[116] In the same issue, another article noted that the 'street pogo', that is, rioting, had become less popular with every 'arrest warrant and every smashed skull'. 'More and more we feel like beaten victims after a demo – and less as living actors of unchaining.' Meanwhile, the number of clandestine attacks increased, but those required more organization than 'spontaneity and joy'. Crucial was the media attention in this regard, the author argued, as only sufficient media coverage turned a riot or an attack into a meaningful event. Yet, with the increased escalation, only clandestine attacks (*Anschläge*), but no 'stolen cheese or street

---

[112] Anon., 'AZ, was sonst!?', in *Stadtzeitung für Freiburg 76*, February 1983, 29.
[113] Anon., 'Keine Träume: 10 Thesen für die Schließung des AZ', in *Stadtzeitung für Freiburg 70/71*, August/September 1982, 32–33.
[114] Anon., untitled poem, in *Vollautonom 300*, March/April 1981, 45.
[115] Personal conversation with D. Z., Berlin, December 2011.
[116] Anon., 'Eruptionen, oder: Der Vulkan bittet zum Tanz', in *radikal: Zeitung für Jagd aus Leidenschaft 104*, May 1982, 8.

riot' made headlines.[117] Street rioting, once joyfully celebrated, lost its appeal. It was thus perhaps not surprising that activists called for 'cancelling the battle' with the police during Reagan's visit. After all, the organized riot would be anything but spontaneous and result only in 'military' defeat.[118]

But these critical voices not withstanding, the demonstration on 12 June 1982 turned into a heavy riot that, as noted earlier in the chapter, was, by some activists at least, joyfully celebrated as another instant of transgression. An activist described the rioting as 'joyful hours of alternative urban planning. Above all one feeling remains: the Controllix-AG can't do magic. Its logic is statistical ordering; no computer can be programmed for the art of permanent change and the permanent new birth of mobile amoebae.'[119] But other activists were more critical. After three months of excited preparation for *the* event, one text argued, nothing but 'painful emptiness' remained which showed how much the scene had been fixated on 'that little guy' (the American president).[120] Another writer claimed that mostly comrades from West Germany had been involved in the riots, while the Berlin scene had remained absent. For those who were there, the 'masochistic program of one's own defeat' produced a 'deep feeling of alienation, of non-participation'. It was a 'feeling of being a planned [*verplanter*], unpaid and unconscious background actor [*Statist*] in a performance [*Inszenierung*] whose logic ran counter our own spontaneity, and that was, furthermore, never that uncontrollable for us, but controllable for the other side'.[121] The more common riots became, these activists argued, the easier it was for the police to tame them, and the less spontaneous and hence joyful and subversive the riots became.

These experiences of stagnation point to a fundamental dilemma activists faced in their search for transgressions. Once they had transgressed a boundary, it could not be transgressed a second time; or at least the transgression became a predictable and controllable ritual rather than a contingent and chaotic moment of change.[122] An author for *radikal* clearly

---

[117] Dr. Seltsam, 'Käseklau und Bombenbau', in *radikal: Zeitung für Jagd aus Leidenschaft* 104, May 1982, 11.

[118] Fernando, 'die schlacht absagen', in *radikal: Zeitung für den unkontrollierten Ernstfall* 105, June 1982, 12.

[119] Glüh-Fix, 'Do it & Ex', in *radikal: Zeitung für den reißenden Absatz* 106, July 1982, 12–13.

[120] Anon., 'Weg isser', in *radikal: Zeitung für den reißenden Absatz* 106, July 1982, 6.

[121] Cunctator, 'Das inszenierte Szenario', in *radikal: Zeitung für den reißenden Absatz* 106, July 1982, 11.

[122] For a theoretical perspective developed by left-wing Agentur Bilwet, drawing on examples from Amsterdam, see Agentur BILWET, *Bewegungslehre: Botschaften aus einer autonomen Wirklichkeit* (Berlin: Edition ID-Archiv, 1991). See also my discussion in Häberlen, 'Sekunden der Freiheit'.

understood this: 'And what now, when there are no more new boundaries to transgress? Eventually you have sprayed for a first time, you have thrown a rock at a demo for a first time, you have participated a decentralized action [*dezentrale Aktion*; that is a clandestine attacked committed by a small group rather than a public riot] ... you've always experienced these moments of freedom, and now: the logical escalation would be a gun in your pockets ... but at exactly this point you reject this logic, your lived life is more important. Or isn't it possible to think about transgressions on a very different terrain than that violent terrain? But we have been looking for those new terrains for half a year now.'[123] The feelings of intensity and exuberance were tied to unpredictable moments of transgression and change. When situations of rioting became predictable and the riot itself turned into a mere ritual, the rioting lost its transgressive and transformative character; it was only part of a scripted performance whose logics were clear. Once this happened, the euphoria and intensity were gone.

Conclusion

In February 1984, *radikal* published an interview with French philosopher Jean Baudrillard. It is an opaque text, and it is not always clear whether interviewer and interviewee actually understood each other. Ultimately, the interview is more interesting for what the *radikal* interviewer had to say. He quoted Michel Foucault to argue that revolts resemble fireworks, shot into the sky to fade away immediately. May 1968 in France had been such an event: it remained without consequences, but was 'passionate'. Later on in the interview, the *radikal* interviewer explained 'their' – the interviewer used the collective 'us' – perspective on the revolts, which by then had finished. For the left, the 1970s had been a time of frustration; and then, suddenly, a revolt had started in Zurich, Amsterdam, Freiburg, and Berlin that no one had theoretically anticipated. During the revolt, the interviewer claimed, there was the sense that 'causes and consequences' no longer existed, but simply merged, 'and that there was no more time. But the after is an intrusion of time, an intrusion of continuity.'[124] This understanding of the revolt as an eruption was not new. Already in February 1982, *radikal* had described the 'movement' as an 'eruption' that had made 'time, clotted into an unbearable duration [*die zu einer*

---

[123] Das "reale" no future, '[No title]', in *radikal: Zeitung für den reißenden Absatz* 106, July 1982, 10.
[124] 'Der Tod des politischen Subjekts. Interview mit Baudrillard', in *radikal: Fachblatt für alles, was Terroristen Spaß macht* 126/127, March/April 1984, 14–19.

unerträglichen Dauer geronnene Zeit]', explode.[125] The revolt was, these texts suggest, a peculiar moment, distinct from the normal and 'unbearable' time. It was a moment of intense exuberance.

To produce feelings of intensity and exuberance, activists engaged in transgressive acts that disrupted the sense of normalcy and that created the feeling of being in a topsy-turvy situation. Whether they strove to overcome their allegedly normal isolation in squatted houses or fought the police in street riots, normality seemed to be turned it on its head; for a brief moment, reason and logic did not matter anymore. Yet rioting or living in a squatted house did not naturally, as it were, yield feelings of intense exuberance. Of course, rioting could also be fear-inducing, and living with other people in a squatted house could be a nerve-wracking experience, which is why squatters constantly moved in and out. For practices such as collective living and rioting to feel intense and exuberant, activists had to draw on emotional knowledge that allowed them to understand such situations to be carnivalesque and exuberant. The knowledge about feelings was, in other words, essential for the production of these feelings. Not least, the textual and visual aesthetics of the revolt (re)produced this emotional knowledge that had been developed in the alternative left at least since the late 1970s. Yet this does not mean that activists simply followed an emotional script during the revolts, and that, as historians, we should deconstruct their narratives of spontaneity. Whether a riot did occur, whether the police lost control of the situation, whether houses could be squatted – all of this was indeed unpredictable. The revolt disrupted the ordinary routines of everyday life. In that sense, the revolt was recognized by its protagonists as an event in Sewell's sense. It was, however, not a transformative event, but a disruptive one. Arguably, this lack of a concern with the future was essential for the emotional intensity of the revolt. The revolt was, then, a liminal moment, but unlike the liminal moments Victor Turner describes, it was hardly ritualized. Indeed, once riots became ritualized, and hence predictable for both the protestors and the police, they ceased to create feelings of intensity and exuberance. They had become part of the normal routine of everyday life for protestors.

---

[125] Anon., 'Eingemachtes', in *radikal: Zeitung für unbeschwerte Stunden* 103, April 1982, 6.

Conclusion

In 1984, the Freiburg-based group *Initiative Sozialistisches Forum* (ISF), a group that would become one of the sharpest and most pronounced critics of the left from a decidedly leftist perspective, published a book called *The Dictatorship of Friendliness: On Bhagwan, the Coming Psychocracy and Delivery Entrances to Charitable Insanity*. The book provided a trenchant critique of the Neo-Sannyas Movement, formed by former professor of philosophy Bhagwan Shree Rajneesh, whose orange-dressed followers, many of them former leftist activists, became a common sight in West-German cities during the mid-1970s.[1] But Bhagwan himself was not the real object of the ISF's critique. Rather, the ISF and its author Joachim Bruhn discussed him as the 'ideal-type theoretician [*ideeller Gesamttheoretiker*] of the "new social movements"'. According to Bruhn, the popularity of Bhagwan indicated a broader 'transformation of bourgeois society into a therapeutic support-community based on mutuality'.[2] This transformation, he argued, turned capitalism into a giant, 'over-dimensioned consciousness-raising group [*Selbsterfahrungsgruppe*], an all-embracing and permanent encounter [English in the original]'. As Bhagwan had written: 'Capitalism helps you to express yourself, to present yourself, to display yourself in your totality [*Dich in Deiner Totalität zu entfalten*].' A 'new aggregate state of power', dubbed 'psychocracy' by Bruhn,[3] had developed, in which the way power functioned had changed: 'In the psychocracy, the seventh sense of the subaltern takes the place of orders and command; [the seventh sense makes the subaltern] foresee that which is commanded already before it is proclaimed, [and it makes them] present it [i.e., the

---

[1] On Bhagwan and his German followers, see Maik Tändler, *Das therapeutische Jahrzehnt: Der Psychoboom in den siebziger Jahren* (Göttingen: Wallstein, 2016), 349–358.

[2] Joachim Bruhn, 'Unter den Zwischenmenschen', in *Diktatur der Freundlichkeit: Über Bhagwan, die kommende Psychokratie und Lieferanteneingänge zum wohltätigen Wahnsinn*, ed. Initiative Sozialistisches Forum (Freiburg: Ça-Ira-Verlag, 1984), 59.

[3] Ibid., 9.

anticipated command] to the points of command as their own wish, which is then happily approved.'[4]

Bruhn was also deeply critical of the search for authenticity and the 'true self' that characterized leftist politics in the psychocracy. In a situation where therapy had become a 'form of life', the truth of an argument no longer mattered; what mattered was only one's inner state, one's feelings, and one's thoughts while expressing an argument. A 'meta-reflection' about the conversation and what it revealed about someone's psychic state had replaced the actual conversation, and thus the potential for a genuine social critique, Bruhn argued.[5] The left, he charged, had ceased critically analysing society, but tried to find the 'true self' through careful self-reflection. And to truly find one's inner self, it would be necessary to stop the 'flow of thinking', since, together with thoughts, 'wishes and hopes' would disappear, as a follower of Bhagwan named Swami Satyanda had claimed. 'If you do all this, then you are authentic, then you don't wear any mask', Bruhn quoted Satyanda. But tearing off all masks in search for the 'true self' only revealed, Bruhn noted, that people are nothing but 'quivering batches of reflexes, autistic amoebae'.[6]

The book as a whole, and Bruhn's contributions in particular, are still worth reading, not least because of its unerring polemics. It is a sharp condemnation of the alternative left. Far from undermining capitalist rationality, the alternative left with its countless therapy groups and its focus on the self had, in Bruhn's reading, contributed to a transformation and stabilization of capitalism; it had helped give birth to a new form of domination for which psychological experts play a fundamental role because they ensure that what people want as best for themselves is also best for capitalist society as a whole. The potentially subversive tension between individual wishes, dreams, or desires and capitalist rationality has disappeared, and self-imposed coercion (*Selbstzwang*) has replaced open coercion by others (*Fremdzwang*). Whereas the traditional bourgeois state had relied, in the last instance, on brute force, Bruhn argued that this would no longer be necessary, as people now have internalized the necessities of capitalism. Fulfilling one's dreams and wishes has become perfectly in line with what capitalism demands. Ultimately, the entire search for 'authenticity' would only help capitalism function. Skilfully mocking the various techniques that would allow people to find their 'true selves', Bruhn denounced the jargon of authenticity: there is no true self behind all the masks leftists wanted to tear down, Bruhn argued, but only shapeless amoebae.

---

[4] Ibid., 73.   [5] Ibid., 63.   [6] Ibid., 68.

Bruhn never employs a Foucauldian terminology (his occasional theoretical point of reference is Theodor W. Adorno); nevertheless, his critical analysis strikingly resembles the arguments scholars have made when drawing on Foucault's work, albeit in a less polemical and engaging tone. This scholarship, which is usually associated with the name 'governmentality studies', has argued for broadening the concept of governing beyond the state and its institutions, and beyond governing others to include the 'government of the self' into the analysis.[7] Governing happens, as Sabine Maasen writes, by instructing people how to govern themselves. A peculiar mixture of technologies of governing guides people to constantly work on themselves, both for their own sake (to be authentic, successful, beautiful, healthy, etc.), and for the sake of the public good (to be productive, not to be a burden for the public health, etc.). Those who refuse to work on themselves not only harm themselves, but also society.[8] Practices of governing and self-determination are thus not (perhaps no longer) seen in opposition. Rather, as Thomas Lemke, Susanne Krasmann, and Ulrich Bröckling note, 'in the context of neoliberal governmentality, self-determination, responsibility and freedom of choice do not signal the limits of governing [*Regierungshandeln*], but are themselves an instrument and medium [*Vehikel*] to change how subjects relate to themselves and to others'.[9] In his study of the 'entrepreneurial self', Bröckling has elaborated the various and contradictory requirements the neoliberal self is facing: it has to be able to work in a team, and it has to be able to lead; it has to be flexible, creative, and autonomous, always willing to build new networks.[10]

---

[7] See only Thomas Lemke, Susanne Krasmann, and Ulrich Bröckling, eds., *Gouvernementalität der Gegenwart: Studien zur Ökonomisierung des Sozialen* (Frankfurt a.M.: Suhrkamp, 2000); Thomas Lemke, *Eine Kritik der politischen Vernunft: Foucaults Analyse der modernen Gouvernementalität* (Berlin: Argument, 1997); Graham Burchell, Colin Gordon, and Peter Miller, eds., *The Foucault Effect: Studies in Governmentality* (Chicago: University of Chicago Press, 1991).

[8] Sabine Maasen, 'Das beratene Selbst: Zur Genealogie der Therapeutisierung in den "langen" Siebzigern: Eine Perspektivierung', in *Das beratene Selbst: Zur Genealogie der Therapeutisierung in den 'langen' Siebzigern*, ed. Sabine Maasen et al. (Bielefeld: transcript, 2011).

[9] Thomas Lemke, Susanne Krasmann, and Ulrich Bröckling, 'Gouvernementalität, Neoliberalismus und Selbsttechnologien: Eine Einleitung', in *Gouvernementalität der Gegenwart: Studien zur Ökonomisierung des Sozialen*, ed. Thomas Lemke, Susanne Krasmann, and Ulrich Bröckling (Frankfurt a.M.: Suhrkamp, 2000), 30.

[10] See Ulrich Bröckling, 'Das demokratisierte Panopticon: Subjektivierung und Kontrolle im 360° Feedback', in *Michel Foucault: Zwischenbilanz einer Rezeption. Frankfurter Foucault-Konferenz 2001*, ed. Axel Honneth and Martin Saar (Frankfurt a.M.: Suhrkamp, 2003); Ulrich Bröckling, *Das unternehmerische Selbst: Soziologie einer Subjektivierungsform* (Frankfurt a.M.: Suhrkamp, 2007); chs. 3 & 4. See along similar lines Jens Elberfeld, 'Befreiung des Subjekts, Management des Selbst: Therapeutisierungsprozesse im deutschsprachigen Raum seit den 1960er Jahren', in *Zeitgeschichte des Selbst: Therapeutisierung – Politisierung – Emotionalisierung*, ed. Pascal Eitler and Jens Elberfeld (Bielefeld: transcript, 2015), 78; Maik Tändler, 'Erziehung der Erzieher: Lehrer als problematische

These are the qualities, rather than subordination and conformity, that matter for the 'new spirit of capitalism' that Luc Boltanski and Eve Chiapello have examined.[11]

These comments about the new capitalism and the neoliberal subject are strikingly similar to what Bruhn had argued in 1984. Capitalism ceases to rely on direct forms of coercion, and instead relies on people's longings for creative and meaningful work that are in harmony with the requirements of a capitalist economy. Both Bröckling and Boltanski and Chiapello note the origins of what they identify as new or neoliberal capitalism at least in part in the alternative left.[12] Without linking the alternative left to the rise of neoliberal capitalism, Sven Reichardt comes to a similarly critical conclusion, reminiscent of Bruhn's account: 'External coercion [*Fremdzwang*] was replaced by internalized coercion [*Selbstzwang*], which pretended to be freedom.' In Reichardt's account, the requirements of the alternative self not only enabled people to talk about themselves, to reflect on their private lives from a political perspective, but, even more importantly, required them to do so. 'In the consensus-society of the alternative left, the self-designing [*das sich Entwerfen*], interpreted as a governing technology of freedom [*Regierungstechnologie der Freiheit*], could take the form of destructive self-coercion.'[13] Ultimately, the alternative left, with its emphasis on self-improvement, contributed, these arguments imply, to a new form of capitalism that requires people, and especially managers, to work autonomously and to build nonhierarchical – 'rhizomatic', as it were – networks. Rather than undermining the capitalist system, the alternative left helped transform and stabilize it. The history of the

Subjekte zwischen Bildungsreform und antiautoritärer Pädagogik', in *Zeitgeschichte des Selbst: Therapeutisierung – Politisierung – Emotionalisierung*, ed. Pascal Eitler and Jens Elberfeld (Bielefeld: transcript, 2015), 111–112.

[11] Luc Boltanski and Eve Chiapello, *The New Spirit of Capitalism* (London: Verso, 2005). They cite authors such as Deleuze, Foucault, Baudillard and Marcuse, all popular within the alternative left, as examples for an 'artisitic critique' of capitalism that informed the 'new spirit of capitalism' that emerged in the 1970s. See also Eve Chiapello, 'Capitalism and Its Criticisms', in *New Spirits of Capitalism? Crises, Justifications, and Dynamics*, ed. Paul du Gay and Glenn Morgan (Oxford: Oxford University Press, 2012), 71–73.

[12] Bröckling, *Unternehmerische Selbst*, 257–260; Boltanski and Chiapello, *Spirit*, 199–202. See also the contemporary critique by André Béjin, 'Auf dem Weg zur "Allgemeinen Selbst-Verwaltung"?', in *Diktatur der Freundlichkeit: Über Bhagwan, die kommende Psychokratie und Lieferanteneingänge zum wohltätigen Wahnsinn*, ed. Initiative Sozialistisches Forum (Freiburg: Ça-Ira-Verlag, 1984). The text was translated from French. It first appeared as 'Les thérapies de l'identité, de la sexualité, de la communication et de la conscience corporelle', in *Cahier internationaux de sociologie* 63 (1977): 363–370.

[13] Sven Reichardt, *Authentizität und Gemeinschaft: Linksalternatives Leben in den siebziger und frühen achtziger Jahren* (Berlin: Suhrkamp, 2014), 887–888.

alternative left matters, that is, not so much because of the critique of capitalism it had to offer, but because it may help us understand the emergence of a particular form of (capitalist) power that cannot be grasped with traditional Marxist categories of class. This would be a bleak assessment for a movement that sought to criticize and subvert capitalist rationality.[14]

There is something to be said for this perspective. Yet it does not do justice to the complexities and ambiguities that characterize the history of the alternative left. It is worth having a look at the critique Foucault formulated in his 1982 essay, *The Subject and Power*, not least because his arguments inform the critical perspective of Bröckling and others, and who is one of the authors Boltanski and Chiapello associate with the artistic critique that helped transform capitalism since the 1970s.[15] In the essay, he notes a peculiar 'form of political power' that has been developing since the 16th century, and the intertwined emergence of peculiar forms of struggles. In his reading, the 'modern Western state has integrated', and thereby transformed, a 'power technique' that 'originated in Church institutions', which Foucault describes as 'pastoral power'. In Christian institutions, pastoral power's 'ultimate aim is to ensure individual salvation in the next world'. Pastoral power not only looks after the whole community, but it is concerned with each and every individual. To be able to care about the individual spiritual fate, pastoral power needs to know about people's inner souls. The modern state presents, as it were, a secularized form of this 'individualizing' power. In the modern state, it 'was no longer a question of leading people to their salvation in the next world but rather ensuring it in this world. And in this context, the word "salvation" takes on different meanings: health, well-being (that is, sufficient health, standard of living) security, protection against accidents.' In the modern state, pastoral power 'suddenly spread out into the whole social body; it found support in a multitude of institutions', such as the family, the educational system, or medical and psychological institutions. In the modern world, in other words, a multiplicity of powers instructs people how to shape their selves in order to 'safe' themselves in this world.

---

[14] See critically Sabine Donauer, 'Job Satisfaction statt Arbeitszufriedenheit: Gefühlswissen im arbeitswissenschaftlichen Diskurs der 1970er Jahre', in *Zeitgeschichte des Selbst: Therapeutisierung – Politisierung – Emotionalisierung*, ed. Pascal Eitler and Jens Elberfeld (Bielefeld: transcript, 2015). She notes that there is no empirical evidence that would link the desire for autonomy and creativity in leftwing alternative circles to a similar rhetoric in management literature.

[15] Michel Foucault, 'The Subject and Power', *Critical Inquiry* 8 (1982).

The emergence of this particular power also necessitates a different form of critique, Foucault argued. When Kant asked in 1784, 'What Is Enlightenment? [*Was heißt Aufklärung?*]', he effectively asked 'Who are we as *Aufklärer?*', in that precise historical moment of *Aufklärung*. It was thus an inquiry about the present. But by 1982 the question had changed, Foucault claimed. Nowadays, he wrote, the target 'is not to discover what we are, but to refuse what we are ... We have to promote new forms of subjectivity through the refusal of this kind of individuality which has been imposed on us for centuries.' The struggles of the 1970s, 'the opposition to the power of men over women, of parents over children, of psychiatry over the mentally ill, of medicine over the population, of administration over the way people live', can be understood in this sense as a challenge to pastoral powers. These were not simply struggles 'for or against the "individual", but ... against the "government of individualization"'. The struggles of the 1970s were thus distinct from other forms of struggles that were 'against forms of domination (ethnic, social, or religious)', or 'against forms of exploitation which separate individuals form what they produce' – a form of struggling that had been, Foucault claimed, prominent in the 19th century. By the 1970s, a different kind of struggle emerged, a struggle 'against that which ties the individual to himself and submits him to others in this way (struggles against subjection, against forms of subjectivity and submission)', even though other forms of struggles had not disappeared.

Arguably, leftists were engaged in a struggle against a 'regime of individualization', in their view a capitalist regime of individualization that required them to be rational all the time and to avoid showing feelings. The 'politics of the first person' that leftists famously formulated exemplified the point. By pleading for a 'politics of the first person', leftist activists did not simply call for focusing on issues that directly affected them, such as urban renewal projects or the destruction of the local environment. Rather, they made their selves, and the powers that shaped, or, in the parlance of the day, 'damaged' them, their primary political concern. Particularly the constant search for transgressions and the refusal to be 'fixated' can be understood as an attempt to escape from any requirement to build a stable self. While this was, as the first chapter has shown, not a complete novelty, the 1970s nevertheless marked a qualitative change when struggles against a 'government of individualization' pushed struggles 'against forms of exploitation' increasingly to the side. Indeed, Foucault could have easily referred to the alternative left as an example for the new kinds of struggles he was describing; and, of course, leftists themselves were eagerly reading Foucault.

No doubt, alternative leftists simultaneously created a different regime of subjectivity that required them to show feelings in order to be recognized as authentic, as Sven Reichardt has argued. However, by focusing their critique on questions of subjectivity and the powers that shape the self, leftists also provided the grounds for criticizing the very regime of subjectivity they themselves were creating, as the texts by Jörg Bopp, Herbert Nagel, the Militante Panthertanten, and, not least of all, Joachim Bruhn demonstrate. Studying the history of the alternative left, that is, helps us not only to understand how a 'pastoral' form of power spread beyond the institutions of the state, but also how a critique of this form of power developed, as Luc Boltanski and Eve Chiapello have argued in the French case. If the alternative left was one place, amongst others, where a neoliberal subjectivity began to take shape, to put it cautiously, then we can also locate the origins of a critique of a neoliberal subjectivity in this milieu. We could, that is, write the history of the alternative left as part and parcel of a history of a contemporary self, *and* a critique of the impositions and requirements that contemporary forms of subjectivity impose upon people.[16]

Yet, as promising as such a perspective would be, it would also be a limited perspective, because it ignores the emotional productivity of the alternative left that tends to get lost in reconstructions of the contours of an alternative subject. Showing this emotional productivity of the left has been my goal in this book. On the one hand, leftist interpretations of capitalism as inducing fear in people and isolating them from each other created an emotional knowledge that was in itself productive because it instructed leftists how to feel under capitalism. But more importantly, the critical knowledge of the emotional regime of capitalism leftists created also provided them with ideas how to produce the feelings of intimacy and intensity they missed. Activists longed for feelings; they wanted to express their feelings, they sought to feel their bodies, and they wanted to live in an emotionally stimulating and sensually diverse environment that would do away with the boredom of modern cities. This desire for emotions encouraged all kinds of practices that would, activists hoped, yield the feelings they desperately missed in capitalist society. But whether those practices did yield the feelings leftists hoped for was never certain. Activists tried out

---

[16] For a similar argument see Maik Tändler and Uffa Jensen, 'Psychowissen, Politik und das Selbst: Eine neue Forschungsperspektive auf die Geschichte des Politischen im 20. Jahrhundert', in *Das Selbst zwischen Anpassung und Befreiung: Psychowissen und Politik im 20. Jahrhundert*, ed. Uffa Jensen and Maik Tändler (Göttingen: Wallstein, 2012), 18.

feelings, sometimes more successfully, sometimes less so. Interpreting the practices in which leftists engaged as emotional experiments that sometimes worked and sometimes failed, and which leftists constantly tried to develop further, may restore a sense of contingency that gets lost in reconstructions of the demands and requirements of peculiar forms of subjectivity. Not least, the emphasis on experiments and their contingent outcomes provides a perspective on the 1970s that does not treat it as a 'problem-history of the present' or, for that matter, a transformative decade that shaped the years to come.[17] It helps us avoid a too monolithic and static depiction of those years that portrays them, for example, as a decade of fear (of nuclear disaster, total surveillance, environmental destruction, etc.), because it highlights how activists both produced fear, and overcame this fear.

For historians, the search for and the production of emotional intensity, especially during the revolts of 1980–81, present an interesting challenge. Historians are trained to understand change over time.[18] The study of the alternative left might help us grasp how a peculiar form of subjectivity, and struggles against the subjection to this 'government of individualization', emerged in the 1970s. This interest in change over time mirrors the conventional temporality of politics: normally, political action and activism is about accomplishing some change in the future. Radical activists of the late 1970s and above all during the revolts of 1980–81 explicitly rejected this conception of politics. They were not interested in longer-term transformations, but in the exuberant intensity of the moment. Any attempt to integrate this desire for momentary exuberance into narratives of transformation, whether to tell a story of democratization, newly emerging subjectivities, or a transformation of capitalism, would be inadequate, since it fails to make sense of this intensity. In contrast to consciousness-raising or therapy groups, the multiple transgressions that yielded feelings of exuberant intensity did not require working on the self; squatted houses never turned, it seems, into the kind of therapeutic communities that some communes of the 1970s were. Squatted houses and carnivalesque riots with the police were hardly an extension of pastoral

---

[17] Anselm Doering-Manteuffel and Lutz Raphael, *Nach dem Boom: Perspektiven auf die Zeitgeschichte seit 1970*, 2nd edn (Göttingen: Vandenhoeck & Ruprecht, 2008), 25; Hans Günther Hockerts, 'Zeitgeschichte in Deutschland: Begriff, Methoden, Themenfelder', *Historisches Jahrbuch* 113 (1993). See the critical comments by Etienne François in Rainer Eckert et al., 'Die 1970er-Jahre in Geschichte und Gegenwart', *Zeithistorische Forschungen* (2006): 423–424.

[18] See William H. Sewell, Jr., *Logics of History: Social Theory and Social Transformation* (Chicago: The University of Chicago Press, 2005), 7–12.

power. Nor did these temporarily limited moments create any fluid and ever-evolving networks that characterize the new 'rhizomatic' capitalism that Boltanski and Chiapello describe. Rather, they were disruptive moments for any network. Asking questions about change over time would thus be inadequate to grasp what happened during the revolts of 1980–81.

The challenge for historians is then to write the history of such a moment, that is, a history that is not concerned with change over time, but with grasping the intensity of the moment itself. For radical activists, acts of transgression were crucial for producing feelings of exuberance. No matter whether boundaries between individual bodies were crossed at excessive parties, or whether the boundaries of law and order were transgressed by stones thrown at policemen, these acts produced a sense of intensity activists longed for; it was a feeling they missed in the normal world of capitalism where, they believed, strict boundaries reigned that separated people from each other. According to leftist thinking, the collapse of those boundaries could result in joyful festivals that might even turn into revolutions. This is not to say that all parties or all riots indeed produced intense feelings of exuberance. The music at parties could prevent excessive dancing, and ritualized riots only reinforced an existing order. To feel intensely, something unpredicted had to happen. Indeed, riots that no one, including the police, had foreseen were often described as the most intense. Yet activists knew how such events would feel. But the emphasis on unpredictability and spontaneity also meant that boundaries could not be transgressed multiple times. Once a boundary had been crossed, the next crossing was a mere repetition that felt much less exuberant and liberating. The exuberance of a moment, that is, could not last.

Not least, the emphasis on the moment raises the question what matters historically. Typically, we consider events historically relevant if they mark some fundamental change – like the Russian Revolution of 1917, the German Autumn of 1977, or the fall of the Berlin Wall in 1989. The revolts of 1980–81 are hardly historically meaningful events in that sense.[19] Certainly, the political culture of the Federal Republic did not change, nor did the socioeconomic system. One might argue, of course, that these revolts mattered because the German *Autonomen* (autonomous) movement was born here; one might also argue that the revolts had an impact on urban renewal policies in West Berlin and laid the foundation for Kreuzberg to become an attractive neighbourhood. But interestingly,

[19] Ibid., 8–9.

not even the protestors themselves thought about their revolts as transformative events. Quoting Foucault, they described the revolts as fireworks, shot into the night to fade immediately. This suggests a different understanding of what makes an event politically and hence historically meaningful. Rather than being transformative, the revolts were politically meaningful precisely due to their exuberant intensity that, at least for activists, disrupted the normalcy of everyday life. What historian Julian Jackson has written about the French Popular Front might have been true about the revolts of 1980–81 as well: They did not change the world, but, like a theatre play, they enlightened the world for a brief moment.[20] The revolts of 1980–81, and activists' celebration of exuberant moments, might encourage historians to rethink what they consider relevant to the histories they write. Perhaps it would be worthwhile for historians to dwell more on intense, enlightening, and exuberant moments in history.

Studying the alternative left in West Germany is then, to conclude, neither about recovering some unfulfilled radical democratic promise, nor is it about demonstrating how a seemingly emancipatory movement effectively created new forms of self-constraint that were anything but liberating. We need to leave such assessments aside. What makes the study of the alternative left worthwhile is neither that there is some 'unfinished business' (a struggle for radical democracy to be completed in the present), nor that new forms of self-domination emerged in the communes and therapy groups of the alternative left, but the experimental nature of what leftists did. They developed what I have described as emotional experiments that could be highly oppressive 'psycho-terror', but also joyous and exuberant. Experiments create potentialities with inherently unpredictable outcomes. Gaining a sense for the open-endedness of such emotional experiments makes the study of the alternative left worthwhile because it helps us to grasp the ambivalences, contradictions, and, not least, the emotional productivity of the time.

[20] Julian Jackson, *The Popular Front in France: Defending Democracy, 1934–38* (Cambridge: Cambridge University Press, 1988), 287.

Primary Sources

Archives (Magazines are held in these archives)
APO Archiv Berlin
    Boxes 1134 – 1135, Tunix
    S 058 – 060
Archiv der Jugendkulturen, Berlin
Papiertiger Archiv Berlin
    Schuber Häuserkämpfe Berlin (Broschüren)
    Ordner Anti-Nato Bewegung
    Ordner Häuserkämpfe Berlin
    Ordner Schulkämpfe
Schweizerisches Sozialarchiv Zürich
    Ar 201.83.3
Schwules Museum, Berlin
Spinnboden Archiv, Berlin

Magazines
's Blättle
ABBLDIBABBLDIBIBBLDIBABBLDIBU: Schülerzeitung der HCO 2
Anschläge
Autonomie: Materialien gegen die Fabrikgesellschaft
Bambule
Befreiung
Beiträge zur feministischen Theorie und Praxis
Besetzer-Rat Info
Carlo Sponti
Courage
Das Blatt
Der Metzger
Der Schwarze Kanal
Die Andere Zeitung

Die Plünderer
Diskus
Doktorspiele: Zeitung für Körperinstandsetzung
Emanzipation
Erotik und Umbruch: Zeitung zu Sexualität
Fizz
Frankfurter Frauenblatt
Frankfurter Gemeine
Frauenjahrbuch
Frauenzeitung
Große Freiheit
Großstadtpflaster: Eine Zeitung für Asphaltaktivisten
HAW Info
Heim und Erzieher Zeitung
Hundert Blumen
Info Bremer Undogmatischer Gruppen
Info BUG
Info Nürnberg
Instandbesetzerzeitung
Kassler Kursblatt
Kieler Fresse
Klenkes: Zeitung Aachener Bürgerinitiativen
Konkursbuch: Zeitschrift für Vernunftkritik
Kursbuch
Lesbenpresse
Mann-o-Mann
Mannsbild
Montagsnotizen
Päng
Pflasterstrand
Politikon
radikal
Radikalinski
Revolte
Rosa
Rumpelstielzchen
Rundschlag
Schüler Info Charlottenburg
Schülerforum
Schwarze Botin

Schwarze Protokolle
Schwuchtel
Selbermachen: Zeitung des Schöneberger Jungarbeiter- und Schülerzentrums
Sexpol
Stadtzeitung für Freiburg
Stilett
Subito
taz
Traumstadt
Traumzeit
Ulcus Molle
Unter dem Pflaster liegt der Strand
Vollautonom
Wir Wollen Alles

Bibliography

Abromeit, John. 'The Limits of Praxis: The Social-Psychological Foundations of Theodor Adorno's and Herbert Marcuse's Interpretations of the 1960s Protest Movements.' In *Changing the World, Changing Oneself: Political Protest and Collective Identities in West Germany and the U.S. in the 1960s and 1970s*, edited by Belinda Davis, Wilfried Mausbach, Martin Klimke and Carla MacDougall, 13–38. New York: Berghahn, 2010.

Ackermann, Astrid. 'Kleidung, Sexualität und politische Partizipation in der Lebensreformbewegung.' In *'Lebensreform': Die soziale Dynamik der politischen Ohnmacht*, edited by Marc Cluet and Catherine Repussard, 161–182. Tübingen: Francke Verlag, 2013.

Ahrens, Rüdiger. *Bündische Jugend: Eine neue Geschichte, 1918–1933*. Göttingen: Wallstein, 2015.

Anders, Freia. 'Wohnraum, Freiraum, Widerstand: Die Formierung der Autonomen in den Konflikten um Hausbesetzungen Anfang der achtziger Jahre.' In *Das Alternative Milieu: Antibürgerlicher Lebensstil und linke Politik in der Bundesrepublik Deutschland und Europa, 1968–1983*, edited by Sven Reichardt and Detlef Siegfried, 473–498. Göttingen: Wallstein, 2010.

Andritzky, Michael. 'Einleitung.' In *'Wir sind nackt und nennen uns Du': Von Lichtfreunden und Sonnenkämpfern. Eine Geschichte der Freikörperkultur*, edited by Michael Andritzky and Thomas Rautenberg, 4–9. Giessen: Anabas, 1989.

Andritzky, Michael, and Thomas Rautenberg, eds. *'Wir sind nackt und nennen uns Du': Von Lichtfreunden und Sonnenkämpfern. Eine Geschichte der Freikörperkultur*. Giessen: Anabas, 1989.

Anon. 'Instructions for an Insurrection.' In *Situationist International Anthology*, edited by Ken Knabb, 84–86. Berkeley: Bureau of Public Secrets, 1981 (1961).

'The Sound and the Fury.' In *Situationist International Anthology*, edited by Ken Knabb, 47–49. Berkeley: Bureau of Public Secrets, 1981 (1958).

Arens, Esther. 'Lektion in Demokratie: Die "Schwabinger Krawalle" und die Münchner "Interessengemeinschaft zur Wahrung der Bürgerrechte".' In *'Schwabinger Krawalle': Protest, Polizei und Öffentlichkeit zu Beginn der 60er Jahre*, edited by Gerhard Fürmetz, 125–140. Essen: Klartext, 2006.

Aust, Stefan, and Sabine Rosenbladt, eds. *Hausbesetzer: Wofür sie kämpfen, wie sie leben und wie sie leben wollen.* Hamburg: Hoffmann und Campe, 1981.

Autorengruppe. *Männerbilder: Geschichten und Protokolle von Männern.* Munich: Trikont Verlag, 1976.

Autorenkollektiv. *Wir warn die stärkste der Partein: Erfahrungsberichte aus der Welt der K-Gruppen.* Berlin: Rotbuch-Verlag, 1977.

Balz, Hanno, and Jan-Henrik Friedrichs, eds. *'All we ever wanted . . .': eine Kulturgeschichte europäischer Protestbewegungen der 1980er Jahre.* Berlin: Dietz, 2012.

Bänziger, Peter-Paul, Magdalena Beljan, Franz X. Eder, and Pascal Eitler, eds. *Sexuelle Revolution? Zur Geschichte der Sexualität im deutschsprachigen Raum seit den 1960er Jahren.* Bielefeld: transcript, 2015.

Barlösius, Eva. *Naturgemäße Lebensführung: Zur Geschichte der Lebensreform um die Jahrhundertwende.* Frankfurt a.M.: Campus Verlag, 1997.

Baumann, Cordia, Stefan Gehrig, and Nicolas Büchse, eds. *Linksalternative Milieus und Neue Soziale Bewegungen in den 1970er Jahren.* Heidelberg: Universitätsverlag Winter, 2011.

Baumeister, Martin, Bruno Bonomo, and Dieter Schott, eds. *Cities Contested: Urban Politics, Heritage, and Social Movements in Italy and West Germany in the 1970s.* Frankfurt a.M.: Campus, 2017.

Baumgartner, Judith. 'Antialkoholbewegung.' In *Handbuch der deutschen Reformbewegungen, 1880–1933,* edited by Diethart Kerbs and Jürgen Reulecke, 141–154. Wuppertal: Hammer, 1998.

'Ernährungsreform.' In *Handbuch der deutschen Reformbewegungen, 1880–1933,* edited by Diethart Kerbs and Jürgen Reulecke, 115–126. Wuppertal: Hammer, 1998.

'Licht, Luft, Sonne, Bergwelt, Wandern und Baden als Sehnsuchtsziele der Lebensreformbewegung.' In *Die Lebensreform: Entwürfe zur Neugestaltung von Leben und Kunst um 1900,* edited by Kai Buchholz, Rita Lotacha, Hilke Peckmann and Klaus Wolbert, 403–406. Darmstadt: haeusser-media, 2001.

'Vegetarismus.' In *Handbuch der deutschen Reformbewegungen, 1880–1933,* edited by Diethart Kerbs and Jürgen Reulecke, 127–139. Wuppertal: Hammer, 1998.

Behnken, Imbke, and Jürgen Zinnecker. '"Hi ha ho, die Bonzen komm'n ins Klo!" Sozialpädagogische Studentenbewegung und Modernisierung Sozialer Arbeit in Deutschland.' *Westfälische Forschungen* 48 (1998): 257–282.

Béjin, André. 'Auf dem Weg zur "Allgemeinen Selbst-Verwaltung"?' In *Diktatur der Freundlichkeit: Über Bhagwan, die kommende Psychokratie und Lieferanteneingänge zum wohltätigen Wahnsinn,* edited by Initiative Sozialistisches Forum, 130–138. Freiburg: Ça-Ira-Verlag, 1984.

Benhabib, Seyla, ed. *Democracy and Difference: Contesting the Boundaries of the Political.* Princeton: Princeton University Press, 1996.

Benini, Alberto, ed. *Indianer und P 38: Italien, ein neues 68 mit anderen Waffen.* Munich: Trikont Verlag, 1978.

Bergerson, Andrew, Joachim C. Häberlen, Josie McLellan, and Barbara Stollberg-Rilinger. 'The Contours of the Political.' *German History* 33 (2015): 255–273.

'Bericht der Wohngemeinschaft aus Posemuckel.' In *Vor uns die Mühen der Ebenen: Alltagsprobleme und Perspektiven von Wohngemeinschaften*, edited by Johann August Schülein, 31–58. Giessen: Focus-Verlag, 1980.

Bernfeld, Siegfried. *Antiautoritäre Erziehung und Psychoanalyse. Ausgewählte Schriften*. 3 vols. Frankfurt a.M.: März Verlag, 1969–1971.

'Die Psychoanalyse in der Jugendbewegung.' *Imago* 5 (1919): 283–289.

'Sozialismus und Psychoanalyse.' *Der Kampf: Sozialdemokratische Monatsschrift* 19 (1926): 385–384.

Bertsch, Anja. 'Alternative (in) Bewegung: Distinktion und transnationale Vergemeinschaftung im alternativen Tourismus.' In *Das Alternative Milieu: Antibürgerlicher Lebensstil und linke Politik in der Bundesrepublik Deutschland und Europa 1968–1983*, edited by Sven Reichardt and Detlef Siegfried, 115–130. Göttingen: Wallstein, 2010.

Biess, Frank. 'Die Sensibilisierung des Subjekts: Angst und "neue Subjektivität" in den 1970er Jahren.' *WerkstattGeschichte* 49 (2008): 51–72.

Bilwet, Agentur. *Bewegungslehre: Botschaften aus einer autonomen Wirklichkeit*. Berlin: Edition ID-Archiv, 1991.

Bilz, Friedrich Eduard. *Der Zukunftsstaat: Staatseinrichtung im Jahre 2000. Neue Weltanschauung. Jedermann wird ein glückliches und sorgenfreies Dasein gesichert*. Leipzig: F. E. Bilz Verlag, 1904.

Blüher, Hans. *Die deutsche Wandervogelbewegung als erotisches Phänomen: Ein Beitrag zur Erkenntnis der sexuellen Inversion. Mit einem Vorwort von Dr. med. Magnus Hirschfeld*. Berlin: Verlag Bernhard Weise, 1912.

Böckelmann, Frank, and Herbert Nagel, eds. *Subversive Aktion: Der Sinn der Organisation ist ihr Scheitern*. Frankfurt a.M.: Verlag Neue Kritik, 1976.

Böhme, Gernot. 'Monte Verità.' In *Die Lebensreform: Entwürfe zur Neugestaltung von Leben und Kunst um 1900*, edited by Kai Buchholz, Rita Lotacha, Hilke Peckmann and Klaus Wolbert, 473–476. Darmstadt: haeusser-media, 2001.

Bohrer, Karl-Heinz. '1968: Die Phantasie an die Macht? Studentenbewegung – Walter Benjamin – Surrealismus.' In *1968 – Vom Ereignis zum Gegenstand der Geschichtswissenschaft*, edited by Ingrid Gilcher-Holtey, 288–300. Göttingen: Vandenhoeck & Ruprecht, 1995.

Boltanski, Luc, and Eve Chiapello. *The New Spirit of Capitalism*. London: Verso, 2005.

Bondy, Curt, and Jan Braden. *Jugendliche stören die Ordnung: Bericht und Stellungnahme zu den Halbstarkenkrawallen*. Munich: Juventa-Verlag, 1957.

Botsch, Gideon, and Josef Haverkamp, eds. *Jugendbewegung, Antisemitismus und rechtsradikale Politik: Vom Freideutschen Jugendtag bis zur Gegenwart*. Berlin: De Gruyter Oldenbourg, 2014.

Bourg, Julian. *From Revolution to Ethics: May 1968 and Contemporary French Thought*. Montreal: McGill-Queen's University Press, 2007.

Bracke, Maud. *Women and the Reinvention of the Political: Feminism in Italy, 1968–1983.* New York: Routledge, 2014.

Brand, Karl-Werner, Detlef Büsser, and Dieter Rucht. *Aufbruch in eine andere Gesellschaft: Neue soziale Bewegungen in der Bundesrepublik.* Frankfurt a.M.: Campus, 1983.

Brandes, Volkhard, and Bernhard Schön, eds. *Wer sind die Instandbesetzer? Selbstzeugnisse, Dokumente, Analysen.* Bensheim: päd.-extra-Buchverlag, 1981.

Brandstetter, Gabriele. 'Ausdruckstanz.' In *Handbuch der deutschen Reformbewegungen, 1880–1933,* edited by Diethart Kerbs and Jürgen Reulecke, 451–463. Wuppertal: Hammer, 1998.

Breuer, Robert. 'Schönheit als Weltanschauung.' *Deutsche Kunst und Dekoration* 23 (1908/09): 153–158.

Breyvogel, Wilfried. 'Provokation und Aufbruch der westdeutschen Jugend in den 50er und 60er Jahren: Konflikthafte Wege der Modernisierung der westdeutschen Gesellschaft in der frühen Bundesrepublik.' In *Protestierende Jugend: Jugendopposition und politischer Protest in der deutschen Nachkriegsgeschichte,* edited by Ulrich Herrmann, 445–460. Weinheim: Juventa, 2002.

Broca, Philippe de. 'Le Roi de Cœur [King of Hearts].' 102 min. France, 1966.

Bröckling, Ulrich. 'Das demokratisierte Panopticon: Subjektivierung und Kontrolle im 360° Feedback.' In *Michel Foucault: Zwischenbilanz einer Rezeption. Frankfurter Foucault-Konferenz 2001,* edited by Axel Honneth and Martin Saar, 77–93. Frankfurt a.M.: Suhrkamp, 2003.

'Regime des Selbst – Ein Forschungsprogramm.' In *Kulturen der Moderne: Soziologische Perspektiven auf die Gegenwart,* edited by Thomas Bonacker and Andreas Reckwitz, 119–139. Frankfurt a.M.: Campus, 2007.

Das unternehmerische Selbst: Soziologie einer Subjektivierungsform. Frankfurt a. M.: Suhrkamp, 2007.

Bröckling, Ulrich, and Robert Feustel, eds. *Das Politische denken: Zeitgenössische Positionen.* Bielefeld: transcript, 2010.

Brown, Timothy S. 'Music as a Weapon? "Ton Steine Scherben" and the Politics of Rock in Cold War Berlin.' *German Studies Review* 32 (2009): 1–22.

West Germany and the Global Sixties: The Antiauthoritarian Revolt, 1962–1978. Cambridge: Cambridge University Press, 2013.

Brown, Timothy S., and Lorena Anton, eds. *Between the Avant-Garde and the Everyday: Subversive Politics in Europe from 1957 to the Present.* New York: Berghahn, 2011.

Bruhn, Joachim. 'Unter den Zwischenmenschen.' In *Diktatur der Freundlichkeit: Über Bhagwan, die kommende Psychokratie und Lieferanteneingänge zum wohltätigen Wahnsinn,* edited by Initiative Sozialistisches Forum, 59–106. Freiburg: Ça-Ira-Verlag, 1984.

Bruns, Claudia. *Politik des Eros: Der Männerbund in Wissenschaft, Politik und Jugendkultur.* Cologne: Böhlau, 2008.

Brutschin, Mischa. 'Züri brännt.' In *Häuserkampf I: Wir wollen alles – Der Beginn einer Bewegung,* 175–204. Hamburg: Laika Verlag, 2012.

Buchholz, Kai. 'Lebensreform und Lebensgestaltung: Die Revision der Alltagspraxis.' In *Die Lebensreform: Entwürfe zur Neugestaltung von Leben und Kunst um 1900*, edited by Kai Buchholz, Rita Lotacha, Hilke Peckmann and Klaus Wolbert, 363–368. Darmstadt: haeusser-media, 2001.

Buchholz, Kai, Rita Lotacha, Hilke Peckmann, and Klaus Wolbert, eds. *Die Lebensreform: Entwürfe zur Neugestaltung von Leben und Kunst um 1900*. 2 vols. Darmstadt: haeusser-media, 2001.

Buchholz, Kai, and Renate Ulmer. 'Reform des Wohnens.' In *Die Lebensreform: Entwürfe zur Neugestaltung von Leben und Kunst um 1900*, edited by Kai Buchholz, Rita Lotacha, Hilke Peckmann and Klaus Wolbert, 547–550. Darmstadt: haeusser-media, 2001.

Bührmann, Andrea. *Das authentische Geschlecht: Die Sexualitätsdebatte der neuen Frauenbewegung und die Foucaultsche Machtanalyse*. Münster: Westfälisches Dampfboot, 1995.

Bull, Anna, Hanna Diamond, and Rosalind Marsh, eds. *Feminisms and Women's Movements in Contemporary Europe*. Houndmills: Macmillan, 2000.

Burchell, Graham, Colin Gordon, and Peter Miller, eds. *The Foucault Effect: Studies in Governmentality*. Chicago: University of Chicago Press, 1991.

Burian, Wilhelm. *Sexualität, Natur, Gesellschaft*. Freiburg: Ça-Ira-Verlag, 1985.

Büro für anti-utopische Forschungen. *Betonzeit: Ein Pamphlet gegen die Stadtlandschaft und ihre Verbesserungen*. Cologne: Eigenverlag, 1980.

Butler, Judith, and Joan W. Scott, eds. *Feminists Theorize the Political*. New York, London: Routledge, 1992.

Castaneda, Carlos. *Eine andere Wirklichkeit: neue Gespräche mit Don Juan*. Frankfurt a.M.: S. Fischer, 1973.

Die Lehren des Don Juan: ein Yaqui-Weg des Wissens. Frankfurt a.M.: S. Fischer, 1973.

Reise nach Ixtlan: die Lehre des Don Juan. Frankfurt a.M.: S. Fischer, 1975.

Chiapello, Eve. 'Capitalism and Its Criticisms.' In *New Spirits of Capitalism? Crises, Justifications, and Dynamics*, edited by Paul du Gay and Glenn Morgan, 60–81. Oxford: Oxford University Press, 2012.

Cluet, Marc, and Catherine Repussard, eds. *'Lebensreform': Die soziale Dynamik der politischen Ohnmacht*. Tübingen: Francke Verlag, 2013.

Colvin, Sarah. *Ulrike Meinhof and West German Terrorism: Language, Violence, and Identity*. Rochester, NY: Camden House, 2009.

Constant. 'Another City for Another Life.' In *Situationist International Anthology*, edited by Ken Knabb, 71–73. Berkeley: Bureau of Public Secrets, 1981 (1959).

Conti, Christoph. *Abschied vom Bürgertum: Alternative Bewegungen in Deutschland von 1890 bis heute*. Reinbek bei Hamburg: Rowohlt, 1984.

Conze, Eckart. 'Sicherheit als Kultur: Überlegungen zu einer "modernen Politikgeschichte" der Bundesrepublik Deutschland.' *Vierteljahrshefte für Zeitgeschichte* 53 (2005): 357–380.

Die Suche nach Sicherheit: Eine Geschichte der Bundesrepublik Deutschland von 1949 bis in die Gegenwart. Munich: Siedler, 2009.

Cyprian, Gudrun. *Sozialisation in Wohngemeinschaften: Eine empirische Untersuchung ihrer strukturellen Bedingungen.* Stuttgart: Ferdinand Enke Verlag, 1978.

D'Angelo, Ed. 'Anarchism and the Beats.' In *The Philosophy of the Beats*, edited by Sharin N. Elkholy, 227–242. Lexington, KY: University Press of Kentucky, 2012.

Damme, Rudi H. P. *Zur Stabilität von Wohngruppen: Ein Modell aktivierender Sozialforschung zur Theorie und Praxis des kollektiven Alltags.* Bonn: Projektbereich 'Hochschul- und Studentische Sozialpolitik', 1980.

Davis, Belinda. 'The City as Theater of Protest: West Berlin and West Germany, 1962–1983.' In *The Spaces of the Modern City: Imaginaries, Politics and Everyday Life*, edited by Gyan Prakash and Kevin M. Kruse, 247–275. Princeton: Princeton University Press, 2008.

'The Personal is Political: Gender, Politics, and Political Activism in Modern German History.' In *Gendering Modern German History. Rewriting Historiography*, edited by Karen Hagemann and Jean H. Quataert, 107–127. New York: Berghahn, 2007.

'What's Left? Popular and Democratic Political Participation in Postwar Europe.' *American Historical Review* 113 (2008): 363–390.

Davis, Belinda, Wilfried Mausbach, Martin Klimke, and Carla MacDougall, eds. *Changing the World, Changing Oneself: Political Protest and Collective Identities in West Germany and the U.S. in the 1960s and 1970s.* New York: Berghahn, 2010.

De Vito, Christian G. 'Liminoids, Hegemony and Transfers in the Liminal Experiences in Italian Psychiatry, 1960s–1980s.' In *Ausnahmezustände: Entgrenzungen und Regulierungen in Europa während des Kalten Krieges*, edited by Dirk Schumann and Cornelia Rauh, 236–252. Göttingen: Wallstein, 2015.

Debord, Guy. 'Perspectives for Conscious Changes in Everyday Life.' In *Situationist International Anthology*, edited by Ken Knabb, 90–99. Berkeley: Bureau of Public Secrets, 1981 (1961).

'Situationist Theses on Traffic.' In *Situationist International Anthology*, edited by Ken Knabb, 69–70. Berkeley: Bureau of Public Secrets, 1981 (1959).

The Society of the Spectacle. New York: Zone Books, 1995.

'Theses on Cultural Revolution.' In *Situationist International Anthology*, edited by Ken Knabb, 53–54. Berkeley: Bureau of Public Secrets, 1981 (1958).

Dehmlow, Raimund. 'Gefährten: Otto Gross und Franz Jung.' In *Von geschlechtlicher Not zur sozialen Katastrophe*, by Otto Gross, 181–190. Hamburg: Edition Nautilus, 2000.

Deleuze, Gilles, and Félix Guattari. *Rhizome.* Berlin: Merve, 1977.

A Thousand Plateaus, translated by Brian Massumi. Minneapolis: University of Minnesota Press, 1987.

Dieter. *Was wird aus mir werden? Ich hoffe ein Mensch. Ein Männertagebuch.* Berlin (West): Parallel Verlag, 1978.

Dietz, Bernhard, Andreas Rödder, and Christopher Neumaier, eds. *Gab es den Wertewandel? Neue Forschungen zum gesellschaftlich-kulturellen Wandel seit den 1960er Jahren.* Munich: Oldenbourg, 2014.

Dirke, Sabine von. *All Power to the Imagination! The West German Counterculture from the Student Movement to the Greens.* Lincoln, NE: University of Nebraska Press, 1997.

Doering-Manteuffel, Anselm, and Lutz Raphael. *Nach dem Boom: Perspektiven auf die Zeitgeschichte seit 1970,* 2nd edn. Göttingen: Vandenhoeck & Ruprecht, 2008.

Doering-Manteuffel, Anselm, Lutz Raphael, and Thomas Schlemmer, eds. *Vorgeschichte der Gegenwart: Dimensionen des Strukturbruchs nach dem Boom.* Göttingen: Vandenhoeck & Ruprecht, 2016.

Donauer, Sabine. 'Job Satisfaction statt Arbeitszufriedenheit: Gefühlswissen im arbeitswissenschaftlichen Diskurs der 1970er Jahre.' In *Zeitgeschichte des Selbst: Therapeutisierung – Politisierung – Emotionalisierung,* edited by Pascal Eitler and Jens Elberfeld, 343–372. Bielefeld: transcript, 2015.

du Gay, Paul, and Glenn Morgan, eds. *New Spirits of Capitalism? Crises, Justifications, and Dynamics.* Oxford: Oxford University Press, 2013.

Duerr, Hans Peter. *Traumzeit: Über die Grenze zwischen Wildnis und Zivilisation.* Frankfurt a.M.: Syndikat, 1978.

Duhm, Dieter. *Angst im Kapitalismus: Zweiter Versuch der gesellschaftlichen Begründung zwischenmenschlicher Angst in der kapitalistischen Warengesellschaft.* Lampertheim: Kübler, 1973.

Duivenvoorden, Eric. *Een voet tussen de deur: Geschiedenis van de kraakbeweging, 1964–1999.* Amsterdam: Arbeiderspers, 2000.

Echaurren, Pablo. *La casa del desiderio: '77: indiani metropolitani e altri strani.* Lecce: Manni Editore, 2005.

Eckert, Rainer, Etienne François, Ingrid Gilcher-Holtey, Christoph Kleßmann, and Krzysztof Ruchniewicz. 'Die 1970er-Jahre in Geschichte und Gegenwart.' *Zeithistorische Forschungen* 3 (2006): 422–438.

Edwards, Phil. *More Work! Less Pay! Rebellion and Repression in Italy, 1972–77.* Manchester, UK: Manchester University Press, 2009.

Ege, Moritz. 'Becoming-Black: Patterns and Politics of West-German "Afro-Americanophilia" in the Late 1960s.' *PORTAL Journal of Multidisciplinary International Studies* 12 (2015).

Schwarz werden: 'Afroamerikanophilie' in den 1960er und 1970er Jahren. Bielefeld: transcript, 2007.

Eitler, Pascal. '"Alternative" Religion: Subjektivierungspraktiken und Politisierungsstrategien im "New Age" (Westdeutschland 1970–1990).' In *Das Alternative Milieu: Antibürgerlicher Lebensstil und linke Politik in der Bundesrepublik Deutschland und Europa, 1968–1983,* edited by Sven Reichardt and Detlef Siegfried, 335–352. Göttingen: Wallstein, 2010.

'Privatisierung und Subjektivierung: Religiöse Selbstverhältnisse im "New Age".' In *Privatisierung: Idee und Praxis seit den 1970er Jahren,* edited by Norbert Frei and Dietmar Süß, 140–156. Göttingen: Wallstein, 2012.

'"Selbstheilung": Zur Somatisierung und Sakralisierung von Selbstverhältnissen im New Age (Westdeutschland 1970–1990).' In *Das beratene Selbst: Zur Genealogie der Therapeutisierung in den 'langen' Siebzigern*, edited by Sabine Maasen, Jens Elberfeld, Pascal Eitler and Maik Tändler, 161–182. Bielefeld: transcript, 2011.

'Die "sexuelle Revolution" – Körperpolitik um 1968.' In *1968: Handbuch zur Kultur- und Mediengeschichte der Studentenbewegung*, edited by Martin Klimke and Joachim Scharloth, 235–246. Stuttgart: Metzler, 2007.

Eitler, Pascal, and Jens Elberfeld. 'Von der Gesellschaftsgeschichte zur Zeitgeschichte des Selbst – und zurück.' In *Zeitgeschichte des Selbst: Therapeutisierung – Politisierung – Emotionalisierung*, edited by Pascal Eitler and Jens Elberfeld, 7–30. Bielefeld: transcript, 2015.

eds. *Zeitgeschichte des Selbst: Therapeutisierung – Politisierung – Emotionalisierung*. Bielefeld: transcript, 2015.

Eitler, Pascal, and Monique Scheer. '"Emotionengeschichte als Körpergeschichte: Eine heuristische Perspektive auf religiöse Konversionen im 19. und 20. Jahrhundert.' *Geschichte und Gesellschaft* 35 (2009): 282–313.

Elberfeld, Jens. 'Befreiung des Subjekts, Management des Selbst: Therapeutisierungsprozesse im deutschsprachigen Raum seit den 1960er Jahren.' In *Zeitgeschichte des Selbst: Therapeutisierung – Politisierung – Emotionalisierung*, edited by Pascal Eitler and Jens Elberfeld, 49–84. Bielefeld: transcript, 2015.

'Subjekt/Beziehung: Patriarchat – Partnerschaft – Projekt. Psychowissen und Normalisierungspraktiken im Diskurs der Paartherapie (BRD 1960–1990).' In *Das Selbst zwischen Anpassung und Befreiung: Psychowissen und Politik im 20. Jahrhundert*, edited by Uffa Jensen and Maik Tändler, 85–114. Göttingen: Wallstein, 2012.

'Von der Sünde zur Selbstbestimmung: Zum Diskurs "kindlicher Sexualität" (Bundesrepublik Deutschland 1960–1990).' In *Sexuelle Revolution? Zur Geschichte der Sexualität im deutschsprachigen Raum seit den 1960er Jahren*, edited by Peter-Paul Bänziger, Magdalena Beljan, Franz X. Eder and Pascal Eitler, 247–284. Bielefeld: transcript, 2015.

Elberfeld, Jens, and Marcus Otto, eds. *Das schöne Selbst: Zur Genealogie des modernen Subjekts zwischen Ethik und Ästhetik*. Bielefeld: transcript, 2009.

Eley, Geoff. *Forging Democracy: The History of the Left in Europe, 1850–2000*. Oxford: Oxford University Press, 2002.

'Wie denken wir über die Politik? Alltagsgeschichte und die Kategorie des Politischen.' In *Alltagskultur, Subjektivität und Geschichte: Zur Theorie und Praxis von Alltagsgeschichte*, edited by Berliner Geschichtswerkstatt, 17–36. Münster: Westphälisches Dampfboot, 1994.

Elkholy, Sharin N. 'Introduction.' In *The Philosophy of the Beats*, edited by Sharin N. Elkholy, 1–6. Lexington, KY: University Press of Kentucky, 2012.

Ellwanger, Karen, and Elisabeth Meyer-Renschhause. 'Kleidungsreform.' In *Handbuch der deutschen Reformbewegungen, 1880–1933*, edited by Diethart Kerbs and Jürgen Reulecke, 87–102. Wuppertal: Hammer, 1998.

Ende, Michael. *The Grey Gentlemen*, translated by Frances Lobb. London & Toronto: Burke Books, 1974.

Eustace, Nicole, Eugenia Lean, Julie Livingston, Jan Plamper, William M. Reddy, and Barbara H. Rosenwein. '*AHR* Conversation: The Historical Study of Emotions.' *American Historical Review* 117 (2012): 1487–1531.

Faulenbach, Bernd. 'Die Siebziger Jahre – ein sozialdemokratisches Jahrzehnt?' *Archiv für Sozialgeschichte* 44 (2004): 1–37.

Feenberg, Andrew, and Jim Freedman. *When Poetry Ruled the Streets: The French May Events of 1968*. Albany, NY: State University of New York Press, 2001.

Fehrmann, Helma, and Peter Weismann. *Und plötzlich willste mehr: Die Geschichte von Paul und Paulas erster Liebe*. Munich: Weismann, 1979.

Felsch, Philipp. *Der lange Sommer der Theorie: Geschichte einer Revolte*. Munich: Beck, 2015.

'Der Leser als Partisan.' *Zeitschrift für Ideengeschichte* 6 (2012): 35–49.

'Merves Lachen.' *Zeitschrift für Ideengeschichte* 2 (2008): 11–30.

Fischer, Lothar. 'Getanzte Körperbefreiung.' In *'Wir sind nackt und nennen uns Du': Von Lichtfreunden und Sonnenkämpfern. Eine Geschichte der Freikörperkultur*, edited by Michael Andritzky and Thomas Rautenberg, 106–123. Giessen: Anabas, 1989.

Fleischmann, Peter. 'Herbst der Gammler.' 67 min. Germany, 1967.

Föllmer, Moritz. 'Cities of Choice: Elective Affinities and the Transformation of Western European Urbanity from the mid-1950s to the early 1980s.' *Contemporary European History* 24 (2015): 577–596.

'Forum: 1977, The German Autumn.' *German History* 25 (2007): 401–421.

Foucault, Michel. 'The Subject and Power.' *Critical Inquiry* 8 (1982): 777–795.

'Technologies of the Self.' In *Technologies of the Self: A Seminar with Michel Foucault*, edited by Luther H. Martin, Huck Gutman and Patrick H. Hutton, 16–49. Amherst, MA: University of Massachusetts Press, 1988.

Frei, Norbert. *1968: Jugendrevolte und globaler Protest*. Munich: Deutscher Taschenbuchverlag, 2008.

Frese, Matthias, Julia Paulus, and Karl Teppe, eds. *Demokratisierung und gesellschaftlicher Aufbruch: Die sechziger Jahre als Wendezeit der Bundesrepublik*. Paderborn: Ferdinand Schöningh, 2003.

Frevert, Ute, and Heinz-Gerhard Haupt, eds. *Neue Politikgeschichte: Perspektiven einer historischen Politikforschung*. Frankfurt a.M.: Campus Verlag, 2005.

Friedrichs, Jan-Henrik. 'Revolt or Transgression? Squatted Houses and Meeting Places of the Heroin Scene in Zurich and Berlin as Spaces of Transgressive Youth.' In *A European Youth Revolt: European Perspectives on Youth Protest and Social Movements in the 1980s*, edited by Bart van der Steen and Knud Andresen, 81–96. Basingstoke, UK: Palgrave Macmillan, 2016.

Fromm, Erich, D. T. Suzuki, and Richard De Martino. *Zen Buddhism & Psychoanalysis*. New York: Harper, 1960.

Fulda, Leopold. *Im Lichtkleid! Stimmen für und gegen das gemeinsame Nacktbaden von Jungend und Mädchen im Familien- und Freundeskreise*. Rudolstadt: Verlag Gesundes Leben, 1924.

Fürmetz, Gerhard. 'Die "Schwabinger Krawalle" von 1962: Vom Ereignis zum Forschungsgegenstand.' In *'Schwabinger Krawalle': Protest, Polizei und Öffentlichkeit zu Beginn der 60er Jahre*, edited by Gerhard Fürmetz, 9–23. Essen: Klartext, 2006.

ed. *'Schwabinger Krawalle': Protest, Polizei und Öffentlichkeit zu Beginn der 60er Jahre*. Essen: Klartext, 2006.

Gammerl, Benno. 'Emotional Styles: Concepts and Challenges.' *Rethinking History* 16 (2012): 161–175.

Gassert, Philipp. 'Narratives of Democratization: 1968 in Postwar Europe.' In *1968 in Europe: A History of Protest and Activism, 1956–1977*, edited by Martin Klimke and Joachim Scharloth, 307–324. New York: Palgrave Macmillan, 2008.

Gehrig, Sebastian. 'Sympathizing Subcultures? The Milieus of West German Terrorism.' In *Between Prague Spring and French May: Opposition and Revolt in Europe, 1960–1980*, edited by Martin Klimke, Jacco Pekelder and Joachim Scharloth. New York: Berghahn, 2011.

Geisthövel, Alexa. 'Anpassung: Disco und Jugendbeobachtung in Westdeutschland, 1975–1981.' In *Zeitgeschichte des Selbst: Therapeutisierung – Politisierung – Emotionalisierung*, edited by Pascal Eitler and Jens Elberfeld, 239–260. Bielefeld: transcript, 2015.

Gilcher-Holtey, Ingrid, ed. *1968 – Vom Ereignis zum Gegenstand der Geschichtswissenschaft, Geschichte und Gesellschaft, Sonderheft*. Göttingen: Vandenhoeck & Ruprecht, 1998.

'Die Phantasie an die Macht': Der Mai 68 in Frankreich. Frankfurt a.M.: Suhrkamp, 1995.

Ginsberg, Allen. *Howl, and Other Poems*. San Francisco: City Lights Pocket Bookshop, 1956.

Golowin, Sergius. *Hexen, Hippies, Rosenkreuzer: 500 Jahre magische Morgenlandfahrt*. Hamburg: Merlin-Verlag, 1977.

Gould, Deborah. *Moving Politics: Emotion and ACT UP's Fight against AIDS*. Chicago: University of Chicago Press, 2009.

Graf, Rüdiger, and Kim Christian Priemel. 'Zeitgeschichte in der Welt der Sozialwissenschaften: Legitimität und Originalität einer Disziplin.' *Vierteljahrshefte für Zeitgeschichte* 59 (2011): 479–508.

Grauwacke, A. G. *Autonome in Bewegung: Aus den ersten 23 Jahren*. Berlin: Assozation A, 2003.

Gross, Otto. 'Die kommunistische Grundidee in der Paradiessymbolik.' In *Von geschlechtlicher Not zur sozialen Katastrophe*, by Otto Gross, 90–105. Hamburg: Edition Nautilus, 2000 [1913].

'Ludwig Rabiners "Psychoanalyse".' In *Von geschlechtlicher Not zur sozialen Katastrophe*, by Otto Gross, 62–63. Hamburg: Edition Nautilus, 2000 [1913].

Von geschlechtlicher Not zur sozialen Katastrophe. Hamburg: Edition Nautilus, 2000.

'Zur neuerlichen Vorarbeit: vom Unterricht.' In *Von geschlechtlicher Not zur sozialen Katastrophe*, by Otto Gross, 170–176. Hamburg: Edition Nautilus, 2000 [1913].

'Zur Überwindung der kulturellen Krise.' In *Von geschlechtlicher Not zur sozialen Katastrophe*, by Otto Gross, 59–62. Hamburg: Edition Nautilus, 2000 [1913].

Grossmann, Atina. *Reforming Sex: The German Movement for Birth Control and Abortion Reform, 1920–1950*. Oxford: Oxford University Press, 1995.

Grotum, Thomas. *Die Halbstarken: Zur Geschichte einer Jugendkultur der 50er Jahre*. Frankfurt a.M.: Campus Verlag, 1994.

Häberlen, Joachim C. 'The Contemporary Self in German History (Review Article).' *Contemporary European History* 28 (2018). Forthcoming.

'Feeling Like a Child: Visions and Practices of Sexuality in the West German Alternative Left during the Long 1970s.' *Journal for the History of Sexuality* 25 (2016): 219–245.

'Ingrid's Boredom.' In *Learning How to Feel: Children's Literature and Emotional Socialization, 1870–1970*, by Ute Frevert, Pascal Eitler, Stephanie Olsen et al., 228–244. Oxford: Oxford University Press, 2014.

'Sekunden der Freiheit: Zum Verhältnis von Gefühlen, Macht und Zeit in Ausnahmesituationen am Beispiel der Revolte 1980/81 in Berlin.' In *Ausnahmezustände: Entgrenzungen und Regulierungen in Europa während des Kalten Krieges*, edited by Dirk Schumann and Cornelia Rauh, 195–213. Göttingen: Wallstein, 2015.

Häberlen, Joachim C., and Jake Smith. 'Struggling for Feelings: The Politics of Emotions in the Radical New Left in West Germany, c. 1968–84.' *Contemporary European History* 23 (2014): 615–637.

Häberlen, Joachim C., and Russell A. Spinney. 'Introduction.' *Contemporary European History* 23 (2014): 489–503.

Häberlen, Joachim C., and Maik Tändler. 'Spaces for Feeling Differently: Emotional Experiments in the Alternative Left in West Germany during the 1970s.' *Emotion, Space and Society* 25 (2017): 103–110.

Hanisch, Carol. 'The Personal is Political.' In *Notes from the Second Year: Women's Liberation*, edited by Shulamit Firestone and Anne Koedt, 76–78. New York: Radical Feminism, 1970.

Hanshew, Karrin. '"Sympathy for the Devil?" The West German Left and the Challenge of Terrorism.' *Contemporary European History* 21 (2012): 511–532.

Terror and Democracy in West Germany. Cambridge: Cambridge University Press, 2012.

Haumann, Sebastian. '"Indiani Metropolitani" and "Stadtindianer": Representing Autonomy in Italy and West-Germany.' In *Between Prague Spring and French May: Opposition and Revolt in Europe, 1960–1980*, edited by Martin Klimke, Jacco Pekelder and Joachim Scharloth, 141–153. New York: Berghahn, 2011.

'Schade, daß Beton nicht brennt...' Planung, Partizipation und Protest in Philadelphia und Köln, 1940–1990. Stuttgart: Franz Steiner Verlag, 2011.

Haunss, Sebastian. *Identität in Bewegung: Prozesse kollektiver Identität bei den Autonomen und in der Schwulenbewegung.* Wiesbaden: Verlag für Sozialwissenschaften, 2004.

Häuserkampf I: Wir wollen alles – Der Beginn einer Bewegung. Hamburg: Laika Verlag, 2012.

Hecken, Thomas, and Agata Grzenia. 'Situationism.' In *1968 in Europe: A History of Protest and Activism, 1956–1977*, edited by Martin Klimke and Joachim Scharloth, 23–32. New York: Palgrave Macmillan, 2008.

Hegemann, Klaus. *Allen Ginsberg: Zeitkritik und politische Aktivitäten.* Baden-Baden: Nomos-Verlagsgesellschaft, 2000.

Hekma, Gert, and Alain Giami, eds. *Sexual Revolutions.* Basingstoke, UK: Palgrave Macmillan, 2014.

Hemler, Stefan. 'Anstoß für die Studentenbewegung? Warum die "Schwabinger Krawalle" wenig mit "1968" zu tun haben.' In *'Schwabinger Krawalle': Protest, Polizei und Öffentlichkeit zu Beginn der 60er Jahre*, edited by Gerhard Fürmetz, 151–172. Essen: Klartext, 2006.

'Aufbegehren einer Jugendszene: Protestbeteiligte, Verlauf und Aktionsmuster bei den "Schwabinger Krawallen".' In *'Schwabinger Krawalle': Protest, Polizei und Öffentlichkeit zu Beginn der 60er Jahre*, edited by Gerhard Fürmetz, 25–57. Essen: Klartext, 2006.

Herbert, Ulrich, ed. *Wandlungsprozesse in Westdeutschland: Belastung, Integration, Liberalisierung 1945–1980.* Göttingen: Wallstein, 2002.

Herrenknecht, Albrecht, Wolfgang Hätscher, and Stefan Koospal. *Träume, Hoffnungen, Kämpfe... Ein Lesebuch zur Jugendzentrumsbewegung.* Frankfurt a.M.: Verlag Jugend und Politik, 1977.

Herzog, Dagmar. *Sex after Fascism: Memory and Morality in Twentieth-Century Germany.* Princeton: Princeton University Press, 2005.

Hesse, Hermann. *Der Steppenwolf.* Berlin: S. Fischer, 1927.

Hink, Gunnar. *Wir waren wie Maschinen: Die bundesdeutsche Linke der 70er-Jahre.* Berlin: Rotbuch Verlag, 2012.

Hockerts, Hans Günther. 'Zeitgeschichte in Deutschland: Begriff, Methoden, Themenfelder.' *Historisches Jahrbuch* 113 (1993): 98–127.

Hof, Gérard. *Hunde wollt ihr ewig sterben!?* Munich: Trinkont Verlag, 1976.

Je ne serai plus psychiatre. Paris: Stock, 1976.

Hofmann-Oedenkoven, Ida. *Monte Verità: Wahrheit ohne Dichtung.* Lorsch: Karl Röhm, 1906.

Hohmann, Joachim S., ed. *Pädophilie Heute: Berichte, Meinungen und Interviews zur sexuellen Befreiung des Kindes.* Frankfurt a.M.: Foerster Verlag, 1980.

Holladay, Hilary, and Robert Holton, eds. What's Your Road, Man? Critical Essays on Jack Kerouac's *On the Road*. Carbondale, IL: Southern Illinois University Press, 2009.

Hollstein, Walter. 'Autonome Lebensformen: Über die transbürgerliche Perspektive der Jugendbewegung.' In *Aussteigen oder rebellieren: Jugendliche gegen Staat und Gesellschaft*, edited by Michael Haller, 197–216. Reinbek bei Hamburg: Rowohlt, 1981.

Holm, Andrej. *Wir bleiben alle! Gentrifizierung – Städtische Konflikte um Aufwertung und Verdrängung*. Münster: Unrast Verlag, 2010.

Holm, Andrej, and Armin Kuhn. 'Squatting and Urban Renewal: The Interaction of Squatter Movements and Strategies of Urban Restructuring in Berlin.' *International Journal of Urban and Regional Research* 35 (2011): 644–658.

Horn, Gerd-Rainer. *The Spirit of '68: Rebellion in Western Europe and North America, 1956–1976*. Oxford: Oxford University Press, 2007.

Huber, Margaretha. *Rätsel: Ich schaue in den geheimnisvollen Raum eines verschollenen Denkens, dessen Tür die Romantik einen Spalt weit geöffnet hat*. Frankurt a.M.: Verlag Roter Stern, 1978.

Hurwitz, Emanuel. *Otto Gross: Paradies-Sucher zwischen Freud und Jung*. Frankfurt a.M.: Suhrkam, 1979.

Illouz, Eva. *Consuming the Romantic Utopia: Love and the Cultural Contradictions of Capitalism*. Berkeley: University of California Press, 1997.

Inglehart, Ronald. *The Silent Revolution: Changing Values and Political Styles among Western Publics*. Princeton: Princeton University Press, 1977.

Jackson, Julian. *The Popular Front in France: Defending Democracy, 1934–38*. Cambridge: Cambridge University Press, 1988.

Jander, Martin. 'Isolation oder Isolationsfolter: Die Auseinandersetzung um die Haftbedingungen der RAF-Häftlinge.' In *Der 'Deutsche Herbst' und die RAF in Politik, Medien und Kunst: nationale und internationale Perspektiven*, edited by Nicole Colin, Beatrice de Graaf, Jacco Pekelder and Joachim Umlauf, 141–155. Bielefeld: transcript, 2008.

Jarausch, Konrad H., ed. *Das Ende der Zuversicht? Die siebziger Jahre als Geschichte*. Göttingen: Vandenhoeck & Ruprecht, 2008.

'Verkannter Strukturwandel: Die siebziger Jahre als Vorgeschichte der Probleme der Gegenwart.' In *Das Ende der Zuversicht? Die siebziger Jahre als Geschichte*, edited by Konrad H. Jarausch, 9–28. Göttingen: Vandenhoeck & Ruprecht, 2008.

Jay, Martin. *The Dialectical Imagination: A History of the Frankfurt School and the Institute of Social Research, 1923–1950*. Berkley, Los Angeles: University of California Press, 1996.

Jefferies, Matthew. 'Lebensreform: A Middle-Class Antidote to Wilhelminism?' In *Wilhelminism and Its Legacies: German Modernities, Imperialism, and the Meanings of Reform, 1890–1930*, edited by Geoff Eley and James Retallack, 91–106. New York: Berghahn, 2003.

Jensen, Uffa. 'The Lure of Authenticity: Emotions and Generation in the German Youth Movement of the Early 20th Century.' In *History by Generations: Generational Dynamics in Modern History*, edited by Harmut Berghoff, Uffa Jensen, Christina Lubinski and Bernd Weisbrod, 109–124. Göttingen: Wallstein, 2013.

'Die Utopie der Authentizität und ihre Grenzen: Die Politisierung der Psychoanalyse im frühen 20. Jahrhundert.' In *Das Selbst zwischen*

Anpassung und Befreiung: Psychowissen und Politik im 20. Jahrhundert, edited by Uffa Jensen and Maik Tändler, 39–59. Göttingen: Wallstein, 2012.

Jensen, Uffa, and Maik Tändler, eds. *Das Selbst zwischen Anpassung und Befreiung: Psychowissen und Politik im 20. Jahrhundert.* Göttingen: Wallstein, 2012.

Kadritzke, Till. 'Bewegte Männer. Men's Liberation und Autonome Männergruppen in den USA und Deutschland, 1970–1995.' In *Feminismus in historischer Perspektive. Eine Reaktualisierung,* edited by Feminismus Seminar, 221–251. Bielefeld: transcript, 2014.

Katsiaficas, Georgy. *The Subversion of Politics: European Autonomous Social Movements and the Decolonization of Everyday Life.* Oakland: AK Press, 2006.

Kauders, Anthony D. 'Drives in Dispute: The West German Student Movement, Psychoanalysis, and the Search for a New Emotional Order, 1967–1971.' *Central European History* 44 (2011): 711–731.

Kempton, Richard. *Provo: Amsterdam's Anarchist Revolt.* Brooklyn: Autonomedia, 2007.

Kerbs, Diethart. 'Die Welt im Jahre 2000: Der Prophet von Oberlößnitz und die Gesellschafts-Utopien der Lebensreform.' In *Die Lebensreform: Entwürfe zur Neugestaltung von Leben und Kunst um 1900,* edited by Kai Buchholz, Rita Lotacha, Hilke Peckmann and Klaus Wolbert, 61–66. Darmstadt: haeusser-media, 2001.

Kerbs, Diethart, and Jürgen Reulecke, eds. *Handbuch der deutschen Reformbewegungen, 1880–1933.* Wuppertal: Hammer, 1998.

Kerouac, Jack. *On the Road.* London: Penguin, 1991.

Kersting, Franz-Werner. 'Juvenile Left-wing Radicalism, Fringe Groups, and Anti-psychiatry in West Germany.' In *Between Marx and Coca-Cola: Youth Cultures in Changing European Societies, 1960–1980,* edited by Axel Schildt and Detlef Siegfried, 353–375. New York: Berghahn, 2006.

Kinder- und Jugendtheater Rote Grütze. *Darüber spricht man nicht: Ein Spiel zur Sexualaufklärung.* Munich: Weismann, 1973.

Kindt, Werner, ed. *Grundschriften der deutschen Jugendbewegung.* Düsseldorf, Cologne: Eugen Diederichs Verlag, 1963.

Klimke, Martin. *The Other Alliance: Student Protest in West Germany and the United States in the Global Sixties.* Princeton: Princeton University Press, 2010.

Klimke, Martin, Jacco Pekelder, and Joachim Scharloth, eds. *Between Prague Spring and French May: Opposition and Revolt in Europe, 1960–1980.* New York: Berghahn, 2011.

Klimke, Martin, and Joachim Scharloth, eds. *1968 in Europe: A History of Protest and Activism, 1956–1977.* New York: Palgrave Macmillan, 2008.

Klönne, Arno. 'Eine deutsche Bewegung, politisch zweideutig.' In *Die Lebensreform: Entwürfe zur Neugestaltung von Leben und Kunst um 1900,* edited by Kai Buchholz, Rita Lotacha, Hilke Peckmann and Klaus Wolbert, 31–32. Darmstadt: haeusser-media, 2001.

Klose-Lewerentz, Cornelia. 'Der "ideale Körper" und seine "Herstellung": Körperdiskurse der Lebensreformbewegung zwischen Utopie und Normativität.' In *'Lebensreform': Die soziale Dynamik der politischen Ohnmacht*, edited by Marc Cluet and Catherine Repussard, 147–159. Tübingen: Francke Verlag, 2013.

Knabb, Ken, ed. *Situationist International Anthology*. Berkeley: Bureau of Public Secrets, 1981.

Koch, Adolf. *Wir sind nackt und nennen uns Du! Bunte Bilder aus der Freikörperkulturbewegung*. Leipzig: Ernst Oldenburg Verlag, 1932.

Koenen, Gerd. *Das rote Jahrzehnt: Unsere kleine deutsche Kulturrevolution 1967–1977*. Cologne: Kiepenheuer & Witsch, 2001.

Koerber, Rolf. 'Freikörperkultur.' In *Handbuch der deutschen Reformbewegungen, 1880–1933*, edited by Diethart Kerbs and Jürgen Reulecke, 103–114. Wuppertal: Hammer, 1998.

Körper, Netzwerk, ed. *What Can a Body Do? Praktiken und Figurationen des Körpers in den Kulturwissenschaften*. Frankfurt a.M.: Campus Verlag, 2012.

Kosel, Margret. *Gammler, Beatniks, Provos: Die schleichende Revolution*. Frankfurt a.M.: Verlag Bärmeier & Nickel, 1967.

Krabbe, Wolfgang R. *Gesellschaftsveränderung durch Lebensreform: Strukturmerkmale einer sozialreformerischen Bewegung im Deutschland der Industrialisierungsperiode*. Göttingen: Vandenhoeck & Ruprecht, 1974.

Kraushaar, Wolfgang. *1968 als Mythos, Chiffre und Zäsur*. Hamburg: Hamburger Edition, 2000.

——— 'Thesen zum Verhältnis von Alternativ- und Fluchtbewegung: Am Beispiel der frankfurter scene.' In *Autonomie oder Ghetto? Kontroversen über die Alternativbewegung*, edited by Wolfgang Kraushaar, 8–67. Frankfurt a.M.: Verlag Neue Kritik, 1978.

——— 'Time Is on My Side: Die Beat-Ära.' In *Schock und Schöpfung. Jugendästhetik im 20. Jahrhundert*, edited by Willi Bucher and Klaus Pohl, 214–223. Darmstadt: Luchterhand, 1986.

Krechel, Ursula. *Selbsterfahrung und Fremdbestimmung: Bericht aus der neuen Frauenbewegung*. Darmstadt, Neuwied: Luchterhand, 1975.

Kriesi, Hanspeter. *Die Züricher Bewegung: Bilder, Interaktionen, Zusammenhänge*. Frankfurt a.M.: Campus Verlag, 1984.

Kuiper, Yme. 'On Monte Verità: Myth and Modernity in the Lebensreform Movement.' In *Myths, Martyrs, and Modernity: Studies in the History of Religions in Honour of Jan N. Bremmer*, edited by Jitse Dijkstra, Justin Kroesen and Yme Kuiper, 629–650. Leiden: Brill, 2010.

Kurme, Sebastian. *Halbstarke: Jugendprotest in den 1950er Jahren in Deutschland und den USA*. Frankfurt a.M.: Campus Verlag, 2006.

Lecorte, Tomas. *Wir tanzen bis zum Ende: die Geschichte eines Autonomen*. Hamburg: Galgenberg, 1992.

Lee, Mia. 'Gruppe Spur: Art as a Revolutionary Medium during the Cold War.' In *Between the Avant-Garde and the Everyday: Subversive Politics in Europe from 1957 to the Present*, edited by Timothy S. Brown and Lorena Anton. New York: Berghahn, 2011.

Lefebvre, Henri. *The Urban Revolution*. Minneapolis: University of Minnesota Press, 2003.

Leggewie, Claus. '1968 ist Geschichte.' *Aus Politik und Zeitgescichte B* 22–23 (2001): 3–6.

Lemke, Thomas. *Eine Kritik der politischen Vernunft: Foucaults Analyse der modernen Gouvernementalität*. Berlin: Argument, 1997.

Lemke, Thomas, Susanne Krasmann, and Ulrich Bröckling, eds. *Gouvernementalität der Gegenwart: Studien zur Ökonomisierung des Sozialen*. Frankfurt a.M.: Suhrkamp, 2000.

'Gouvernementalität, Neolibealismus und Selbsttechnologien: Eine Einleitung.' In *Gouvernementalität der Gegenwart: Studien zur Ökonomisierung des Sozialen*, edited by Thomas Lemke, Susanne Krasmann and Ulrich Bröckling, 7–40. Frankfurt a.M.: Suhrkamp, 2000.

Lengwiler, Martin, and Jeannette Madarász, eds. *Das präventive Selbst: Eine Kulturgeschichte moderner Gesundheitspolitik*. Bielefeld: transcript, 2010.

Linse, Ulrich. 'Das "natürliche" Leben: Die Lebensreform.' In *Erfindung des Menschen: Schöpfungsträume und Körperbilder, 1500–2000*, edited by Richard van Dülmen, 435–457. Vienna: Böhlau, 1998.

Lumley, Robert. *States of Emergency: Cultures of Revolt in Italy from 1968–1978*. London: Verso, 1990.

Maase, Kaspar. *BRAVO Amerika: Erkunden zur Jugendkultur der Bundesrepublik in den fünfziger Jahren*. Hamburg: Junius, 1992.

Maasen, Sabine. 'Das beratene Selbst: Zur Genealogie der Therapeutisierung in den "langen" Siebzigern: Eine Perspektivierung.' In *Das beratene Selbst: Zur Genealogie der Therapeutisierung in den 'langen' Siebzigern*, edited by Sabine Maasen, Jens Elberfeld, Pascal Eitler and Maik Tändler, 7–32. Bielefeld: transcript, 2011.

Genealogie der Unmoral: Zur Therapeutisierung sexueller Selbste. Frankfurt a.M.: Suhrkamp, 1998.

Maasen, Sabine, Jens Elberfeld, Pascal Eitler, and Maik Tändler, eds. *Das beratene Selbst: Zur Genealogie der Therapeutisierung in den 'langen' Siebzigern*. Bielefeld: transcript, 2011.

MacDougall, Carla. 'In the Shadow of the Wall: Urban Space and Everyday life in Berlin Kreuzberg.' In *Between the Avant-Garde and the Everyday: Subversive Politics in Europe from 1957 to the Present*, edited by Timothy S. Brown and Lorena Anton, 154–174. New York: Berghahn, 2011.

'"We too are Berliners": Protest, Symbolism and the City in Cold War Germany.' In *Changing the World, Changing Oneself: Political Protest and Collective Identities in West Germany and the U.S. in the 1960s and 1970s*, edited by Belinda Davis, Wilfried Mausbach, Martin Klimke and Carla MacDougall, 83–101. New York: Berghahn, 2010.

Maier, Hans. 'Fortschrittsoptimismus oder Kulturpessimismus? Die Bundesrepublik in den 1970er und 1980er Jahren.' *Vierteljahrshefte für Zeitgeschichte* 56 (2008): 1–18.

Marcuse, Herbert. *Eros and Civilization: A Philosophical Inquiry into Freud.* London: Routledge, 1987 [1956].

— *One-Dimensional Man: Studies in the Ideology of Advanced Industrial Society.* Boston: Beacon Press, 1964.

Martinez, Manuel Luis. *Countering the Counterculture: Rereading Postwar American Dissent from Jack Kerouac to Tomás Rivera.* Madison: The University of Wisconsin Press, 2003.

März, Michael. *Linker Protest nach dem Deutschen Herbst: Eine Geschichte des linken Spektrums im Schatten des 'starken Staates', 1977–1979.* Bielefeld: transcript, 2012.

Mecking, Klaus, and Heino Stöver. *Männersexualität: Gespräche, Bilder, Notizen.* Bremen: Verlag Roter Funke, 1980.

Mende, Silke. *'Nicht rechts, nicht links, sondern vorn': Eine Geschichte der Gründungsgrünen.* Munich: Oldenbourg, 2011.

Mergel, Thomas. 'Überlegungen zu einer Kulturgeschichte der Politik.' *Geschichte und Gesellschaft* 28 (2002): 574–606.

Merta, Sabine. *Schlank! Ein Körperkult der Moderne.* Stuttgart: Franz Steiner Verlag, 2008.

Mildenberger, Michael. *Die religiöse Revolte: Jugend zwischen Flucht und Aufbruch* Frankfurt a.M.: Fischer Verlag, 1979.

Möhring, Maren. 'Ethnic Food, Fast Food, Health Food: Veränderungen der Ernährung und Esskultur im letzten Drittel des 20. Jahrhunderts.' In *Vorgeschichte der Gegenwart: Dimensionen des Strukturbruchs nach dem Boom,* edited by Anselm Doering-Manteuffel, Lutz Raphael and Thomas Schlemmer, 309–331. Göttingen: Vandenhoeck & Ruprech, 2016.

— *Marmorleiber: Körperbildung in der deutschen Nacktkultur (1890–1930).* Cologne: Böhlau, 2004.

Moreni, Primo, and Nanni Balestrini. *Die goldene Horde: Arbeiterautonomie, Jugendrevolte und bewaffneter Kampf in Italien.* Berlin: Assoziation A, 2002.

Mosler, Peter. *Was wir wollten, was wir wurden: Studentenrevolte, 10 Jahre danach.* Reinbek bei Hamburg: Rowohlt, 1977.

Mosse, George. *The Crisis of German Ideology: Intellectual Origins of the Third Reich.* New York: Grosset & Dunlap, 1964.

Mühsam, Erich. *Ascona: Eine Broschüre. Locarno: Carlson, 1905.* Reprint, Berlin: Verlag Klaus Guhl, 1982.

Müller, Gerd-Gustl. *Der Job: Roman.* Munich: Weismann Verlag, 1977.

Müller, Hedwig. 'Tanz der Natur: Lebensreform und Tanz.' In *Die Lebensreform: Entwürfe zur Neugestaltung von Leben und Kunst um 1900,* edited by Kai Buchholz, Rita Lotacha, Hilke Peckmann and Klaus Wolbert, 329–334. Darmstadt: haeusser-media, 2001.

Müller, Tim B. *Krieger und Gelehrte: Herbert Marcuse und die Denksystem im Kalten Krieg.* Hamburg: Hamburger Edition, 2010.

Nagel, Katja. *Die Provinz in Bewegung: Studentenunruhen in Heidelberg 1967–1973*. Heidelberg: Verlag für Regionalkultur, 2009.

Nigg, Heinz, ed. *Wir wollen alles, und zwar subito! Die Achtziger Jugendunruhen in der Schweiz und ihre Folgen*. Zurich: Limmat Verlag, 2001.

Nolte, Paul. 'Jenseits des Westens? Überlegungen zu einer Zeitgeschichte der Demokratie.' *Vierteljahrshefte für Zeitgeschichte* 61 (2013): 275–301.

Owens, Lynn. *Cracking under Pressure: Narrating the Decline of the Amsterdam Squatters' Movement*. University Park, PA: Pennsylvania State University Press, 2009.

Paasche, Hans. *Die Forschungsreise des Afrikaners Lukanga Mukara ins innerste Deutschlands*. Hamburg: Verlag Junge Menschen, 1921.

Pas, Niek. 'Mediatisation of Provo: From a Local Movement to a European Phenomenon.' In *Between Prague Spring and French May: Opposition and Revolt in Europe, 1960–1980*, edited by Martin Klimke, Jacco Pekelder and Joachim Scharloth, 157–176. New York: Berghahn, 2011.

'Subcultural Movements: The Provos.' In *1968 in Europe: A History of Protest and Activism, 1956–1977*, edited by Martin Klimke and Joachim Scharloth, 13–22. New York: Palgrave Macmillan, 2008.

Passmore, Leith. 'The Art of Hunger: Self-Starvation in the Red Army Faction.' *German History* 27 (2009): 32–59.

Ulrike Meinhof and the Red Army Faction: Performing Terrorism. New York: Palgrave Macmillan, 2011.

Pausewang, Gudrun. *Die letzten Kinder von Schewenborn oder . . . sieht so unsere Zukunft aus?* Ravensburg: Maier, 1983.

Die Wolke. Ravensburg: Maier, 1987.

Peinemann, Steve. *Wohngemeinschaft: Problem oder Lösung?* Frankfurt a.M.: Verlag Rieta Hau, 1975.

Perinelli, Massimo. 'Longing, Lust, Violence, Liberation: Discourses on Sexuality on the Radical Left in West Germany, 1969–1972.' In *After the History of Sexuality: German Interventions*, edited by Dagmar Herzog, Helmut Puff and Spector Scott, 248–281. New York: Berghahn, 2011.

Pilzweger, Stefanie. *Männlichkeit zwischen Gefühl und Revolution: Eine Emotionsgeschichte der bundesdeutschen 68er-Bewegung*. Bielefeld: transcript, 2015.

Piper, Otto. 'Rückblick auf den Wandervogel.' In *Dokumentation der Jugendbewegung, vol 2: Die Wandervogelzeit*, edited by Werner Kindt, 215–230. Düsseldorf and Cologne: Diederichs, 1968.

Plamper, Jan. *The History of Emotions: An Introduction*, translated by Keith Tribe. Oxford: Oxford University Press, 2015.

Plant, Sadie. *The Most Radical Gesture: The Situationist International in a Postmodern Age*. London: Routledge, 1992.

Postone, Moishe. *Time, Labor, and Social Domination: A Reinterpretation of Marx's Critical Theory*. Cambridge: Cambridge University Press, 1993.

Pretzl, Andreas, and Volker Weiß, eds. *Rosa Radikale: Die Schwulenbewegung der 1970er Jahre*. Hamburg: Männerschwarm Verlag, 2012.

Rackelmann, Marc. 'Wilhelm Reich und der Einheitsverband für proletarische Sexualreform und Mutterschutz: Was war die Sexpol?' *Emotion. Beiträge zum Werk von Wilhelm Reich* 11 (1993): 56–93.

Raithel, Thomas, Andreas Rödder, and Andreas Wirsching, eds. *Auf dem Weg in eine neue Moderne? Die Bundesrepublik Deutschland in den siebziger und achtziger Jahren.* Munich: R. Oldenbourg Verlag, 2009.

Ras, Marion E. P. de. *Körper, Eros und weibliche Kultur: Mädchen im Wandervogel und in der Bündischen Jugend.* Pfaffenweiler: Centaurus, 1988.

Raschke, Joachim. *Soziale Bewegungen: Ein historisch-systematischer Grundriss.* Frankfurt a.M.: Campus Verlag, 1985.

Raskin, Jonah. *American Scream: Allen Ginsberg's Howl and the Making of the Beat Generation* Berkeley: University of California Press, 2004.

Reckwitz, Andreas. 'Auf dem Weg zu einer praxeologischen Analyse des Selbst.' In *Zeitgeschichte des Selbst: Therapeutisierung – Politisierung – Emotionalisierung,* edited by Pascal Eitler and Jens Elberfeld, 31–45. Bielefeld: transcript, 2015.

Das hybride Subjekt: eine Theorie der Subjektkulturen von der bürgerlichen Moderne zur Postmoderne. Weilerswist: Velbrück, 2006.

Reddy, William M. 'Emotional Liberty: History and Politics in the Anthropology of Emotions.' *Cultural Anthropology* 14 (1999): 256–288.

The Navigation of Feeling: A Framework for the History of Emotions. Cambridge: Cambridge University Press, 2001.

Regener, Sven. *Neue Vahr Süd.* Frankfurt a.M.: Eichborn, 2004.

Reich, Wilhelm. *Dialektischer Materialismus und Psychoanalyse.* Copenhagen: Verlag für Sexualpolitik, 1934.

Die Funktion des Orgasmus: Zur Psychopathologie und zur Soziologie des Geschlechtslebens. Amsterdam: Thomas de Munter, 1965.

Massenpsychologie des Faschismus: Zur Sexualökonomie der politischen Reaktion und zur proletarischen Sexualpolitik. Copenhagen: Verlag für Sexualpolitik, 1933.

Der sexuelle Kampf der Jugend. Berlin: Verlag für Sexualpolitik, 1932.

Die sexuelle Revolution. Frankfurt a.M.: Fischer, 1966.

Was ist Klassenbewusstsein? Ein Beitrag zur Diskussion über die Neuformierung der Arbeiterbewegung. Kopenhagen: Verlag für Sexualpolitik, 1934.

Reichardt, Sven. *Authentizität und Gemeinschaft: Linksalternatives Leben in den siebziger und frühen achtziger Jahren.* Berlin: Suhrkamp, 2014.

'Von "Beziehungskisten" und "offener Sexualität".' In *Das Alternative Milieu: Antibürgerlicher Lebensstil und linke Politik in der Bundesrepublik Deutschland und Europa 1968–1983,* edited by Sven Reichardt and Detlef Siegfried, 267–289. Göttingen: Wallstein, 2010.

Reichardt, Sven, and Detlef Siegfried, eds. *Das Alternative Milieu: Antibürgerlicher Lebensstil und linke Politik in der Bundesrepublik Deutschland und Europa 1968–1983.* Göttingen: Wallstein, 2010.

'Das Alternative Milieu: Konturen einer Lebensform.' In *Das Alternative Milieu: Antibürgerlicher Lebensstil und linke Politik in der Bundesrepublik*

Deutschland und Europa 1968–1983, edited by Sven Reichardt and Detlef Siegfried, 9–24. Göttingen: Wallstein, 2010.

Reimann, Aribert. *Dieter Kunzelmann: Avantgardist, Protestler, Radikaler.* Göttingen: Vandenhoeck & Ruprecht, 2009.

Reinecke, Christiane. 'Am Rande der Gesellschaft? Das Märkische Viertel – eine West-Berliner Großsiedlung und ihre Darstellung als urbane Problemzone.' *Zeithistorische Forschungen* 11 (2014): 212–234.

'Localising the Social: The Rediscovery of Urban Poverty in Western European "Affluent Societies".' *Contemporary European History* 24 (2015): 555–576.

Reitmayer, Morten, and Thomas Schlemmer, eds. *Die Anfänge der Gegenwart: Umbrüche in Westeuropa nach dem Boom.* Munich: Oldenbourg, 2014.

Richter, Horst-Eberhardt. *Die Gruppe: Hoffnung auf einen neuen Weg, sich selbst und andere zu befreien. Psychoanalyse in Kooperation mit Gruppeninitiativen.* Reinbek bei Hamburg: Rowohlt, 1972.

Flüchten oder Standhalten. Reinbek bei Hamburg: Rowohlt, 1976.

Lernziel Solidarität. Reinbek bei Hamburg: Rowohlt, 1974.

Riederer, Christoph. *Die RAF und die Folterdebatte der 1970er Jahre.* Wiesbaden: Springer, 2014.

Rigoll, Dominik. *Staatsschutz in Westdeutschland: Von der Entnazifizierung zur Extremistenabwehr.* Göttingen: Wallstein Verlag, 2013.

Rinner, Susanne. *The German Student Movement and the Literary Imagination: Transnational Memories of Protest and Dissent.* New York: Berghahn, 2013.

Rochefort, Christiane. *Encore heureux qu'on va vers l'été.* Paris: Grasset, 1975.

Zum Glück gehts dem Sommer entgegen. Frankfurt a.M.: Suhrkamp, 1977.

Rödder, Andreas. 'Das "Modell Deutschland" zwischen Erfolgsgeschichte und Verfallsdiagnose.' *Vierteljahrshefte für Zeitgeschichte* 54 (2006): 345–363.

Wertewandel und Postmoderne: Gesellschaft und Kultur der Bundesrepublik Deutschland 1965–1990. Stuttgart: Stiftung Bundespräsident-Theordor-Heuss-Haus, 2004.

Rödder, Andreas, and Wolfgang Elz, eds. *Alte Werte – neue Werte: Schlaglichter des Wertewandels.* Göttingen: Vandenhoeck & Ruprecht, 2008.

Rödner, Helmut. *Männergruppen: Versuche einer Veränderung der traditionellen Männerrolle. Ursachen, Wege, Schwierigkeiten.* Berlin: Editora Queimada, 1978.

Rohkrämer, Thomas. *Eine andere Moderne? Zivilisationskritik, Natur und Technik in Deutschland, 1880–1933.* Paderborn: Schöningh, 1999.

Ross, Kristin. *May '68 and Its Afterlives.* Chicago: University of Chicago Press, 2002.

Roth, Roland. '"Die Macht liegt auf der Straße": Zur Bedeutung des Straßenprotests für die neuen sozialen Bewegungen.' In *Straße und Straßenkultur: Interdisziplinäre Beobachtungen eines öffentlichen Sozialraumes in der fortgeschrittenen Moderne*, edited by Hans-Jürgen Hohm, 195–214. Konstanz: Universitätsverlag Konstanz, 1997.

Rebellische Subjektivität. Herbert Marcuse und die neuen Protestbewegungen. Frankfurt a.M.: Campus, 1985.

Roth, Roland, and Dieter Rucht, eds. *Neue soziale Bewegungen in der Bundesrepublik Deutschland*. Bonn: Bundeszentrale für Politische Bildung, 1987.

———. *Die sozialen Bewegungen in Deutschland seit 1945: Ein Handbuch*. Frankfurt a. M.: Campus, 2008.

Rothschuh, Karl E. *Naturheilbewegung, Reformbewegung, Alternativbewegung*. Darmstadt: Wissenschaftliche Buchgesellschaft, 1983.

Röttgen, Herbert, and Florian Rabe. *Vulkantänze: Linke und alternative Ausgänge*. Munich: Trikont-Verlag, 1978.

Rucht, Dieter. *Modernisierung und neue soziale Bewegungen: Deutschland, Frankreich und USA im Vergleich*. Frankfurt a.M.: Campus, 1995.

Rutschky, Michael. *Erfahrungshunger: Ein Essay über die siebziger Jahre*. Cologne: Kiepenheuer und Witsch, 1980.

Sander, Tobias. 'Der Wertewandel der 1960er und 1970er Jahre und soziale Ungleichheit: Neue Befunde zu widersprüchlichen Interpretamenten.' *Comparativ: Zeitschrift für Globalgeschichte und vergleichende Gesellschaftsforschung* 7 (2007): 101–118.

Scharloth, Joachim. *1968: Eine Kommunikationsgeschichte*. Paderborn: Wilhelm Fink, 2011.

Scheer, Monique. 'Are Emotions a Kind of Practice (and Is That What Makes Them Have a History)? A Bourdieuan Approach to Understanding Emotion.' *History and Theory* 51 (2012): 193–220.

Scherer, Klaus-Jürgen. 'Berlin (West): Hauptstadt der Szenen. Ein Porträt kultureller und anderer Revolten Anfang der achtziger Jahre.' In *Pöbelexzesse und Volkstumulte in Berlin: Zur Sozialgeschichte der Straße (1830–1980)*, edited by Manfred Gailus, 197–222. Berlin: Verlag Europäische Perspektiven, 1984.

Scheurmann, Erich. *Der Papalagi: Die Reden des Südsee-Häuptlings Tuiavii aus Tiavea*. Buchenbach: Felsen-Verlag, 1920.

Schildt, Axel, and Detlef Siegfried, eds. *Between Marx and Coca-Cola: Youth Cultures in Changing European Societies, 1960–1980*. New York: Berghahn, 2006.

Schildt, Axel, Detlef Siegfried, and Karl Christian Lammers, eds. *Dynamische Zeiten: Die 60er Jahre in den beiden deutschen Gesellschaften*. Hamburg: Christians, 2000.

Schmincke, Imke. 'Sexualität als "Angelpunkt" der Frauenbewegung? Zum Verhältnis von sexueller Revolution und Frauenbewegung.' In *Sexuelle Revolution? Zur Geschichte der Sexualität im deutschsprachigen Raum seit den 1960er Jahren*, edited by Peter-Paul Bänziger, Magdalena Beljan, Franz X. Eder and Pascal Eitler, 199–222. Bielefeld: transcript, 2015.

———. 'Von der Befreiung der Frau zur Befreiung des Selbst: Eine kritische Analyse der Befreiungssemantik in der neuen Frauenbewegung.' In *Zeitgeschichte des Selbst: Therapeutisierung – Politisierung – Emotionalisierung*, edited by Pascal Eitler and Jens Elberfeld, 217–238. Bielefeld: transcript, 2015.

Schmitt, Carl. *Der Begriff des Politischen. Text von 1932 mit einem Vorwort und drei Corollarien.* Berlin: Dunker und Humblot, 1987.

Schönberg, Volkhart. 'Freiburg: Bewegungen in den besetzten Häusern.' In *Häuserkampf I: Wir wollen alles – Der Beginn einer Bewegung,* 149–158. Hamburg: Laika Verlag, 2012.

Schülein, Johann August. 'Beziehungsprobleme.' In *Vor uns die Mühen der Ebenen: Alltagsprobleme und Perspektiven von Wohngemeinschaften,* edited by Johann August Schülein, 145–168. Giessen: Focus-Verlag, 1980.

'Einige Bemerkungen zur Entwicklung der Wohngemeinschaftsbewegung.' In *Vor uns die Mühen der Ebenen: Alltagsprobleme und Perspektiven von Wohngemeinschaften,* edited by Johannes August Schülein, 13–30. Giessen: Focus-Verlag, 1980.

Schulz, Kristina. '1968: Lesarten der "sexuellen Revolution".' In *Demokratisierung und gesellschaftlicher Aufbruch: Die sechziger Jahre als Wendezeit der Bundesrepublik,* edited by Matthias Frese, Julia Paulus and Karl Teppe, 121–133. Paderborn: Ferdinand Schöningh, 2003.

'Echoes of Provocation: 1968 and the Women's Movements in France and Germany.' In *Transnational Moments of Change: Europe 1945, 1968, 1989,* edited by Gerd-Rainer Horn and Padraic Kenney, 137–156. Lanham, MD.: Rowman & Littlefield, 2004.

Der lange Atem der Provokation: Die Frauenbewegung in der Bundesrepublik und in Frankreich. Frankfurt a.M.: Campus, 2002.

Schwäbisch, Lutz, and Martin Siems. *Anleitung zum sozialen Lernen für Paare, Gruppen und Erzieher: Kommunikations- und Verhaltenstraining.* Reinbek bei Hamburg: Rowohlt, 1974.

Schwendter, Rolf. *Theorie der Subkultur.* Cologne and Berlin: Kiepenheuer und Witsch, 1971.

Sedgwick, Eve Kosofsky. *Touching Feeling: Affect, Pedagogy, Performativity.* Durham, NC: Duke University Press, 2003.

Sedlmaier, Alexander. *Consumption and Violence: Radical Protest in Cold-War West Germany.* Ann Arbor, MI: University of Michigan Press, 2014.

Seiler, Wolfgang. *Grenzüberschreitungen: Zur Sprache des Wahnsinns.* Giessen: Focus, 1980.

Sewell, Jr., William H. *Logics of History: Social Theory and Social Transformation.* Chicago: The University of Chicago Press, 2005.

Sharma, Avi. *We Lived for the Body: Natural Medicine and Public Health in Imperial Germany.* DeKalb, IL: Northern Illinois University Press, 2014.

Shinder, Jason, ed. *The Poem That Changed America: 'Howl' Fifty Years Later.* New York: Farrar, Straus and Giroux, 2006.

Siegfried, Detlef. '"Einstürzende Neubauten": Wohngemeinschaften, Jugendzentren und private Präferenzen kommunistischer "Kader" als Formen jugendlicher Subkultur.' *Archiv für Sozialgeschichte* 44 (2004): 39–66.

'Die Entpolitisierung des Privaten: Subjektkonstruktionen im alternativen Milieu.' In *Privatisierung: Idee und Praxis seit den 1970er Jahren,* edited by Norbert Frei and Dietmar Süß, 124–139. Göttingen: Wallstein, 2012.

Time Is on My Side: Konsum und Politik in der westdeutschen Jugendkultur der 6oer Jahre. Göttingen: Wallstein, 2006.

Silies, Eva-Maria. 'Ein, zwei, viele Bewegungen? Die Diversität der neuen Frauenbewegung in den 1970er Jahren der Bundesbewegung.' In *Linksalternative Milieus und neue soziale Bewegungen in den 1970er Jahren,* edited by Cordia Baumann, Stefan Gehrig and Nicolas Büchse, 87–106. Heidelberg: Winter, 2011.

Liebe, Lust und Last: Die Pille als weibliche Generationserfahrung in der Bundesrepublik 1960–1980. Göttingen: Wallstein Verlag, 2010.

Slobodian, Quinn. *Foreign Front: Third World Politics in Sixties West Germany.* Durham, NC: Duke University Press, 2012.

Sonnenberg, Uwe. *Von Marx zum Maulwurf: Linker Buchhandel in Westdeutschland in den 1970er Jahren.* Göttingen: Wallstein, 2016.

Sontheimer, Kurt. *So war Deutschland nie: Anmerkungen zur politischen Kultur der Bundesrepublik.* Munich: C. H. Beck, 1999.

Springer, Anna. *Vegetarisches Kochebuch. Mit einer Einleitung: 'Wie sollen wir leben?' von Joseph Springer.* Berlin: Verlag Lebensreform, 1907.

Stachura, Peter. *The German Youth Movement: An Interpretative and Documentary History.* London: Macmillan, 1981.

Stahel, Thomas. *Wo-Wo-Wonige: Stadt- und wohnpolitische Bewegungen in Zürich nach 1968.* Zurich: Paranoia City, 2006.

Stefan, Verena. *Häutungen.* Munich: Verlag Frauenoffensive, 1975.

Steinacker, Sven. '"... daß die Arbeitsbedingungen im Interesse aller verändert werden müssen !!!" Alternative Pädagogik und linke Politik in der Sozialen Arbeiten der sechziger und siebziger Jahre.' In *Das Alternative Milieu: Antibürgerlicher Lebensstil und linke Politik in der Bundesrepublik Deutschland und Europa 1968–1983,* edited by Sven Reichardt and Detlef Siegfried, 353–372. Göttingen: Wallstein, 2010.

Straub, Ute, and Barbara Schröder. *Kinder in Wohngemeinschaften.* Herford: Zündhölzchen, 1978.

Streng, Marcel. 'Führungsverhältnisse im Hungerstreik: Ein Kapitel zur Geschichte des westdeutschen Strafvollzugs (1973–1985).' In *Zeitgeschichte des Selbst: Therapeutisierung – Politisierung – Emotionalisierung,* edited by Pascal Eitler and Jens Elberfeld, 113–146. Bielefeld: transcript, 2015.

'Der Körper im Ausnahmezustand: Hungern als politische Praxis im westdeutschen Strafvollzug (1973–1985).' In *Ausnahmezustände: Entgrenzungen und Regulierungen in Europa während des Kalten Krieges,* edited by Dirk Schumann and Cornelia Rauh, 214–235. Göttingen: Wallstein, 2015.

Stüdemann, Natalia. *Dionysos in Sparta: Isadora Duncan in Russland. Eine Geschichte von Tanz und Körper.* Bielefeld: transcript, 2008.

Sutter, Barbara. '"Selbstveränderung und Sozialveränderung": Von der Selbsthilfegruppe und ihren Verheißungen zum Bürgerschaftlichen Engagement und seinen Zumutungen.' In *Das beratene Selbst: Zur Genealogie der Therapeutisierung in den 'langen' Siebzigern,* edited by Sabine

Maasen, Jens Elberfeld, Pascal Eitler and Maik Tändler, 293–312: Bielefeld: transcript, 2011.

Suttner, Andreas. *'Beton brennt': Hausbesetzer und Selbstverwaltung im Berlin, Wien und Zürich der 8oer*. Vienna: Lit-Verlag, 2011.

Szeemann, Harald, ed. *Monte Verità: Lokale Anthropologie als Beiträge zur Wiederentdeckung einer neuzeitlichen sakralen Topographie*. Milan: Electa Editrice, 1979.

Tändler, Maik. 'Erziehung der Erzieher: Lehrer als problematische Subjekte zwischen Bildungsreform und antiautoritärer Pädagogik.' In *Zeitgeschichte des Selbst: Therapeutisierung – Politisierung – Emotionalisierung*, edited by Pascal Eitler and Jens Elberfeld, 85–112. Bielefeld: transcript, 2015.

——— '"Psychoboom": Therapeutisierungsprozesse in Westdeutschland in den späten 1960er und 1970er Jahren.' In *Das beratene Selbst: Zur Genealogie der Therapeutisierung in den 'langen' Siebzigern*, edited by Sabine Maasen, Jens Elberfeld, Pascal Eitler and Maik Tändler, 59–94. Bielefeld: transcript, 2011.

——— *Das therapeutische Jahrzehnt: Der Psychoboom in den siebziger Jahren*. Göttingen: Wallstein, 2016.

——— 'Therapeutische Vergemeinschaftung: Demokratie, Emanzipation und Emotionalisierung in der "Gruppe", 1963–1976.' In *Das Selbst zwischen Anpassung und Befreiung: Psychowissen und Politik im 20. Jahrhundert*, edited by Maik Tändler and Uffa Jensen, 141–169. Göttingen: Wallstein, 2012.

Tändler, Maik, and Uffa Jensen. 'Psychowissen, Politik und das Selbst: Eine neue Forschungsperspektive auf die Geschichte des Politischen im 20. Jahrhundert.' In *Das Selbst zwischen Anpassung und Befreiung: Psychowissen und Politik im 20. Jahrhundert*, edited by Uffa Jensen and Maik Tändler, 9–35. Göttingen: Wallstein, 2012.

Templin, David. *Freizeit ohne Kontrollen: Die Jugendzentrumsbewegung in der Bundesrepublik der 1970er Jahre*. Göttingen: Wallstein, 2015.

Terhoeven, Petra. *Deutscher Herbst in Europa: Der Linksterrorismus der siebziger Jahre als transnationales Phänomen*. Berlin: De Gruyter Oldenbourg, 2016.

Thrift, Nigel. *Non-Representational Theory: Space, Politics, Affect*. London: Routledge, 2007.

Thurn, Christiane, and Herbert Röttgen, eds. *Die Rückkehr des Imaginären: Märchen, Magie, Mystik, Mythos, Anfänge einer anderen Politik*. Munich: Trikon-Dianus Buchverlag, 1981.

Tripold, Thomas. *Die Kontinuität romantischer Ideen*. Bielefeld: transcript, 2012.

Trumann, Andrea. *Feministische Theorie: Frauenbewegung und weibliche Subjektbildung im Spätkapitalismus*. Stuttgart: Schmetterlingsverlag, 2002.

Turner, Victor. *The Ritual Process: Structure and Anti-Structure* Ithaca, NY: Cornell University Press, 1969.

van der Steen, Bart, and Knud Andresen, eds. *A European Youth Revolt: European Perspectives on Youth Protest and Social Movements in the 1980s*. Basingstoke, UK: Palgrave Macmillan, 2016.

Vaneigm, Raoul. 'Basic Banalities (Part 2).' In *Situationist International Anthology*, edited by Ken Knabb, 154–173. Berkeley: Bureau of Public Secrets, 1981 (1963).

The Revolution of Everyday Life. London: Rebel Press, 2003.

Vasudevan, Alexander. *Metropolitan Preoccupations: The Spatial Politics of Squatting in Berlin* Chichester, UK: John Wiley and Sons, 2015.

Ventrone, Angelo. '*Vogliamo tutto*': *Perché due generazioni hanno creduto nella rivoluzione 1960–1988*. Rome: Editori Laterza, 2012.

Verheyen, Nina. 'Der ausdiskutierte Orgasmus: Beziehungsgespräche als kommunikative Praxis in der Geschichte des Intimen seit den 1960er Jahren.' In *Sexuelle Revolution? Zur Geschichte der Sexualität im deutschsprachigen Raum seit den 1960er Jahren*, edited by Peter-Paul Bänziger, Magdalena Beljan, Franz X. Eder and Pascal Eitler, 181–198. Bielefeld: transcript, 2015.

Diskussionslust: Eine Kulturgeschichte des 'besseren Arguments' in Westdeutschland Göttingen: Vandenhoeck & Ruprecht, 2010.

Vogel, Sophie von, and Lars Schultze-Kossack, eds. *Zür(e)ich brennt*. Zurich: Europa Verlag AG, 2010.

Voigts, Hanning. *Entkorkte Flaschenpost: Herbert Marcuse, Theodor W. Adorno und der Streit um die Neue Linke*. Münster: LIT Verlag, 2010.

Voswinckel, Ulrike. *Freie Liebe und Anarchie: Schwabing – Monte Verità. Entwürfe gegen das etablierte Leben*. Munich: Allitera-Verlag, 2009.

Walter, Franz, Stephan Klecha, and Alexander Hensel, eds. *Die Grünen und die Pädosexualität: Eine bundesdeutsche Geschichte*. Göttingen: Vandenhoeck & Ruprecht, 2015.

Wandmalereien & Texte: Nehmt der Langeweile ihren Sinn. Berlin: Kramer, 1979.

Wark, McKenzie. *The Beach Beneath the Street: The Everyday Life and Glorious Times of the Situationist International*. London: Verso Books, 2011.

Wartenberg, Johann Christoph. *Kreuzberg, K36, Leben in (der) Bewegung: Kreuzberg inside bis zum Fall der Mauer*. Bockenem: Lühmann, 2003.

Weidner, Tobias. *Die Geschichte des Politischen in der Diskussion: Das Politische als Kommunikation*. Göttingen: Wallstein, 2012.

Weinhauer, Klaus. 'Zwischen Aufbruch und Revolte: Die 68er Bewegung und die Gesellschaft der Bundesrepublik Deutschland der sechziger Jahre.' *Neue Politische Literatur* 3 (2001): 412–432.

Wetzel, Wolf. 'Die Besetzung der Siesmayerstraße.' In *Häuserkampf: Teil 1. Der Beginn einer Bewegung*, 101–106. Hamburg: LAIKA Verlag, 2012.

Wienhaus, Andrea. *Bildungswege zu '1968': Eine Kollektivbiografie des Sozialistischen Deutschen Studentenbundes*. Bielefeld: transcript, 2014.

Wigman, Mary. *Die Sprache des Tanzes*. Stuttgart: Battenberg, 1963.

Wilson, Steve. 'The Author as Spiritual Pilgrim: The Search for Authenticity in Jack Kerouac's *On the Road* and *The Subterraneans*.' In *The Beat Generation. Critical Essays*, edited by Kostas Myrsiades, 77–91. New York: Peter Lang, 2001.

Wolbert, Klaus. 'Körper: Zwischen animalischer Leiblichkeit und ästhetisierender Verklärung der Physis.' In *Die Lebensreform: Entwürfe zur Neugestaltung von*

Leben und Kunst um 1900, edited by Kai Buchholz, Rita Lotacha, Hilke Peckmann and Klaus Wolbert, 339–340. Darmstadt: haeusser-media, 2001.

'Die Lebensreform – Anträge zur Debatte.' In *Die Lebensreform: Entwürfe zur Neugestaltung von Leben und Kunst um 1900*, edited by Kai Buchholz, Rita Lotacha, Hilke Peckmann and Klaus Wolbert, 13–21. Darmstadt: haeusser-media, 2001

'"Unbekleidet" oder "ausgezogen"? Die befreite Nacktheit in der Kunst.' In *Die Lebensreform: Entwürfe zur Neugestaltung von Leben und Kunst um 1900*, edited by Kai Buchholz, Rita Lotacha, Hilke Peckmann and Klaus Wolbert, 369–372. Darmstadt: haeusser-media, 2001.

Wolfrum, Edgar. *Die geglückte Demokratie: Geschichte der Bundesrepublik Deutschland von ihren Anfängen bis zur Gegenwart*. Stuttgart: Klett-Cotta, 2006.

Wyneken, Gustav. 'Der weltgeschichtliche Sinn der Jugendbewegung.' In *Der Kampf für die Jugend*, edited by Gustav Wyneken, 149–179. Jena: Diederichs, 1919.

Ziemann, Benjamin. 'Zwischen sozialer Bewegung und Dienstleistung am Individuum: Katholiken und katholische Kirche im therapeutischen Jahrzehnt.' *Archiv für Sozialgeschichte* 44 (2004): 357–393.

Zinnecker, Jürgen. '"Halbstarke" – Die andere Seite der 68er-Generation.' In *Protestierende Jugend: Jugendopposition und politischer Protest in der deutschen Nachkriegsgeschichte*, edited by Ulrich Herrmann. Weinheim: Juventa, 2002.

Zürich, Videoladen. 'Züri brännt.' 190 min. Switzerland, 1980.

Zwick, Michael M. *Neue soziale Bewegungen als politische Subkultur: Zielsetzungen, Anhängerschaft, Mobilisierung – eine empirische Analyse*. Frankfurt a.M.: Campus, 1990.

Index